商事仲裁翻译

Theory and Case Study
of Commercial Arbitration

金春岚　编著

上海三联书店

目　录

第一章　商事仲裁翻译简介

仲裁是在一般法院以外,根据争议各方书面订立的仲裁协议解决民事争议的机制。仲裁的启动源于当事人的意愿(party-consensus)与合约关系,当事人有自主权(party autonomy),仲裁地法院最好不插手,或尽量少插手,特别是对于国际仲裁,这已是近三十年来被普遍接受的说法。但是,仲裁毕竟是一种"司法行为"(judicial process),它可以保护法定时效(《Limitation Act 1980》),并且裁决的结果可以像法院判决一样得到强制执行。

国际商事仲裁是为"解决法人及/或自然人之间产生于国际商业交易过程中的争议所进行的仲裁"[①],其特点在于,仲裁的当事人均为私法上的主体,即法人或自然人。通常,争议双方当事人分属不同的国家,争议自商业交易中所产生的法律争议而来。商事仲裁仅处理私人间(法人或自然人)的商事争议。

仲裁语言是仲裁程序所使用的语言,一般包括通讯(通知)、当事人提交的文书和证明材料、证据、开庭及裁决书所使用的语言。虽然仲裁语言看上去不是什么大问题,但在国际商事仲裁中如果忽略了仲裁语言的约定,轻则会拖延仲裁程序进度、增加成本,重则甚至可能因为影响正当程序而阻碍仲裁裁决的执行。

[①] 郑远民:《国际私法——国际民事诉讼法与国际商事仲裁法》,中信出版社 2002 年版,第224 页。

例如,在 CEEG（Shanghai）Solar Science v. LUMOS LLC. 一案①中,双方就是因为没有约定仲裁语言而导致其中一方没能参与仲裁庭的组成,结果执行地法院认为这违背了仲裁正当程序原则的要求,因此判决拒绝承认与执行。

该案中,中国公司 CEEG 与美国公司 LUMOS 签订了主合同品牌合作协议以及在主合同项下的一系列销售合同,其中的仲裁条款均约定将双方争议提交到 CIETAC 进行仲裁,但没有约定具体的仲裁语言。纠纷产生后,CEEG 向 CIETAC 提起了对 LUMOS 的仲裁。根据 CIETAC 规则,在双方对仲裁语言无约定的情况下,以中文为仲裁语言。② 于是,CIETAC 将中文的仲裁通知寄给在科罗拉多的 LUMOS,而 LUMOS 的老总看到写着中文的信件就没觉得这会是什么急事,从而错过了 15 天的指定仲裁员期限,因此 CIETAC 又根据仲裁规则指定了仲裁员。③ LUMOS 直到后来收到 CEEG 律师回复的英文邮件才知道要仲裁,于是手忙脚乱地找翻译员、请中国律师。

商事仲裁翻译一般是为国际商事仲裁服务的,其本质与商事仲裁的特点息息相关。国际仲裁公约的适用范围很广,涉及投资、人权、合同、知识产权等商务事务或者产权等。仲裁最初是作为一种解决争论或者问题的方法而产生的。法国律师 Fouchard（1965）将仲裁定义为解决争端的基本方法,因为它通过被仲裁者选择的人来进行。也就是说,只要被选择,任何人都可以成为仲裁者。Holdsworth（1965）将仲裁定义为:"仲裁来自于法律的最初体系。在国家设立法庭之后,诉诸法庭就成为而且一直是解决争端的方法。而当争端各方希望用少于向

---

① CEEG（Shanghai）Solar Sci. & Tech. Co. Ltd. v. LUMOS LLC. , n/k/a/LUMOS SOLAR LLC, 829 F. 3d 1201(10th Cir. 2016).

② 《中国国际经济贸易仲裁委员会仲裁规则(2015 版)》第八十一条第(一)款:"当事人对仲裁语言有约定的,从其约定。当事人对仲裁语言没有约定的,以中文为仲裁语言。仲裁委员会也可以视案件的具体情形确定其他语言为仲裁语言。"

③ 《中国国际经济贸易仲裁委员会仲裁规则(2015 版)》第二十七条第(一)款:"申请人和被申请人应各自在收到仲裁通知后 15 天内选定或委托仲裁委员会主任指定一名仲裁员。当事人未在上述期限内选定或委托仲裁委员会主任指定的,由仲裁委员会主任指定。"

法院提起诉讼所涉及的手续和费用来解决争端时，就仍选择仲裁的方式。"①在 Alan Martin（2005）的定义中，仲裁是自愿的、请中立的第三方参与的解决纠纷的手段，"在仲裁协议之外，根据当事人的愿望，为仲裁的进行设定一套规则。但国际仲裁并不局限于一国之内。"②

　　经过最近半个世纪的发展，商事仲裁已成为解决商务、航运和贸易纠纷的主要舞台，其改变了以前法律纠纷必须由法院解决、由律师处理的状况。随着仲裁的普及化，商业人士也得到大量的参与机会，因为仲裁的原意是鼓励一些懂商务也懂法律的"内行人"去解决商业纠纷。因此，理想的仲裁员需要精通商务和法律，了解国际商事惯例，公平敬业地完成使命。自改革开放以及尤其是"一带一路"政策实行以来，中国的商务、航运和贸易量不断增加。国际商场如战场，中国在与世界各地产生密切联系的过程中也必然会遭遇大量纠纷。中国不能逃避纠纷，也不可能指望"竞争者"不会来，只能自己严阵以待，以强大的商务实力和法律知识来装备自己。然而，国际商务、航运和贸易仲裁的舞台目前基本被西方人垄断。虽然一般仲裁条款不会规定仲裁员国籍其他特色，但华人仲裁员被委任还是少见的情形。因此，商事仲裁文本翻译则成为"重中之重"，其可以成为商事仲裁过程中的依据和前提，而有瑕疵的甚至错误的翻译可能导致整个仲裁的失败及商业的损失。

第一节　商事仲裁翻译定义

　　商事仲裁是解决商事主体间贸易纠纷的常用途径，在现代经济生活中，企业间常通过仲裁这一较经济的方式解决纠纷。根据《中华人民

---

① "The practice of arbitration therefore, comes, so to speak, naturally to primitive bodies of law, and after courts have been established by the state and a recourse to them has become the natural method of setting disputes the practice continues because the parties to a dispute want to settle it with less formality and expense than is involved in a recourse to the courts."

② "A body of rules which sets a standard external to the arbitration agreement, and the wishes of the parties, for the conduct of the arbitration. But interactional arbitration does not stay within national boundaries."

共和国仲裁法》第二十一条的规定,当事人申请仲裁应当符合下列条件:(1)有仲裁协议;(2)有具体的仲裁请求和事实、理由;(3)属于仲裁委员会的受理范围。根据《中华人民共和国仲裁法》第二条的规定,平等主体的公民、法人和其他组织之间发生的合同纠纷和其他财产权益纠纷,可以仲裁。据此,提交仲裁解决的纠纷必须符合下列条件:(1)发生纠纷的双方应当属于平等主体的当事人;(2)仲裁的事项应当是当事人有权处分的财产权益;(3)仲裁的范围限定为合同纠纷和其他财产权益纠纷。根据《中华人民共和国仲裁法》第三条、第七十七条的规定,下列纠纷不能仲裁:(1)婚姻、收养、监护、扶养、继承纠纷;(2)依法应当由行政机关处理的行政争议;(3)劳动争议;(4)农业集体经济组织内部的农业承包合同纠纷。《中华人民共和国仲裁法》第六条规定:"仲裁委员会应由当事人协议选定。仲裁不实行级别管辖和地域管辖。"这条规定说明,当事人在仲裁中可以自行选择解决纠纷的仲裁机构,这是仲裁区别于诉讼的一个重要特点。参与仲裁的当事人最关心的,是纠纷能否得到公正、及时和低成本的解决,所以准确选择仲裁机构是极为重要的。

　　商事仲裁翻译则是商事仲裁过程中相关文本(包括法律文本、合同等)的书面翻译和协商过程中的口头翻译。碍于篇幅,本书将以商事仲裁的书面翻译为主,兼有少量口头翻译的内容。

　　法律翻译是一个涵盖范围甚广的概念,其主要涉及四大类文本:(1)国际公约及双边或多边条约、宪法、法规、条例;(2)司法机构的各种公文,如法庭判决、案例报告、各种诉状、答辩书以及各种举证、取证文书等;(3)合同、协议、契约以及各种具有法律效力的证书,如遗嘱、文凭、出生证等;(4)公司、法人组织的章程、规定等。法律文书的性质不同,对其译文精确程度的要求也不可能相同,针对其中被称为"准法律文件"(quasi legal documents)的部分,如第(4)类及第(2)类中的某些文件,只要译文能符合"准确"这一要求,便已是务实了。商事仲裁翻译中的相关仲裁法律之翻译属于第(1)类和第(2)类,而当事人签订的合约或者公司的章程属于第(3)类和第(4)类。

　　对商事仲裁翻译的研究和学习非常重要,因为虽然仲裁的过程在强制性执行等方面没有法律那样要求的严格,但是其中的文本理解和传述也不容半点含糊。在跨境的商事仲裁中,要想获得主动性,首先就涉及对商事仲裁语言的了解和精准阐释,以避免耗费大量人力、物力,却仍然得不到理想的结果。

例如,在 London & leeds Estates Ltd. v. Paribas Ltd.(No. 2)(1995)2 E. G. 134 一案中,一方认为另一方的专家意见与其之前的不一致,于是要求提供该专家证人在此之前的意见。Mince 法官认为,在该案中,判断有关指控比维护仲裁的机密性更为重要,他说:

"If a witness were proved to have expressed himself in a materially different sense when acting for different sides,that could be a factor which should be brought out in the interests of individual litigants involved and in the public interest."

但是,Mince 法官提到的"公众利益"(public interest),实为"公正利益"(the interest of justice),所以大家不要错以为凡涉公众利益者皆可避开仲裁的机密性而向外披露,事实上该案考虑的是公正的问题。在 Ali Shipping Corporation v. Shipyard Trogir(1998)Lloyd's Rep. 643 一案中,Potter 大法官对 Mince 法官所指的公众利益有以下看法:

"It seems to me clear that,in that context,Mr. Justice Mince was referring to the 'public interest' in the sense of 'the interest of justice',namely the importance of a judicial decision being reached upon the basis of the truthful or accurate evidence of the witnesses concerned."

由此可见,通常的那些简单、表面的"准确"翻译,有时候在商事仲裁中是不一定能够真正传达原意的,因此只有对法理、法规及实践足够熟悉,才能做到"不逾矩"。

第二节　商事仲裁翻译准则

李克兴教授认为,"法律文本的翻译有三项基本原则,分别为:

(1)准确性及精确性;(2)一致性及同一性;(3)清晰及简练。"①在商事仲裁翻译中,准确性及精确性毋庸置疑是首要条件。对于商事仲裁翻译而言,除了准确性及精确性还需加上表达多样性及同一性与专业性两条原则。

1. 准确性及精确性(Accuracy and Precision)

准确性及精确性是所有翻译的基本要求。一般翻译的基本要求就是忠实于原文,这就是要求译文有较高程度的准确性,在传递原文所包含的基本信息方面较少失真。但是,这样的要求对于法律文献翻译来说仍然过于笼统,并且很不全面。法律文书本身在写作上的严肃性决定了法律文书翻译工作的特殊性。《法律语言》一书的作者 David Mellink 写道:"... that opposing themselves to 'the inherent vagueness' of language attempts at precision of expression."(Chen, 1992:164‐165) 在论述法律文书的写作风格时,Henry Weihofen 也阐明了对法律文书写作的精确性之要求及其重要意义:

"The lawyer must be more precise in his writing than almost anyone else. Most writers can expect their work to be read in good faith,that is,with an honest desire to understand what was meant. But the lawyer must write in constant fear of what we might call the reader in bad faith,the man looking for loopholes in the contract so as to avoid liability for his failure to perform,the disappointed heir who wants the will read in a way that would defeat the testator's intention,the criminal defendant who the statute interpreted so as not to cover his act,and all the others who will want to twist the meaning of words for their own ends."(Chen,1992:164‐165)

在这里,上文作者提出的,对法律文书写作时的用词遣句之要求不只是要"准确",而是要"更加精确"。在大多数情况下,法律文书是由训练有素的律师、法官和其他司法专家按照一定格式撰写的,其在表达思

---

① 李克兴:《法律翻译 译·注·评》(翻译名师讲评系列),清华大学出版社 2018 年版,第 39 页。

想、叙述事实、说明法理、确立职责、规定奖罚等方面均比其他类型的著作更加严谨，措辞也更加确切。

在 Union of India v. McDonnell Douglas（1993）2 Lloyd's Rep. 48 一案中，一个涉及人造卫星发射的协议第 8 条的仲裁条文规定如下：

"in the event of a dispute ⋯ arising out of or in connection with this agreement ⋯ the same shall be referred to an Arbitration Tribunal ⋯ The arbitration shall be conducted in accordance with the procedure provided in the India Arbitration Act of 1940 or any reenactment or modification thereof. The arbitration shall be conducted in the English language ⋯ The seat of the arbitration proceedings shall be London, United Kingdom ⋯"

另外，协议第 11 条说："本协议以印度法适用与解释。"[①]显然，根据第 11 条，该协议所依照的实体法是印度法。但是，协议第 8 条说明，如果要依照印度 1940 年《仲裁法》，那么就要给它一定的解释了。好的合约解释就是尽量给双方约定的条文与文字一个合理解释，而不随意去删除或否定条文内容，因为法官或仲裁员不是订约方。如果是作为程序法来解释，那么就会带来非常不完满的结果，如当事人动不动就要去印度法院寻求救济。在 1940 年《仲裁法》中，印度仍允许"特殊案件"（pecial case）中的当事人通过裁决书将法律问题提交上诉法院，但英国适用的已经是 1979 年《仲裁法》，其规定当事人需要上诉批文才能上诉。这只是许多差异中的一个，但足见情况是令人非常不满意与不确定的。所以，Saville 大法官说：

"The choice of a procedural law different from the law of the place of arbitration will at least where that place was England, necessarily mean that the parties had actually chosen to have their arbitrable proceedings at least potentially governed both by their

---

① "... the agreement is to be governed by, interpreted and construed in accordance with the laws of India."

express choice and by the laws of England; such a state of affairs was clearly highly unsatisfactory and the question was whether the parties had agreed to such a potentially unsatisfactory method of regulating their arbitration proceedings."

结果，Saville 大法官判定，明示的印度仲裁法只能针对仲裁的内部操作(internal conducts)，而外部的法院监督(external supervision)仍由英国法院而不是印度法院负责，估计这样做就意味着把印度仲裁法当作仲裁规则(arbitration rules)来解释。上述解释主要是依据第 8 仲裁条文中的"操作"(conducted)一词，Saville 大法官说："I agree 'conducted' is more apt to describe the way in which the parties and the Tribunal are to carry on their proceedings than the supervision of those proceedings by the Indian Court."英国法律有这样一个说法，即把双方当事人之间及双方当事人与仲裁庭之间的关系当作内部法律(internal law)，而针对国家通过法院与参与仲裁的人士所形成之关系的是外部法(external law)。

为此，在法律翻译中，我们将准确性和精确性作为标准一并提出。具体言之，在翻译准法律文件时，我们可将准确性作为准则；而在对待正式程度较高的法律文件时，我们就要非以精确性为原则不可。

2. 表达多样性及同一性(Diversification and Identity)

与其他法律文书相比，商事仲裁提交的文书请求的写作要求相对宽松。文书请求有许多不同名称，但本质与作用相同。"索赔请求"可以是"statement of claim""statement of case""memorial""claim submissions"或"points of claim"，而抗辩请求可以是"statement of defence""rebuttal"或"points of defence"，"statement of case""memorial"或"claim submissions"则含有全面抗辩的味道。但是，准确名称在现实中也并不重要，实质内容才重要。笔者多次见过名为"points of claim"的文件，但其内容却包括全面陈述案情与法律争辩，这在法院诉讼中是不可以的。

在法律文献的翻译中，整篇文章甚至整个法律体系坚持用同一词语表示同一概念是值得推崇的，即便这样做有时会使译文读起来味同嚼蜡,因为法律文献的最高翻译准则是准确性和精确性,任何同义词、等义词或近义词的使用都不得以牺牲这个准则为代价。因此,重复使用同一词语表达同一概念也是法律文献写作和法律翻译中值得提倡的做法。反之,为了避免词语的重复,绞尽脑汁地用五花八门的同义词取而代之,其效果将适得其反。《法律文体》一书的作者 Henry Weihofen 强调说:

"Tactness often demands repeating the same term to express the same idea. Where that is true never be afraid of using the same word over and over again."(Chen,1992:164-165)

在同一法律体系的不同法律条例中,译文如此刻板但如此高度统一,这不仅代表了法律语言的独特风格,而且体现了译者在翻译过程中所奉行的一致性和同一性之原则。如上所述,正因为日常的法律文献翻译中违反译名同一原则的错误相当普遍,而撰写司法文章本身又有概念同一、表述一致的要求,并且权威的法律条例翻译实践也素来奉行同一原则,故笔者认为完全有必要将"同一性"列为一条法律翻译的准则。在无官方释义可循的法律文献中(如跨国公司之间的专业合约、经济合同等),译者应采取"界定术语"(defined terms)的方式,以使同一系宗的法律文献译文中的关键词在表述上前后一致,概念上始终同一。

3. 专业性

国家贸仲委的规则和实践对书面翻译的形式并无强制性规定,但在涉及域外形成的证据时,仲裁庭是否需参照《最高人民法院关于民事诉讼证据的若干规定》第十一条,要求当事人提供证据翻译件的公证和认证呢? 惯常实践是,仲裁庭在收到一方当事人提交的证据及其翻译件后,转交对方当事人质证,如对方当事人要求提供证据翻译件的公证和认证,仲裁庭出于审慎,会要求提交证据一方完善证据形式。当事人提交书面翻译的必要性,均由仲裁庭在征求双方当事人意见后作出决定。为保障仲裁程序之快捷便利,并非所有与仲裁语言的文字形式不同的文件均需提交书面翻译。例如,在以中文进行的仲裁程序中,如果作为证据提交的双方往来电邮是英文形式,但各方均可明了电邮内容,且非证据提供方同意就英文电邮进行质证,那么仲裁庭并不强求当事人提供相应的中文译本。仲裁涉及的另一重要书面翻译类型，是裁决书的翻译。根据《承认及执行外国仲裁裁决公约》第四条，如裁决书所用文字非承认及执行国的正式文字，申请承认及执行裁决的当事人需提交裁决书的翻译件，"译本应由公设或宣誓之翻译员或外交或领事人员认证"。为便利当事人，贸仲委在当事人提交书面申请、说明翻译件的用途，以及预交翻译费后，提供裁决书的翻译，并附具译本与裁决书原文内容一致的证明。

国际商事仲裁中的"商事性"一词是表述国际经济贸易活动的惯用语，确定一项争议是否属于商事争议，是仲裁制度中的先决事项，它关系到争议能否以仲裁方式解决，以及裁决作出后能否得到本国法院或外国法院的承认与执行。这是因为大多数国家的法律都将某些争议排除在仲裁管辖的范围之外，当事人无权将非商事性质的争议交付仲裁解决。例如，1997 年 7 月 1 日生效的新西兰仲裁法对实施了长达 90 年之久的原仲裁法进行了修订，该法规定消费争议不属于可仲裁的事项。1996 年 9 月 23 日通过的巴西仲裁法明确规定，家庭和有关身份的争议不能仲裁解决。商事仲裁的专业性源于其所包含的主要内容非常专业，其涉及的领域包括"供应或交换商品或劳务的任何贸易交易；销售协议；商事代表或代理；租赁；建造工厂；咨询；工程；设计；许可证；投资；银行；保险；开发协议或特许权；合营或其他形式的工业或商业合作；货物或旅客的航空、海上、铁路或公路的运输"[①]。

第三节　商事仲裁翻译特点

商事仲裁的目的是迅速、实际和有效地解决商事问题。与早期的仲裁法相比，现代仲裁法变得更加复杂化、法制化、制度化。一般而言，商事仲裁翻译应该具有以下特点：

---

① 郑远民：《国际私法——国际民事诉讼法与国际商事仲裁法》，中信出版社 2002 年版，第 215 页。

（1）保持原有仲裁的公正性（Impartiality）；

（2）不影响裁决的可执行性（Enforceability）——仲裁裁决是终局性的，只在非常有限的情况下才能被质疑；

（3）正式性和专业性（Formality and specialty）——国际仲裁公约的法律起草人使用正式和专业的语言，双方可以选择具有技术背景的仲裁员，这些仲裁员将能够理解案件中的具体问题；

（4）一致性（Uniformity）——具体的仲裁程序可能因国而异，但国际公约对仲裁的影响是，对于世界上大多数重要的贸易国而言，仲裁裁决的承认和执行是相当一致的，因此商事仲裁翻译应该努力促成其一致性。

第二章　商事仲裁翻译分析

第一节　商事仲裁词汇翻译

与其他法律语言相似,商事仲裁的词汇具有专门性、排他性等特点,详情请参见下表。

中文词汇	英语翻译
仲裁	arbitration
调解	conciliation
调停	mediation
裁判	adjudication
申诉	grievance naming
请求	claims
故意	deliberate
恶意	bad faith
调解	mediation
先例	precedent
约定	agree
和解	conciliation
域名	domain names

续　表

中文词汇	英语翻译
裁判型	adjudicational type
契约型	contractual type
不适任	disqualification
警察法	lois de police
场所化	localization
博弈论	game theory
特权法	privilege law
实时讯	instant messaging
出庭权	jus standi
不履行	non-performance
冷却期	cooling off period
丝绒锤（为互建信任提供契机来解决矛盾冲突的方法）	the velvet hammer
程序公正	procedural justice
实体公正	substantive justice
仲裁协议	arbitration agreement
往来函电	in an exchange of letters or telegrams
临时仲裁	ad hoc arbitration
显名代理	agency of named principal
隐名代理	agency of unnamed principal
地方标准	local standard
发回重审	remission
特殊类型	sui genceris
剩余条款	residual clause
宪法权利	novel constitutional claims
最终机构	ultimate agency

续　表

中文词汇	英语翻译
私人审判	private judging
取消传唤	moves to quash the subpoena
调解协商	mediation consultation
开示义务	duty to disclosure
混合程序	mixed process
电子签名	digital signatures
在线监察	Online ombuds
发现程序	discovery
微型审判	mini-trial
监察专员	ombudsman
租借法官	rent a judge
地理标准	geographical criterion
法律标准	juridical criterion
网络和解	Cyber-settle
直接磋商	direct negotiation
模拟调解	simulated mediation
点击和解	Click'n' settle
汽油条例	gasoline rules
海事争议	maritime dispute （广义包括 maritime matters 或 maritime affairs）
杰森条款	Jason clause
法定基准	statutory baseline
合并诉求	consolidation of claims
追索诉讼	pursuit litigation
艰难条款	hardship clause
政府机构	state organs

续　表

中文词汇	英语翻译
审查机制	screening mechanism
专家裁断	expert determination
特许协议	concession
国家契约	state contract
稳定条款	stabilization clause
调整条款	adaptation clause
排他性的	exclusively
契约地法	lex contractus
非国内化	denationalized
保证机制	guarantee scheme
索还机制	chargeback system
事实认定	fact finding
行为守则	codes of conduct
联络中心	the clearing house
控诉中心	call centre
域名系统	Domain Name System，DNS
联邦仲裁法	Federal Arbitration Act，FAA
专家研究所	the academic of experts
短员仲裁庭	truncated arbitral tribunal
非国内裁决	non-domestic award
国际流通币	international currency
英美普通法	common law
民事调停法	the law for civil affairs
从表面上看	prima facie
依职权自行	sua sponte
否认性言论	negative commitment

中文词汇	英语翻译
预防性方法	preventive means
特别主事人	special master
对人管辖权	personal Jurisdiction
合同自始无效	uoid ab initio
双重许可制度	double exequatur
无中不能生有	ex nitil nil fit
美国仲裁协会	American Arbitration Association，AAA
国际律师协会	International Bar Association，IBA
美国律师协会	American Bar Association，ABA
撤销仲裁裁决	setting aside of award
准司法的性质	quasi-judicial
近邻司法中心	neighborhood justice centers
公共资源中心	center for public resources
自动移转规则	automatic assignment rule
简易陪审审判	summary jury trial
电子数据交换	Electronic Data Interchange，EDI
最终仲裁条款	terminal arbitration clause
双边投资条约	bilateral investment treaties
投资保证协定	investment guarantee agreement
重新协商条款	re-negotiation clause
能源宪章条约	energy charter treaty
高额低额仲裁	high-low arbitration
最后要约仲裁	final-offer arbitration
信誉标志机制	trust mark scheme
监察专员制度	ombudsman
半约束性调解	semi-binding mediation

续　表

中文词汇	英语翻译
早期中立评议	early neutral evaluation
进一步活动说	additional activity
原告法院管辖	forum actoris
信息社会服务	information society services
按比例增减说	sliding scale
有知觉的阶段	perceived injurious experiences
小额索赔程序	small claims procedures
反托拉斯诉讼	antitrust litigation
实质性连结因素	material connecting factors
审判前文件开示	discovery of document
仲裁条款独立性理论/（又称）仲裁条款自治性理论/仲裁条款分离性理论/仲裁条款分割性理论	doctrine of arbitration clause/autonomy reparability of arbitration clause/severability of arbitration clause/theory of autonomy of the arbitration clause
显然漠视法律原则	manifest disregard of law
仲裁的质量取决于仲裁员	arbitration is as good as arbitrators
国际仲裁员行为准则	ethics for international arbitrators
国际大会及会议协会	International Council of Chemical Associations，ICCA
双方当事人陈述	audi alteram partem
有利害关系的案件	nemo index in parte sua
仲裁庭审判不公	miscarriage of justice
不具有可仲裁性	non-habitability
无知觉的伤害经验	unperceived injurious experiences
选择性争议解决方法法	alternative dispute resolution act 1998
中立专家事实认定	neutral expert finding
披露本人的代理	agency of disclosed principal

续　表

中文词汇	英语翻译
未披露本人的代理	agency of undisclosed principal
司法仲裁和调解服务机构	Judicial Arbitration and Mediation Services，JAMS
在线争议解决网络周	online dispute resolution cyberweek
国际在线争议解决论坛	international forum on online dispute resolution
民事司法改革法	Civil Justice Reform Act of 1990，CJRA
城市争议专家小组	the City Dispute Panel，CDP
创造和平的功能	peace-making function
家庭关系调停法	the law for adjustment of domestic relations
国际商会选择性调解规则	optional conciliation rules，ICC
世界知识产权组织	World Intellectual Property Organization，WIPO
WIPO 仲裁和调解中心	the WIPO arbitration and mediation centre
互联网名称与数字地址分配机构	the Internet corporation for assigned names and numbers
WIPO 的加速仲裁规则	the WIPO expedited arbitration rules
全球和国内商业电子签名法	the electronic signatures in global and national commerce act
快速低廉仲裁规则	fast and low cost arbitration rules
美国环境保护署	environment protection agency
美国国家海洋渔业服务机构	national marine fisheries service
濒临野生动植物物种国际贸易公约	Convention on International Trade in Endangered Species of Wild Fauna and Flora，CITES
小额标的的特别程序	small claims special procedures
加纳 1994 年投资法	Ghana Investment Promotion Centre Act

续　表

中文词汇	英语翻译
解决国家与他国国民之间投资争议公约	Convention on the Settlement of Investment Dispute Between States and Nationals of Other States
解决投资争端国际中心	International Centre for Settlement of Investment Disputes ICSID
ICSID 附加功能规则	the ICSID additional facility rules
结构测试和功能测试法	structural and functional test
少数、非控制和间接股东	minority non-controlling and indirect shareholders
最优惠投资者或东道国条款	most favored investor/host state clause
特定事实与整体评估	fact-specific and holistic assessment
必须与东道国法律保持一致	in accordance with the laws of the host state
北美自由贸易协定	North American Free Trade Agreement，NAFTA
既决事项或定案	res judicata
否定或肯定的禁令	negative or positive injunction
友好通商航海条约	friendship，commerce and navigation treaties
促进与保护投资协定	agreement for promotion and protection of investment
避免无义请求的机制	mechanism to avoid "frivolous claims"
改进岔路口条款	improving the "fork in the road"
东南亚国家联盟促进与保护协定	the agreement of the members of the association of southeast Asian nations for the promotion and protection of investments，ASEAN agreement
南方共同市场关于促进与相互保护投资的科洛尼亚议定书	colonia investment of the common market of the southern cone，mercosur
布宜诺斯艾利斯投资议定书	Buenos Aires investment protocol of mercosur

中文词汇	英语翻译
卡塔赫纳自由贸易协定	cartagena free trade agreement
股权式合营合同	Equity joint venture contract
不正当契约理论	the doctrine of unconscionability
直接适用的法	direct applicable rules
契约式合营合同	contractual joint venture contract
强制性仲裁条款	mandatory arbitration clause
跟单信用证争议解决规则	rules for documentary credit dispute resolution expertise，DOCDEX Rules
跟单信用证银行偿付统一规则	uniform rules for bank to bank reimbursement under documentary credits URR
欧洲信息技术观测组	European information technology observatory
欧盟电子商务动议	A European initiative in electronic commerce
法院外争议解决机制	out-of-court dispute settlement system
双赢的解决方法	win-win solution
消费者投诉机制	consumer complaint system
欧洲司法外争议解决机制网络	the European Extra-Judicial Network，EEJ-NET
冲突管理或协商	conflict management or negotiations
欧洲自由贸易区	European Free Trade Association，EFTA
北欧消费者专员监察机构	the nordic consumer ombudsman
与标的有关的管辖权	Jurisdiction relating to subject-matter
欧洲直接销售者联合会	federation of european direct marketing
统一计算机信息交易法	the Uniform Computer Information Transaction Act

第二节 商事仲裁句式翻译

1. 仲裁句式多以被动句为主,体现公正性和客观性,例如:

(1) The parties who may be appointed or designated as arbitrators must meet the following requirements:(《印度尼西亚商事仲裁法》,第 12 条)

可指定或任命为仲裁员的当事人必须符合下列要求:

(2) This Act comes into operation on a date to be appointed by the Minister by notification in the Gazette. (《马来西亚仲裁法》2005,第一部分)

本法案于部长在宪报上指定的日期生效。

(3) Representative is a person duly authorized in writing by a party to a dispute, who could be a counsel, a person in his/her employ or any other person of his/her choice, duly authorized to represent said party in the arbitration proceedings.(《菲律宾仲裁法》,适用于国际商业一章的术语 12)

代表是指争议一方当事人以书面形式正式授权的人,他可以是律师、受雇的人或他选择的任何其他人,有权在仲裁程序中代表该方当事人。

2. 仲裁句式多利用情态动词成句来标识指令性、承诺性和宣告性的特点。比如,汉语中的"必须""应当""可以""不得""严禁""禁止"等,以及英语中的"shall""should""may""be obliged"等。例如:

(4)A mediator shall make reasonable efforts to ensure that each party understands the nature and character of the mediation proceedings including private caucuses, the issues, the available options, the alternatives to non-settlement, and that each party is free and able to make whatever choices he/she desires regarding participation in mediation generally and regarding specific settlement options. If a mediator believes that a party，who is not represented by counsel，is unable to understand，or fully participate in，the mediation proceedings for any reason，a mediator may either：(《马来西亚仲裁法》,第 3.9 条)

调解人应付出合理努力,确保每一方了解调解程序的性质和特征,包括私人核心小组、问题、现有选择、非解决办法,并确保每一方在一般参与调解和具体解决办法方面可以自由做出自己希望的任何选择。如果调解人认为没有律师代理的当事方因任何原因不能理解或充分参与调解程序,调解人也可以:

(5) A reference in a bill of lading to a charterparty or other document containing an arbitration clause shall constitute an arbitration agreement if the reference is such as to make that clause part of the bill of lading.(《文莱商事仲裁法》,仲裁协议 4.5)

提单中提及的租船合同或其他含仲裁条款的文件,若提及该条款是提单的一部分,即构成仲裁协议。

(6) This Law shall not affect any other law of the Kingdom of Cambodia by virtue of which certain dispute may be submitted to arbitration or other dispute resolution procedures，or by virtue of which certain disputes may not be submitted to arbitration.(《柬埔寨商事仲裁法》,第 1 条)

本法不影响柬埔寨王国的任何其他法律,某些争议可以提交仲裁或其他争端解决程序,某些争议不能提交仲裁。

第三章　商事仲裁文本范例

第一节　印度尼西亚商事仲裁法英汉对照

Law No. 30 of 1999
CONCERNING
  ARBITRATION AND ALTERNATIVE DISPUTE RESOLUTION
1999 年第 30 号法律
事关仲裁和替代性争议解决机制
  WITH THE GRACE OF GOD ALMIGHTY
  THE PRESIDENT OF THE REPUBLIC OF INDONESIA
  以全能之神和印度尼西亚共和国总统的恩典

CONSIDERING，*that*：
考虑到：
a. Whereas，under prevailing regulations having the force of law，
civil dispute resolution besides being submitted to the public courts
also has the possibility of being submitted to arbitration and/or
alternative dispute resolution；
a. 根据现行的具有法律效力的条例,民事争议的解决办法除了提交公
共法院之外,还有可能提交仲裁或以其他方式解决争议；
b. Whereas，the current regulations having the force of law applicable to

dispute resolution by means of arbitration are no longer in sufficient to address developments in the business world and law in general;

b. 然而,现行的可以通过仲裁手段解决争议的有法律效力的条例,已经不足以应对商业和一般法律发展中出现的问题;

c. Whereas, based on the considerations specified in points a and b, above, it is necessary to stipulate an Act concerning Arbitration and Alternative Dispute Resolution.

c. 而根据上文 a 和 b 所述的考虑,有必要规定一项关于仲裁和替代性争议解决的法案。

In View Of:

鉴于:

1. Article 5 paragraph (1) and Article 20 paragraph (1) of the 1945 constitution;

1. 1945 年《宪法》第 5 条第(1)款和第 20 条第(1)款;

2. Basic Provisions of Judicial Authority Act (Law No. 14 of 1970 (State Gazette Book

Number 74 of 1970, Supplement Number 2951);

2.《司法权力法》的基本规定(1970 年第 14 号法律《国家公报》1970 年第 74 号,补编第 2951 号);

WITH THE APPROVAL OF

THE PEOPLE'S LEGISLATIVE ASSEMBLY OF THE REPUBLIC OF INDONESIA HAS DECIDED:

To promulgate this

ARBITRATION and ALTERNATIVE DISPUTE RESOLU-TION ACT

经印度尼西亚共和国人民议会批准

公布此

仲裁和替代性争议解决法案

CHAPTER I
GENERAL PROVISIONS
第一章 总则

Article 1

第1条

In this Act the following terms have the following meanings：.

在本法中，下列术语具有以下含义：

（1）Arbitration shall mean a mechanism of settling civil disputes outside the general courts based upon an arbitration agreement entered into in writing by the disputing Parties；

（1）仲裁是指在一般法院以外根据争议各方书面订立的仲裁协议解决民事争议的机制；

（2）Parties shall be legal entities，based upon civil and/or public law；

（2）当事人应当是以民法和公法为基础的法人；

（3）Arbitration agreement shall mean a written agreement in the form of an arbitration clause entered into by the parties before a dispute arises，or a separate written arbitration agreement made by the parties after a dispute arises.

（3）仲裁协议是指当事人在争议发生前订立的仲裁条款形式的书面协议或者当事人在争议发生后订立的单独的书面仲裁协议。

（4）District Court shall mean the District Court having jurisdiction over the Respondent.

（4）地区法院是指对被告有管辖权的地区法院。

（5）Claimant shall mean the party submitting the request for resolution of the dispute by arbitration.

（5）原告是指提出仲裁请求的当事人。

（6）Respondent shall mean the party opposing the Claimant in the resolution of the dispute by arbitration.

（6）被申请人是指在仲裁解决争议中反对原告的一方。

（7）Arbitrator(s)(or arbitrator(s)) shall mean one or more persons designated by the parties in dispute or appointed by the District Court or by an arbitration institution to render an award regarding the particular dispute submitted for resolution by arbitration.

（7）仲裁员是指争议各方指定或地区法院或仲裁机构指定的一名或多名人员，负责就提交仲裁解决的特定争议作出裁决。

（8）Arbitration Institution shall mean a body designated by the parties in dispute to render an award with regard to a particular dispute. This institution may also give a binding opinion concerning a particular legal relationship where a dispute has not yet arisen.

（8）仲裁机构是指争议各方指定就某一特定争议作出裁决的机构。该机构还可就尚未发生争议的特定法律关系提出具有约束力的意见。

（9）International Arbitration Awards shall mean awards handed down by an arbitration institution or individual arbitrator(s) outside the jurisdiction of the Republic of Indonesia，or an award by an arbitration institution or individual arbitrators(s) which under the provisions of Indonesian law are deemed to be International arbitra-tion awards.

（9）国际仲裁裁决是指由印度尼西亚共和国管辖范围以外的仲裁机构或个人仲裁员作出的裁决，或仲裁机构或个人仲裁员作出的裁决，根据印度尼西亚法律的规定，这些裁决被视为国际仲裁裁决。

（10）Alternative Dispute Resolution（or "ADR"）shall mean a mechanism for the resolution of disputes or differences of opinion through procedures agreed upon by the parties，i.e. resolution outside the courts by consultation，negotiation，mediation，conciliation，or expert assessment.

（10）替代性争议解决机制是指通过当事方商定的程序解决争议或意

见分歧的机制,即通过协商、谈判、调解、和解或专家评估在法庭外解决。

Article 2

This Act shall regulate the resolution of disputes or differences of opinion between parties having a particular legal relationship who have entered into an arbitration agreement which explicitly states that all disputes or differences of opinion arising or which may arise from such legal relationship will be resolved by arbitration or through alternative dispute resolution.

第 2 条

本法应规范具有特定法律关系的当事方之间达成仲裁协议的争议或意见分歧的解决,该协议明确规定,所有由这种法律关系引起或可能引起的争议或意见分歧将通过仲裁或以替代性争议解决方式解决。

Article 3

The District Court shall have no jurisdiction to try disputes between parties bound by an arbitration agreement.

第 3 条

地区法院无权审理受仲裁协议约束的当事人之间的争议。

Article 4
第 4 条

（1）In the event the parties have previously agreed that disputes between them are to be resolved through arbitration and have granted such authority，the arbitrators are competent to determine in their award the rights and obligations of the parties if these matters are not regulated in their agreement.

（1）如果当事各方先前已商定通过仲裁解决双方之间的争议并授予此

种权力,对于未在其协议中加以规定的事项,仲裁员有权在其裁决中确定当事各方的权利和义务。

（2）The agreement to resolve disputes through arbitration, as specified in paragraph（1）, shall be contained in a document signed by the parties.

（2）第（1）款规定的通过仲裁解决争议的协议,应载于双方当事人签署的文件中。

（3）In the event the agreement for resolution of disputes by arbitration is contained in an exchange of correspondence, including letters, telexes, telegrams, faxes, e-mail, or any other form of communication, the same shall be accompanied by a record of receipt of such correspondence by the parties.

（3）如果通过仲裁解决争议的协议载于一份换文,包括信件、电传、电报、传真、电子邮件或任何其他形式的通信,该换文应附有当事各方收到此种通信的记录。

Article 5

第 5 条

（1）Only disputes of a commercial nature, or those concerning rights which, under the law and regulations, fall within the full legal authority of the disputing parties, may be settled through arbitration.

（1）只有具有商业性质的争议,或涉及根据法律和条例属于争议各方充分法律权力范围的权利的争议,才可通过仲裁解决。

（2）Disputes which may not be resolved by arbitration are disputes where according to regulations having the force of law no amicable settlement is possible.

（2）不能通过仲裁解决的争议是指根据具有法律效力的条例无法友好解决的争议。

CHAPTER II
ALTERNATIVE DISPUTE RESOLUTION
第二章　替代性争议解决机制

Article 6

第 6 条

（1） Disputes or differences of opinion that are not of a criminal nature may be resolved by the parties through Alternative Dispute Resolution（"ADR"）based on their good faith，by waiving such resolution by litigation in the District Court.

（1）非刑事性质的争议或意见分歧可由当事方根据其诚意，通过替代性争议解决机制放弃通过在地区法院的诉讼解决。

（2） Resolution of disputes or differences of opinion through ADR，as contemplated in paragraph（1），shall be carried out through a direct meeting of the parties not later than fourteen（14）days and the outcome shall be set out in a written agreement.

（2）如按第(1)款通过替代性争议解决机制解决争议或意见分歧，应在不迟于 14 天的缔约方直接会议上执行，其结果应在一份书面协议中列明。

（3） In the event the dispute or difference of opinion cannot be resolved，as contemplated in paragraph（2），then by a written agreement of the parties，the dispute or difference of opinion between the parties may be resolved through the assistance of one or more expert advisors or a mediator.

（3）如果争议或意见分歧不能如第(2)款所规定的那样得到解决，则当事方之间的争议或意见分歧可通过一名或多名专家顾问或调解人的协助加以解决。

（4） If the parties fail to reach an agreement as to the resolution of such dispute within fourteen（14）days with the assistance of one or more expert advisors or a mediator，or the mediator is not successful in reconciling the parties concerned，such parties may request an Arbitration or ADR Institution to appoint a mediator.

（4）如果当事各方在一名或多名专家顾问或调解人的协助下，在 14 天内达成后或在调解人未能成功调解有关各方的情况下，这些当事方可请求仲裁或代理机构指定调解人。

（5）After the appointment of the mediator by such arbitration or ADR institution，the mediation process shall be commenced within seven（7）days.

（5）该仲裁或仲裁机构指定调解人后，调解程序应在 7 天内开始。

（6）Efforts to resolve disputes or differences of opinion through mediation，as contemplated in paragraph（5），shall be undertaken in confidentiality. The settlement reached shall be set out in a written agreement，signed by all parties concerned，within thirty（30）days.

（6）第（5）款所规定的通过调解解决争议或意见分歧的努力应保密进行。达成的协议应在 30 天内由有关各方签署书面协议。

（7）The written agreement for such resolution of the dispute or difference of opinion shall be final and binding on the parties concerned，shall be implemented in good faith，and shall be registered in the District Court within no more than thirty（30）days after it has been signed.

（7）有关解决争议或意见分歧的书面协议为最终协议，对有关各方具有约束力，应本着诚意予以执行，并应在协议签署后 30 天内在地区法院登记。

（8）The agreement for resolution of the dispute or difference of opinion contemplated in paragraph（7）shall be completely implemented within no more than thirty（30）days after its registration.

（8）第（7）款所规定的解决争议或意见分歧的协议应在其登记后 30 天内完全执行。

（9）If attempts to reach an amicable settlement，as contemplated in paragraphs（1）to（6），are unsuccessful，the parties，based on a written agreement，may submit the matter to resolution by an arbitration institution or ad-hoc arbitration.

（9）如果试图按照第（1）款至第（6）款的规定达成友好解决的努力失败，当事各方可根据书面协议将该事项提交仲裁机构或特别仲裁解决。

CHAPTER III
CONDITIONS OF ARBITRATION，APPOINTMENT OF ARBITRATORS AND RIGHT OF RECUSAL
第三章　仲裁条件、指定仲裁员和回避权
First Part
Conditions of Arbitration
第一部分　仲裁条件

Article 7

The parties may agree that a dispute which arises，or which may arise，between them shall be resolved by arbitration.

第 7 条

双方当事人可以约定，双方之间发生的或可能发生的争议应以仲裁方式解决。

Article 8
第 8 条

（1）In the event that a dispute arises，the Claimant shall inform the Respondent by registered letter，telegram，telex，fax，e-mail，or by courier that the conditions for arbitration to be entered into by the Claimant and Respondent are applicable.

（1）发生争议时，申请人应当以挂号信、电报、电传、传真、电子邮件或者信使的形式通知被申请人，以申请人与被申请人订立的仲裁条件适用的方式为准。

(2) The notification of Arbitration，as contemplated in paragraph (1)，shall expressly state at least the following：

(2) 第(1)款所规定的仲裁通知至少应明确规定：

a. The names and addresses of the parties；

a. 当事方的名称和地址；

b. Reference to the applicable arbitration clause or agreement；

b. 提及适用的仲裁条款或协议；

c. The agreement or matter being the subject of the dispute；

c. 作为争议标的的协议或事项；

d. The basis for the claim and the amount claimed，if any；

d. 索赔依据和索赔额（如有）；

e. The method of resolution desired；and

e. 所需的解决方法；以及

f. The agreement entered into by the parties concerning the number of arbitrators or，if no such agreement has been entered into，the Claimant may propose the total number of arbitrators，provided such is an odd number.

f. 当事各方就仲裁员人数达成的协议，或者如果尚未达成协议，申请人可提出仲裁员总数，且该总数应当是奇数。

Article 9
第 9 条

(1) In the event the parties choose resolution of the dispute by arbitration after a dispute has arisen，their designation of arbitration as the means of resolution of such dispute must be given in a written agreement signed by the parties.

(1) 当事人在争议发生后选择仲裁方式解决的，应当以书面协议的形式指定仲裁方式解决。

(2) In the event the parties are unable to sign the written agreement as contemplated in paragraph (1)，such written agreement must

be drawn by by a Notary in the form of a notarial deed.

（2）如果当事人不能按照第（1）款的规定签署书面协议，该书面协议必须由公证人以公证契约的形式签署。

（3）The written agreement contemplated in paragraph（1）must contain：

（3）第（1）款所规定的书面协议必须包括：

  a. The subject matter of the dispute；

  a. 争议的主题事项；

  b. The full names and addresses of residence of the parties；

  b. 当事方的全名和住址；

  c. The full name and place of residence of the arbitrator or arbitrators；

  c. 仲裁员的全名和居住地；

  d. The place the arbitrator or arbitration panel will make their decision；

  d. 仲裁员或仲裁小组作出决定的地点；

  e. The full name of the secretary；

  e. 秘书的全名；

  f. The period in which the dispute shall be resolved；

  f. 解决争议的期限；

  g. A statement of willingness by the arbitrator(s)；and

  g. 仲裁员表示愿意的声明；以及

  h. A statement of willingness of the disputing parties that they will bear all costs necessary for the resolution of the dispute through arbitration

  h. 表明争议各方愿意承担通过仲裁解决争议所需一切费用的声明

（4）A written agreement not containing the matters specified in paragraph（3）will be null and void.

（4）不包含第（3）款所述事项的书面协议无效。

Article 10

第 10 条

An arbitration agreement shall not become null or void under any of the following circumstances：

有下列情形之一的，仲裁协议不得无效：

a. the death of one of the parties；

a. 其中一方死亡；

b. the bankruptcy of one of the parties；

b. 一方当事人破产；

c. novation；

c. 更新；

d. the insolvency of one of the parties；

d. 一方当事人资不抵债；

e. inheritance；

e. 继承；

f. effectivity of requirements for the cancellation of the main contract；

f. 取消主合同要求的有效性；

g. if the implementation of the agreement is transferred to one or more third parties，with the consent of the parties who made the agreement to arbitrate；or

g. 协议的执行经达成仲裁协议的当事方同意，移交给一个或多个第三方；或

h. the expiration of voidance of the main contract.

h. 主合同失效。

Article 11

第 11 条

（1）The existence of a written arbitration agreement shall eliminate the right of the parties to seek resolution of the dispute or difference of opinion contained in the agreement through the District Court.

（1）书面仲裁协议的存在应消除当事方通过地区法院寻求解决协议中所载争议或意见分歧的权利。

（2）The District Court shall refuse and not interfere in settlement of any dispute which has been determined by arbitration except in particular cases determined in this Act.

（2）区法院应拒绝和不干预仲裁所确定的任何争议的解决，但本法确定的特定案件除外。

Second Part

Conditions of Appointment of Arbitrators

第二部分　指定仲裁员的条件

Article 12

第 12 条

（1）The parties who may be appointed or designated as arbitrators must meet the following requirements：

（1）可指定或任命为仲裁员的当事人必须符合下列要求：

　　a. Being authorised or competent to perform legal actions；

　　a. 被授权或有能力采取法律行动；

　　b. Being at least 35 years of age；

　　b. 至少 35 岁；

　　c. Having no family relationship by blood or marriage，to the third degree，with either of the disputing parties；

　　c. 与争议任何一方均无三级血缘或婚姻关系；

　　d. Having no financial or other interest in the arbitration award；and

　　d. 在仲裁裁决中没有经济或其他利益；以及

　　e. Having at least 15 years experience and active mastery in the field.

e. 具有 15 年以上相关工作经验,并在该领域具有一定的专业水平。

（2）Judges, prosecutors, clerks of courts, and other government or court officials may not be appointed or designated as arbitrators.

（2）法官、检察官、法院书记员和其他政府官员、法院工作人员不得被指定为仲裁员。

Article 13
第 13 条

（1）In the event the parties cannot reach agreement on the choice of arbitrators, or no terms have been set concerning the appointment of arbitrators, the Chief Judge of the District Court shall be authorised to appoint the arbitrator or arbitration tribunal.

（1）如果当事各方不能就仲裁员的选择达成协议,或没有就指定仲裁员做出任何规定,则应授权地区法院首席法官指定仲裁员或仲裁庭。

（2）In an ad hoc arbitration, where there is any disagreement between the parties with regard to the appointment of one or more arbitrators, the parties may request the Chief Judge of the District Court to appoint one or more arbitrators for resolution of such dispute.

（2）在特别仲裁中,如果当事各方对指定一名或多名仲裁员有任何分歧,当事各方可请求地区法院首席法官指定一名或多名仲裁员解决此类争议。

Article 14
第 14 条

（1）In the event the parties have agreed that a dispute arising shall be heard and decided upon by a sole arbitrator, the parties must endeavour to reach an agreement concerning the appointment of such sole arbitrator.

（1）如果双方当事人同意由一名独任仲裁员审理和裁决所产生的争议，双方当事人必须努力就该独任仲裁员的任命达成协议。

（2）The Claimant shall propose to the Respondent，by registered letter，telegram，telex，telefax，e-mail or courier service，the name of a person eligible to be appointed as sole arbitrator.

（2）申请人应通过挂号信、电报、电传、传真、电子邮件或信使服务，向被申请人提出有资格被指定为独任仲裁员的人的姓名。

（3）If the parties have not reached agreement as to the sole arbitrator within fourteen（14）days after the Respondent receives the Claimant's proposal contemplated in paragraph（2），then at the request of one of the parties，the Chief Judge of the District Court may appoint the sole arbitrator.

（3）如果双方当事人未能在 14 天内就独任仲裁员达成协议，则应其中一方当事人的请求，区法院首席法官可指定独任仲裁员。

（4）The Chief Judge of the District Court shall appoint a sole arbitrator from a list of names submitted by the parties or obtained from the arbitration organization or institution contemplated in Article 34，with due consideration of the recommendation of or objections to the person concerned submitted by the parties.

（4）区域法院首席法官应根据当事各方提交的名单或根据第 34 条从仲裁组织或机构获得的名单指定一名独任仲裁员，并适当考虑当事各方提交的对独任仲裁员的推荐或反对。

Article 15
第 15 条

（1）The appointment of two arbitrators by the parties shall constitute authority to the two arbitrators to elect and appoint a third arbitrator.

（1）双方当事人指定两名仲裁员应构成两名仲裁员选举和指定第三名

仲裁员的权力。

（2）The third arbitrator contemplated by paragraph（1）shall be appointed as the chair of the arbitration tribunal.

（2）第(1)款规定的第三名仲裁员应被任命为仲裁庭主席。

（3）If within no more than thirty（30）days after notification is received by the Respondent as contemplated in Article 8 paragraph（1），one of the parties has failed to appoint a person as member of the arbitration panel，the arbitrator chosen by the other party shall act as sole arbitrator and his/her award shall be binding upon both parties.

（3）如果在被申请人收到第八条第(1)款的通知后 30 天内，一方当事人未指定一人担任仲裁小组成员，则另一方当事人选定的仲裁员应担任独任仲裁员，其裁决应对双方当事人具有约束力。

（4）In the event the two arbitrators appointed by the parties as contemplated in paragraph（1）do not succeed in appointing a third arbitrator within fourteen（14）days after the last arbitrator was appointed，then at the request of one of the parties the Chief Judge of the District Court may appoint the third arbitrator.

（4）如果双方当事人按照第(1)款的规定指定的两名仲裁员未能在最后一名仲裁员被指定后的 14 天内成功地指定第三名仲裁员，则应其中一方当事人的请求，区法院首席法官可指定第三名仲裁员。

（5）No attempt may be made to nullify the appointment of an arbitrator made by the Chief Judge of the District Court as contemplated in paragraph（4）.

（5）不得试图取消第(4)款中规定的地区法院首席法官对仲裁员的任命。

Article 16

第 16 条

（1）An arbitrator appointed or designated may accept or refuse the appointment or nomination.

（1）指定的仲裁员可以接受或者拒绝指定。

（2）The parties must be advised by the arbitrator(s), in writing, of the acceptance or rejection of the appointment, as contemplated in paragraph (1) within fourteen (14) days from the date of the appointment or designation.

（2）根据第(1)款的规定,仲裁员必须在指定或指定之日起 14 天内书面通知当事人接受或拒绝指定。

Article 17

第十七条

（1）By the appointment of one or more arbitrators by the parties in writing and the acceptance in writing of the appointment by the arbitrator (s), there is a civil contract between the appointing parties and the arbitrator(s) accepting the appointment.

（1）通过双方当事人以书面形式指定一名或多名仲裁员以及仲裁员书面接受指定,指定方与接受指定的仲裁之间订立民事合同。

（2）The appointment contemplated in paragraph (1) shall have the effect that the arbitrator or arbitrators will render an award fairly, justly, and in accordance with the prevailing stipulations (of law and contract), and the parties will accept such award as final and binding as mutually agreed.

（2）第(1)款所规定的指定应具有这样的效果,即仲裁员将根据法律和合同的现行规定公正地作出裁决,而且当事各方将接受该裁决为最终裁决,并具有相互约定的约束力。

Article 18

第 18 条

（1）A prospective arbitrator asked by one of the parties to sit on the arbitration panel shall be obliged to advise the parties of any matter which could influence his independence or give rise to bias in the rendering of the award.

（1）一名未来的仲裁员应有义务就任何可能影响其独立性或在作出裁决时引起偏见的事项向当事各方提供咨询。

（2）Anyone accepting an appointment as arbitrator as contemplated in paragraph（1）shall inform the parties of his appointment.

（2）接受第（1）款所规定的仲裁员任命的任何人，应将其任命通知各方当事人。

Article 19
第 19 条

（1）In the event that an arbitrator states his/her acceptance of the appointment or designation as contemplated in Article 16，the arbitrator concerned may not withdraw his/her acceptance except with the approval of the parties.

（1）如果仲裁员声明接受第 16 条所规定的任命或指定，除非得到当事各方的同意，有关仲裁员不得撤回接受。

（2）In the event the arbitrator contemplated in paragraph（1）who has accepted the appointment or designation，wishes to withdraw，such arbitrator shall submit a written request to the parties.

（2）如果第（1）款所规定的接受任命或指定的仲裁员希望退出，该仲裁员应向各方当事人提交书面请求。

（3）In the event the parties may consent to the request to withdraw contemplated in paragraph（2）the arbitrator concerned may be released from his/her duties as arbitrator.

（3）如果当事各方同意第（2）款所规定的撤回请求，有关仲裁员可解除其仲裁员职责。

（4）In the event the request for withdrawal does not receive the consent of the parties the Chief Judge of the District Court may release such release of the arbitrator from his/her duties.

（4）如果撤回请求未得到当事各方的同意，地区法院首席法官可解除仲裁员的这一职责。

Article 20

In the event an arbitrator or arbitration panel，without valid reason，fails to render its an award within the period specified，such arbitrator(s) may be ordered to pay to the parties compensation for the costs and losses caused by the delay.

第 20 条

如果仲裁员或仲裁小组无正当理由不能在规定的期限内作出裁决，可以命令该仲裁员就迟延造成的费用和损失向当事方支付赔偿。

Article 21

The arbitrator or arbitration tribunal may not be held legally responsible for any action taken during the proceedings to carry out the function of arbitrator or arbitration tribunal unless it is proved that there was bad faith in the action.

第 21 条

除非证明在诉讼程序期间为履行仲裁员或仲裁庭的职能而采取的任何行动有恶意，否则不得追究仲裁员或仲裁庭的法律责任。

Third Part
Right of Recusal
第三部分　回避权

Article 22
第 22 条

（1）A demand for recusal may be submitted against an arbitrator if there is found sufficient cause and authentic evidence to give rise to doubt that such arbitrator will not perform his/her duties independently or will be biased in rendering an award.

（1）如果有充分理由和真实证据使人怀疑仲裁员不会独立履行其职责

或在作出裁决时有偏见，则可请求仲裁员回避。

（2）Request for recusal of an arbitrator may also be made if it is proven that there is any familial，financial，or employment relationship with one of the parties or its respective legal representatives.

（2）如果证明与当事一方或其各自的法律代表有任何家庭、财务或雇用关系，也可请求仲裁员回避。

Article 23
第 23 条

（1）Application for recusal of an arbitrator appointed by the President of a District Court shall be submitted to the District Court concerned.

（1）地区法院院长指定的仲裁员申请回避，应当向有关地区法院提出。

（2）Application for recusal of a sole arbitrator shall be submitted to the arbitrator concerned.

（2）独任仲裁员的回避申请应当提交有关仲裁员。

（3）Application for recusal of a member of an arbitration tribunal shall be submitted to the arbitration tribunal concerned.

（3）仲裁庭组成人员申请回避，应当向仲裁庭提出。

Article 24
第 24 条

（1）An arbitrator who was not appointed by the Court，may only be recused for a reason which become known to the party applying for such recusal after the appointment of the arbitrator concerned.

（1）不是法院指定的仲裁员，只有在有关仲裁员被指定后，申请回避的一方当事人有理由才可回避。

（2）An arbitrator appointed by the Court may only be recused for a reason which became known to the Court after acceptance of such appointment.

（2）法院指定的仲裁员，只有在其接受这种任命后，法院有理由才能撤销其职务。

（3）The party objecting to the appointment of an arbitrator made by the other party must submit its demand for recusal within fourteen （14） days after the appointment.

（3）反对另一方当事人指定仲裁员的一方当事人必须在指定后 14 天内提出回避请求。

（4）In the event that matters，as contemplated in Article 22 paragraphs （1） and （2），become known at a later date，the request for recusal must be submitted not more than fourteen （14） days after such matters become known.

（4）如果第 22 条第（1）款和第（2）款所规定的重要事项在稍后日期被告知，则应在获悉此类事项后 14 天内提出回避请求。

（5）The demand for recusal must be submitted in writing，either to the other party or to the arbitrator concerned，stating the reason for the demand.

（5）回避请求必须以书面形式提交给另一方当事人或有关仲裁员，说明提出回避请求的理由。

（6）In the event the demand for recusal submitted by one of the parties is consented to by the other party，the arbitrator concerned must resign and a replacement arbitrator shall be appointed in accordance with the procedures set out in this Act.

（6）如果一方当事人提出的回避请求得到另一方当事人的同意，有关仲裁员必须辞职，并应按照本法规定的程序指定一名替代仲裁员。

Article 25

第 25 条

（1）In the event the request for recusal submitted by one of the parties is not consented to by the other party and the arbitrator concerned is unwilling to resign，the party concerned may submit its request for recusal to the Chief Judge of the District Court，whose decision on the matter shall bind the two parties，and shall not be subject to appeal.

（1）如果一方当事人提出的回避请求未得到另一方当事人的同意，且有关仲裁员不愿辞职，该方当事人可向地区法院首席法官提出回避请求，地区法院首席法官对该事项的裁决对双方当事人具有约束力，不得上诉。

（2）In the event the Chief Judge of the District Court decides that the request for recusal，contemplated in paragraph（1），is well founded，a replacement arbitrator shall be appointed in the manner applied to the appointment of the arbitrator to be replaced.

（2）如果地区法院首席法官决定，第（1）款中所规定的回避请求有充分的理由，应按照指定被替换仲裁员的方式任命一名替代仲裁员。

（3）In the event the Chief Judge of the District Court rejects the demand for recusal，the arbitrator shall continue to perform his/her duties.

（3）如果地区法院首席法官拒绝回避要求，仲裁员应继续履行其职责。

Article 26

第 26 条

（1）An arbitrator's authority shall not be nullified by the death of the arbitrator and the authority shall thereupon be continued by a successor arbitrator appointed in accordance with this Act.

（1）仲裁员的权力不因其死亡而丧失，该权力由根据本法指定的继任仲裁员继续行使。

（2）An arbitrator may be dismissed from his/her mandate in the event that he/she is shown to be biased or demonstrates disgraceful conduct，which must be legally proven.

（2）仲裁员如果被证明有偏见或表现出可耻的行为，可解除其职务，但应依法证明。

（3）In the event that during hearing of the dispute an arbitrator dies，is incapacitated，or resigns，and so is unable to meet his/her obligations，a replacement arbitrator shall be appointed in the manner applicable to the appointment of the arbitrator concerned.

（3）如果在审理争议期间，一名仲裁员死亡、丧失工作能力或辞职，因而无法履行其义务，应按照指定有关仲裁员的方式指定一名替代仲裁员。

（4）In the event a sole arbitrator or the chair of the arbitration tribunal is replaced，all hearings previously held shall be repeated.

（4）如果独任仲裁员或仲裁庭庭长被替换，以前举行的所有审理应重新进行。

（5）In the event a member of the arbitration tribunal replaced，the hearing of the dispute shall only be repeated among the arbitrators themselves.

（5）如果仲裁法庭的一名成员被替换，则只有在仲裁员之间争议审理程序重新进行。

CHAPTER IV
PROCEDURES APPLICABLE BEFORE THE ARBITRATION TRIBUNAL
First Part
Arbitration Procedures
第四章 仲裁审判之前适用的程序
第一部分 仲裁程序

Article 27

All hearings of arbitration disputes shall be closed to the public.

第 27 条

仲裁争议的审理不公开。

Article 28

The language to be used in all arbitration proceedings is Indonesian，except that the parties may choose another language to be used，subject to consent of the arbitrator or arbitration tribunal.

第 28 条

在所有仲裁程序中使用的语言是印尼语；当事各方可选择使用另一种语言，但须经仲裁员或仲裁庭同意。

Article 29

第 29 条

（1）The parties in dispute shall have the same right and opportunity to put forward their respective opinions.

（1）争议各方有提出各自意见的同等权利和机会。

（2）The parties in dispute may be represented by counsel，pursuant to special power of attorney.

（2）争议各方可根据特别委托书由律师代理。

Article 30

Third parties outside the arbitration agreement may participate and join themselves into the arbitral process，if they have related interests and their participation is agreed to by the parties in dispute and by the arbitrator or arbitration tribunal hearing the dispute.

第 30 条

仲裁协议以外的第三方可以参与仲裁进程，条件是其具有相关利益，而且其参与得到争议各方以及审理争议的仲裁员或仲裁庭的同意。

Article 31

第 31 条

（1）The parties are free to determine，in an explicit written agreement，the arbitration procedures to be applied in hearing the dispute，provided this does not conflict with the provisions of this Act.

（1）当事人可以通过书面协议自行决定仲裁在审理争议时适用的程序，但不得与本法规定相冲突。

（2）In the event that the parties do not themselves determine the procedures to be applied，and the arbitrator or arbitration tribunal has been constituted in accordance with Articles 12，13，and 14，all disputes which have been so referred to the arbitrator or arbitration tribunal shall be heard and decided upon in accordance with the provisions in this Act.

（2）如果当事各方不能自行确定适用的程序，而仲裁员或仲裁法庭已根据第 12 条、第 13 条和第 14 条组成，则提交仲裁员或仲裁法庭的所有争议均应根据本法的规定进行审理和裁决。

（3）In the event that the parties have chosen an arbitration procedure as contemplated in paragraph（1），the time frame and venue of the arbitration must be agreed upon，and if these have not been so determined by the parties，they shall be decided upon by the arbitrator or arbitration tribunal.

（3）如果当事各方根据第(1)款之规定自行选择了仲裁程序，则必须商定仲裁的时限和地点；如果当事各方未商定，则应由仲裁员或仲裁庭决定。

Article 32

第 32 条

（1）At the request of one of the parties，the arbitrator or arbitration tribunal may make a provisional award or other interlocutory decision to regulate the manner of running the examination of

the dispute，including decreeing a security attachment，ordering
the deposit of goods with third parties，or the sale of perishable
goods.

（1）应一方当事人的请求，仲裁员或仲裁法庭可作出临时裁决或其他
中间裁决，以规范对争议的审理方式，包括下达保证金通知、命令
向第三方交存货物或出售易腐货物。

（2）The period of implementation of the provisional award or other
interlocutory decision contemplated in paragraph（1）shall not
be counted into the period contemplated in Article 48.

（2）执行第（1）款所规定的临时裁决或其他中间裁决的期间，不应计入
第 48 条所规定的期间。

Article 33
第 33 条

The arbitrator or arbitration tribunal has the authority to extend its
term of office：

在下列情况下，仲裁员或仲裁庭有权延长其任期：

（1）if a request is made by one of the parties in specific special
circumstances；

（1）当事一方在特殊情况下提出请求；

（2）as result of a provisional award or other interlocutory ruling
being made；or

（2）由于作出临时裁决或其他中间裁决；或

（3）if it is deemed necessary by the arbitrator or arbitration tribunal
in the interests of the hearing.

（3）为了审理的顺利进行，仲裁员或仲裁庭认为有必要。

Article 34
第 34 条

（1）Resolution of a dispute through arbitration may be referred to a national or international arbitration institution if so agreed upon by of the parties.

（1）通过仲裁解决争议，经当事方同意，可提交国家或国际仲裁机构。

（2）Resolution of a dispute through institutional arbitration，as contemplated in paragraph（1），shall be done according to the rules and procedures of such designated institution，except to the extent otherwise agreed upon by the parties.

（2）通过机构仲裁解决争议，如第（1）款所述，应根据该指定机构的规则和程序进行，除非当事方另有约定。

Article 35

The arbitrator or arbitration tribunal may order that any document or evidence be accompanied by a translation into such language as determined on by the arbitrator or arbitration tribunal.

第 35 条

仲裁员或仲裁庭可命令将任何文件或证据附有仲裁员或仲裁庭确认的译文。

Article 36

第 36 条

（1）The arbitral hearings of the dispute shall be done by written documents.

（1）对争议的仲裁应当以书面文件进行。

（2）Verbal hearings may be conducted with the approval of the parties concerned or if deemed necessary by the arbitrator or arbitration tribunal.

（2）口头听证经当事人同意，或者经仲裁员或者仲裁庭认为必要的，可以进行。

Article 37

第 37 条

（1）Unless the parties have themselves determined the venue of the arbitration, the same shall be determined by the arbitrator or arbitration tribunal.

（1）除非当事各方自行确定仲裁地点,否则应由仲裁员或仲裁庭确定。

（2）The arbitrator or arbitration tribunal may hear witness testimony or hold meetings, if deemed necessary, at a place or places outside the place where the arbitration is being held.

（2）仲裁员或仲裁法庭可听取证人证词或在认为必要时在仲裁地点以外的一个或多个地点举行会议。

（3）Examination of witnesses and expert witnesses before the arbitrator or arbitration tribunal shall be carried out on accordance with the provisions of the Code of Civil Procedure.

（3）由仲裁员或者仲裁庭对证人、鉴定人进行讯问,应当依照民事诉讼法的规定进行。

（4）The arbitrator or arbitration tribunal may conduct examination of property in dispute, or of same other matter connected with the dispute, at the location of such property. If such is deemed necessary the parties shall be properly summoned so that they may also be present at such examination.

（4）仲裁员或仲裁庭可在争议财产所在地对该财产或与争议有关的同一其他事项进行审查。如果认为有必要,应适当传唤当事方,以便他们也能出席审查。

Article 38

第 38 条

（1）The Claimant shall submit its statement claim to the arbitrator or arbitration tribunal within the period of time as determined by the arbitrator or arbitration tribunal.

（1）申请人应在仲裁员或仲裁庭确定的期限内向仲裁员或仲裁庭提交其陈述请求。

（2）The statement of claim shall contain at the least：

（2）索赔说明至少应包括：

    a. The full name and residence or domicile of the parties；

    a. 当事人的全名、住所或者居住地；

    b. A short description of the dispute，accompanied by evidence；and

    b. 对争议的简短描述，并附上证据；以及

    c. Clear contents of the claim being asserted.

    c. 明确的索赔内容。

Article 39

After receiving the statement of claim from the Claimant，the arbitrator or the chair of the arbitration tribunal shall forward a copy of such claim to the Respondent，accompanied by an order that the Respondent must file its response in writing within a period of not more than fourteen（14）days as from Respondent's receipt of the copy of Claimant's claim.

第 39 条

仲裁员或仲裁庭庭长在收到申请人的索偿说明后，应将该索偿要求的副本转交被申请人，并附上一项命令，规定被申请人必须在收到申请人索偿要求副本后不超过 14 天的期限内提交书面答复。

Article 40

第 40 条

（1）Immediately upon receipt of the response from the Respondent，the arbitrator or the chair of the arbitration tribunal shall provide a copy of thereof to the Claimant.

（1）收到被申请人的答复后，仲裁员或仲裁庭庭长应向申请人提供答复副本。

（2）At the same time, the arbitrator or chair of the arbitration tribunal shall order the parties or their representatives to appear at an arbitration hearing fixed for no more than fourteen（14）days from the issuance of the order.

（2）同时，仲裁庭的仲裁员或庭长应命令当事各方或其代表出席自命令发布之日起 14 天内举行的仲裁听讯。

Article 41

In the event that the Respondent has not responded to Claimant's claim within the fourteen（14）day period contemplated in Article 39, the Respondent shall be summoned to a hearing pursuant to the provisions set out in Article 40 paragraph（2）.

第 41 条

如果被申请人未在第 39 条规定的 14 天期限内对申请人的请求作出答复，应根据第 40 条第（2）款的规定传唤被申请人参加听讯。

Article 42
第 42 条

（1）In the response or no later than the first hearing the Respondent may submit a counterclaim and the Claimant shall be given an opportunity to respond thereto.

（1）在答辩中或不迟于第一次听讯时，被申请人可提出反诉，申请人应有机会做出答辩。

（2）Any counterclaim, as contemplated in paragraph（1）, shall be heard and decided upon by the arbitrator or arbitration tribunal together with the main dispute.

（2）任何反诉，如第（1）款所述，应由仲裁员或仲裁法庭与主要争议一并审理和裁决。

Article 43

If on the day determined as contemplated in Article 40 paragraph (2) the Claimant for no good reason does not appear after being duly summoned，the statement of claim shall be declared null and void and the mandate of the arbitrator or arbitration tribunal deemed to have been completed.

第 43 条

如果在根据第四十条第(2)款确定的日期,无正当理由的申请人在被正式传唤后没有出庭,则应宣布申请书无效,并认为仲裁员或仲裁庭的任务已经完成。

Article 44
第 44 条

(1) If on the day determined pursuant to Article 40 paragraph (2)，the Respondent for no good reason does not appear，but has been duly summoned，the arbitrator or arbitration tribunal shall immediately summon the Respondent again.

(1) 如果在根据第四十条第(2)款确定的日期,由于没有正当理由被申请人不出庭,但已被正式传唤,仲裁员或仲裁庭应立即再次传唤被申请人。

(2) If the Respondent for no good reason still does not appear at the hearing，within ten (10) days after receipt by it of the second summons，the hearing shall continue without the presence of the Respondent and the Claimant's claim shall be granted as a whole，unless the claim is unfounded or contrary to law.

(2) 如果被告没有正当理由在收到第二次传票后 10 天内仍然没有出庭,则应在被告不在场的情况下继续进行审理,除非原告的请求没有根据或违反法律,否则应准予整个请求。

Article 45

第 45 条

（1）In the event that the parties appear on the day determined，the arbitrator or arbitration tribunal shall first endeavour to encourage an amicable settlement between the disputing parties.

（1）如果双方当事人在确定的日期出庭，仲裁员或仲裁庭应首先努力鼓励争议双方当事人之间达成友好解决。

（2）In the event such attempt at amicable settlement，as contemplated in paragraph （1），is successful，the arbitrator or arbitration tribunal shall draw up a deed setting out such amicable settlement，which deed shall be binding on both parties and shall order the parties to comply with the terms of such amicable settlement.

（2）如果第（1）款中所规定的这种友好解决的尝试获得成功，仲裁员或仲裁法庭应起草一份列明这种友好解决的契约，该契约应对双方具有约束力，并应命令双方遵守这种友好解决的条款。

Article 46

第 46 条

（1）The hearing(s) on the merits of the dispute shall proceed if the attempt at amicable settlement，as contemplated in Article 45 paragraph （1），should not prove successful.

（1）如果第 45 条第（1）款所规定的友好解决的尝试不成功，则应就争议的是非曲直进行审理。

（2）The parties shall be afforded a final opportunity to explain in writing their respective positions，and to submit evidence deemed necessary to support such position，within such time limitation as shall be determined by the arbitrator or arbitration tribunal.

（2）应在仲裁员或仲裁庭确定的时限内，给予各方当事人最后机会，以书面解释各自的立场,并提交被认为支持这一立场所必需的证据。

（3）The arbitrator or arbitration tribunal shall be empowered to require the parties to provide such supplementary written submissions of explanations, documentary or other evidence as may be deemed necessary, within such time limitation as shall be determined by the arbitrator or arbitration tribunal.

（3）应授权仲裁员或仲裁庭要求各方当事人在仲裁员或仲裁庭确定的时限内,提供其认为必要的补充书面解释、书面证据或其他证据。

Article 47
第 47 条

（1）Before there has been any response from the Respondent, the Claimant shall be entitled to withdraw its request for dispute resolution by arbitration.

（1）在被申请人做出任何答复之前,申请人有权撤回其通过仲裁解决争议的请求。

（2）In the event that there has already been a response from the Respondent, any amendment or supplement to the Claimant's statement of claim shall be allowed only upon the consent of the Respondent; and any such amendment or supplement may only involve matters of fact and not the legal basis of the claim.

（2）如果被申请人已经做出答复,只有在被申请人同意的情况下,才允许对申请人的索赔说明做出任何修正或补充;任何此种修正或补充只能涉及事实事项,而不是索赔的法律依据。

Article 48
第 48 条

（1）The hearings on the dispute must be completed within not more than one hundred eighty（180）days from the formulation of the arbitral panel.

（1）关于争议的审理必须在仲裁小组成立后不超过 180 天内完成。

（2）Such time limitation may be extended upon consent of the parties or if required in accordance with the provisions of Article 33 hereof.

（2）这种时间限制经当事方同意或根据本法第三十三条的规定的要求可以延长。

Second Part
Witnesses and Expert Witnesses
第二部分
证人和鉴定人

Article 49

第 49 条

（1）Upon the order of the arbitrator or arbitration tribunal, or at the request of the parties, one or more witnesses or expert witnesses may be summoned to give testimony.

（1）根据仲裁员或仲裁庭的命令，或应当事人的请求，可以传唤一名或多名证人或专家证人作证。

（2）The costs of summoning such witnesses, or expert witnesses, and their travel expenses shall be borne by the party requesting such testimony.

（2）传唤此类证人或专家证人的费用及其旅费应由要求提供此类证词的一方承担。

（3）Any such witnesses or expert witnesses shall testify upon oath, given prior to such testimony.

（3）任何此类证人或专家证人在作证前应宣誓作证。

Article 50

第 50 条

（1）The arbitrator or arbitration tribunal may request the assistance of one or more expert witnesses to provide a written report concerning any specific matter relating to the merits of the dispute.

（1）仲裁员或仲裁庭可请求一名或多名专家证人协助，就与争议案情实质有关的任何具体事项提供书面报告。

（2）The parties shall be required to provide all details and information that may be deemed necessary by such expert witnesses.

（2）当事方应提供这些专家证人认为必要的所有细节和资料。

（3）The arbitrator or arbitration tribunal shall provide copies of any report provided by such expert witnesses to the parties，in order to allow the parties to respond in writing.

（3）仲裁员或仲裁法庭应向当事各方提供此类专家证人提供的任何报告的副本，以便当事各方能够做出书面答复。

（4）In the event that any matters opined upon by any such expert witness is insufficiently clear，upon request of either of the parties，such expert witness may be requested to give testimony in a hearing before the arbitrator(s) and the parties，or their legal representatives.

（4）如果任何这类专家证人对任何事项的看法不够明确，经任何一方当事人请求，可以请这类专家证人在仲裁员和当事方或其法律代理人的听讯中作证。

Article 51

Minutes of the hearings，and examination of witnesses，shall be drawn up by a secretary and shall cover all activities in the examination and arbitration hearings.

第 51 条

听讯的记录和对证人的讯问应由秘书草拟，并应涵盖复核和仲裁听讯的所有活动。

CHAPTER V

OPINION AND ARBITRAL AWARD

第五章 意见和仲裁裁决

Article 52

The parties to an agreement have the right to request a binding opinion from an arbitration institution concerning any particular legal point or points contained in or concerning their agreement

第 52 条

协议的当事人有权要求仲裁机构就协议中所载的或涉及其协议的任何特定法律要点提出具有约束力的意见。

Article 53

No appeal whatsoever may be filed against any binding opinion，as contemplated in Article 52.

第 53 条

根据第五十二条的规定，不得对任何具有约束力的意见提出任何上诉。

Article 54

第 54 条

（1）An arbitration award must contain：

（1）仲裁裁决必须包括：

    a. A heading to the award containing the words "Demi Keadilan Berdasarkan Ketuhanan Yang Maha Esa"（for the sake of Justice based on belief in the Almighty God）；

    a. 一个判决的标题，上面写着"基于至尊神格的正义［马来语］"（为了正义，基于对全能的神的信仰）；

    b. The full name and addresses of the disputing parties；

    b. 争议各方的全名和地址；

    c. A brief description of the matter in dispute；

    c. 对争议事项的简要说明；

d. The respective position of each of the parties；

d. 双方各自的立场；

e. The full names and addresses of the arbitrators；

e. 仲裁员的姓名和地址；

f. The considerations and conclusions of the arbitrator or arbitra-tion tribunal concerning the dispute as a whole；

f. 仲裁员或仲裁庭对整个争议的考虑和结论；

g. The opinion of each arbitrator in the event that there is any difference of opinion within the arbitration tribunal；

g. 仲裁庭内部存在意见分歧的，各仲裁员的意见；

h. The order of the award；

h. 裁决的顺序；

i. The place and date of the award；and

i. 裁决的地点和日期；以及

j. The signature(s) of the arbitrator or arbitration tribunal.

j. 仲裁员或仲裁庭的签名。

（2）The effectivity of the award shall not be frustrated by the failure of one arbitrator（where there are three）to sign the award if such failure to sign is caused by illness or demise of such non-signing arbitrator.

（2）裁决的有效性不应因一名仲裁员（共有三名仲裁员）未签署裁决而受到影响，如果这种未签署裁决是由于该仲裁员生病或死亡所致。

（3）The reason for the failure of such arbitrator to sign，as contemplated in paragraph（2），must be set out in the award.

（3）如第（2）款所述，该仲裁员未能签字的原因必须在裁决中说明。

（4）The award shall state a time limitation within which the award must be implemented.

（4）裁决应规定执行裁决的时限。

Article 55

When the examination of the dispute is complete the hearing shall be concluded，and a date shall be fixed for the rendering of the arbitration award.

第 55 条

审查争议结束，应当终结审理，并确定作出仲裁裁决的日期。

Article 56

第 56 条

（1）The arbitrator or arbitration tribunal shall render its decision based upon the relevant provisions of law，or based upon justice and fairness.

（1）仲裁员或仲裁法庭应根据有关法律规定或根据公正和公平作出裁决。

（2）The parties are entitled to designate the choice of law to be applied to the resolution of disputes which may arise，or which have arisen，between or among them.

（2）当事各方有权指定适用于解决他们之间可能产生或已经产生的争议的法律。

Article 57

The award shall be rendered not later than thirty （30） days after the conclusion of hearings.

第 57 条

裁决应在听讯结束后 30 天内作出。

Article 58

Within not more than fourteen （14） days after receipt of the award，the parties may submit a request to the arbitrator or arbitration tribunal to correct any administrative errors and/or to make additions or deletions to the award if a matter claimed has not been dealt with in such award.

第 58 条

在收到裁决后 14 天内,当事人可以向仲裁员或仲裁庭提出纠正任何行政错误的请求,或在裁决中未涉及所称事项的情况下对裁决进行增删。

CHAPTER VI
ENFORCEMENT OF THE ARBITRATION AWARD
First Part
Domestic Arbitration
第六章　仲裁裁决的执行
第一部分　国内仲裁

Article 59

第 59 条

(1) Within thirty (30) days from the date the arbitral award is rendered, the original or an authentic copy of the award shall be submitted for registration to the Clerk of the District Court by the arbitrator(s) or a legal representative of the arbitrator(s).

(1) 在仲裁裁决作出之日起 30 天内,仲裁员或法律代表应将裁决原件或正本提交区法院书记官登记。

(2) The submission and registration, as contemplated in paragraph (1), shall be carried out by recording and signature at the end, or on the margin, of the award by the Clerk of the District Court and by the arbitrator or his/her representative, and such submission shall constitute a deed of registration.

(2) 如第(1)款所规定的,提交和登记应在地区法院书记官和或仲裁员或其代表裁决结束时或在空白处记录和签署,提交和登记应构成登记契据。

(3) The arbitrator(s) or legal representative(s) shall deliver the

original, or authentic copy, of the award and of the instrument of appointment of such arbitrator(s) to the Clerk of the District Court.

（3）仲裁员或法律代表应将裁决和指定该仲裁员的文书的原件或正本送交地区法院书记官。

（4）Failure to comply with the requirements set out in paragraph （1）above shall render the arbitration award unenforceable.

（4）未遵守上文第（1）款中规定的要求，仲裁裁决不可执行。

（5）All costs connected with the making of the deed of registration shall be borne by the parties.

（5）与登记契据的制作有关的所有费用应由当事人承担。

Article 60

The arbitration award shall be final and binding upon both parties to the dispute.

第 60 条

仲裁裁决为终局裁决，对争议双方具有约束力。

Article 61

In the event that the parties fail voluntarily to implement the arbitration award，the award may be enforced on the basis of an order from the Chief Judge of the District Court at the request of one of the parties to the dispute.

第 61 条

如果当事各方未能自愿执行仲裁裁决，可根据地区法院首席法官应争议一方的请求下达的命令执行裁决。

Article 62

第 62 条

（1）The order referred to in Article 61 shall be issued not later than thirty（30）days after an application for execution of the award is submitted to the Clerk to the District Court.

（1）第 61 条所指的命令应在向地区法院提出执行裁决的申请后 30 天内发出。

（2）Prior to issuance of the order of execution，the Chief Judge of the District Court contemplated in paragraph（1）shall examine whether the arbitration award fulfils the requirements set out in Articles 4 and 5，and is not in conflict with public morality or order.

（2）在执行令下达之前，第（1）款所规定的地区法院首席法官应审查仲裁裁决是否符合第 4 条和第 5 条规定的要求，并且不与公共道德或秩序相冲突。

（3）In the event the arbitration award does not meet the requirements set out in paragraph（2）above，the Chief Judge of the District Court shall reject the request for execution and shall not order such execution，and there shall be no recourse whatsoever to the judgement of the Chief Judge of the District Court.

（3）如果仲裁裁决不符合上文第（2）款规定的要求，区法院首席法官应驳回执行请求，不应下令执行，也不得诉诸区法院首席法官的判决。

（4）The Chief Judge of the District Court shall not examine the substantive reasons or considerations upon which the arbitration award was based.

（4）地区法院首席法官不得审查仲裁裁决所依据的实质性理由或考虑。

Article 63

The order of the Chief Judge of the District Court shall be set out in writing upon the original text and authentic copy of the arbitration award.

第 63 条

地区法院首席法官的裁定，应当以书面形式的裁决书原件和正本为准。

Article 64

An arbitration award bearing an order of execution from the Chief Judge of the District Court shall be enforced in accordance with the provisions（of the Code of Civil Procedure）on execution of judgements in civil cases which are final and binding.

第 64 条

载有地区法院首席法官执行令的仲裁裁决，应根据民事诉讼法中关于执行民事案件判决的规定执行。

Second Part
International Arbitration
第二部分
国际仲裁

Article 65

The District Court of Central Jakarta shall be the court vested with the authority to handle matters of the recognition and enforcement of International Arbitration Awards.

第 65 条

雅加达地区法院是有权处理承认和执行国际仲裁裁决事项的法院。

Article 66
第 66 条

International Arbitration Awards will only be recognised and may only be enforced within the jurisdiction of the Republic of Indonesia if they fulfill the following requirements：

国际仲裁裁决只有在符合以下要求的情况下才会得到承认，并在印度尼西亚共和国管辖范围内执行：

（a）The International Arbitration Award must have been rendered by an arbitrator or arbitration tribunal in a country which， together with the Republic of Indonesia，is a party to a bilateral or multilateral treaty on the recognition and enforcement of Interna-tional Arbitration Awards.

(a) 国际仲裁裁决必须由一国的仲裁员或仲裁庭作出，该国与印度尼西亚联合共和国是关于承认和执行国际仲裁裁决的双边或多边条约的缔约方。

(b) International Arbitration Awards，as contemplated in item（a），above，are limited to awards which，under the provisions of Indonesian law，fall within the scope of commercial law.

(b) 如上文(a)项所规定的那样，国际仲裁裁决仅限于根据印度尼西亚法律规定属于商法范围的裁决。

(c) International Arbitration Awards，as contemplated in item（a），above，may only be enforced in Indonesia if they do not violate public order.

(c) 上述条款所规定的国际仲裁裁决只有在不违反公共秩序的情况下才能在印度尼西亚执行。

(d) An International Arbitration Award may be enforced in Indonesia only after obtaining an order of Exequatur from the Chief Judge of the District Court of Central Jakarta.

(d) 国际仲裁裁决只有在获得雅加达中部地区法院首席法官的许可令之后才能在印度尼西亚执行。

(e) An International Arbitration Award，as contemplated in item（a），in which the Republic of Indonesia is one of the parties to the dispute，may only be enforced after obtaining an order of Exequatur from the Supreme Court of the Republic of Indonesia，which order is then delegated to the District Court of Central Jakarta for execution.

(e) (a)项所规定的一项印度尼西亚共和国是争议的当事方之一的国际仲裁裁决，只有在获得印度尼西亚共和国最高法院的执行令之后才能执行，该命令随后委托雅加达中部地区法院执行。

Article 67

第 67 条

（1） Application for enforcement of an International Arbitration Award shall be made after the award is submitted for registration to the Clerk to the District Court of Central Jakarta Pusat by the arbitrator(s) or the legal representative thereof.

（1） 要求执行国际仲裁裁决的申请应在仲裁员或其法律代表将裁决提交雅加达中部地区法院书记官登记后提出。

（2） The submission of the file of the application for enforcement, as contemplated in　paragraph（1）above, must be accompanied by：

（2） 按照上文第（1）款的规定提交执行申请的档案时，必须附有：

　　a. the original International Arbitration Award, or a copy authenticated in accordance with the provisions on authentica-tion of foreign documents, together with an official translation of the text thereof into the Indonesian language；

　　a. 国际仲裁裁决原件，或根据外国文件认证规定认证的副本，及其译为印度尼西亚文的正式翻译文件；

　　b. the original agreement which is the basis for the International Arbitration Award, or a copy authenticated in accordance with the provisions on authentication of foreign documents, together with an official translation of the text thereof into the Indone-sian language；

　　b. 作为国际仲裁裁决依据的原始协议，或根据外国文件认证规定认证的副本，及其译为印度尼西亚文的正式翻译文件；

　　c. a certification from the diplomatic representative of the Republic of Indonesia in the country in which the International Arbitra-tion Award was rendered stating that such country and the Republic of Indonesia are both bound by a bilateral or multilateral treaty on the recognition and implementation of International Arbitration Awards.

c. 印度尼西亚共和国驻作出国际仲裁裁决的国家的外交代表出具的证明,说明该国和印度尼西亚联合共和国都受关于承认和执行国际仲裁裁决的双边或多边条约的约束。

Article 68

第68条

(1) No appeal to either the High Court or the Supreme Court may be lodged against a decision of the Chief Judge of the District Court, as contemplated in Article 66 (d), above, recognising and enforcing an International Arbitration Award.

(1) 对于第66条(d)项规定的地区法院首席法官承认和执行国际仲裁裁决的决定,不得向高等法院或最高法院提出上诉。

(2) An appeal may be filed with the Supreme Court against a decision of the Chief Judge of the District court contemplated in Article 66 (d), refusing to recognise and enforce an International Arbitration Award.

(2) 对于第66条(d)项所规定的地区法院首席法官拒绝承认和执行国际仲裁裁决的决定,可向最高法院提出上诉。

(3) The Supreme Court shall consider and rule upon an appeal submitted to it, as contemplated in paragraph (2) above, within a period of nor more than ninety (90) days after the application for appeal has been received by the Supreme Court.

(3) 最高法院在收到第(2)款规定之上诉申请后,应在90天内审议并作出裁决。

(4) No appeal may be submitted against a decision of the Supreme Court, as contemplated in Article 66 (e).

(4) 不得对最高法院的裁决提出上诉,正如第66条第(e)项之所述。

Article 69

第 69 条

(1) After the Chief Judge of the District Court of Jakarta Pusat has issued a writ of execution，as contemplated in Article 64，further enforcement shall be delegated to the Chief Judge of the District Court having jurisdiction to enforce it.

（1）根据第 64 条的规定，在雅加达省区法院首席法官发出执行令状后，应将进一步的执行委托给有管辖权的区法院首席法官。

(2) An order of attachment may be made upon such assets and property of the party against whom the award was rendered as shall be requested in the application for such order.

（2）可根据命令申请书的要求，对裁决所针对的一方的资产和财产发出扣押令。

(3) The procedure for seizure and attachment in enforcement of the award shall follow the procedures therefor as set out in the Code of Civil Procedure.

（3）执行裁决的扣押程序应遵循民事诉讼法规定的程序。

CHAPTER VIII
ANNULMENT OF ARBITRATION AWARDS
第八章　仲裁裁决的撤销

Article 70

第 70 条

An application to annul an arbitration award may be made if any of the following conditions are alleged to exist：

如果声称存在下列条件之一，可以申请撤销仲裁裁决：

(a) letters or documents submitted in the hearings are acknowledged to be false or forged or are declared to be forgeries after the award has been rendered；

（a）在审理中提交的信件或文件被确认为虚假或伪造，或在作出裁决后被宣布为伪造；

(b) after the award has been rendered documents are founded which are decisive in nature and which were deliberately concealed by the opposing party; or

(b) 在作出裁决后,即建立了具有决定性的文件,但被对方当事人故意隐瞒;或

(c) the award was rendered as a result of fraud committed by one of the parties to the dispute.

(c) 裁决是由于争议当事一方的欺诈行为而作出的。

Article 71

An application for annulment of an arbitration award must be submitted in writing within not more than thirty (30) days from the date such arbitration award was submitted for registration to the Clerk to the District Court.

第 71 条

撤销仲裁裁决的申请必须在仲裁裁决提交地区法院书记官登记之日起三十天内以书面形式提交。

Article 72

第 72 条

(1) An application for annulment of an arbitration award must be submitted to the Chief Judge of the applicable District Court.

(1) 要求撤销仲裁裁决的申请必须提交给适用的地区法院首席法官。

(2) If the application as contemplated in paragraph (1) above is granted the Chief Judge of the District Court shall determine further the consequences of the annulment of the whole, or a part, of the arbitration award.

(2) 如果第(1)款所述之申请获得批准,地区法院首席法官应进一步确

定取消仲裁裁决的全部或部分裁决的后果。

(3) The decision on the application for annulment shall be made by the Chief Judge of the District Court within not more than thirty (30) days from receipt of the aforesaid application.

(3) 关于撤销申请的决定应由地区法院首席法官在收到上述申请后 30 天内作出。

(4) An application for an appeal against the decision of the District Court may be made to the Supreme Court, which latter shall decide the matter as the court of final instance.

(4) 对地区法院的裁决提出上诉的申请可向最高法院提出,最高法院应作为终审法院裁决该事项。

(5) The Supreme Court shall consider and decide upon any such application to appeal, as contemplated in paragraph (4) above, within not more than thirty (30) days after such application to appeal is received by the Supreme Court.

(5) 最高法院应在收到上诉申请后 30 天内,按照上文第(4)款的规定,审议并决定任何此类上诉申请。

CHAPTER VIII
THE TERMINATION OF THE ARBITRATORS' MANDATE
第八章　仲裁员任期的终止

Article 73
第 73 条

The mandate of the arbitrator (s) shall terminate under the following circumstances:

在下列情况下,仲裁员的任期终止:

a. An award has been rendered with respect to the matters in dispute;

a. 已就争议事项作出裁决;

b. The time limitation, as determined in the arbitration agreement, including any extension thereto agreed upon by the parties, has expired; or

b. 仲裁协议中所确定的时限,包括当事人约定的任何展期,已经期满;或

c. The parties mutually agree to rescind the arbitrators' appointment.

c. 双方当事人同意撤销对仲裁员的任命。

Article 74

第 74 条

(1) The death of one of the parties shall not cause the mandate of the arbitrators to terminate.

(1) 任何一方当事人的死亡不引起仲裁员任期的终止。

(2) The term of the mandate of the arbitrators, as contemplated in Article 48, may be postponed for a period of not greater than sixty (60) days from the death of one of the parties.

(2) 第 48 条所规定的仲裁员任期可延期至其中一方当事人死亡后不超过 60 天。

Article 75

第 75 条

(1) In the event that one of the arbitrators passes away, or a demand for recusal or dismissal of one or more arbitrators is granted, the parties must appoint a replacement arbitrator.

(1) 如果其中一名仲裁员去世,或请求回避或解雇一名或多名仲裁员被准予,当事各方必须指定一名替代仲裁员。

(2) If the parties are unable to reach an agreement as to the appointment of the replacement arbitrator, as contemplated in paragraph (1) above, within thirty (30) days, the Chief Judge of the District Court shall, at the request of the interested party, appoint one or more replacement arbitrator(s).

(2) 如果当事各方不能按照上文第(1)款的规定,在 30 天内就替代仲裁员的任命达成协议,则区法院首席法官应根据有关当事方的请求,任命一名或多名替代仲裁员。

(3) The replacement arbitrators shall have the duty to continue the resolution of the dispute concerned based on the most recent conclusions drawn.

(3) 替换仲裁员有责任根据最近得出的结论继续解决有关争议。

CHAPTER IX
ARBITRATION FEES
第九章 仲裁费

Article 76

第 76 条

(1) The arbitrators shall determine the arbitration fee.

(1) 仲裁费用由仲裁员决定。

(2) The fee contemplated in paragraph (1) above shall include:

(2) 上文第(1)款中规定的费用应包括:

    a. the arbitrators' honoraria;

    a. 仲裁员的酬金;

    b. travel expenses and other costs incurred by the arbitrators;

    b. 仲裁员的旅费和其他费用;

    c. the costs of witnesses and expert witnesses required in the hearings on the dispute; and

    c. 审理争议所需的证人和专家证人费用;以及

    d. administrative costs.

    d. 行政费用。

Article 77

第 77 条

(1) The arbitration fees shall be charged to the losing party.

（1）仲裁费用应由败诉方承担。

（2）In the event that a claim is only partially granted，the arbitration fees shall be charged to the parties equally.

（2）如果一项要求只是部分获准，仲裁费用应平等地向双方收取。

CHAPTER IX

TRANSITIONAL PROVISIONS

第九章 过渡条款

Article 78

Disputes which have already been submitted to an arbitrator or arbitration tribunal by the time this Act comes into effect，but for which no hearings have as yet been held，shall be resolved based upon the provisions of this Act.

第78条

在本法生效时已提交仲裁员或仲裁庭，但尚未进行审理的争议，应根据本法规定解决。

Article 79

Disputes which have already been submitted to an arbitrator or arbitration tribunal and with respect to which hearings have already been held by the time this Act comes into effect，but for which no award has as yet been rendered，shall be resolved based upon the laws and regulations prevailing prior to the enactment hereof.

第79条

凡在本法生效时已提交仲裁员或仲裁庭审理，但尚未作出裁决的争议，应根据本法颁布前有效的法律和条例解决。

Article 80

Disputes with respect to which an award has already been rendered by the time this Act comes into effect，which awards have been invested with permanent legal force，shall be implemented based upon the provisions of this Act.

第 80 条

在本法令生效时已经作出裁决，且裁决具有永久法律效力的争议，应根据本法的规定执行。

CHAPTER XI
CLOSING PROVISIONS
第十一章　终结条款

Article 81

Upon the coming into effect of this Act，Articles 615 through 651 of the Civil Procedure Rules（Reglemen Acara Perdata〈Reglemen op de Rechtsvordering〉，Staatsblad 1847：52），Article 377 of the Renewed Indonesian Rules（Reglemen Indonesia Yang Diperbaharui〈het Herziene Indoneisisch Reglement〉，Staatsblad 1941：44）and Article 705 of the Procedural Rules for Areas Outside Java and Madura（Reglemen Acara Untuk Daerah Luar Jawa dan Madura（〈Rechstreglement Buitengewesten〉，Staatsblad 1927：227）are declared null and void.

第 81 条

本法生效后，《民事诉讼规则》第 615 条至第 651 条（法令全书 1847：52），《印度尼西亚更新规则》第 377 条（法令全书 1941：44）以及《爪哇和马杜拉以外地区程序规则》第 705 条（法令全书 1927：227）被宣布无效。

Article 82

This Act shall come into effect as of the date of its promulgation. For public notice，it is ordered that the enactment of this act be announced in the State Gazette of the Republic of Indonesia.

第82条

本法自公布之日起施行。为引起公众注意,命令在印度尼西亚共和国政府公报上宣布该法的颁布。

Ratified in Jakarta

On August 12,1999

在雅加达批准

一九九九年八月十二日

PRESIDENT OF THE REPUBLIC OF INDONESIA

BACHRUDDIN JUSUF HABIBIE

印度尼西亚共和国总统

BACHRUDDIN JUSUF HABIBIE

Enacted in Jakarta on 12 August 1999

一九九九年八月十二日在雅加达颁布

MINISTER OF STATE FOR THE STATE SECRETARIAT

OF THE REPUBLIC OF INDONESIA

MULADI

印度尼西亚共和国国务秘书

MULADI

STATE GAZETTE OF THE REPUBLIC OF INDONESIA 1999

NO. 138

一九九九年印度尼西亚共和国政府公报第一百三十八号

第二节　马来西亚商事仲裁法英汉对照

LAWS OF MALAYSIA

马来西亚法

ONLINE VERSION OF UPDATED

TEXT OF REPRINT

最新重印版之网络通行版

Act 646

法令第 646 号

ARBITRATION ACT 2005

2005 年《仲裁法》

As at 1 December 2011

施行于 2011 年 12 月 1 日

ARBITRATION ACT 2005

2005 年《仲裁法》

Date of Royal Assent ··· ··· ··· ···	30 December 2005
皇室批准日期	2005 年 12 月 30 日
Date of publication in the *Gazzette* ··· ···	31 December 2005
在《宪报》刊登日期	2005 年 12 月 31 日
English text to be authoritative ··· ···	P. U.（B）61/2006
具有权威性的英文文本	P. U.（B）61/2006
Latest amendment made by	
Act A1395 which came	
最新修正案由第 1395 号法案修正并	
into operation on ··· ··· ··· ···	1 July 2011
	2011 年 7 月 1 日

生效于

PREVIOUS REPRINTS

以前的重印版

First Reprint	·········	*2006*
第一个重印版	·········	2006

ARRANGEMENT OF SECTIONS

各条款的编排

PART I

PRELIMINARY

第一部分　序言

Section

条款

1. Short title and commencement　简称和生效

2. Interpretation　解释

3. Application to arbitrations and awards in Malaysia
   对马来西亚仲裁和裁决的适用

4. Arbitrability of subject matter　事由可否仲裁

5. Government to be bound　政府受到约束

PART II

ARBITRATION

第二部分　仲裁

Chapter 1

General Provisions

第一章　一般规定

6. Receipt of　written communications 收到书面来文

7. Waiver of right to object 放弃反对权

8. Extent of court intervention 法院干预的程度

Chapter 2

Arbitration agreement

第二章　仲裁协议

9. Definition and form of arbitration agreement
   仲裁协议的定义和形式

10. Arbitration agreement and substantive claim before court
    仲裁协议和向法院提出的实质性索赔

11. Arbitration agreement and interim measures by High Court

仲裁协议和高等法院的临时措施

Chapter 3
Composition of arbitrators
第三章　仲裁员的组成

Section
条款

12. Number of arbitrators 仲裁员人数

13. Appointment of arbitrators 仲裁员的任命

14. Grounds for challenge 质疑理由

15. Challenge procedure 质疑程序

16. Failure or impossibility to act 未能或不可能采取的行动

17. Appointment of substitute arbitrator 指定替代仲裁员

Chapter 4
Jurisdiction of arbitral tribunal
第四章　仲裁庭的管辖权

18. Competence of arbitral tribunal to rule on its jurisdiction
仲裁庭就其管辖权作出裁决的权限

19. Power of arbitral tribunal to order interim measures
仲裁庭下令采取临时措施的权力

Chapter 5
Conduct of arbitral proceedings
第五章　仲裁程序的执行

20. Equal treatment of parties 平等对待各方

21. Determination of rules of procedure 程序规则的决定

22. Seat of arbitration 仲裁地

23. Commencement of arbitral proceedings 仲裁程序的启动

24. Language 语言

25. Statements of claim and defence 申请书和答辩书

26. Hearings 听讯

27. Default of a party 一方违约

28. Expert appointed by arbitral tribunal 仲裁庭指定的专家

29. Court assistance in taking evidence 法庭协助取证

Chapter 6

Making of award and termination of proceedings

第六章 作出裁决和终止诉讼程序

30. Law applicable to substance of dispute 适用于争议实质的法律

31. Decision making by panel of arbitrators 仲裁员小组的决定

32. Settlement 处理

33. Form and contents of award 裁决的形式和内容

34. Termination of proceedings 程序的终止

35. Correction and interpretation of award or additional award
更正和解释裁决或补充裁决

36. An award is final and binding
裁决是具有约束力的最终裁决

Chapter 7

Recourse against award

第七章 对裁决的追诉

37. Application for setting aside 申请撤销

Chapter 8

Recognition and enforcement of awards

第八章 裁决的认可和执行

38. Recognition and enforcement 认可和执行

39. Grounds for refusing recognition or enforcement
拒绝承认或执行的理由

PART III
ADDITIONAL PROVISIONS RELATING TO ARBITRATION
第三部分 关于仲裁的补充规定

40. Consolidation of proceedings and concurrent hearings
合并诉讼程序和同时举行听讯

41. Determination of preliminary point of law by court
法院确定初步法律问题

42. Reference on questions of law 关于法律问题的参考

43. Appeal 上诉

44. Costs and expenses of an arbitration 仲裁费用和开支

45. Extension of time for commencing arbitration proceedings
延长启动仲裁程序的时间

46. Extension of time for making award 延长裁决时间

PART IV
MISCELLANEOUS
第四部分 杂项

47. Liability of arbitrator 仲裁员的责任

48. Immunity of arbitral institutions 仲裁机构的豁免

49. Bankruptcy 破产

50. Mode of application 适用方式

51. Repeal and savings 废除和保留

An Act to reform the law relating to domestic arbitration，provide for international arbitration，the recognition and enforcement of awards and for related matters.

[15 March 2006；P. U.（B）65/2006]

关于改革国内仲裁相关法律、规定国际仲裁、承认和执行裁决及相关事项的法案。

[2006 年 3 月 15 日；P. U.（B）65/2006]

ENACTED by the Parliament of Malaysia as follows：

马来西亚议会颁布如下：

PART I
PRELIMINARY
第一部分 序言

Short title and commencement

简称和生效

1. (1) This Act may be cited as the Arbitration Act 2005.

(1) 该法案可被援引为 2005 年仲裁法案。

(2) This Act comes into operation on a date to be appointed by the Minister by notification in the *Gazette*.

(2) 本法案于部长在宪报上指定的日期生效。

Interpretation

释意

2. (1) In this Act，unless the context otherwise requires —

(1) 在本法令中，除非上下文另有要求：

"award" means a decision of the arbitral tribunal on the substance of the dispute and includes any final，interim or partial award and any award on costs or interest but does not include interlocutory orders；

"裁决"是指仲裁庭就争议实质作出的裁决，包括任何最终裁决、临时裁决或部分裁决以及关于费用或利息的任何裁决，但不包括中间命令；

"High Court" means the High Court in Malaya and the High Court in Sabah and Sarawak or either of them，as the case may require

"高等法院"是指马拉亚的高等法院，以及萨巴赫和沙捞越的高等法院，或者两者中的任何一个，视情况而定。

"Minister" means the Minister charged with the responsibility for arbitration；

"部长"是指负责仲裁的部长；

"State" means a sovereign State and not a component state of Malaysia, unless otherwise specified;

"国家"是指主权国家而非马来西亚的组成国家,除非另有说明;

"presiding arbitrator" means the arbitrator designated in the arbitration agreement as the presiding arbitrator or chairman of the arbitral tribunal, a single arbitrator or the third arbitrator appointed under subsection 13(3);

"首席仲裁员"是指仲裁协议中指定为仲裁庭首席仲裁员或主席的仲裁员,根据第13条第(3)款指定的一名仲裁员或第三名仲裁员;

"arbitration agreement" means an arbitration agreement as defined in section 9;

"仲裁协议"是指第9条所界定的仲裁协议;

"party" means a party to an arbitration agreement or, in any case where an arbitration does not involve all the parties to the arbitration agreement, means a party to the arbitration;

"当事人"是指仲裁协议的当事人,或者,在任何情况下,仲裁不涉及仲裁协议的所有当事人,是指仲裁的当事人;

"seat of arbitration" means the place where the arbitration is based as determined in accordance with section 22;

"仲裁地"是指根据第22条确定的仲裁地;

"international arbitration" means an arbitration where —

"国际仲裁"是指下述情形下的仲裁:

(a) one of the parties to an arbitration agreement, at the time of the conclusion of that agreement, has its place of business in any State other than Malaysia;

(a) 仲裁协议的一方当事人在订立该协议时营业地位于马来西亚以外的任何国家;

(b) one of the following is situated in any State other than Malaysia in which the parties have their places of business:

(b) 以下之一位于当事方营业地所在的马来西亚以外的任何州

（i）the seat of arbitration if determined in，or pursuant to，the arbitration agreement；

（i）如果仲裁协议已确定仲裁所在地，则依照之；若未确定，则根据仲裁协议而定；

（ii）any place where a substantial part of the obligations of any commercial or other relationship is to be *Arbitration*

performed or the place with which the subject matter of the dispute is most closely connected；or

（ii）任何地方，任何商业关系或其他关系的大部分义务都是仲裁

（c）the parties have expressly agreed that the subject matter of the arbitration agreement relates to more than one State；

"domestic arbitration" means any arbitration which is not an international arbitration；

"arbitral tribunal" means a sole arbitrator or a panel of arbitrators.

（c）双方当事人明确约定，若仲裁协议的主题事项涉及一个以上国家；

"国内仲裁"是指任何非国际仲裁的仲裁；

"仲裁庭"是指独任仲裁员或仲裁员小组。

（2）For the purposes of this Act —

（2）就本条例而言

（a）in the definition of "international arbitration"—

（a）在"国际仲裁"的定义中

（i）where a party has more than one place of business，reference to the place of business is that which has the closest relationship to the arbitration agreement；or

（i）当事人有一个以上营业地的，提及营业地是与仲裁协议关系最密切的营业地；

（ii）where a party does not have a place of business，reference to the place of business is that party's habitual residence；

（ii）当事人没有营业地的，以营业地为准的是该当事人的惯常居住地；

（b）where a provision of this Act，except section 3，leaves the parties free to determine a certain issue, such freedom shall include the right of the parties to authorize a third party, including an institution, to determine that issue;

(b) 如果本法的一项规定,除第 3 条外,允许当事方自由决定某一问题, 这种自由应包括当事方有权授权第三方,包括机构,决定该问题;

(c) where a provision of this Act refers to the fact that the parties have agreed or that they may agree or in any other way refers to an agreement of the parties, that agreement shall include any arbitration rules referred to in that agreement;

(c) 如果本法的一项规定提及当事各方已约定或可以约定或以任何其 他方式提及当事各方的约定,该约定应包括该协议中提及的任何 仲裁规则;

(d) where a provision of this Act refers to a claim, other than in paragraphs 27 (a) and 34 (2) (a), it shall also apply to a counterclaim, and where it refers to a defence, it shall also apply to a defence to that counterclaim.

(d) 如果本法的一项规定是指一项请求,除了第 27 条(a)项和第 34 条 第(2)款(a)项之外,它也应适用于反诉,如果它涉及抗辩,它也应 适用于该反诉的辩护。

Application to arbitrations and awards in Malaysia
对马来西亚仲裁和裁决的适用

3. (1) This Act shall apply throughout Malaysia.

(1) 本法案将适用于整个马来西亚。

(2) In respect of a domestic arbitration, where the seat of arbitration is in Malaysia —

(2) 关于国内仲裁,仲裁地点在马来西亚

(a) Parts I, II and IV of this Act shall apply; and

(a) 本法第一部分、第二部分和第四部分适用;以及

(b) Part III of this Act shall apply unless the parties agree otherwise in writing.

　　（b）除非当事人另有书面约定,本法第三部分适用。

（3）In respect of an international arbitration，where the seat of arbitration is in Malaysia —

（3）关于国际仲裁,仲裁地点在马来西亚

　　（a）Parts I，II and IV of this Act shall apply；and

　　（a）本法第一部分,第二部分和第四部分适用；

　　（b）Part III of this Act shall not apply unless the parties agree otherwise in writing.

　　（b）除非当事人另有书面约定,本法第三部分不适用。

（4）For the purposes of paragraphs（2）（b）and（3）（b），the parties to a domestic arbitration may agree to exclude the application of Part III of this Act and the parties to an international arbitra-tion may agree to apply Part III of this Act，in whole or in part.

（4）为达成第(2)款(b)项和第(3)款(b)项所述的目的,国内仲裁的当事人可以同意排除适用本法第三部分,国际仲裁的当事人可以同意全部或部分适用本法第三部分。

Arbitrability of subject matter

事由可否仲裁

4.（1）Any dispute which the parties have agreed to submit to arbitration under an arbitration agreement may be determined by arbitration unless the arbitration agreement is contrary to public policy.

（1）当事人约定根据仲裁协议交付仲裁的任何争议,可以通过仲裁裁决,除非仲裁协议违背公共政策。

（2）The fact that any written law confers jurisdiction in respect of any matter on any court of law but does not refer to the determination of that matter by arbitration shall not，by itself，indicate that a dispute about that matter is not capable of determination by arbitration.

（2）任何成文法赋予任何法院对任何事项的管辖权，但未提及通过仲裁确定该事项，这一事实本身并不表明有关该事项的争议不能通过仲裁确定。

Government to be bound
政府受到约束

5. This Act shall apply to any arbitration to which the Federal Government or the Government of any component state of Malaysia is a party.

本法令适用于联邦政府或任何组成马来西亚州的政府所参加的任何仲裁。

PART II
ARBITRATION
第二部分　仲裁
Chapter 1
General provisions
第一章　总则

Receipt of written communications
收到书面来文

6.（1）Unless otherwise agreed by the parties —

（1）除非当事方另有约定

(a) a written communication is deemed to have been received if it is delivered to the addressee personally or if it is delivered at his place of business, habitual residence or mailing address; and

（a）一项书面通信，如果直接送交收件人，或如果送达收件人的营业地，惯常居所或通信地址，即视为已收到；以及

(b) where the places referred to in paragraph (a) cannot be

found after making a reasonable inquiry，a written communication is deemed to have been received if it is sent to the addressee's last known place of business，habitual residence or mailing address by registered post or any other means which provides a record of the attempt to deliver it.

（b）如果经合理查询后找不到（a）项提到的地方，则以挂号邮递或任何其他方式将书面函件送交收件人最后已知的营业地点、惯常居所或邮寄地址，即视为已收到。

（2）Unless otherwise agreed by the parties，a written communication sent electronically is deemed to have been received if it is sent to the electronic mailing address of the addressee.

（2）除非各方当事人另有约定，以电子方式发送的书面函件，如发送至收件人的电子邮件地址，即视为已收到。

（3）The communication is deemed to have been received on the day it is so delivered.

（3）来文被认为是在发送当天收到的。

（4）This section shall not apply to any communications in respect of court proceedings.

（4）本条不适用于与法院诉讼有关的任何来文。

Waiver of right to object
放弃反对权

7. A party who knows —

若一方知悉

（a）of any provision of this Act from which the parties may derogate；or

（a）当事各方可以减损的本法的任何规定；或

（b）that any requirement under the arbitration agreement has not been complied with.

（b）或者仲裁协议中的任一要求未得到遵守。

And yet it proceeds with the arbitration without stating its objection to such non-compliance without undue delay or，if a time limit is provided for stating that objection，within that period of time，shall be deemed to have waived its right to object.

然而,在进行仲裁时却没有说明其对这种不遵守行为的反对意见,也没有做出不应有的拖延;或者,如果规定了说明反对意见的时限,则应认为在该期限内放弃了反对意见的权利。

Extent of court intervention

法院干预的程度

8. No court shall intervene in matters governed by this Act，except where so provided in this Act.

除本法另有规定外,法院不得干涉本法管辖的事项。

Chapter 2

Arbitration agreement

第二章　仲裁协议

Definition and form of arbitration agreement

仲裁协议的定义和形式

9. (1) In this Act，"arbitration agreement" means an agreement by the parties to submit to arbitration all or certain disputes which have arisen or which may arise between them in respect of a defined legal relationship，whether contractual or not.

   (1) 在本法中,"仲裁协议"是指当事各方同意将双方之间就合同或非合同性质的特定法律关系已经产生或可能产生的全部或某些争议提交仲裁。

   (2) An arbitration agreement may be in the form of an arbitration clause in an agreement or in the form of a

separate agreement.

（2）仲裁协议可以采取协议中仲裁条款的形式，也可以采取单独协议的形式。

（3）An arbitration agreement shall be in writing.

（3）仲裁协议应为书面形式。

（4）An arbitration agreement is in writing where it is contained in —

（4）仲裁协议为书面形式，应存在于下述材料之中

　　（a）a document signed by the parties；

　　（a）各方签署的文件；

　　（b）an exchange of letters，telex，facsimile or other means of communication which provide a record of the agreement；or

　　（b）提供协议记录的换文，电传，传真或其他通信手段；或者

　　（c）an exchange of statement of claim and defence in which the existence of an agreement is alleged by one party and not denied by the other.

　　（c）索赔和答辩的交换声明，其中一方声称存在协议，另一方没有否认。

（5）A reference in an agreement to a document containing an arbitration clause shall constitute an arbitration agreement，provided that the agreement is in writing and the reference is such as to make that clause part of the agreement.

（5）在协议中提及载有仲裁条款的文件，应构成仲裁协议，条件是该协议为书面形式，且提及使该条款成为协议的一部分。

Arbitration agreement and substantive claim before court
仲裁协议和向法院提出的实质性索赔

10.（1）A court before which proceedings are brought in respect of a matter which is the subject of an arbitration agreement shall，where a party makes an application before taking any other steps in the proceedings, stay those proceedings and refer the parties to arbitration unless it finds that the agreement is null and void, inoperative or incapable of being performed.

(1) 就仲裁协议所涉事项提起诉讼的法院,如果一方当事人在采取程序中的任何其他步骤之前提出申请,应中止这些程序并将双方当事人交付仲裁,除非该法院认定该协议无效、不生效或无法履行。

(2) The court, in granting a stay of proceedings pursuant to subsection (1), may impose any conditions as it deems fit.

(2) 法院在依据第(1)款准予中止诉讼时,可施加任何适当的条件。

(2A) Where admiralty proceedings are stayed pursuant to subsection (1), the court granting the stay may, if in those proceedings property has been arrested or bail or other security has been given to prevent or obtain release from arrest—

(2A) 在根据第(1)款中止海事诉讼的情况下,如果在这些诉讼中财产被扣押或提供保释金或其他担保以防止扣押或解除扣押,准予中止的法院可以

　　(a) order that the property arrested be retained as security for the satisfaction of any award given in the arbitration in respect of that dispute; or

　　(a) 命令将被扣押的财产保留作为履行仲裁中就该纠纷做出的任何裁决的担保;或

　　(b) order that the stay of those proceedings be conditional on the provision of equivalent security for the satisfaction of any such award.

　　(b) 命令中止这些程序的条件是为任何此类裁决的执行提供同等的担保。

(2B) Subject to any rules of court and to any necessary

modifications，the same law and practice shall apply in relation toproperty retained in pursuance of an order under subsection（2A）as would apply if it were held for the purposes of proceedings in the court making the order.

（2B）在不违反任何法院规则和任何必要修改的情况下，对于根据第(2A)项命令所保留的财产，应适用同一法律和惯例，如果该财产是为作出命令的法院诉讼的目的而保留的。

（2C）For the purpose of this section，admiralty proceedings refer to admiralty proceedings under Order 70 of the Rules of the High Court 1980［*P. U.（A）50/1980*］and proceedings commenced pursuant to paragraph *24（b）* of the Courts of Judicature Act 1964［*Act 91*］.

（2C）就本节而言，海事诉讼程序是指根据 1980 年高等法院规则第 70 号命令进行的海事诉讼程序，以及根据 1964 年《司法法院法》第 24 条(b)款进行的诉讼程序。

（3）Where the proceedings referred to in subsection（1）have been brought，arbitral proceedings may be commenced or continued，and an award may be made，while the issue is pending before the court.

（3）在已经提起第(1)款所指的程序的情况下，可以启动或继续仲裁程序，并可以作出裁决，但该问题仍有待法院裁决。

（4）This section shall also apply in respect of an international arbitration，where the seat of arbitration is not in Malaysia.

（4）本节也适用于仲裁地点不在马来西亚的国际仲裁。

Arbitration agreement and interim measures by High Court
仲裁协议和高等法院的临时措施

11.（1）A party may，before or during arbitral proceedings，apply to a High Court for any interim measure and the High Court may make the following orders for：

(1) 一方当事人可在仲裁程序之前或期间向高等法院申请采取任何临时措施,高等法院可下达以下命令:

(a) security for costs；

(a) 费用担保；

(b) discovery of documents and interrogatories；

(b) 文件开示和询问；

(c) giving of evidence by affidavit；

(c) 提供证据并宣誓；

(d) appointment of a receiver；

(d) 指定接收人；

(e) securing the amount in dispute，whether by way of arrest of property or bail or other security pursuant to the admiralty jurisdiction of the High Court；

(e) 根据高等法院的海事管辖权,通过扣押财产或保释金或其他担保方式,确保争议金额；

(f) the preservation，interim custody or sale of any property which is the subject-matter of the dispute；

(f) 保存、临时保管或出售属于争议标的任何财产；

(g) ensuring that any award which may be made in the arbitral proceedings is not rendered ineffectual by the dissipation of assets by a party；and

(g) 确保在仲裁程序中作出的任何裁决不致因一方当事人挥霍资产而无效；

(h) an interim injunction or any other interim measure.

(h) 临时禁令或任何其他临时措施。

(2) Where a party applies to the High Court for any interim measure and an arbitral tribunal has already ruled on any matter which is relevant to the application，the High Court shall treat any findings of fact made in the course of such ruling by the arbitral tribunal as conclusive for the purposes

of the application.

（2）如果一方当事人就任何临时措施向高等法院提出申请，而仲裁庭已经就与申请有关的任何事项作出裁决，高等法院应就申请而言，将仲裁庭在这种裁决过程中作出的任何事实认定视为是结论性的。

（3）This section shall also apply in respect of an international arbitration，where the seat of arbitration is not in Malaysia.

（3）本节也适用于仲裁地点不在马来西亚的国际仲裁。

Chapter 3
Composition of arbitrators
第三章　仲裁员的组成

Number of arbitrators

仲裁员人数

12.（1）The parties are free to determine the number of arbitrators.

（1）双方当事人可自由决定仲裁员人数。

（2）Where the parties fail to determine the number of arbitrators，the arbitral tribunal shall —

（2）如果当事方未能确定仲裁员人数，仲裁庭应：

（a）in the case of an international arbitration，consist of three arbitrators；and

（a）在国际仲裁中，由三名仲裁员组成；以及

（b）in the case of a domestic arbitration，consist of a single arbitrator.

（b）在国内仲裁中，只有一名仲裁员。

Appointment of arbitrators

仲裁员的任命

13.（1）Unless otherwise agreed by the parties，no person shall be precluded by reason of nationality from acting as an arbitrator.

(1) 除非当事人另有约定,任何人不得因国籍限制而不能担任仲裁员。

(2) The parties are free to agree on a procedure for appointing the arbitrator or the presiding arbitrator.

(2) 双方当事人可自由商定指定仲裁员或首席仲裁员的程序。

(3) Where the parties fail to agree on the procedure referred to in subsection (2), and the arbitration consists of three arbitrators, each party shall appoint one arbitrator, and the two appointed arbitrators shall appoint the third arbitrator as the presiding arbitrator.

(3) 如果当事各方未能就第(2)款所述程序达成协议,且仲裁由三名仲裁员组成,每一方应指定一名仲裁员,两名指定的仲裁员应指定第三名仲裁员为首席仲裁员。

(4) Where subsection (3) applies and —

(4) 当第(3)款适用且下述情形发生时

(a) a party fails to appoint an arbitrator within thirty days of receipt of a request in writing to do so from the other party; or

(a) 一方当事人未能在收到另一方当事人书面请求后 30 天内指定仲裁员;

(b) the two arbitrators fail to agree on the third arbitrator within thirty days of their appointment or such extended period as the parties may agree,

(b) 两名仲裁员未能在指定后 30 天内或双方当事人可能同意的延长期限内就第三名仲裁员达成协议,

either party may apply to the Director of the Kuala Lumpur Regional Centre for Arbitration for such appointment.

任何一方当事人均可向吉隆坡区域中心主任申请任命仲裁员。

(5) Where in an arbitration with a single arbitrator —

(5) 在一个独任仲裁员的仲裁中,当

    (a) the parties fail to agree on the procedure referred to in subsection (2); and

    (a) 当事各方未能就第(2)款所述程序达成协议;以及

    (b) the parties fail to agree on the arbitrator,

    (b) 双方未能就仲裁员达成一致,

either party may apply to the Director of the Kuala Lumpur Regional Centre for Arbitration for the appointment of an arbitrator.

任何一方均可向吉隆坡区域仲裁中心主任申请指定仲裁员。

(6) Where, the parties have agreed on the procedure for appointment of the arbitrator —

(6) 若各方当事人已就任命仲裁员的程序事宜达成一致

    (a) a party fails to act as required under such procedure;

    (a) 一方未能按照这种程序的要求行事;

    (b) the parties, or two arbitrators, are unable to reach an agreement under such procedure; or

    (b) 当事各方或两名仲裁员无法根据这种程序达成协议;或

    (c) a third party, including an institution, fails to perform any function entrusted to it under such procedure,

    (c) 包括一个机构在内的第三方未能履行该程序赋予它的任何职能,

any party may request the Director of the Kuala Lumpur Regional Centre for Arbitration to take the necessary measures, unless the agreement on the appointment procedure provides other means for securing the appointment.

任何一方均可要求吉隆坡区域仲裁中心主任采取必要措施,除非关于任命程序的协议规定了确保任命的其他手段。

(7) Where the Director of the Kuala Lumpur Regional Centre for

Arbitration is unable to act or fails to act under subsections (4)，(5) and (6) within thirty days from the request，any party may apply to the High Court for such appointment.

（7）吉隆坡区域仲裁中心主任不能或没有根据第(4)(5)(6)款采取行动的,任何一方均可在提出请求后 30 天内向高等法院申请这种任命。

（8）In appointing an arbitrator the Director of the Kuala Lumpur Regional Centre for Arbitration or the High Court，as the case may be，shall have due regard to —

（8）在指定仲裁员时,必要时吉隆坡区域仲裁中心主任或高等法院的院长应适当考虑到

（a）any qualifications required of the arbitrator by the agreement of the parties；

（a）当事各方协议要求仲裁员具备的任何资格；

（b）other considerations that are likely to secure the appointment of an independent and impartial arbitrator；and

（b）可能确保指定独立和公正的仲裁员的其他考虑；以及

（c）in the case of an international arbitration，the advisability of appointing an arbitrator of a nationality other than those of the parties.

（c）在国际仲裁的情况下,应指定一名非当事方国籍的仲裁员。

（9）No appeal shall lie against any decision of the Director of the Kuala Lumpur Regional Centre for Arbitration or the High Court under this section.

（9）对于吉隆坡地区仲裁中心主任或高等法院院长根据本条做出的任何决定,不得提出上诉。

Grounds for challenge
质疑理由

14.（1）A person who is approached in connection with that person's possible appointment as an arbitrator shall disclose any circumstances likely to give rise to justifiable doubts as to that person's impartiality or independence.

（1）可能被任命为仲裁员的人应披露可能对其公正性或独立性产生合理怀疑的任何情况。

（2）An arbitrator shall，without delay，from the time of appointment and throughout the arbitral proceedings，disclose any circumstances referred to in subsection（1）to the parties unless the parties have already been informed of such circumstances by the arbitrator.

（2）仲裁员应当从指定之时起和在整个仲裁程序中毫不拖延地向各方当事人披露第一款中提及的任何情形，除非仲裁员已将此种情形通知各方当事人。

（3）An arbitrator may be challenged only if —

（3）一名仲裁员只有在下述情况下才可被质疑

　　（a）the circumstances give rise to justifiable doubts as to that arbitrator's impartiality or independence；or

　　（a）情况引起对仲裁员的公正性或独立性的合理怀疑；

　　（b）that arbitrator does not possess qualifications agreed to by the parties.

　　（b）仲裁员不具备获取双方当事人同意的资格。

（4）A party may challenge an arbitrator appointed by that party，or in whose appointment that party has participated，only for reasons which that party becomes aware of after the appointment has been made.

（4）一方当事人可以对其指定或其参与指定的仲裁员提出异议，但仅限于该方当事人在仲裁员被任命后才知道的理由。

Challenge procedure
质疑程序

15.（1）Unless otherwise agreed by the parties，any party who

intends to challenge an arbitrator shall, within fifteen days after becoming aware of the constitution of the arbitral tribunal or of any reasons referred to in subsection 14(3), send a written statement of the reasons for the challenge to the arbitral tribunal.

(1) 除非各方当事人另有约定,任何一方当事人如打算对仲裁员提出异议,应在知悉仲裁庭组成或了解第 14 条第(3)款所述任何理由后 15 天内向仲裁庭提交一份书面陈述,说明提出异议的理由。

(2) Unless the challenged arbitrator withdraws from office or the other party agrees to the challenge, the arbitral tribunal shall make a decision on the challenge.

(2) 除非被质疑的仲裁员辞职或另一方同意该项异议,仲裁庭应对该异议作出裁决。

(3) Where a challenge is not successful, the challenging party may, within thirty days after having received notice of the decision rejecting the challenge, apply to the High Court to make a decision on the challenge.

(3) 如果异议不成功,提出异议的一方可以在收到驳回异议的决定通知后 30 天内,向高等法院申请对异议作出裁决。

(4) While such an application is pending, the arbitral tribunal, including the challenged arbitrator, may continue the arbitral proceedings and make an award.

(4) 在此类申请待决期间,仲裁庭,包括被质疑的仲裁员,可继续仲裁程序并作出裁决。

(5) No appeal shall lie against the decision of the High Court under subsection (3).

(5) 对于高等法院根据第(3)款作出的裁决,不得提出上诉。

Failure or impossibility to act

未能或不可能采取行动

16.（1）Where an arbitrator becomes in law or in fact unable to perform the functions of that office, or for other reasons fails to act without undue delay, that arbitrator's mandate terminates on withdrawal from office or if the parties agree on the termination.

（1）如果仲裁员在法律上或事实上无法履行其职务，或由于其他原因未能及时采取行动，则该仲裁员的任期在其离职时，或如果当事方同意终止时终止。

（2）Where any party disagrees on the termination of the mandate of the arbitrator, any party may apply to the High Court to decide on such termination and no appeal shall lie against the decision of the High Court.

（2）如果任何一方对终止仲裁员的任期有异议，任何一方均可向高等法院申请对终止任期作出裁决，且不得对高等法院的裁决提出上诉。

（3）Where, under this section or subsection 15（2）, an arbitrator withdraws from office or a party agrees to the termination of the mandate of an arbitrator, it shall not imply acceptance of the validity of any ground referred to in this section or subsection 14(3).

（3）根据本节或第 15 条第（2）款，仲裁员辞职或当事一方同意终止仲裁员的任期，并不意味着接受本节或第 14 条第（3）款提及的任何理由的有效性。

Appointment of substitute arbitrator

指定替代仲裁员

17.（1）A substitute arbitrator shall be appointed in accordance with the provisions of this Act where —

（1）若发生下述情形，应根据本法规定指定一名替代仲裁员

（a）the mandate of an arbitrator terminates under section 15 or 16；

（a）根据第 15 条或第 16 条，仲裁员的授权终止；

（b）an arbitrator withdraws from office for any other reason；

（b）仲裁员因任何其他原因辞职；

（c）the mandate of the arbitrator is revoked by agreement of the parties；or

（c）经当事各方同意撤销仲裁员的授权；或

（d）in any other case of termination of mandate.

（d）在任何其他终止的情况下。

（2）Unless otherwise agreed by the parties—

（2）除非双方另有协议

（a）where a single or the presiding arbitrator is replaced，any hearings previously held shall be repeated before the substitute arbitrator；or

（a）如果替换了一名独任或首席仲裁员，先前举行的任何审理应在替代仲裁员面前重复进行；或

（b）where an arbitrator other than a single or the presiding arbitrator is replaced，any hearings previously held may be repeated at the discretion of the arbitral tribunal.

（b）如果替换了独任或首席仲裁员以外的仲裁员，以前举行的任何审理可以由仲裁庭酌情决定重复进行。

（3）Unless otherwise agreed by the parties，any order or ruling of the arbitral tribunal made prior to the replacement of an arbitrator under this section shall not be invalid solely on the ground there has been a change in the composition of the arbitral tribunal.

（3）除当事人另有约定外，仲裁庭根据本节规定对更换仲裁员所

作的任何其他裁决,不得仅以仲裁庭的组成发生变化为理由
而无效。

Chapter 4
Jurisdiction of arbitral tribunal
第四章　仲裁庭的管辖权

Competence of arbitral tribunal to rule on its jurisdiction

仲裁庭就其管辖权作出裁决的权限

18.（1）The arbitral tribunal may rule on its own jurisdiction,
including any objections with respect to the existence or
validity of the arbitration agreement.

（1）仲裁庭可就其管辖权作出裁决,包括就仲裁协议的存在或有
效性提出的任何异议。

（2）For the purposes of subsection（1）—

（2）就第（1）款而言

（a）an arbitration clause which forms part of an agreement
shall be treated as an agreement independent of the
other terms of the agreement; and

（a）仲裁条款构成协议的一部分,应视为独立于协议其他条款
的协议;以及

（b）a decision by the arbitral tribunal that the agreement is
null and void shall not *ipso jure* entail the invalidity of
the arbitration clause.

（b）仲裁庭关于协议无效的裁决,在法律上并不一定导致仲裁
条款的无效。

（3）A plea that the arbitral tribunal does not have jurisdiction
shall be raised not later than the submission of the
statement of defence.

（3）仲裁庭没有管辖权的抗辩的提出,应不迟于提交答辩书。

（4）A party is not precluded from raising a plea under

subsection（3）by reason of that party having appointed or participated in the appointment of the arbitrator.

（4）一方当事人已经指定或参与指定仲裁的事实不得成为阻碍其依据第(3)款提出抗辩的理由。

（5）A plea that the arbitral tribunal is exceeding the scope of its authority shall be raised as soon as the matter alleged to be beyond the scope of its authority is raised during the arbitral proceedings.

（5）在仲裁程序中,一旦指称的超出其权限的事项被提出,即应提出关于仲裁庭正在超出其权限的抗辩。

（6）Notwithstanding subsections（3）and（5）, the arbitral tribunal may admit such plea if it considers the delay justified.

（6）尽管有第(3)款和第(5)款的规定,如果仲裁庭认为延误是合理的,仲裁庭可以接受这种指认。

（7）The arbitral tribunal may rule on a plea referred to in subsection（3）or（5）, either as a preliminary question or in an award on the merits.

（7）仲裁庭可对第(3)款或第(5)款所指的事项作出裁定,无论是作为初步问题或对案情进行裁决。

（8）Where the arbitral tribunal rules on such a plea as a preliminary question that it has jurisdiction, any party may, within thirty days after having received notice of that ruling appeal to the High Court to decide the matter.

（8）如果仲裁庭对作为初步问题的这一请求作出裁决,规定其具有管辖权,则任何一方可在收到该裁定上诉通知之后 30 日内向高等法院提出上诉。

（9）While an appeal is pending, the arbitral tribunal may continue the arbitral proceedings and make an award.

(9) 在上诉待决期间，仲裁庭可继续仲裁程序并作出裁决。

(10) No appeal shall lie against the decision of the High Court under subsection (8).

(10) 对于高等法院根据第(8)款做出的裁决，不得提出上诉。

Power of arbitral tribunal to order interim measures

仲裁庭下令采取临时措施的权力

19. (1) Unless otherwise agreed by the parties, a party may apply to the arbitral tribunal for any of the following orders：

(1) 除非当事人另有约定，当事一方可以向仲裁庭申请下列任何一项命令：

(a) security for costs；

(a) 费用担保；

(b) discovery of documents and interrogatories；

(b) 文件的开示和询问；

(c) giving of evidence by affidavit；

(c) 提供证据并宣誓；

(d) the preservation, interim custody or sale of any property which is the subject-matter of the dispute.

(d) 保存，临时保管或出售任何属于争议标的财产。

(2) The arbitral tribunal may require any party to provide appropriate security in connection with such measure as ordered under subsection (1).

(2) 仲裁庭可要求任何一方当事人提供与根据第(1)款下达的命令有关的措施的适当担保。

(3) Unless otherwise agreed by the parties, sections 38 and 39 shall apply to orders made by an arbitral tribunal under this section as if a reference in those sections to an award were a reference to such an order.

（3）除非各方当事人另有约定，第38条和第39条应适用于仲裁庭根据本条做出的命令，如同这两条中提及的裁决是提及此种命令一样。

Chapter 5
Conduct of arbitral proceedings
第五章　仲裁程序的执行

Equal treatment of parties

平等对待各方

20. The parties shall be treated with equality and each party shall be given a fair and reasonable opportunity of presenting that party's case.

应平等对待各当事方，并应给予每一当事方公平合理的陈述其案情的机会。

Determination of rules of procedure

程序规则的决定

21. （1）Subject to the provisions of this Act，the parties are free to agree on the procedure to be followed by the arbitral tribunal in conducting the proceedings.

（1）在不违反本法规定的情况下，各方当事人可自由商定仲裁庭在进行程序时应遵循的程序。

（2）Where the parties fail to agree under subsection（1），the arbitral tribunal may，subject to the provisions of this Act，conduct the arbitration in such manner as it considers appropriate.

（2）如果当事各方未能根据第（1）款达成协议，仲裁庭可在不违反本法令规定的情况下，以其认为适当的方式进行仲裁。

（3）The power conferred upon the arbitral tribunal under subsection（2）shall include the power to —

（3）第（2）款中赋予仲裁庭的权力应包括下述权力：

（a）determine the admissibility，relevance，materiality and weight of any evidence；

（a）确定任何证据的可采性、相关性、实质性和重要性；

（b）draw on its own knowledge and expertise；

（b）利用自己的知识和专长；

（c）order the provision of further particulars in a statement of claim or statement of defence；

（c）命令在索赔书或答辩书中提供进一步的细节；

（d）order the giving of security for costs；

（d）要求为费用提供担保；

（e）fix and amend time limits within which various steps in the arbitral proceedings must be completed；

（e）修正仲裁程序中必须完成各种步骤的时限；

（f）order the discovery and production of documents or materials within the possession or power of a party；

（f）在一方拥有或权力范围内发现和提供文件或材料；

（g）order the interrogatories to be answered；

（g）命令回答问题；

（h）order that any evidence be given on oath or affirmation；and

（h）命令在宣誓或确认后提供任何证据；以及

（i）make such other orders as the arbitral tribunal considers appropriate.

（i）仲裁庭认为适当的其他命令。

Seat of arbitration

仲裁地

22.（1）The parties are free to agree on the seat of arbitration.

（1）双方当事人可以自由约定仲裁地。

（2）Where the parties fail to agree under subsection（1），the seat of arbitration shall be determined by the arbitral tribunal having regard to the circumstances of the case, including the convenience of the parties.

（2）如果当事各方未能根据第（1）款达成协议，仲裁庭应根据案情，包括当事人的方便程度，确定仲裁的地点。

（3）Notwithstanding subsections（1）and（2），the arbitral tribunal may, unless otherwise agreed by the parties, meet at any place it considers appropriate for consultation among its members, for hearing witnesses, experts or the parties, or for inspection of goods, other property or documents.

（3）尽管有第（1）款和第（2）款，仲裁庭仍可在其认为适当的任何地点举行会议，以便在其成员之间进行协商，听取证人、专家或当事方的意见，或检查货物、其他财产或文件。

Commencement of arbitral proceedings
仲裁程序的启动

23. Unless otherwise agreed by the parties, the arbitral proceedings in respect of a particular dispute shall commence on the date on which a request in writing for that dispute to be referred to arbitration is received by the respondent.

除非当事各方另有协议，关于某一特定争议的仲裁程序应自被申请人收到将该争议提交仲裁的书面请求之日起开始。

Language
语言

24.（1）The parties are free to agree on the language to be used in the arbitral proceedings.

（1）双方当事人可自由商定仲裁程序中使用的语言。

（2）Where the parties fail to agree under subsection（1），the

arbitral tribunal shall determine the language to be used in the arbitral proceedings.

（2）如果当事各方未能根据第（1）款达成协议，仲裁庭应决定仲裁程序中使用的语言。

（3）The agreement or the determination referred to in subsections（1）and（2）respectively shall，unless otherwise specified in the agreement or determination，apply to any written statement made by a party，any hearing and any award，decision or other communication by the arbitral tribunal.

（3）除非在协议或决定中另有规定，第（1）款中提及的协议或决定应分别适用于当事方的任何书面陈述、任何听讯以及仲裁庭的任何裁决、决定或其他通信。

（4）The arbitral tribunal may order that any documentary evidence shall be accompanied by a translation into the language agreed upon by the parties or determined by the arbitral tribunal.

（4）仲裁庭可下达命令：任何书面证据应附有一份翻译成各方当事人商定或仲裁庭确定的语言的译文。

Statements of claim and defence
申请书和答辩书

25.（1）Within the period of time agreed by the parties or，failing such agreement，as determined by the arbitral tribunal，the claimant shall state —

（1）在当事各方商定的期限内，如未达成仲裁庭确定的此种协议，申请人应说明

（a）the facts supporting his claim；

（a）申请的事实依据；

（b）the points at issue；and

(b) 有争议的问题；以及

(c) the relief or remedy sought，

(c) 所寻求的救济或补救，

and the respondent shall state his defence in respect of the particulars set out in this subsection，unless the parties have otherwise agreed to the required elements of such statements.

被申请人应就本款所列细节提出抗辩，除非当事人另有约定。

(2) The parties may —

(2) 各方当事人可以

(a) submit with their statements any document the parties consider relevant；or

(a) 提交双方认为相关的任何文件；或

(b) add a reference to the documents or other evidence that the parties may submit.

(b) 增加文件的参考资料或双方可以提交的其他证据。

(3) Unless otherwise agreed by the parties，either party may amend or supplement the claim or defence during the course of the arbitral proceedings，unless the arbitral tribunal considers it inappropriate to allow such amendment having regard to the delay in making it.

(3) 除非各方当事人另有约定，任何一方当事人均可在仲裁程序过程中修改或补充其请求或答辩，除非仲裁庭认为不宜允许在做出此种修改时出现拖延。

Hearings

听讯

26. (1) Unless otherwise agreed by the parties，the arbitral tribunal shall decide whether to hold oral hearings for the presentation of evidence or oral arguments，or whether the proceedings shall be conducted on the basis of documents and other materials.

（1）除非当事各方另有约定，仲裁庭应决定是否举行口头听讯以提出证据或口头辩论，或是否应根据文件和其他材料进行仲裁程序。

（2）Unless the parties have agreed that no hearings shall be held，the arbitral tribunal shall upon the application of any party hold oral hearings at an appropriate stage of the proceedings.

（2）除非当事各方同意不举行任何听讯，仲裁庭应根据任何当事方的申请在程序的适当阶段举行口头听讯。

（3）The parties shall be given reasonable prior notice of any hearing and of any meeting of the arbitral tribunal for the purposes of inspection of goods，other property or documents.

（3）为达成检查货物、其他财产或文件的目的，应事先合理通知各方当事人仲裁庭的任何听讯和任何会议。

（4）All statements，documents or other information supplied to the arbitral tribunal by one party shall be communicated to the other party.

（4）一方当事人向仲裁庭提供的所有陈述、文件或其他资料均应送交另一方当事人。

（5）Any expert report or evidentiary document on which the arbitral tribunal may rely in making its decision shall be communicated to the parties.

（5）仲裁庭在做出决定时可依据的任何专家报告或证据文件应送交各方当事人。

Default of a party
一方违约

27. Unless otherwise agreed by the parties，if without showing sufficient cause —

除非双方另有协议,如没有证明有充分理由

(a) the claimant fails to communicate the statement of claim in accordance with subsection 25（1）, the arbitral tribunal shall terminate the proceedings;

(a) 原告未能按照第 25 条第（1）款提交索赔说明,仲裁庭应终止仲裁程序;

(b) the respondent fails to communicate the statement of defence in accordance with subsection 25（1）, the arbitral tribunal shall continue the proceedings without treating such failure in itself as an admission of the claimant's allegations;

(b) 被申请人未能根据第 25 条第（1）款提交答辩书,仲裁庭应继续进行仲裁程序,但其本身不应将这种未提交视为承认申请人的指控;

(c) any party fails to appear at a hearing or to produce documentary evidence, the arbitral tribunal may continue the proceedings and make the award on the evidence before it; or

(c) 任何一方当事人未出席庭审或未出示书面证据,仲裁庭可继续进行程序并根据其收到的证据作出裁决;或

(d) the claimant fails to proceed with the claim, the arbitral tribunal may make an award dismissing the claim or give directions, with or without conditions, for the speedy determination of the claim.

(d) 申请人未能继续处理该请求,仲裁庭可作出驳回该请求的裁决,或就迅速裁定该请求做出附带或无条件的指示。

Expert appointed by arbitral tribunal
仲裁庭指定的专家

28.（1）Unless otherwise agreed by the parties, the arbitral tribunal may —

（1）除非各方当事人另有约定，仲裁庭可以

（a）appoint one or more experts to report to it on specific issues to be determined by the arbitral tribunal；or

（a）指定一名或多名专家就仲裁庭确定的具体问题向仲裁庭报告；或

（b）require a party to give the expert any relevant information or to produce or to provide access to any relevant documents，goods or other property for the expert's inspection.

（b）要求一方向专家提供任何相关信息，或提供任何相关文件、货物或其他财产供专家检查。

（2）Unless otherwise agreed by the parties，if a party so requests or if the arbitral tribunal considers it necessary，the expert shall，after delivery of a written or oral report，participate in a hearing where the parties have the opportunity to put questions to the expert and to present other expert witnesses in order to testify on the points at issue.

（2）除非当事各方另有约定，如当事一方提出请求，或仲裁庭认为有必要，专家应在做出书面或口头报告后，在当事各方有机会向专家提出问题和介绍其他专家证人以便就有关问题作证的情况下，参加听讯。

Court assistance in taking evidence

法庭协助取证

29.（1）Any party may with the approval of the arbitral tribunal，apply to the High Court for assistance in taking evidence.

（1）经仲裁庭批准，任何一方当事人均可向高等法院申请取证协助。

（2）The High Court may order the attendance of a witness to

give evidence or, where applicable, produce documents on oath or affirmation before an officer of the High Court or any other person, including the arbitral tribunal.

(2) 高等法院可命令证人出庭作证,或在适用情况下,向高等法院官员或包括仲裁庭在内的任何其他人提供宣誓或确认的文件。

Chapter 6
Making of award and termination of proceedings
第六章　作出裁决和终止诉讼程序

Law applicable to substance of dispute
适用于争议实质的法律

30. (1) Unless otherwise agreed by the parties, in respect of a domestic arbitration where the seat of arbitration is in Malaysia, the arbitral tribunal shall decide the dispute in accordance with the substantive law of Malaysia.

(1) 除非当事各方另有协议,对于仲裁地点在马来西亚的国内仲裁,仲裁庭应根据马来西亚实体法对争议作出裁决。

(2) In respect of an international arbitration, the arbitral tribunal shall decide the dispute in accordance with the law as agreed upon by the parties as applicable to the substance of the dispute.

(2) 对于国际仲裁,仲裁庭应根据当事各方商定的适用于争议实质内容的法律对争议作出裁决。

(3) Any designation by the parties of the law of a given State shall be construed, unless otherwise expressed, as directly referring to the substantive law of that State and not to its conflict of laws rules.

(3) 除非另有表示,当事各方对某一特定国家法律的任何指定均应被解释为直接提及该国的实体法而不是其法律冲突规则。

（4）Failing any agreement under subsection（2），the arbitral tribunal shall apply the law determined by the conflict of laws rules.

（4）如未根据第（2）款达成任何协议，仲裁庭应适用由法律冲突规则确定的法律。

（5）The arbitral tribunal shall，in all cases，decide in accordance with the terms of the agreement and shall take into account the usages of the trade applicable to the transaction.

（5）仲裁庭在所有情况下均应根据协议条款做出决定，并应考虑到适用于交易的行业惯例。

Decision making by panel of arbitrators
仲裁员小组的决定

31.（1）Unless otherwise agreed by the parties，in any arbitral proceedings with more than one arbitrator，any decision of the arbitral tribunal shall be made by a majority of all its members.

（1）除非当事各方另有协议，在有一名以上仲裁员的任何仲裁程序中，仲裁庭的任何裁决应由仲裁庭全体仲裁员的过半数作出。

（2）Where so authorized by the parties or by all the members of the arbitral tribunal，questions of procedure may be decided by the presiding arbitrator.

（2）经当事各方或仲裁庭全体成员授权，程序问题可由首席仲裁员裁决。

Settlement
处理

32.（1）If，during arbitral proceedings，the parties settle the dispute，the arbitral tribunal shall terminate the proceedings and，if requested by the parties and not objected to by the arbitral tribunal, record the settlement in the form of an award on agreed terms.

(1) 如果在仲裁程序期间,当事各方解决了争端,仲裁庭应终止仲裁程序,并在当事各方提出请求且未遭到仲裁庭反对的情况下,以协议条款的裁决形式记录该和解。

(2) An award on agreed terms shall be made in accordance with the provisions of section 33 and shall state that it is an award.

(2) 按约定条件作出裁决,应根据第 33 条的规定作出,并应说明这是一项裁决。

(3) An award made under subsection (1) shall have the same status and effect as an award on the merits of the case.

(3) 根据第(1)款作出的裁决应具有与关于案情实质的裁决相同的地位和效力。

Form and contents of award

裁决的形式和内容

33. (1) An award shall be made in writing and subject to subsection (2) shall be signed by the arbitrator.

(1) 根据第(2)款的要求,裁决应以书面形式作出,由仲裁员签署。

(2) In arbitral proceedings with more than one arbitrator, the signatures of the majority of all members of the arbitral tribunal shall be sufficient provided that the reason for any omitted signature is stated.

(2) 在有一名以上仲裁员的仲裁程序中,要说明任何省略签名的理由,仲裁庭全体成员的多数之签名即已足够。

(3) An award shall state the reasons upon which it is based, unless —

（3）裁决应说明其所依据的理由，除非

（a）the parties have agreed that no reasons are to be given；or

（a）各当事方商定不提出理由；或

（b）the award is an award on agreed terms under section 32.

（b）裁决是根据第 32 条下的约定条款作出的裁决。

（4）An award shall state its date and the seat of arbitration as determined in accordance with section 22 and shall be deemed to have been made at that seat.

（4）裁决应说明其日期和根据第 22 条确定的仲裁地，并应视为在该地作出。

（5）After an award is made，a copy of the award signed by the arbitrator in accordance with subsections（1）and（2）shall be delivered to each party.

（5）作出裁决后，应向每一方当事人送交仲裁员根据第（1）款和第（2）款签署的裁决副本。

（6）Unless otherwise provided in the arbitration agreement，the arbitral tribunal may —

（6）除非仲裁协议另有规定，仲裁庭可以

（a）award interest on any sum of money ordered to be paid by the award from the date of the award to the date of realisation；and

（a）从裁决之日起至实现之日止，裁定由裁决支付的任何款项的裁定利息；以及

（b）determine the rate of interest.

（b）确定利率。

Termination of proceedings

程序的终止

34.（1）The arbitral proceedings shall be terminated by a final award or by an order of the arbitral tribunal in accordance with subsection（2）.

（1）仲裁程序应根据第（2）款以终止裁决或仲裁庭命令终止。

（2）The arbitral tribunal shall order the termination of the arbitral proceedings where —

（2）仲裁庭应在下列情况下，下令终止仲裁程序：

(a) the claimant withdraws the claim，unless the respondent objects to the withdrawal and the arbitral tribunal recognizes the respondent's legitimate interest in obtaining a final settlement of the dispute；

(a) 申请人撤回了请求，除非被申请人反对撤回，而且仲裁庭承认被申请人的合法权益；

(b) the parties agree on the termination of the proceedings；or

(b) 获得争端的最后解决；或

(c) the arbitral tribunal finds that the continuation of the proceedings has for any other reason become unnecessary or impossible.

(c) 仲裁庭认为，由于任何其他原因，程序的继续是没有必要或不可能的。

（3）Subject to the provisions of section 35 and subsection 37（6），the mandate of the arbitral tribunal shall terminate with the termination of the arbitral proceedings.

（3）在不违反第35条和第37条第（6）款规定的情况下，仲裁庭的任务随着仲裁程序的终止而终止。

（4）Unless otherwise provided by any written law, the death of a party does not terminate —

（4）除非任何成文法另有规定，否则不能因一方的死亡而终止

(a) the arbitral proceedings；or

(a)仲裁程序；或

(b) the authority of the arbitral tribunal.

（b）仲裁庭的权力。

Correction and interpretation of award or additional award
更正和解释裁决或补充裁决

35.（1）A party，within thirty days of the receipt of the award，unless any other period of time has been agreed upon by the parties —

（1）一方在收到裁决后 30 天内，除非当事双方商定任何其他期限

（a）upon notice to the other party，may request the arbitral tribunal to correct in the award any error in computation，any clerical or typographical error or other error of similar nature；or

（a）一经通知另一方当事人，可要求仲裁庭更正裁决中的计算错误、任何文书或印刷错误或其他类似性质的错误；

（b）upon notice to and with the agreement of the other party，may request the arbitral tribunal to give an interpretation of a specific point or part of the award.

（b）经通知另一方当事人并征得其同意，可请求仲裁庭对裁决的某一具体内容或部分做出解释。

（2）Where the arbitral tribunal considers the request made under subsection（1）to be justified，it shall make the correction or give the interpretation within thirty days of the receipt of the request and such interpretation shall form part of the award.

（2）仲裁庭认为根据第（1）款提出的请求有正当理由的，应在收到该请求后 30 天内做出更正或做出解释，此种解释应构成裁决的一部分。

（3）The arbitral tribunal may correct any error of the type referred to in paragraph（1）(a)on its own initiative within thirty days of the date of the award.

（3）仲裁庭可在裁决之日起 30 天内自行纠正第（1）款（a）项任何类型的错误。

（4）Unless otherwise agreed by the parties，a party may，within thirty days of the receipt of the award and upon notice to the other party，request the arbitral tribunal to make an additional award as to claims presented in the arbitral proceedings but omitted from the award.

（4）除非各方当事人另有约定，一方当事人可以在收到裁决后 30 天内，在通知另一方当事人后，请求仲裁庭就仲裁程序中提出但从裁决中删除的请求作出补充裁决。

（5）Where the arbitral tribunal considers the request under subsection（4）to be justified，it shall make the additional award within sixty days from the receipt of such request.

（5）仲裁庭认为根据第（4）款提出的请求有正当理由的，应在收到该请求后 60 天内作出补充裁决。

（6）The arbitral tribunal may，where it thinks necessary，extend the period of time within which it shall make a correction，interpretation or an additional award under this section.

（6）仲裁庭认为必要时，可以延长根据本条做出更正、解释，或作出补充裁决的期限。

（7）The provisions of section 33 shall apply to a correction or interpretation of the award or to an additional award.

（7）第 33 条的规定应适用于对裁决的更正或解释或附加裁决。

An award is final and binding
裁决是具有约束力的最终裁决

36.（1）An award made by an arbitral tribunal pursuant to an arbitration agreement shall be final and binding on the parties and may be relied upon by any party by way of defence，set-off or otherwise in any proceedings in any court.

（1）仲裁庭根据仲裁协议作出的裁决应为最终裁决，对各方当事人具有约束力，任何一方当事人均可在任何法院的任何程序中以答辩、抵消或其他方式援用该裁决。

（2）The arbitral tribunal shall not vary, amend, correct, review, add to or revoke an award which has been made except as specifically provided for in section 35.

（2）仲裁庭不得变更、修改、更正、复核、增补或撤销已作出的裁决，除非第 35 条有具体规定。

Chapter 7
Recourse against award
第七章　对裁决的追诉

Application for setting aside

申请撤销

37.（1）An award may be set aside by the High Court only if —

（1）高等法院只有在下列情况下才可撤销裁决：

(a)the party making the application provides proof that —

（a）提出申请的一方提供了证据证明

(i) a party to the arbitration agreement was under any incapacity；

（i）仲裁协议的一方当事人无行为能力；

(ii) the arbitration agreement is not valid under the law to which the parties have subjected it，or，failing

（ii）仲裁协议根据当事各方所依据的法律无效，或者在没有任何说明的情况下根据马来西亚法律无效；

(iii) the party making the application was not given proper notice of the appointment of an arbitrator or of the arbitral proceedings or was otherwise unable to present that party's case；

（iii）提出申请的一方未得到指定仲裁员或仲裁程序的适当

通知,或未能以其他方式获得通知陈述当事人的案情;

（iv）the award deals with a dispute not contemplated by or not falling within the terms of the submission to arbitration;

（iv）裁决涉及提交仲裁的条款未考虑到或不属于该条款范围的争议;

（v）subject to subsection （3）, the award contains decisions on matters beyond the scope of the submission to arbitration; or

（v）但须遵守第（3）款,裁决包含超出提交仲裁范围的事宜;

（vi）the composition of the arbitral tribunal or the arbitral procedure was not in accordance with the agreement of the parties, unless such agreement was in conflict with a provision of this Act from which the parties cannot derogate, or, failing such agreement, was not in accordance with this Act; or

（vi）仲裁庭或仲裁程序的组成不符合当事各方的协议,除非此种协议与当事各方不能减损的本行为的一项规定发生冲突,或者如果没有此种协议,则不符合本行为;或

any indication thereon, under the laws of Malaysia;

马来西亚法律规定的任何指示;

（b）the High Court finds that —

（b）高等法院认为

（i）the subject matter of the dispute is not capable of settlement by arbitration under the laws of Malaysia; or

（i）争端的事由不能根据马来西亚法律通过仲裁解决;或

（ii）the award is in conflict with the public policy of

Malaysia.

(ii) 该裁决与马来西亚的公共政策相冲突。

(2) Without limiting the generality of subparagraph (1)(b)(ii), an award is in conflict with the public policy of Malaysia where —

(2) 在不限制第(1)款(b)项(ii)目的普遍性的情况下,一项裁决与马来西亚的公共政策相冲突,其中

(a) the making of the award was induced or affected by fraud or corruption; or

(a) 裁决的作出受到欺诈或腐败的诱导或影响;或

(b) a breach of the rules of natural justice occurred —

(b) 违反自然正义的规则

(i) during the arbitral proceedings; or

(i) 在仲裁程序期间;

(ii) in connection with the making of the award.

(ii) 与裁决有关。

(3) Where the decision on matters submitted to arbitration can be separated from those not so submitted, only that part of the award which contains decisions on matters not submitted to arbitration may be set aside.

(3) 如果关于提交仲裁的事项的决定可以与未提交的事项分开,则只可撤销裁决中载有关于未提交仲裁事项的决定的部分。

(4) An application for setting aside may not be made after the expiry of ninety days from the date on which the party making the application had received the award or, if a request has been made under section 35, from the date on which that request had been disposed of by the arbitral tribunal.

(4) 撤销申请不得在提出申请的一方当事人收到裁决之日起 90 天后提出,如已根据第 35 条提出请求,则不得在该请求经仲裁庭处理之日起 90 天后提出。

（5）Subsection（4）does not apply to an application for setting aside on the ground that the award was induced or affected by fraud or corruption.

（5）第（4）款不适用于以裁决受到欺诈或腐败的诱导或影响为由提出的撤销申请。

（6）On an application under subsection（1）the High Court may，where appropriate and so requested by a party，adjourn the proceedings for such period of time as it may determine in order to allow the arbitral tribunal an opportunity to resume the arbitral proceedings or to take such other action as in the arbitral tribunal's opinion will eliminate the grounds for setting aside.

（6）对于根据第（1）款提出的申请，高等法院可酌情并根据一方当事人的请求，将程序延期，期限由其确定，以便仲裁庭有机会恢复仲裁程序或采取仲裁庭认为将消除撤销理由的其他行动。

（7）Where an application is made to set aside an award，the High Court may order that any money made payable by the award shall be brought into the High Court or otherwise secured pending the determination of the application.

（7）在申请撤销裁决的情况下，高等法院可命令将裁决支付的任何款项提交高等法院，或在对申请作出裁定之前以其他方式担保。

Chapter 8
Recognition and enforcement of awards
第八章　裁决的认可和执行

Recognition and enforcement

认可和执行

38.（1）On an application in writing to the High Court，an award made in respect of an arbitration where the seat of arbitration is in Malaysia or an award from a foreign State shall，subject to this section and section 39 be recognized as binding and be enfor ced by entry as a judgment in terms of the award or by action.

（1）根据向高等法院提出的书面申请，仲裁地在马来西亚的仲裁裁决或外国作出的裁决，在不违反本节和第 39 条的情况下，应被承认具有约束力，并通过作为裁决或诉讼判决的方式予以执行。

（2）In an application under subsection （1） the applicant shall produce —

（2）在根据第（1）款提出的申请中，申请人应出示经正式认证的裁决原件或

（a）the duly authenticated original award or a duly certified copy of the award；and

（a）经正式认证的裁决副本；或

（b）the original arbitration agreement or a duly certified copy of the agreement.

（b）仲裁协议原件或经正式认证的协议副本。

（3）Where the award or arbitration agreement is in a language other than the national language or the English language，the applicant shall supply a duly certified translation of the award or agreement in the English language.

（3）如果裁决或仲裁协议使用的是本国语言或英文以外的语言，申请人应提供正式证明的英文裁决或协议译文。

（4）For the purposes of this Act，"foreign State" means a State which is a party to the Convention on the Recognition and Enforcement of Foreign Arbitral Awards adopted by the United Nations Conference on International Commercial Arbitra-tion in 1958.

（4）就本法而言，"外国"是指作为 1958 年国际商事仲裁会议通过的
《联合国通过承认和执行外国仲裁裁决公约》缔约国的国家。

Grounds for refusing recognition or enforcement
拒绝承认或执行的理由

39.（1）Recognition or enforcement of an award，irrespective of the
State in which it was made，may be refused only at the
request of the party against whom it is invoked —

（1）裁决的承认或执行，不论其作出的国家为何，只有在其所援引
的当事一方的请求下才可予以拒绝

　（a）where that party provides to the High Court proof
that —

　（a）该方向高等法院提供的证据证明

　　（i）a party to the arbitration agreement was under any
incapacity；

　　（i）仲裁协议的一方无行为能力；

　　（ii）the arbitration agreement is not valid under the law
to which the parties have subjected it，or，failing
any indication thereon，under the laws of the State
where the award was made；

　　（ii）仲裁协议根据当事各方所依据的法律无效，或者在没有
任何说明的情况下根据国家的法律进行裁决的地方；

　　（iii）the party making the application was not given
proper notice of the appointment of an arbitrator
or of the arbitral proceedings or was otherwise
unable to present that party's case；

　　（iii）提出申请的当事人没有得到适当的关于指定仲裁员
或仲裁程序的通知，或者无法提出该当事人的案件；

　　（iv）the award deals with a dispute not contemplated by
or not falling within the terms of the submission to

arbitration；

（iv）裁决涉及不属于提交仲裁的条款所考虑的或者不属于该条款的争端；

（v）subject to subsection（3），the award contains decisions on matters beyond the scope of the submission to arbitration；

（v）除第（3）款另有规定外，裁决包含有关提交仲裁范围以外事宜的决定；

（vi）the composition of the arbitral tribunal or the arbitral procedure was not in accordance with the agreement of the parties，unless such agreement was in conflict with a provision of this Act from which the parties cannot derogate，or，failing such agreement，was not in accordance with this Act；or

（vi）仲裁庭的组成或仲裁程序不符合当事各方的协议，除非该协议与当事人不能减损的本法之规定相抵触，或者如果达不成协议，不符合本法；或

（vii）the award has not yet become binding on the parties or has been set aside or suspended by a court of the country in which，or under the law of which，that award was made；or

（vii）裁决尚未对当事人具有约束力，或已由裁决所在的国家之法院或裁决所依据的国家之法院予以搁置或中止；或

（b）if the High Court finds that —

（b）如高等法院认定

（i）the subject-matter of the dispute is not capable of settlement by arbitration under the laws of Malaysia；or （i）根据马来西亚法律，争议无法通过仲裁解决；或

（ii）the award is in conflict with the public policy of Malaysia.

（ii）该裁决与马来西亚的公共政策相抵触。

（2）If an application for setting aside or suspension of an award has been made to the High Court on the grounds referred to in subparagraph （1）（a）（vii）, the High Court may, if it considers it proper, adjourn its decision and may also, on the application of the party claiming recognition or enforcement of the award, order the other party to provide appropriate security.

（2）如高等法院根据第（1）款（a）项（vii）目所述的理由向高等法院申请撤销或中止裁决，高等法院如认为适当，可延期其决定，也可以根据申请承认或执行裁决的当事人的申请，命令另一方提供适当的担保。

（3）Where the decision on matters submitted to arbitration can be separated from those not so submitted, only that part of the award which contains decisions on matters submitted to arbitration may be recognized and enforced.

（3）如果提交仲裁的事项的决定可以与未提交的决定分开，那么只有包含提交仲裁事项决定的那部分裁决才能得到承认和执行。

PART III
ADDITIONAL PROVISIONS RELATING TO ARBITRATION
第三部分　有关仲裁的其他规定

Consolidation of proceedings and concurrent hearings
合并诉讼程序和同时举行听讯

40.（1）The parties may agree —

（1）当事各方可以同意

（a）that the arbitration proceedings shall be consolidated with other arbitration proceedings; or

（a）仲裁程序应与其他仲裁程序合并；或

（b）that concurrent hearings shall be held，

（b）应同时举行听证会，

on such terms as may be agreed.

按可能达成的协议条款。

（2）Unless the parties agree to confer such power on the arbitral tribunal，the tribunal has no power to order consolidation of arbitration proceedings or concurrent hearings.

（2）除非双方同意授予仲裁庭这种权力，否则仲裁庭无权命令合并仲裁程序或同时进行听讯。

Determination of preliminary point of law by court
法院确定法律的初步问题

41.（1）Any party may apply to the High Court to determine any question of law arising in the course of the arbitration —

（1）任何一方可以向高等法院申请确定在仲裁过程中出现的任何法律问题

（a）with the consent of the arbitral tribunal; or

（a）经仲裁庭同意；或

（b）with the consent of every other party.

（b）在每一方的同意下。

（2）The High Court shall not consider an application under subsection（1）unless it is satisfied that the determination —

（2）高等法院不得根据第（1）款考虑申请，除非该项决定

（a）is likely to produce substantial savings in costs; and

（a）可能会大量节省成本；或

（b）substantially affects the rights of one or more of the

parties.

（b）实质影响一方或多方的权利。

（3）The application shall identify the question of law to be determined and, except where made with the agreement of all parties to the proceedings, shall state the grounds that support the application.

（3）申请书应确定待确定的法律问题,除非裁决在诉讼各方同意的情况下作出,否则应说明支持申请的理由。

（4）While an application under subsection（1）is pending, the arbitral proceedings may be continued and an award may be made.

（4）虽然根据第(1)款提出的申请悬而未决,仲裁程序可继续并可作出裁决。

Reference on questions of law

关于法律问题的参考

42.（1）Any party may refer to the High Court any question of law arising out of an award.

（1）任何一方可以向高等法院提出由于裁决而引起的任何法律问题。

（1A）The High Court shall dismiss a reference made under subsection（1）unless the question of law substantially affects the rights of one or more of the parties.

（1A）除非法律问题严重影响一方或多方的权利,否则高等法院须驳回根据第(1)款提出的申请。

（2）A reference shall be filed within forty-two days of the publication and receipt of the award, and shall identify the question of law to be determined and state the grounds on which the reference is sought.

（2）应在公布和收到裁决后 42 天内提交一份参考资料,并应确定待确定的法律问题,并说明提出该参考资料的理由。

(3) The High Court may order the arbitral tribunal to state the reasons for its award where the award —

(3) 高等法院可命令仲裁庭陈述其裁决的理由

(a) does not contain the arbitral tribunal's reasons; or

(a) 不包含仲裁庭的理由;或

(b) does not set out the arbitral tribunal's reasons in sufficient detail.

(b) 没有详细列出仲裁庭的理由。

(4) The High Court may, on the determination of a reference —

(4) 高等法院可在确定参考时

(a) confirm the award;

(a) 确认裁决;

(b) vary the award;

(b) 更改裁决;

(c) remit the award in whole or in part, together with the High Court's determination on the question of law to the arbitral tribunal for reconsideration; or

(c) 将裁决全部或部分地连同高等法院对法律问题的裁决一并交给仲裁庭重新审理;或

(d) set aside the award, in whole or in part.

(d) 全部或部分撤销裁决。

(5) Where the award is varied by the High Court, the variation shall have effect as part of the arbitral tribunal's award.

(5) 如果高等法院对裁决做出了变更,则该裁决作为仲裁庭裁决的一部分生效。

(6) Where the award is remitted in whole or in part for reconsideration, the arbitral tribunal shall make a fresh

award in respect of the matters remitted within ninety days of the date of the order for remission or such other period as the High Court may direct.

（6）如果裁决全部或部分被重新审理，则仲裁庭应在缓解令发出之日起 90 日内或在高等法院可能会指示的其他期间内对汇出的事项重新作出裁决。

（7）Where the High Court makes an order under subsection （3），it may make such further order as it thinks fit with respect to any additional costs of the arbitration resulting from that order.

（7）高等法院根据第(3)款做出命令时，可就其因该命令而产生的任何额外仲裁费用做出其认为合适的进一步命令。

（8）On a reference under subsection （1）the High Court may —

（8）根据第(1)款的申请，高等法院可以

(a) order the applicant to provide security for costs；or

(a) 命令申请人提供成本保证；

(b) order that any money payable under the award shall be brought into the High Court or otherwise secured pending the determination of the reference.

(b) 命令根据裁决应付的任何款项应在高等法院提出或以其他方式获得担保，直至确定参考。

Appeal
上诉

43. A decision of the High Court under section 42 shall be deemed to be a judgment of the High Court within the meaning of section 67 of the Courts of Judicature Act 1964 ［*Act 91*］.

高等法院根据第 42 条做出的决定应被视为 1964 年《司法法院法令》［第 91 号法令］第 67 条所界定的高等法院的判决。

Costs and expenses of an arbitration

仲裁的成本和费用

44.（1）Unless otherwise agreed by the parties —

（1）除非当事各方另有协议

（a）the costs and expenses of an arbitration shall be in the discretion of the arbitral tribunal who may —

（a）仲裁的费用和开支由仲裁庭酌情决定，而仲裁庭可以

（i）direct to and by whom and in what manner those costs or any part thereof shall be paid;

（i）指示这些费用或其任何部分应支付给谁以及由谁支付;

（ii）tax or settle the amount of such costs and expenses; and

（ii）纳税或结算这些成本和费用的金额;以及

（iii）award such costs and expenses to be paid as between solicitor and client;

（iii）裁决律师与客户之间支付的费用和开支;

（b）any party may apply to the High Court for the costs to be taxed where an arbitral tribunal has in its award directed that costs and expenses be paid by any party，but fails to specify the amount of such costs and expenses within thirty days of having being requested to do so; or

（b）任何一方当事人可以向高等法院申请仲裁庭在裁决中指示成本和费用由任何一方支付的费用，但未在 30 天内具体说明费用和费用的数额被要求这样做;或

（c）each party shall be responsible for its own legal and other expenses and for an equal share of the fees and expenses of the arbitral tribunal and any other expenses relating to the arbitration in the absence of an award or additional award fixing and allocating the costs and expenses of the arbitration.

(c) 各方应对其自身的法律和其他开支以及仲裁庭的费用和支出以及与仲裁相关的任何其他费用的平等分摊负责，因为没有裁决或额外的决定确定和分配仲裁的成本和费用。

(2) Unless otherwise agreed by the parties, where a party makes an offer to the other party to settle the dispute or part of the dispute and the offer is not accepted and the award of the arbitral tribunal is no more favourable to the other party than was the offer, the arbitral tribunal, in fixing and allocating the costs and expenses of the arbitration, may take the fact of the offer into account in awarding costs and expenses in respect of the period from the making of the offer to the making of the award.

(2) 除非当事人另有约定，当事人向另一方提出解决争议或部分争议的要约，并且该要约不被接受且仲裁庭的裁决不再有利于另一方仲裁庭在确定和分配仲裁的费用和开支时可能会考虑到这一要约，即从提出要约到作出该裁决。

(3) An offer to settle made under subsection (2) shall not be communicated to the arbitral tribunal until it has made a final determination of all aspects of the dispute other than the fixing and allocation of costs and expenses.

(3) 根据第(2)款做出的和解要约，除非确定和分配费用和开支，否则不得将其转交给仲裁庭，直至最终确定了争议的各个方面。

(4) Where an arbitral tribunal refuses to deliver its award before the payment of its fees and expenses, the High Court may order the arbitral tribunal to deliver the award on such conditions as the High Court thinks fit.

(4) 如仲裁庭在支付其费用及开支前拒绝交付裁决，高等法院可命令仲裁庭以高等法院认为合适的条件交付裁决。

(5) A taxation of costs, fees and expenses under this section may be reviewed in the same manner as a taxation of costs.

（5）根据本条征收的费用，费用和开支可以与费用征税相同的方式进行审查。

Extension of time for commencing arbitration proceedings

延长启动仲裁程序的时间

45. Where an arbitration agreement provides that arbitral proceedings are to be commenced within the time specified in the agreement, the High Court may, notwithstanding that the specified time has expired, extend the time for such period and on such terms as it thinks fit, if it is of the opinion that in the circumstances of the case undue hardship would otherwise be caused.

如果仲裁协议规定仲裁程序应在协议规定的时间内启动，则尽管规定的时间已到期，高等法院仍可延长该期限并按其认为合适的条件延长，如果它认为在这种情况下会导致不适当的困难。

Extension of time for making award

延长裁决时间

46. (1) Where the time for making an award is limited by the arbitration agreement, the High Court may, unless otherwise agreed by the parties, extend that time.

（1）裁决时间受仲裁协议限制的，除当事人另有约定外，高等法院可延长该期限。

(2) An application under subsection (1) may be made —

（2）根据第（1）款，可在下述情况下提出申请

(a) upon notice to the parties, by the arbitral tribunal; or

（a）由仲裁庭通知当事各方；或

(b) upon notice to the arbitral tribunal and the other parties, by any party to the proceedings.

（b）通过诉讼的任何一方向仲裁庭和其他当事人发出通知。

（3）The High Court shall not make an order unless —

（3）高等法院不得作出命令，除非

　　（a）all available tribunal processes for obtaining an extension of time have been exhausted; and

　　（a）所有可用的延长时间的法庭程序已经用尽；

　　（b）the High Court is satisfied that substantial injustice would otherwise be done.

　　（b）高等法院认为不这样做会造成实质性的不公正。

（4）The High Court may exercise its powers under subsection（1）notwithstanding that the time previously fixed by or under the arbitration agreement or by a previous order has expired.

（4）即使先前由仲裁协议或根据仲裁协议或先前命令所确定的时间已届满，高等法院仍可行使其根据第（1）款所能行使的权力。

PART IV
MISCELLANEOUS
第四部分　杂项

Liability of arbitrator
仲裁员的责任

47. An arbitrator shall not be liable for any act or omission in respect of anything done or omitted to be done in the discharge of his functions as an arbitrator unless the act or omission is shown to have been in bad faith.

仲裁员对履行其作为仲裁员职能时所做或所做的任何事情的任何作为或不作为不承担责任，除非该作为或不作为被证明是恶意的。

Immunity of arbitral institutions
仲裁机构的豁免

48. The Director of the Kuala Lumpur Regional Centre for

Arbitration or any other person or institution designated or requested by the parties to appoint or nominate an arbitrator, shall not be liable for anything done or omitted in the discharge of the function unless the act or omission is shown to have been in bad faith.

吉隆坡区域仲裁中心主任或当事各方指定或要求任命或提名仲裁员的任何其他人员或机构,对于在履行职能时所做或所做的任何事情均不承担责任,除非该作为或不作为是虚假的。

Bankruptcy
破产

49. （1）Where a party to an arbitration agreement is a bankrupt and the person having jurisdiction to administer the property of the bankrupt adopts the agreement，the arbitration agreement shall be enforceable by or against that person.

（1）仲裁协议当事人为破产人,管辖破产财产的管辖人接受协议的,仲裁协议应当可以由该人强制执行或者可以强制执行。

（2）The High Court may direct any matter in connection with or for the purpose of bankruptcy proceedings to be referred to arbitration if —

（2）如有以下情况,高等法院可指示与破产程序有关的任何事宜或为破产程序的目的而提交仲裁的事宜

　（a）the matter is one to which the arbitration agreement applies；

　（a）仲裁协议适用的事项；

　（b）the arbitration agreement was made by a person who has been adjudged a bankrupt before the commencement of the bankruptcy proceedings；and

　（b）仲裁协议是由在破产程序开始前被判定为破产人的人制定的；以及

(c) the person having jurisdiction to administer the property does not adopt the agreement.

(c) 管辖财产的人不会采用该协议。

(3) An application under subsection (2) may be made by —

(3) 根据第(2)款,下列人员可提出破产申请:

    (a) any other party to the arbitration agreement; or

    (a) 仲裁协议的任何其他方;

    (b) any person having jurisdiction to administer the property of the bankrupt.

    (b) 有管辖权来管理破产人的财产之人。

Mode of application

适用方式

50. Any application to the High Court under this Act shall be by an originating summons as provided in the Rules of the High Court 1980 [*P. U. (A) 50/1980*].

根据本法向高等法院提出的任何申请均应按照 1980 年高等法院规则的规定提出原诉传票[P. U. (A)50/1980]。

Repeal and savings

废除和保留

51. (1) The Arbitration Act 1952 [*Act 93*] and the Convention on the Recognition and Enforcement of Foreign Arbitral Awards Act 1985 [*Act 320*] are repealed.

(1) 1952 年《仲裁法》[第 93 号法]和 1985 年《承认及执行外国仲裁裁决公约》[第 320 号法]已被废除。

(2) Where the arbitral proceedings were commenced before the coming into operation of this Act, the law governing the arbitration agreement and the arbitral proceedings shall be the law which would have applied as if this Act had not

been enacted.

（2）如果在本法实施之前启动仲裁程序，则仲裁协议和仲裁程序的法律应为本法尚未颁布的法律。

（3）Nothing in this Act shall affect any proceedings relating to arbitration which have been commenced in any court before the coming into operation of this Act.

（3）本法的任何规定均不影响在本法实施之前在任何法院启动的任何与仲裁有关的程序。

（4）Any court proceedings relating to arbitration commenced after the commencement of this Act shall be governed by this Act notwithstanding that such proceedings arose out of arbitral proceedings commenced before the commencement of this Act.

（4）在本法生效后开始的与仲裁有关的任何法院程序应受本法管辖，即使该程序是在本法生效之前开始的仲裁程序之外发生的。

LIST OF AMENDMENTS

修正案清单

Amending law	Short title	In force from
修正法案	简称	生效日期
Act A1395	Arbitration（Amendment）Act 2011	01 - 07 - 2011
法案 A1395	仲裁法（修正版）法案 2011	2011 年 7 月 1 日

LIST OF SECTIONS AMENDED

修正案清单

Section	Amending authority	In force from
条款	修正授权	生效日期
	Act A1395	01 - 07 - 2011
2	法案 A1395	2011 年 7 月 1 日
	Act A1395	01 - 07 - 2011
8	法案 A1395	2011 年 7 月 1 日

	Act A1395	01 - 07 - 2011
10	法案 A1395	2011 年 7 月 1 日
	Act A1395	01 - 07 - 2011
11	法案 A1395	2011 年 7 月 1 日
	Act A1395	01 - 07 - 2011
30	法案 A1395	2011 年 7 月 1 日
	Act A1395	01 - 07 - 2011
38	法案 A1395	2011 年 7 月 1 日
39	Act A1395	01 - 07 - 2011
	法案 A1395	2011 年 7 月 1 日
42	Act A1395	01 - 07 - 2011
	法案 A1395	2011 年 7 月 1 日
51	Act A1395	01 - 07 - 2011
	法案 A1395	2011 年 7 月 1 日

第三节　菲律宾商事仲裁法英汉对照

Republika ng Pilipinas

菲律宾共和国

KAGAWARAN NG KATARUNGAN

Department of Justice Manila

马尼拉司法部

DEPARTMENT CIRCULAR NO. 98

第 98 号通告

IMPLEMENTING RULES AND REGULATIONS

OF THE ALTERNATIVE DISPUTE RESOLUTION ACT OF 2004

2004 年《替代性争议解决法实施细则与条例》

Whereas，pursuant to Section 52 of Republic Act No. 9285，
otherwise known as the "Alternative Dispute Resolution Act of

2004"("ADR Act"), the Secretary of Justice is directed to convene a Committee for the formulation of the appropriate rules and regulations necessary for the implementation of the ADR Act；

根据《第 9285 号共和法》第 52 条,也被称为《替代性争议解决法》("ADR 法案"),司法部长按照指示召开委员会,以制定实施《替代性争议解决法案》所需的适当规则和条例；

Whereas，the Committee was composed of representatives from the Department of Justice，the Department of Trade and Industry，the Department of the Interior and Local Government，the President of the Integrated Bar of the Philippines，a representative from the arbitration profession，a representative from the mediation profession and a representative from the ADR organizations.

该委员会由来自司法部、工业贸易部、内政部和地方政府的代表,以及菲律宾综合律师协会会长,仲裁行业、调解行业和 ADR 组织的代表构成。

Wherefore，the following rules and regulations are hereby adopted as the Implementing Rules and Regulations of Republic Act No.9285.

鉴于此,《第 9285 号共和法》条例施行细则如下。

IMPLEMENTING RULES AND REGULATIONS OF THE ALTERNA-TIVE DISPUTE RESOLUTION ACT OF 2004(R.A. No.9285)

2004 替代性争议解决法案实施细则和条例(R.A.第 9285 号)

Pursuant to Section 52 of Republic Act No.9285，otherwise known as the "Alternative Dispute Resolution Act of 2004"("ADR Act")，the following Rules and Regulations (these "Rules") are hereby promulgated to implement the provisions of the ADR Act：

根据《第 9285 号共和法》第 52 条,也被称为《替代性争议解决法》("ADR 法案"),现颁布以下细则和条例(这些细则),以执行《ADR 法案》的规定：

CHAPTER 1　GENERAL PROVISIONS
第一章　总则

RULE 1 - Policy and Application
细则 1——政策和应用

Article 1.1. Purpose. These Rules are promulgated to prescribe the procedures and guidelines for the implementation of the ADR Act.

第 1.1 条　目的。为明确实施《替代性争议解决法案》的程序和指导方针颁布本法。

Article 1.2. Declaration of Policy. It is the policy of the State：

第 1.2 条　政策宣言。这是国家的政策：

(a) To promote party autonomy in the resolution of disputes or the freedom of the parties to make their own arrangements to resolve their disputes；

(a) 在争议解决中保障当事人的自主权，促进当事人自行努力解决争议；

(b) To encourage and actively promote the use of Alternative Dispute Resolution ("ADR") as an important means to achieve speedy and impartial justice and to declog court dockets；

(b) 鼓励和积极推动替代性争议解决机制的使用作为实现快速、公正司法和协商解决法院诉讼事件的重要手段；

(c) To provide means for the use of ADR as an efficient tool and an alternative procedure for the resolution of appropriate cases；and

(c) 提供多种方式保障替代性争议解决机制的使用，作为解决适当案件的有效工具和替代程序；以及

(d) To enlist active private sector participation in the settlement of disputes through ADR.

(d) 争取积极的私营主体通过替代性争议解决机制参与争议解决。

Article 1. 3. Exception to the Application of the ADR Act. The provisions of the ADR Act shall not apply to the resolution or settlement of the following:

第1.3条　《替代性争议解决法案》的规定不适用于下列决议的处理和解决:

(a) labor disputes covered by Presidential Decree No. 442, otherwise known as the "Labor Code of the Philippines, as amended", and its Implementing Rules and Regulations;

(a) 第442号总统令所涵盖的劳动争议,又称为《经修订的菲律宾劳工法典》及其实施细则和条例;

(b) the civil status of persons;

(b) 人的民事地位;

(c) the validity of marriage;

(c) 婚姻的合法性;

(d) any ground for legal separation;

(d) 合法分离的任何理由;

(e) the jurisdiction of courts;

(e) 法院的管辖权;

(f) future legitime;

(f) 未来的合法性

(g) criminal liability;

(g) 刑事责任;

(h) those disputes which by law cannot be compromised; and

(h) 法律不能解决的争议

(i) disputes referred to court-annexed mediation.

(i) 涉及法院附设调解的争议。

Article 1. 4. Electronic Signatures in Global and E-Commerce Act. The provisions of the Electronic Signatures in Global and E-

Commerce Act, and its Implementing Rules and Regulations shall apply to proceedings contemplated in the ADR Act.

第 1.4 条 《全球电子签名和电子商务法案》。《全球电子签名和电子商务法案》的规定及其实施细则和条例应适用于《替代性争议解决法案》所设定的诉讼程序。

Article 1.5. Liability of ADR Providers/Practitioners. The ADR providers/practitioners shall have the same civil liability for acts done in the performance of their official duties as that of public officers as provided in Section 38(1), Chapter 9, Book I of the Administrative Code of 1987, upon a clear showing of bad faith, malice or gross negligence.

第 1.5 条 《替代性争议解决法案》的提供者和当事人的责任。《替代性争议解决法案》的提供者和当事人在履行他们的职责时,一旦具有明显的恶意和重大过失,对于已完成的案件应有相同的民事责任,如同公职人员在 1987 年行政法典的第一册书第九章第 38 条第(1)款中所述。

RULE 2 - Definition of Terms
细则 2——术语的解释

Article 1.6. Definition of Terms. For purposes of these Rules, the terms shall be defined as follows:

第 1.6 条 术语的解释。为本议事规则的目的,这些用语的解释如下:

A. Terms Applicable to all Chapters

A. 适用于所有章节的术语

1. ADR Provider means the institutions or persons accredited as mediators, conciliators, arbitrators, neutral evaluators or any person exercising similar functions in any Alternative Dispute Resolution system. This is without prejudice to the rights of the parties to choose non-accredited individuals to act as mediator, conciliator, arbitrator or neutral evaluator of their dispute.

1. 替代性争议解决机制的提供者指的是机构或个人，经过认证，作为调解员、仲裁员、中立的评价者或任何在各替代性争议解决机制中承担类似的职责的人员。当事人有权选择未经过认证的个人担任其争议的调解人、仲裁员或中立评价者。

2. Alternative Dispute Resolution System means any process or procedure used to resolve a dispute or controversy，other than by adjudication of a presiding judge of a court or an officer of a government agency，as defined in the ADR Act，in which a neutral third person participates to assist in the resolution of issues，including arbitration， mediation， conciliation， early neutral evaluation，mini-trial or any combination thereof.

2. 替代性争议解决机制是指在任何用于解决争议或争议的过程或程序中，除了由主审法院的法官或政府机构的官员作出裁决，可以由中立的第三人参与协助解决问题，包括仲裁、调解、和解，早期中立评估、小型审判或他们的任意组合。

3. Arbitration means a voluntary dispute resolution process in which one or more arbitrators，appointed in accordance with the agreement of the parties or these Rules，resolve a dispute by rendering an award.

3. 仲裁是指根据各当事方或本规则的一致同意指定一个或多个仲裁人通过仲裁裁决争议的自愿的争议解决程序。

4. Arbitration Agreement means an agreement by the parties to submit to arbitration all or certain disputes which have arisen or which may arise between them in respect of a defined legal relationship， whether contractual or not. An arbitration agreement may be in the form of an arbitration clause in a contract or in the form of a separate agreement.

4. 仲裁协议是指当事人在约定的法律关系中，无论是以合同的还是非合同的形式，提交仲裁的全部或某些争议。仲裁协议可以是合同中的仲裁条款，也可以是单独的协议。

5. Authenticate means to sign，execute，adopt a symbol or encrypt a

record in whole or in part, intended to identify the authenticating party and to adopt, accept or establish the authenticity of a record or term.

5. 认证意味着全部或部分地签署、执行、采用一个符号或加密一个记录，目的是识别认证方，并采纳、接受或确立备案或条款的真实性。

6. Award means any partial or final decision by an arbitrator in resolving the issue or controversy.

6. 裁决是指仲裁人在解决问题或争议时做出的部分或最终决定。

7. Confidential Information means any information, relative to the subject of mediation or arbitration, expressly intended by the source not to be disclosed, or obtained under circumstances that would create a reasonable expectation on behalf of the source that the information shall not be disclosed. It shall include：

7. 保密信息是指与调解或仲裁的标的有关的任何有意不披露的信息，或在为信息来源创造合理期望的情况下获得的信息不应披露。它应包括：

（a）communication, oral or written, made in a dispute resolution proceeding, including any memoranda, notes or work product of the neutral party or non-party participant；

（a）在争议解决过程中的口头或书面沟通，包括任何备忘录、笔记或参与其中的中立方的工作成果；

（b）an oral or written statement made or which occurs during mediation or for purposes of considering, conducting, participating, initiating, continuing or reconvening mediation or retaining a mediator；and

（b）在调解或准备、参与、发起、继续、重新召开或维持调解中的口头或书面声明；

（c）pleadings, motions, manifestations, witness statements, reports filed or submitted in arbitration or for expert evaluation.

（c）在仲裁中或为了专家评估而提交的诉状、议案、目击者的陈述和报告。

8. Counsel means a lawyer duly admitted to the practice of law in the Philippines and in good standing who represents a party in any ADR process.

8. 律师是指在替代性争议解决机制中，任何正式承认的在菲律宾执业的律师，以及代表某一方当事人的有资格的律师。

9. Court means Regional Trial Court except insofar as otherwise defined under the Model Law.

9. 除非示范法另有规定，法院指的是区域审判法院。

10. Government Agency means any governmental entity，office or officer，other than a court，that is vested by law with quasi-judicial power or the power to resolve or adjudicate disputes involving the government，its agencies and instrumentalities or private persons.

10. 政府机构是指除了法院以外，有法律赋予的准司法权或权力来解决或裁决涉及政府及其代理、机构或私人争议的任何政府实体、办公室或官员。

11. Model Law means the Model Law on International Commercial Arbitration adopted by the United Nations Commission on International Trade Law on 21 June 1985.

11. 示范法是指联合国国际贸易法委员会于 1985 年 6 月 21 日通过的《国际商事仲裁示范法》。

12. Proceedings means a judicial，administrative or other adjudicative process，including related pre-hearing or post hearing motions，conferences and discovery.

12. 诉讼是指司法、行政或其他审判过程，包括相关的庭审前后的议案、会议和开示程序。

13. Record means information written on a tangible medium or stored in an electronic or other similar medium，retrievable in a perceivable form.

13. 记录是指写在有形介质或存储在电子或其他介质的信息，以可被检索的形式存在。

14. Roster means a list of persons qualified to provide ADR services as neutrals or to serve as arbitrators.

14. 名册是指有资格作为中立者提供替代性争议解决机制服务或担任仲裁员的人员名单。

15. Special ADR Rules means the Special Rules of Court on Alternative Dispute Resolution issued by the Supreme Court on September 1,2009.

15. 特殊的替代性争议解决规则是指由最高法院在 2009 年 9 月 1 日颁布的实行替代性争议解决机制的法院的特殊规则。

B. Terms Applicable to the Chapter on Mediation

B. 适用于调解章节的术语

1. Ad hoc Mediation means any mediation other than institutional or court-annexed.

1. 特别调解是指除机构调解或法院附议调解之外的任何调解。

2. Institutional Mediation means any mediation administered by, and conducted under the rules of, a mediation institution.

2. 机构调解是指在调解机构的规则下进行的、由调解机构进行的调解。

3. Court-Annexed Mediation means any mediation process conducted under the auspices of the court and in accordance with Supreme Court approved guidelines, after such court has acquired jurisdiction of the dispute.

3. 法院附设调解是指在法院主持下，根据最高法院核准的准则，在法院获得争议管辖权后进行的任何调解程序。

4. Court-Referred Mediation means mediation ordered by a court to be conducted in accordance with the agreement of the parties when an action is prematurely commenced in violation of such agreement.

4. 法院调解是指在提前出现违背协议的行为时,法院根据各方协议启动的调解。

5. Certified Mediator means a mediator certified by the Office for ADR as having successfully completed its regular professional training program.

5. 经认证的调解人是指由替代性争议解决机制办公室认证的顺利地完成了正规的专业培训计划的调解员。

6. Mediation means a voluntary process in which a mediator, selected by the disputing parties, facilitates communication and negotiation, and assists the parties in reaching a voluntary agreement regarding a dispute.

6. 调解是指由争议方选定的调解人促进沟通和谈判,并协助当事人就争议达成自愿协议的自愿过程。

7. Mediation Party means a person who participates in a mediation and whose consent is necessary to resolve the dispute.

7. 调解方是指参与调解并同意解决争议所必需的人。

8. Mediator means a person who conducts mediation.

8. 调解人是指承担调解工作的人。

9. Non-Party Participant means a person, other than a party or mediator, who participates in a mediation proceeding as a witness, resource person or expert.

9. 非当事人是指当事人、调解人以外的人作为证人、资源人或专家参加调解程序的人。

C. Terms Applicable to the Chapter on International Commercial Arbitration

C. 适用于国际商业一章的术语

1. Appointing Authority as used in the Model Law shall mean the person or institution named in the arbitration agreement as the appointing authority; or the regular arbitration institution under whose rules the arbitration is agreed to be conducted. Where the

parties have agreed to submit their dispute to institutional arbitration rules, and unless they have agreed to a different procedure, they shall be deemed to have agreed to the procedure under such arbitration rules for the selection and appointment of arbitrators. In ad hoc arbitration, the default appointment of an arbitrator shall be made by the National President of the Integrated Bar of the Philippines (IBP) or his/her duly authorized representative.

1. 示范法中指定的指定机关是指仲裁协议中指定为指定机构的人或机构;或根据其规则进行仲裁的常设仲裁机构。若当事人同意用仲裁机构的仲裁规则解决争议,除非当事人自愿选择不同的程序,否则应视为已同意根据仲裁规则选择和任命仲裁员。临时仲裁中,仲裁员的任命须由默认的菲律宾综合律师协会会长或其正式授权的代表做出。

2. Arbitral Tribunal (under the Model Law) means a sole arbitrator or a panel of arbitrators.

2. 仲裁法庭(根据示范法)指独任仲裁员或仲裁员小组。

3. Arbitration means any arbitration whether or not administered by a permanent arbitration institution.

3. 仲裁是指由常设仲裁机构管理的或未管理的任何仲裁。

4. Commercial Arbitration means an arbitration that covers matters arising from all relationships of a commercial nature, whether contractual or not. Relationships of a commercial nature include, but are not limited to, the following commercial transactions: any trade transaction for the supply or exchange of goods or services; distribution agreements; construction of works; commercial representation or agency; factoring; leasing; consulting; engineering; licensing; investment; financing; banking; insurance; joint venture and other forms of industrial or business cooperation; carriage of goods or passengers by air, sea, rail or road.

4. 商事仲裁是指涉及商事关系的，不论是否具有合同性质的所有事项的仲裁。商事关系包括但不限于以下商业交易：任何关于商品或服务的供应或交换的交易行为；分配协议；工程建设；商业代表或代理；保理；租赁；咨询；工程；许可；投资；融资；银行；保险；合资企业或其他形式的工业或商业合作；通过飞机、轮船、铁路或公路来运输旅客或货物。

5. Convention Award means a foreign arbitral award made in a Convention State.

5. 公约裁决是指在公约缔约国作出的外国仲裁裁决。

6. Convention State means a state that is a member of the New York Convention.

6. 公约国家指作为《纽约公约》成员国的国家。

7. Court（under the Model Law）means a body or organ of the judicial system of the Philippines（i. e.，the Regional Trial Court，Court of Appeals and Supreme Court）.

7. 法院（根据示范法）是指菲律宾司法系统的一个机构或机关（即区域审判法院、上诉法院和最高法院）。

8. International Arbitration means an arbitration where：

8. 国际仲裁是指以下仲裁：

（a）the parties to an arbitration agreement have，at the time of the conclusion of that agreement，their places of business in different states；or

（a）仲裁协议的当事人在订立该协议时，在不同的国家有各自的营业场所；或

（b）one of the following places is situated outside the Philippines in which the parties have their places of business：

（b）下列地点之一位于菲律宾境外，当事人有各自的营业场所：

（i）the place of arbitration if determined in，or pursuant to，the arbitration agreement；

（i）仲裁的地点可以在仲裁协议中约定或根据仲裁协议确定；

（ii）any place where a substantial part of the obligations of the commercial relationship is to be performed or the place with which the subject matter of the dispute is most closely connected; or

（ii）任何履行商业关系义务的地方或争议标的所在地最密切联系的地方；或

（c）the parties have expressly agreed that the subject matter of the arbitration agreement relates to more than one country.

（c）双方明确同意仲裁协议的标的涉及多个国家。

For this purpose：

为了这些目标

（a）if a party has more than one place of business, the place of business is that which. has the closest relationship to the arbitration agreement；

（a）如果一方当事人有一个以上的营业地,则其营业地是指与仲裁协议有最密切关系的营业地；

（b）if a party does not have a place of business, reference is to be made to his/her habitual residence.

（b）当事人没有营业地的,参照其惯常居住地。

9. New York Convention means the United Nations Convention on the Recognition and Enforcement of Foreign Arbitral Awards approved in 1958 and ratified by the Philippine Senate under Senate Resolution NO.71.

9.《纽约公约》是指 1958 年联合国对外国仲裁裁决承认和批准的并由菲律宾参议院 71 号决议批准执行的公约。

10. Non-Convention Award means a foreign arbitral award made in a state，which is not a Convention State.

10. 非公约裁决是指在一个国家内作出的外国仲裁裁决,该国不是一个公约缔约国。

11. Non-Convention State means a state that is not a member of the

New York Convention.

11. 非公约国家指不属于《纽约公约》成员国的国家。

D. Terms Applicable to the Chapter on Domestic Arbitration

D. 适用于国内仲裁一章的术语

1. Ad hoc Arbitration means an arbitration administered by an arbitrator and/or the parties themselves. An arbitration administered by an institution shall be regarded as an ad hoc arbitration if such institution is not a permanent or regular arbitration institution in the Philippines.

1. 临时仲裁是指由仲裁员和（或）当事人自己管理的仲裁。如果该机构不是菲律宾的常设或定期仲裁机构，则由一个机构管理的仲裁应视为一次临时仲裁。

2. Appointing Authority in Ad Hoc Arbitration means，in the absence of an agreement，the National President of the IBP or his/her duly authorized representative.

在特设仲裁中任命主管当局，在没有协议的情况下，是指菲律宾综合律师协会会长或其正式授权的代表。

3. Appointing Authority Guidelines means the set of rules approved or adopted by an appointing authority for the making of a Request for Appointment，Challenge，Termination of the Mandate of Arbitrator/s and for taking action thereon.

3. 指定机构准则是指指定机构为提出指定、请求、质疑、终止仲裁人的任务授权和就此采取行动而核准或通过的一套规则。

4. Arbitration means a voluntary dispute resolution process in which one or more arbitrators，appointed in accordance with the agreement of the parties or these Rules，resolve a dispute by rendering an award.

4. 仲裁是指根据当事各方的协议或本规则指定的一名或多名仲裁员通过作出裁决解决争议的自愿争议解决程序。

5. Arbitral Tribunal means a sole arbitrator or a panel，board or

committee of arbitrators.

5. 仲裁庭是指独任仲裁员或仲裁员组成的专门小组、理事会或委员会。

6. Claimant means a person/s with a claim against another and who commence/s arbitration against the latter.

6. 求偿人是指对他人提出权利主张并参与对他人进行仲裁的人。

7. Court means，unless otherwise specified in these Rules，a Regional Trial Court.

7. 法院是指区域审判法院，除非本规则另有规定。

8. Day means calendar day.

8. 天是指日历日。

9. Domestic Arbitration means an arbitration that is not international as defined in Article 1(3) of the Model Law.

9. 国内仲裁是指示范法第 1 条第（3）款所界定的不属于国际的仲裁。

10. Institutional arbitration means arbitration administered by an entity，which is registered as a domestic corporation with the Securities and Exchange Commission（SEC）' and engaged in，among others，arbitration of disputes in the Philippines on a regular and permanent basis.

10. 机构仲裁是指由某一实体管理的仲裁，该机构是注册在美国证券交易委员会的国内公司，并经常和长期从事菲律宾争议的仲裁。

11. Request for Appointment means the letter-request to the appointing authority of either or both parties for the appointment of arbitrator/s or of the two arbitrators first appointed by the parties for the appointment of the third member of an arbitral tribunal.

11. 指定请求是指向指定机构发出的关于指定仲裁人或双方当事人之一或双方当事人为指定仲裁庭第三名仲裁员而首先指定的两名仲裁员的请求。

12. Representative is a person duly authorized in writing by a party

to a dispute, who could be a counsel, a person in his/her employ or any other person of his/her choice, duly authorized to represent said party in the arbitration proceedings.

12. 代表是指争议一方当事人以书面形式正式授权的人,他可以是律师、受雇的人或他选择的任何其他人,有权在仲裁程序中代表该方当事人。

13. Respondent means the person/s against whom the claimant commence/s arbitration.

13. 被申请人是指被申请人提起仲裁的人。

14. Written communication means the pleading, motion, manifestation, notice, order, award and any other document or paper submitted or filed with the arbitral tribunal or delivered to a party.

14. 书面通信是指书状、动议、表示、通知、命令、裁决以及向仲裁庭提交或送交某一当事方的任何其他文件。

E. Terms Applicable to the Chapter on Other ADR Forms

E. 适用于其他替代性争议解决形式一章的术语

1. Early Neutral Evaluation means an ADR process wherein parties and their lawyers are brought together early in the pre-trial phase to present summaries of their cases and to receive a non-binding assessment by an experienced neutral person, with expertise in the subject matter or substance of the dispute.

1. 早期中立评价是指一种替代性争议解决程序,在这一程序中,当事方及其律师在预审阶段的早期就被召集起来,提出其案件摘要,并接受一位经验丰富的中立人士的不具约束力的评估,该人具有争议标的或实质内容方面的专门知识。

2. Mediation-Arbitration or Med-Arb is a two-step dispute resolution process involving mediation and then followed by arbitration.

2. 调解仲裁或混合式仲裁是指一个分两步走的争议解决程序,包括调解,然后是仲裁。

3. Mini-trial means a structured dispute resolution method in which the merits of a case are argued before a panel comprising of senior decision-makers, with or without the presence of a neutral third person, before which the parties seek a negotiated settlement.

3. 微型审判是指一种分阶段解决争议的方法。在这种方法中,由高级决策者组成的小组对案件的是非曲直进行辩论,无论是否有中立的第三人在场,在此之前双方都寻求谈判解决。

CHAPTER 2
THE OFFICE FOR ALTERNATIVE DISPUTE RESOLUTION
第二章　替代性争议解决办公处
RULE 1 - Office for Alternative Dispute Resolution (OADR)
细则1——替代性争议解决办公处

Article 2. 1. Establishment of the Office for Alternative Dispute Resolution. There is hereby established the OADR as an agency attached to the Department of Justice. It shall have a Secretariat and shall be headed by an Executive Director, who shall be appointed by the President of the Philippines, taking into consideration the recommendation of the Secretary of Justice.

第2.1条　设立替代性争议解决办公处。兹设立替代性争议解决办公处,作为隶属于司法部的机构。该办公处应有一个秘书处,由一名执行主任领导,执行主任应由菲律宾主席根据司法部长的推荐任命。

Article 2. 2. Powers of the OADR. The OADR shall have the following powers:

第2.2条　替代性争议解决办公处的权力。替代性争议解决办公处具有以下权力:

(a) To act as appointing authority of mediators and arbitrators when the parties agree in writing that it shall be empowered to do so;

（a）当各方当事人书面授权时，担任调解人和仲裁员的指定机构；

（b）To conduct seminars, symposia, conferences and other public fora and publish proceedings of said activities and relevant materials/information that would promote, develop and expand the use of ADR;

（b）举办研讨会、座谈会、会议及其他公众论坛，并发表有关上述活动的记录及相关资料，以促进、发展和扩大替代性争议解决机制的使用；

（c）To establish an ADR library or resource center where ADR laws, rules and regulations, jurisprudence, books, articles and other information about ADR in the Philippines and elsewhere may be stored and accessed;

（c）建立一个替代性争议解决机制图书馆或资源中心，以便存放和查阅菲律宾和其他地区有关替代性争议解决机制的法律、规章、判例、书籍、文章和其他信息；

（d）To establish a training programs for ADR providers/practitioners, both in the public and private sectors; and to undertake periodic and continuing training programs for arbitration and mediation and charge fees on participants. It may do so in conjunction with or in cooperation with the IBP, private ADR organizations, and local and foreign government offices and agencies and international organizations;

（d）为公营机构及私营机构的替代性争议解决机制提供者制订培训计划；并定期及持续举办仲裁及调解培训计划，并向参加者收费。可与菲律宾综合律师协会会长、私营替代性争议解决机制提供组织、地方和外国政府办事处和机构以及国际组织合作进行；

（e）To certify those who have successfully completed the regular professional training programs provided by the OADR;

（e）对那些成功完成替代性争议解决办公处提供的定期专业培训课程

的人进行认证；

(f) To charge fees for services rendered such as, among others, for training and certifications of ADR providers;

(f) 就提供的服务,如培训和替代性争议解决机制认证服务等收费；

(g) To accept donations, grants and other assistance from local and foreign sources; and

(g) 接受本地及外国的捐赠、赠款及其他援助；

(h) To exercise such other powers as may be necessary and proper to carry into effect the provisions of the ADR Act.

(h) 行使其他必要和适当的权力,以实施《替代性争议解决法案》的规定。

Article 2.3. Functions of the OADR. The OADR shall have the following functions:

第2.3条　替代性争议解决办公处的功能。替代性争议解决办公处应具有下列职能:

(a) To promote, develop and expand the use of ADR in the private and public sectors through information, education and communication;

(a) 通过信息、教育和交流,促进、发展和扩大公共部门和私营部门对替代性争议解决机制的使用；

(b) To monitor, study and evaluate the use of ADR by the private and public sectors for purposes of, among others, policy formulation;

(b) 监督、研究和评估私人与公众对替代性争议解决机制的使用情况；

(c) To recommend to Congress needful statutory changes to develop, strengthen and improve ADR practices in accordance with international professional standards;

(c) 向国会建议进行必要的法律改革,按照国际标准加强和改进替代性争议解决机制；

(d) To make studies on and provide linkages for the development, implementation，monitoring and evaluation of government and private ADR programs and secure information about their respective administrative rules/procedures，problems encountered and how they were resolved；

（d）研究、实施、监测和评估政府与私营企业的替代性争议解决程序，并建立联系，确保了解各自的行政规则、程序、遇到的问题和解决办法；

（e）To compile and publish a list or roster of ADR providers/practitioners，who have undergone training by the OADR，or by such training providers/institutions recognized or certified by the OADR as performing functions in any ADR system. The list or roster shall include the addresses，contact numbers，e-mail addresses，ADR service/s rendered（e. g. arbitration，mediation）and experience in ADR of the ADR providers/practitioners；

（e）编制并公布一份替代性争议解决机制从业人员的名单或名册，这些人要经过替代性争议解决机制办公处的训练，也可以由被替代性争议解决机制办公处承认或认证的能在替代性争议解决机制中发挥作用的个人或机构训练。名单或名册应包括替代性争议解决机制从业人员的地址、联系号码、电子邮件地址、提供的替代性争议解决服务（如仲裁、调解）和替代性争议解决机制的经验；

（f）To compile a list or roster of foreign or international ADR providers/practitioners. The list or roster shall include the addresses，contact numbers，e-mail addresses，ADR service/s rendered（e. g. arbitration，mediation）and experience in ADR of the ADR providers/practitioners；and

（f）编制一份外国或国际替代性争议解决机制从业人员的名单或花名册。名单或名册应包括替代性争议解决机制从业人员的地址、联系号码、电子邮件地址、提供的替代性争议解决服务（如仲裁、调解）和替代性争议解决机制的经验；以及

(g) To perform such other functions as may be assigned to it.

(g) 履行赋予它的其他职能。

Article 2.4. Divisions of the OADR. The OADR shall have the following staff and service divisions, among others:

第2.4条 替代性争议解决机制办公处的分支。除其他外主管机构应设有下列人员及服务科:

(a) Secretariat-shall provide necessary support and discharge such other functions and duties as may be directed by the Executive Director.

(a) 秘书处——应提供必要的支持并履行其他职能,执行董事可能指示的职能和职责。

(b) Public Information and Promotion Division-shall be charged with the dissemination of information, the promotion of the importance and public acceptance of mediation, conciliation, arbitration or any combination thereof and other ADR forms as a means of achieving speedy and efficient means of resolving all disputes and to help in the promotion, development and expansion of the use of ADR.

(b) 宣传及推广科——负责传播信息,增强调解、和解、仲裁或其组合和其他替代性争议解决机制的重要性和公众对这些形式的接受程度,以此作为迅速有效地解决所有争端的手段,并帮助促进调解、和解、仲裁或其他形式的仲裁,发展和扩大替代性争议解决机制的使用。

(c) Training Division-shall be charged with the formulation of effective standards for the training of ADR practitioners; conduct of trainings in accordance with such standards; issuance of certifications of training to ADR practitioners and ADR service providers who have undergone the professional training provided by the OADR; and the coordination of the development，implementation，monitoring and evaluation of government and private sector ADR programs.

(c) 训练科——负责制订有效的替代性争议解决机制从业人员培训标准;按照这些标准进行培训;向已接受替代性争议解决机制办公处提供的专业训练的替代性争议解决机制从业人员和替代性争议解决服务提供者颁发培训证书;协调发展、实施、监测和评价政府和私营部门的替代性争议解决程序。

(d) Records and Library Division-shall be charged with the establishment and maintenance of a central repository of ADR laws，rules and regulations，jurisprudence，books，articles，and other information about ADR in the Philippines and elsewhere.

(d) 档案及图书馆科——负责建立以及维护一个包含替代性争议解决法规则和关于菲律宾和其他地方替代性争议解决机制的法规、判例、书籍、文章和其他信息。

RULE 2 - The Advisory Council
细则 2——顾问委员会

Article 2.5. Composition of the Advisory Council. There is also created an Advisory Council composed of a representative from each of the following：

第2.5条 顾问委员会的组成。还设立了一个咨询委员会,由以下各方的代表组成:

(a) Mediation profession；

(a) 调解业;

(b) Arbitration profession；

(b) 仲裁业;

(c) ADR organizations；

(c) 替代性争议解决机制组织;

(d) IBP；and

(d) 菲律宾综合律师协会会长;以及

（e）Academe.

The members of the Council，who shall be appointed by the Secretary of Justice upon the recommendation of the OADR Executive Director，shall choose a Chairman from among themselves.

（e）学术机构。

理事会成员由司法部长根据替代性争议解决机制办公处的执行董事推荐任命，并在其中选出一名主席。

Article 2.6. Role of the Advisory Council. The Advisory Council shall advise the Executive Director on policy，operational and other relevant matters. The Council shall meet regularly，at least once every two（2）months，or upon call by the Executive Director.

第 2.6 条　咨询委员会的作用。咨询委员会应就政策、运作及其他有关事宜向执行董事提供意见。理事会应定期举行会议，至少每两个月举行一次，或应执行主任的要求举行。

CHAPTER 3
MEDIATION
第三章　调解

RULE 1‐General Provisions
细则 1—总则

Article 3.1. Scope of Application. These Rules apply to voluntary mediation，whether ad hoc or institutional，other than court-annexed mediation and only in default of an agreement of the parties on the applicable rules. These Rules shall also apply to all cases pending before an administrative or quasi-judicial agency that are subsequently agreed upon by the parties to be referred to mediation.

第3.1条　适用范围。这些规则适用于自愿调解，无论是临时调解还是机构调解，但法院附属调解除外，而且只有在当事方未就适用规则达成协议的情况下才适用。本规则还应适用于行政或准司法机构的所有待决案件，这些案件随后经当事方同意交付调解。

Article 3. 2 Statement of Policy. In applying and construing the provisions of these Rules，consideration must be given to the need to promote candor of parties and mediators through confidentiality of the mediation process，the policy of fostering prompt，economical and amicable resolution of disputes in accordance with principles of integrity of determination by the parties and the policy that the decision-making authority in the mediation process rests with the parties.

第3.2条　政策声明。在适用和解释这些规则的规定时，必须考虑到需要通过调解过程的保密性促进各方和调解人的坦率，促进根据各方确定的廉正原则迅速、经济和友好地解决争端的政策，以及调解过程中的决策权力属于各方的政策。

A party may petition a court before which an action is prematurely brought in a matter which is the subject of a mediation agreement，if at least one party so requests，not later than the pre-trial conference or upon the request of both parties，thereafter，to refer the parties to mediation in accordance with the agreement of the parties.

一方当事人可以请求法院对调解协议所涉事项过早提起的诉讼，根据双方当事人的协议将当事人交付调解；但在预审会议前应有至少一方当事人请求，或此后经双方当事人请求。

RULE 2 - Selection of a Mediator
细则2——调解人的甄选

Article 3. 3. Freedom to Select Mediator. The parties have the freedom to select their mediator. The parties may request the OADR to provide them with a list or roster or the resumes of its certified mediators. The OADR may be requested to inform the mediator of his/her selection.

第 3.3 条　选择调解人的自由。各方有选择调解人的自由。当事各方可要求替代性争议解决办公室向其提供一份名单或名册或经认证的调解人的简历,并将其选择通知调解人。

Article 3.4. Replacement of Mediator. If the mediator selected is unable to act as such for any reason, the parties may, upon being informed of such fact, select another mediator.

第 3.4 条　替换调解人。如果选定的调解人因任何原因不能担任,各方在获悉这一事实后,可选择另一调解人。

Article 3.5. Refusal or Withdrawal of Mediator. A mediator may refuse from acting as such, withdraw or may be compelled to withdraw, from the mediation proceedings under the following circumstances:

第 3.5 条　拒绝或退任调解人。调解人可在下列情况下拒绝、退出或被迫退出调解程序:

(a) If any of the parties so requests the mediator to withdraw;

(a) 如果任何一方要求调解人退出;

(b) The mediator does not have the qualifications, training and experience to enable him/her to meet the reasonable expectations of the parties;

(b) 调解人不具备满足各方合理期望的资格、培训和经验;

(c) Where the mediator's impartiality is in question;

(c) 调解人的公正性受到质疑;

(d) If continuation of the process would violate any ethical standards;

（d）如果继续这一程序将违反任何道德标准；

（e）If the safety of any of the parties would be jeopardized；

（e）任何一方的安全将受到损害；

（f）If the mediator is unable to provide effective services；

（f）如果调解人不能提供有效的服务；

（g）In case of conflict of interest；and

（g）发生利益冲突时；以及

（h）In any of the following instances，if the mediator is satisfied that：

（h）调解人确信：

（i）one or more of the parties is/are not acting in good faith；

（i）一方或多方当事人没有本着诚意行事；

（ii）the parties' agreement would be illegal or involve the commis-sion of a crime；

（ii）当事方的协议是非法的，或涉及犯罪；

（iii）continuing the dispute resolution would give rise to an appearance of impropriety；

（iii）如果继续解决争端，就会出现不当行为；

（iv）continuing with the process would cause significant harm to a non-participating person or to the public；or

（iv）继续进行这一进程会对非参与人员或公众造成重大损害；或

（v）continuing discussions would not be in the best interest of the parties，their minor children or the dispute resolution process.

（v）继续讨论不符合当事方、其未成年子女或争端解决程序的最佳利益。

RULE 3 - Ethical Conduct of a Mediator
细则 3——调解人的道德行为

Article 3.6. Competence. It is not required that a mediator shall have special qualifications by background or profession unless the special qualifications of a mediator are required in the mediation agreement or by the mediation parties. However，the certified mediator shall：

第 3.6 条　能力。除非调解协议或调解各方要求调解人具有特殊资格，否则调解人不需要具备背景或专业方面的特殊资格。但经认证的调解人应：

（a） maintain and continually upgrade his/her professional competence in mediation skills；

（a） 保持并不断提升其在调解技能方面的专业能力；

（b） ensure that his/her qualifications，training and experience are known to and accepted by the parties；and

（b） 确保当事方了解并接受其资格、培训和经验；

（c） serve only when his/her qualifications，training and experience enable him/her to meet the reasonable expectations of the parties and shall not hold himself/herself out or give the impression that he/she has qualifications，training and experience that he/she does not have. Upon the request of a mediation party，an individual who is requested to serve as mediator shall disclose his/her qualifications to mediate a dispute.

（c） 只有在其资格、培训和经验使其能够满足当事人的合理期望，并且不应使当事人认为其有其所没有的资格、培训和经验时才能任职。经调解当事人请求，被请求担任调解人的个人应当披露调解争议的资格。

Article 3.7. Impartiality. A mediator shall maintain impartiality.

第 3.7 条　公正。调解人应保持公正。

（a） Before accepting a mediation，an individual who is requested to serve as a mediator shall：

（a） 在接受调解之前，被要求担任调解人的个人应：

（ i ） make an inquiry that is reasonable under the circumstances to determine whether there are any known facts that a reasonable individual would consider likely to affect the impartiality of the mediator，including a financial or personal interest in the outcome of the mediation and any existing or past relationship with a party or foreseeable participant in the mediation；and

（ i ） 根据情况进行合理的调查，以确定是否有任何已知事实，合理的个人会认为这些事实可能影响调解人的公正性，包括调解结果以及与一方或可预见的调解参与者的任何现有或过去关系中的经济利益或个人利益；以及

（ ii ） disclose to the mediation parties any such fact known or learned as soon as is practical before accepting a mediation.

（ ii ） 在接受调解之前，应尽快向调解各方披露已知的事实。

（ b ） If a mediator learns any fact described in paragraph（a）（i）of this Article after accepting a mediation，the mediator shall disclose it as soon as practicable to the mediation parties.

（ b ） 如果调解人在接受调解后获悉本条（a）款（i）项所述的任何事实，调解人应尽快向调解各方披露。

Article 3. 8. Confidentiality. A mediator shall keep in utmost confidence all confidential information obtained in the course of the mediation process. A mediator shall discuss issues of confidentiality with the mediation parties before beginning the mediation process including limitations on the scope of confidentiality and the extent of confidentiality provided in any private sessions or caucuses that the mediator holds with a party.

第3.8条　保密。调解人应将在调解过程中获得的所有机密信息保密。调解人在开始调解进程之前，应与调解方讨论保密问题，包括对保密范围的限制以及调解人与一方举行的任何非公开会议或核心小组会

议所规定的保密程度。

Article 3.9. Consent and Self-Determination.

第 3.9 条　同意和自决。

(a) A mediator shall make reasonable efforts to ensure that each party understands the nature and character of the mediation proceedings including private caucuses, the issues, the available options, the alternatives to non-settlement, and that each party is free and able to make whatever choices he/she desires regarding participation in mediation generally and regarding specific settlement options. If a mediator believes that a party, who is not represented by counsel, is unable to understand, or fully participate in, the mediation proceedings for any reason, a mediator may either：

(a) 调解人应做出合理努力,确保每一方了解调解程序的性质和特征,包括私人核心小组、问题、现有选择、非解决办法,并确保每一方在一般参与调解和具体解决办法方面可以自由做出自己希望的任何选择。如果调解人认为没有律师代理的当事方因任何原因不能理解或充分参与调解程序,调解人也可以:

    (i) limit the scope of the mediation proceedings in a manner consistent with the party's ability to participate，and/or recommend that the party obtain appropriate assistance in order to continue with the process；or

    (i) 以符合当事方参与能力的方式限制调解程序的范围,并建议当事方获得适当协助,以便继续进行调解程序;或

    (ii) terminate the mediation proceedings.

    (ii) 终止调解程序。

(b) A mediator shall recognize and put in mind that the primary responsibility of resolving a dispute and the shaping of a voluntary and uncoerced settlement rests with the parties.

（b）调解人应认识到并铭记解决争端和形成自愿和不受胁迫的解决办法的主要责任在于当事方。

Article 3.10. Separation of Mediation from Counseling and Legal Advice.

第 3.10 条　将调解与咨询和法律意见分开。

（a）Except in evaluative mediation or when the parties so request，a mediator shall：

（a）除在评价调解或当事方提出请求时，调解人应：

　　（i）refrain from giving legal or technical advice and otherwise engaging in counseling or advocacy；and

　　（i）不提供法律或技术意见或以其他方式参与咨询或宣传；以及

　　（ii）abstain from expressing his/her personal opinion on the rights and duties of the parties and the merits of any proposal made.

　　（ii）不就当事方的权利和义务以及所提建议的是非曲直发表个人意见。

（b）Where appropriate and where either or both parties are not represented by counsel，a mediator shall：

（b）在当事一方或双方无律师代理的情况下，调解人应：

　　（i）recommend that the parties seek outside professional advice to help them make informed decision and to understand the implications of any proposal；and

　　（i）建议缔约方寻求外部专业咨询意见，以帮助它们做出知情决定，并了解任何提案的影响；以及

　　（ii）suggest that the parties seek independent legal and/or technical advice before a settlement agreement is signed.

　　（ii）建议双方当事人在和解协议签署之前寻求独立的法律和/或技术意见。

（c）Without the consent of all parties，and for a reasonable time under the particular circumstance，a mediator who also practices another profession shall not establish a professional relationship in that other profession with one of the parties, or any person or entity, in a substantially and factually related matter.

(c) 调解人如未经所有各方同意,在特定情况下,在一段合理时间内也从事另一职业,则不得就实质和与事实相关的事项与另一职业之一或任何个人或实体建立职业关系。

Article 3.11. Charging of Fees.

第3.11条 收费。

(a) A mediator shall fully disclose and explain to the parties the basis of cost, fees and charges.

(a) 调解人应充分披露并向各方解释成本、费用和收费的依据。

(b) The mediator who withdraws from the mediation shall return to the parties any unearned fee and unused deposit.

(b) 调解人退出调解时,应将任何不劳而获的费用和未用的存款退还各方。

(c) A mediator shall not enter into a fee agreement which is contingent upon the results of the mediation or the amount of the settlement.

(c) 调解人不得订立视调解结果或和解金额而定的收费协议。

Article 3. 12. Promotion of Respect and Control of Abuse of Process. The mediator shall encourage mutual respect between the parties, and shall take reasonable steps, subject to the principle of self-determination, to limit abuses of the mediation process.

第3.12条 促进尊重和控制滥用程序。调解人应鼓励双方相互尊重,并应根据自决原则采取合理步骤,限制滥用调解进程。

Article 3.13. Solicitation or Acceptance of any Gift. No mediator or any member of a mediator's immediate family or his/her agent shall request，solicit，receive or accept any gift or any type of compensation other than the agreed fee and expenses in connection with any matter coming before the mediator.

第3.13条　索取或接受任何礼物。调解人或其直系亲属或代理人不得要求、索取、接受任何礼物或任何类型的补偿，但与调解人处理的任何事项有关的商定费用和开支除外。

RULE 4‐ Role of Parties and their Counsels
细则 4——当事方及其律师的作用

Article 3. 14. Designation of Counselor any Person to Assist Mediation. Except as otherwise provided by the ADR Act or by these Rules，a party may designate a lawyer or any other person to provide assistance in the mediation. A waiver of this right shall be made in writing by the party waiving it. A waiver of participation or legal representation may be rescinded at any time.

第3.14条　指定顾问协助调解。除《替代性争议解决法案》或本规则另有规定外，当事人可以指定律师或者其他任何人协助调解。放弃此项权利的一方应以书面形式提出。放弃参与或法律代理可随时撤销。

Article 3.15. Role of Counsel.

第3.15条　律师的作用。

(a) The lawyer shall view his/her role in mediation as a collaborator with the other lawyer in working together toward the common goal of helping their clients resolve their differences to their mutual advantage.

(a) 律师应视其在调解中的作用为其他律师的合作者，为共同的目标努力，即帮助客户解决分歧，使其互利。

(b) The lawyer shall encourage and assist his/her client to actively participate in positive discussions and cooperate in crafting an agreement to resolve their dispute.

（b）律师应鼓励和协助其委托人积极参与讨论，并合作起草解决争议的协议。

（c）The lawyer must assist his/her client to comprehend and appreciate the mediation process and its benefits, as well as the client's greater personal responsibility for the success of mediation in resolving the dispute.

（c）律师必须协助其委托人理解和欣赏调解过程及其好处，以及委托人对调解成功解决争端承担的更大个人责任

（d）In preparing for participation in mediation, the lawyer shall confer and discuss with his/her client the following：

（d）在准备参与调解时，律师应与其委托人商讨下列事项：

（i）The mediation process as essentially a negotiation between the parties assisted by their respective lawyers, and facilitated by a mediator, stressing its difference from litigation, its advantages and benefits, the client's heightened role in mediation and responsibility for its success and explaining the role of the lawyer in mediation proceedings.

（i）调解进程基本上是当事各方在各自律师协助下进行的谈判，由调解人提供便利，强调其与诉讼的不同之处、其优势和好处、客户在调解中的强化作用及其成功的责任，并解释律师在调解程序中的作用。

（ii）The substance of the upcoming mediation, such as：

（ii）即将进行的调解的实质内容，例如：

（aa）The substantive issues involved in the dispute and their prioritization in terms of importance to his/her client's real interests and needs；

（aa）争议所涉及的实质性问题及其对其客户的真正利益和

需求的重要性的轻重缓急；

(bb) The study of the other party's position in relation to the issues with a view to understanding the underlying interests, fears, concerns and needs；

(bb) 研究另一方对问题的立场，以了解其潜在的利益、恐惧、考虑和需要；

(cc) The information or facts to be gathered or sought from the other side or to be exchanged that are necessary for informed decision-making；

(cc) 从另一方收集或索取的、或交换的知情决策所必需的资料或事实；

(dd) The possible options for settlement but stressing the need to be open-minded about other possibilities；and

(dd) 可能的解决方案，但强调必须对其他可能性持开放态度；

(ee) The best, worst and most likely alternatives to a non-negotiated settlement.

(ee) 非谈判解决的最佳、最差和最有可能的替代办法。

Article 3.16. Other Matters which the Counsel shall do to Assist.

第3.16条　律师应协助处理的其他事项。

Mediation. The lawyer：

调解。律师：

(a) shall give support to the mediator so that his/her client will fully understand the rules and processes of mediation；

(a) 应支持调解人，使其当事人充分了解调解规则和程序；

(b) shall impress upon his/her client the importance of speaking for himself/herself and taking responsibility for making decisions during the negotiations within the mediation process；

(b) 应使其客户认识到在调解过程中亲自发言和负责做出决定的重要性；

(c) may ask for a recess in order to give advice or suggestions to his/

her client in private, if he/she perceives that his/her client is unable to bargain effectively;

(c) 如果其认为其当事人不能有效地讨价还价,可以请求休庭,以便私下向该当事人提出建议;

(d) shall assist his/her client and the mediator put in writing the terms of the settlement agreement that the parties have entered into. The lawyers shall see to it that the terms of the settlement agreement are not contrary to law, morals, good customs, public order or public policy.

(d) 应协助其客户和调解人书面订立双方达成的和解协议条款。律师应当确保和解协议的条款不违反法律、道德、良好习俗、公共秩序或者公共政策。

RULE 5 - Conduct of Mediation
细则 5——进行调解

Article 3. 17. Articles to be Considered in the Conduct of Mediation.

第 3.17 条　调解中应考虑的条款。

(a) The mediator shall not make untruthful or exaggerated claims about the dispute resolution process, its costs and benefits, its outcome or the mediator's qualifications and abilities during the entire mediation process.

(a) 在整个调解过程中,调解人不得就争议解决程序、其成本效益、结果或调解人的资格和能力提出不实或夸大的主张。

(b) The mediator shall help the parties reach a satisfactory resolution of their dispute but has no authority to impose a settlement on the parties.

(b) 调解人应帮助当事方圆满解决争端,但无权将解决办法强加给当事方。

(c) The parties shall personally appear for mediation and may be assisted by a lawyer. A party may be represented by an agent who must have full authority to negotiate and settle the dispute.

(c) 当事方应亲自出庭调解,并可由律师协助。当事人可以由代理人代理,代理人必须具有谈判和解决争议的充分权力。

(d) The mediation process shall, in general, consist of the following stages:

(d) 调解进程一般应包括以下阶段:

（i) opening statement of the mediator;

（i) 调解人的开幕词;

（ii) individual narration by the parties;

（ii) 当事方的个人陈述;

（iii) exchange by the parties;

（iii) 双方交换意见;

（iv) summary of issues;

（iv) 问题摘要;

（v) generation and evaluation of options; and

（v) 备选方案的生成和评估;以及

（vi) closure.

（vi) 结束。

(e) The mediation proceeding shall be held in private. Persons, other than the parties, their representatives and the mediator, may attend only with the consent of all the parties.

(e) 调解程序应非公开进行。除当事方、其代表和调解人外,其他人只有在所有当事方同意的情况下才能出席。

(f) The mediation shall be closed:

(f) 调解应在以下情况发生时结束:

（i) by the execution of a settlement agreement by the parties;

（i) 当事人执行和解协议的;

（ii) by the withdrawal of any party from mediation; and

（ii）任何一方退出调解；以及

（iii）by the written declaration of the mediator that any further effort at mediation would not be helpful.

（iii）调解人书面声明任何进一步的调解努力都没有帮助。

RULE 6 - Place of Mediation
细则 6——调解地点

Article 3.18. Agreement of Parties on the Place of Mediation. The parties are free to agree on the place of mediation. Failing such agreement，the place of mediation shall be any place convenient and appropriate to all parties.

第3.18条　各方关于调解地的协议。当事方可自由商定调解地点。在未达成此种协议的情况下，调解地应为任何方便且适合各方当事人的地方。

RULE 7 - Effect of Agreement to Submit Dispute to Mediation Under Institutional Rules
细则 7——根据机构规则将争端提交调解的协议的效力

Article 3.19. Agreement to Submit a Dispute to Mediation by an Institution. An agreement to submit a dispute to mediation by an institution shall include an agreement to be bound by the internal mediation and administrative policies of such institution. Further，an agreement to submit a dispute to mediation under institutional mediation rules shall be deemed to include an agreement to have such rules govern the mediation of the dispute and for the mediator，the parties，their respective counsels and non-party participants to abide by such rules.

第3.19条　同意将争议提交机构调解。将争议提交机构调解的协议应当包括受机构内部调解和行政政策约束的协议。此外,根据机构调解规则将争端提交调解的协议应被视为包括由这些规则管理争端的调解的协议,并由调解人、当事方、其各自的律师和非当事方参与者遵守这些规则。

RULE 8 - Enforcement of Mediated Settlement Agreements
细则 8——执行调解解决协议

Article 3.20. Operative Principles to Guide Mediation. The mediation shall be guided by the following operative principles:

第 3.20 条　指导调解的执行原则。调解应遵循以下执行原则:

(a) A settlement agreement following successful mediation shall be prepared by the parties with the assistance of their respective counsels, if any, and by the mediator. The parties and their respective counsels shall endeavor to make the terms and condition of the settlement agreement complete and to make adequate provisions for the contingency of breach to avoid conflicting interpretations of the agreement.

(a) 调解成功后的和解协议应由各方在各自法律顾问(如果有的话)的协助下和调解人拟定。双方当事人及其各自的律师应努力使和解协议的条款和条件完整,并为违约的意外情况做出适当规定,以避免对协议的解释发生冲突。

(b) The parties and their respective counsels, if any, shall sign the settlement agreement. The mediator shall certify that he/she explained the contents of the settlement agreement to the parties in a language known to them.

(b) 双方及其各自的律师(如有)应签署和解协议。调解人应证明其以当事方熟悉的语言向他们解释了和解协议的内容。

(c) If the parties agree, the settlement agreement may be jointly deposited by the parties or deposited by one party with prior notice to the other party/ies with the Clerk of Court of the Regional Trial Court:

(c) 当事人约定的,可以由当事人共同交存和解协议,也可以由当事人一方向当事人另一方预先通知,向以下区域审判庭书记官交存和解协议:

(a) where the principal place of business in the Philippines of any of the parties islocated:

(a) 任何一方在菲律宾的主要营业地点;

(b) if any of the parties is an individual, where any of those individuals resides; or

(b) 如果当事方中有任何一方是个人,这些个人的居住地;或

(c) in the National Capital Judicial Region. Where there is a need to enforce the settlement agreement, a petition may be filed by any of the parties with the same court, in which case, the court shall proceed summarily to hear the petition, in accordance with the Special ADR Rules.

(c) 国家首都司法区域。在需要执行和解协议的情况下,任何一方当事人均可向同一法院提出申请,在这种情况下,法院应根据替代性争议解决机制特别规则立即审理该申请。

(d) The parties may agree in the settlement agreement that the mediator shall become a sole arbitrator for the dispute and shall treat the settlement agreement as an arbitral award which shall be subject to enforcement under Republic Act No. 876, otherwise known as "The Arbitration Law", notwithstanding the provisions of Executive Order No. 1008, s. 1985, otherwise known as the "Construction Industry Arbitration Law" for mediated disputes outside of the Construction Industry Arbitration Commission.

(d) 当事各方可在和解协议中商定,调解人应成为争端的独任仲裁员,并应将和解协议作为仲裁裁决处理,该裁决应根据第876号共和

国法（又称"仲裁法"）予以执行，尽管有第1008号行政命令第1985节的规定，又称建筑行业仲裁法，是指建筑行业仲裁委员会以外的调解争议。

RULE 9 - Confidentiality of Information
细则9——资料的机密性

Article 3.21. Confidentiality of Information. Information obtained through mediation proceedings shall be subject to the following principles and guidelines：

第3.21条　信息的保密性。通过调解程序获得的信息应遵循以下原则和准则：

(a) Information obtained through mediation shall be privileged and confidential.

(a) 通过调解获得的信息应当保密。

(b) A party，mediator，or non-party participant may refuse to disclose and may prevent any other person from disclosing a confidential information.

(b) 当事一方、调解员或非当事方的参与方可拒绝披露，并可阻止任何其他人披露机密资料。

(c) Confidential information shall not be subject to discovery and shall be inadmissible in any adversarial proceeding，whether judicial or quasi-judicial. However，evidence or information that is otherwise admissible or subject to discovery dbes not become inadmissible or protected from discovery solely by reason of its use in a mediation.

(c) 机密资料不应被发现，在任何对抗性诉讼程序中，无论是司法程序还是准司法程序，都不应予以受理。然而，在其他方面可以接受或被发现的证据或信息不会仅仅因为在调解中使用而变得不可接受或不被发现。

（d） In such an adversarial proceeding，the following persons involved or previously involved in a mediation may not be compelled to disclose confidential information obtained during the mediation：

（d）在这种对抗程序中，不得强迫下列参与或曾参与调解的人披露调解期间获得的机密资料：

（i） the parties to the dispute；

（i）争端各方；

（ii） the mediator or mediators；

（ii）调解人；

（iii） the counsel for the parties；

（iii）当事方的律师；

（iv） the non-party participants；

（iv）非缔约方参与者；

（v） any person hired or engaged in connection with the mediation as secretary，stenographer，clerk or assistant；and

（v）受雇或参与调解的任何人，如秘书、速记员、职员或助理；以及

（vi） any other person who obtains or possesses confidential information by reason of his/her profession.

（vi）任何其他因其职业而获得或拥有机密信息的人。

（e） The protections of the ADR Act shall continue to apply even if a mediator is found to have failed to act impartially.

（e）即使发现调解人未能公正行事，该《替代性争议解决法案》的保护仍将继续适用。

（f） A mediator may not be called to testify to provide confidential information gathered in mediation. A mediator who is wrongfully subpoenaed shall be reimbursed the full cost of his/her attorney's fees and related expenses.

（f）不得传唤调解人作证提供其在调解中收集的机密信息。对于被错误传唤的调解人，应补偿其律师费和相关费用的全部费用。

Article 3.22. Waiver of Confidentiality.

第 3.22 条　放弃保密。

(a) A privilege arising from the confidentiality of information may be waived in a record or orally during a proceeding by the mediator and the mediation parties.

(a) 因资料保密而产生的特权，可以在记录中放弃，也可以在调解人和调解方进行诉讼期间口头放弃。

(b) With the consent of the mediation parties，a privilege arising from the confidentiality of information may likewise be waived by a non-party participant if the information is provided by such non-party participant.

(b) 调解当事人同意非当事人提供信息的，非当事人也可以放弃信息保密特权。

(c) A person who discloses confidential information shall be precluded from asserting the privilege under Article 3.21 (Confidentiality of Information) to bar disclosure of the rest of the information necessary to a complete understanding of the previously disclosed information. If a person suffers loss or damage as a result of the disclosure of the confidential information，he/she shall be entitled to damages in a judicial proceeding against the person who made the disclosure.

(c) 披露机密信息的人不得主张第 3.21 条（信息的保密性）的特权，不得披露完全了解先前披露的信息所必需的其他信息。如果一个人因披露机密信息而遭受损失或损害，他有权在对披露者提起的司法诉讼中获得损害赔偿。

(d) A person who discloses or makes a representation about a mediation is precluded from asserting the privilege mentioned in Article 3.21 to the extent that the communication prejudices another person in the proceeding and it is necessary for the person prejudiced to respond to the representation or disclosure.

(d) 如果其内容在诉讼程序中对另一人造成损害,则披露调解或对调解做出陈述的人不得主张第 3.21 条所述的特权,且受损害的人有必要对该披露或陈述进行答辩。

Article 3. 23. Exceptions to the Privilege of Confidentiality of Information.

第 3.23 条　信息保密特权的例外。

(a) There is no privilege against disclosure under Article 3.21 in the following instances:

(a) 在下列情况下,没有第 3.21 条规定的禁止披露的特权:

(i) in an agreement evidenced by a record authenticated by all parties to the agreement;

(i) 由协议各方认证的记录证明的协议;

(ii) available to the public or made during a session of a mediation which is open, or is required by law to be open, to the public;

(ii) 向公众开放或在对公众开放或法律要求对公众开放的调解期间进行的;

(iii) a threat or statement of a plan to inflict bodily injury or commit a crime of violence;

(iii) 威胁实施或说明实施人身伤害或暴力犯罪的计划;

(iv) intentionally used to plan a crime, attempt to commit, or commit a crime, or conceal an ongoing crime or criminal activity;

(iv) 故意用于策划犯罪、企图实施或实施犯罪,或隐瞒正在进行的犯罪或犯罪活动;

(v) sought or offered to prove or disprove abuse, neglect, abandon-ment or exploitation in a proceeding in which a public agency is protecting the interest of an individual protected by law; but this exception does not apply where a child protection matter is referred to mediation by a court or where a public agency participates in the child protection mediation;

(ⅴ) 在公共机构保护受法律保护的个人利益的诉讼中寻求或提出证明或否认虐待、忽视、遗弃或剥削；但这一例外不适用于儿童保护事项交由法院调解或公共机构参与儿童保护调解的情况；

(ⅵ) sought or offered to prove or disprove a claim or complaint of professional misconduct or malpractice filed against a mediator in a proceeding; or

(ⅵ) 寻求或提出证明或反驳在诉讼程序中针对调解人提出的职业不当行为或不当行为的主张或投诉；或

(ⅶ) sought or offered to prove or disprove a claim or complaint of professional misconduct or malpractice filed against a party, non-party participant, or representative of a party based on conduct occurring during a mediation.

(ⅶ) 寻求或提出证明或反驳对一方当事人、非当事人参与人或一方代表在调解过程中发生的行为提出的职业不当行为或不当行为的申诉或控告。

(b) If a court or administrative agency finds, after a hearing in camera, that the party seeking discovery of the proponent of the evidence has shown that the evidence is not otherwise available, that there is a need for the evidence that substantially outweighs the interest in protecting confidentiality, and the mediation communication is sought or offered in:

(b) 如果法院或行政机构在非公开审理后发现，寻求证据提出者发现的一方当事人证明没有其他证据，需要的证据远远超过保护机密性的利益，并且调解沟通是在：

(ⅰ) a court proceeding involving a crime or felony; or

（i）涉及犯罪或重罪的法院程序；或

（ii）a proceeding to prove a claim or defense that under the law is sufficient to reform or avoid a liability on a contract arising out of the mediation.

（ii）根据法律足以改革或避免因调解而产生的合同责任的索赔或抗辩的程序。

（c）A mediator may not be compelled to provide evidence of a mediation communication or testify in such proceeding.

（c）调解人不得被迫提供调解沟通的证据或在这种程序中作证。

（d）If a mediation communication is not privileged under an exception in sub-section（a）or（b）hereof，only the portion of the communication necessary for the application of the exception for non-disclosure may be admitted. The admission of a particular evidence for the limited purpose of an exception does not render that evidence，or any other mediation communication，admissible for any other purpose.

（d）如果调解沟通不享有本条（a）款和（b）款的例外情况下的特权，只能接受为适用不披露例外情况所必需的沟通部分。为例外的有限目的而接受某一特定证据，并不使该证据或任何其他调解来文为任何其他目的所接受。

Article 3. 24. Non-Reporting or Communication by Mediator. A mediator may not make a report，assessment，evaluation，recommendation，finding or other communication regarding a mediation to a court or agency or other authority that may make a ruling on a dispute that is the subject of a mediation，except：

第3.24条　调解人不报告或沟通。调解人不得就调解事项向法院或机构或可能就调解所涉争端作出裁决的其他当局提出报告、评估、评价、建议、调查结果或其他通信，除非：

（a）to state that the mediation occurred or has terminated，or where a settlement was reached; or

（a）说明调解已经发生或已经结束，或达成了和解；或

（b）as permitted to be disclosed under Article 3.23 （Exceptions to the Privilege of Confidentiality of Information）.

（b）允许根据第 3.23 条披露（信息保密特权的例外）。

The parties may, by an agreement in writing, stipulate that the settlement agreement shall be sealed and not disclosed to any third party including the court. Such stipulation, however, shall not apply to a proceeding to enforce or set aside the settlement agreement.

当事人可以通过书面协议约定，和解协议应当密封，不得向包括法院在内的任何第三方披露。但该规定不适用于执行或撤销和解协议的程序。

RULE 10‐Fees and Cost of Mediation
细则 10——调解费用

Article 3.25. Fees and Cost of Ad hoc Mediation. In ad hoc mediation, the parties are free to make their own arrangement as to mediation cost and fees. In default thereof, the schedule of cost and fees to be approved by the OADR shall be followed.

第 3.25 条　特别调解费用。在临时调解中，各方可自行安排调解费用和收费。如无规定，应当按照替代性争议解决机制办公处规定的费用和收费表办理。

Article 3.26. Fees and Cost of Intitutional Mediation.

第 3.26 条　机构调解费用。

（a）In institutional mediation, mediation cost shall include the administrative charges of the mediation institution under which the parties have agreed to be bound, mediator's fees and associated expenses, if any. In default of agreement of the parties as to the amount and manner of payment of mediation's cost and fees, the same shall be determined in accordance with the applicable internal rules of the mediation service providers under whose rules the mediation is conducted.

(a) 在机构调解中,调解费用应包括各方同意受其约束的调解机构的行政费用、调解员费用和任何相关费用。在当事各方未就支付调解费用和收费的数额和方式达成协议的情况下,应根据调解所依据的规则所适用的调解服务提供者的内部规则确定此种协议和收费。

(b) A mediation service provider may determine such mediation fee as is reasonable taking into consideration the following factors, among others:

(b) 调解服务提供者可根据以下因素确定合理的调解费用:

(i) the complexity of the case;

(i) 案件的复杂性;

(ii) the number of hours spent in mediation; and

(ii) 用于调解的小时数;以及

(iii) the training, experience and stature of mediators.

(iii) 调解人的训练、经验和地位。

CHAPTER 4
INTERNATIONAL COMMERCIAL ARBITRATION
第四章　国际商事仲裁

RULE 1 - General Provisions
细则 1—总则

Article 4.1. Scope of Application.
第 4.1 条　适用范围。

(a) This Chapter applies to international commercial arbitration, subject to any agreement in force between the Philippines and other state or states.

（a）本章适用于国际商事仲裁，但须遵守菲律宾国家与其他国家之间的任何有效协议。

（b）This Chapter applies only if the place or seat of arbitration is the Philippines and in default of any agreement of the parties on the applicable rules.

（b）本章仅适用于仲裁地或所在地为菲律宾，且当事人未就适用规则达成任何协议的情况。

（c）This Chapter shall not affect any other law of the Philippines by virtue of which certain disputes may not be submitted to arbitration or may be submitted to arbitration only according to provisions other than those of the ADR Act.

（c）本章不影响菲律宾的任何其他法律，根据这些法律，某些争端不能提交仲裁，或只能根据《替代性争议解决法案》以外的规定提交仲裁。

Article 4.2. Rules of Interpretation.

第4.2条　解释规则。

（a）International commercial arbitration shall be governed by the Model Law on International Commercial Arbitration.

（a）国际商事仲裁适用《国际商事仲裁示范法》。

（b）In interpreting this Chapter，regard shall be had to the international origin of the Model Law and to the need for uniformity in its interpretation. Resort may be made to the travaux preparatoires and the Report of the Secretary-General of the United Nations Commission on International Trade Law dated March 1985 entitled，"International Commercial Arbitration：Analytical Commentary on Draft Text identifie by reference number A/CN. 9/264".

（b）在解释本章时，应当考虑到示范法的国际渊源以及统一解释的必要性。可以参考1985年3月联合国国际贸易法委员会秘书长题为《国际商事仲裁：关于案文草案的分析性评论》的报告（通过参考编号 A/CN. 9/264 确认）。

(c) Moreover, in interpreting this Chapter, the court shall have due regard to the policy of the law in favor of arbitration and the policy of the Philippines to actively promote party autonomy in the resolution of disputes or the freedom of the parties to make their own arrangement to resolve their dispute.

(c) 此外，法院在解释本章时，应适当考虑到有利于仲裁的法律政策和菲律宾政策，从而积极促进当事人在解决争端方面的自主权，或当事人自行做出解决争端的安排的自由。

(d) Where a provision of this Chapter, except the Rules applicable to the substance of the dispute, leaves the parties free to determine a certain issue, such freedom includes the right of the parties to authorize a third party, including an institution, to make that determination.

(d) 本章规定，除适用于争端实质的规则外，使当事方可以自由决定某一问题，这种自由包括当事方有权授权包括机构在内的第三方做出决定。

(e) Where a provision of this Chapter refers to the fact that the parties have agreed or that they may agree or in any other way refers to an agreement of the parties, such agreement includes any arbitration rules referred to in that agreement.

(e) 本章规定，当事人约定或者可以约定或者以任何其他方式约定当事人约定的，该约定包括该约定中述及的任何仲裁规则。

(f) Where a provision of this Chapter, other than in paragraph (a) of Article 4.25 (Default of a Party) and paragraphs (b) (i) of Article 4.32 (Termination of Proceedings), refers to a claim, it also applies to a counter-claim, and where it refers to a defense, it also applies to a defense to such counter-claim.

(6) 本章规定，除第 4.25 条(a)款(当事方违约)和第 4.32 条(b)款和(i)款(终止诉讼程序)的规定外，还涉及诉讼请求，也适用于反诉。

如果它提到抗辩，它也适用于对这种反诉的抗辩。

Article 4.3. Receipt of Written Communications.

第4.3条　收到书面来文。

(a) Unless otherwise agreed by the parties：

(a) 除非当事方另有协议：

   (i) any written communication is deemed to have been received if it is delivered to the addressee personally or at his/her place of business, habitual residence or mailing address; if none of these can be found after making a reasonable inquiry, a written communication is deemed to have been received if it is sent to the addressee's last known place of business, habitual residence or mailing address by registered letter or any other means which provides a record of the attempt to deliver it；

   (i) 任何书面通信，如果直接送交收件人本人或其营业地、惯常居所或通信地址，即视为已收到；如果经合理查询后未能找到任何上述地址，则如果书面通信以挂号信或任何其他提供做出了送交尝试的记录的方式送交收件人最后为人所知的营业地、惯常居所或通信地址，即视为已收到。

   (ii) the communication is deemed to have been received on the day it is so delivered.

   (ii) 来文被认为是在发送当天收到的。

(b) The provisions of this Article do not apply to communications in court proceedings, which shall be governed by the Rules of Court.

(b) 该条的规定不适用于法院诉讼程序中的通信，而法院规则应对此做出规定。

Article 4.4. Waiver of Right to Object. A party who knows that any provision of this Chapter from which the parties may derogate or any requirement under the arbitration agreement has not been complied with and yet proceeds with the arbitration without stating the objections for such non-compliance without undue delay or if a time limit is provided therefor, within such period of time, shall be deemed to have waived the right to object.

第4.4条 放弃反对的权利。当事人明知本章中当事人可以减损的任何规定或仲裁协议中的任何要求未得到遵守,但仍继续进行仲裁而未就此类不遵守规定提出异议而无不当拖延,或者对此规定了时限的,视为已放弃反对权。

Article 4.5. Extent of Court Intervention. In matters governed by this Chapter, no court shall intervene except where so provided in the ADR Act. Resort to Philippine courts for matters within the scope of the ADR Act shall be governed by the Special ADR Rules.

第4.5条 法院干预的范围。对于本章所规定的事项,除《替代性争议解决法案》有规定外,任何法院不得介入。对于属于《替代性争议解决法案》范围内的事项诉诸菲律宾法院,适用《替代性争议解决法案》的特别规则。

Article 4.6. Court or Other Authority for Certain Functions of Arbitration Assistance and Supervision.

第4.6条 仲裁协助和监督的某些职能。

(a) The functions referred to in paragraphs (c) and(d) of Article 4. 11 (Appointment of Arbitrators) and paragraph (c) of Article 4.13 (Challenge Procedure) and paragraph (a) of Article 4.14 (Failure or Impossibility to Act) shall be performed by the appointing authority as defined in Article 1. 6 C1, unless the latter shall fail or refuse to act within thirty (30) days from receipt of the 20 request in which case the applicant may renew the application with the court. The appointment of an arbitrator is not subject to appeal or motion for reconsideration.

(a) 第 4.11 条(c)款和(d)款(指定仲裁员)、第 4.13 条(c)款(质疑程序)以及第 4.14 条(a)款(法案的不足)中提到的职能应由第 1.6 条 C1 项所界定的指定机构执行,除非后者在收到 20 请求后 30 天内未能或拒绝采取行动,在这种情况下,申请人可以向法院重新提出申请。仲裁员的任命不得上诉或请求复议。

(b) The functions referred to in paragraph (c) of Article 4.16 (c) (Competence of Arbitral Tribunal to Rule on its Jurisdiction), second paragraph of Article 4.34 (Application for Setting Aside an Exclusive Recourse Against Arbitral Award), Article4.35 (Recognition and Enforcement), Article 4.38 (Venue and Jurisdiction), shall be performed by the appropriate Regional Trial Court.

(b) 第 4.16 条(c)款(仲裁庭就其管辖权作出裁决的权限)、第 4.34 条(b)款(申请撤销对仲裁裁决的专属追索权)、第 4.35 条(承认和执行)和第 4.38 条(地点和管辖权)应由适当的区域审判法院执行。

(c) A Court may not refuse to grant, implement or enforce a petition for an interim measure, including those provided for in Article 4.9 (Arbitration Agreement and Interim Measures by Court), Article 4.11 (Appointment of Arbitrators), Article 4.13 (Challenge Procedure), Article 4.27 (Court Assistance in Taking Evidence), on the sole ground that the Petition is merely an ancillary relief and the principal action is pending with the arbitral tribunal.

(c) 法院不得拒绝批准、执行或强制执行临时措施的申请,包括第 4.9 条(仲裁协议和法院的临时措施)、第 4.11 条(指定仲裁员)、第 4.13 条(质疑程序)以及第 4.27 条(法院协助取证),唯一的理由是,该申请只是一种辅助救济,主要诉讼有待仲裁庭裁决。

RULE 2 - Arbitration Agreement
细则2——仲裁协议

Article 4. 7. Definition and Form of Arbitration Agreement. The arbitration agreement, as defined in Article 1. 6 A4, shall be in writing. An agreement is in writing if it is contained in a document signed by the parties or in an exchange of letters, telex, telegrams or other means of telecommunication which provide a record of the agreement, or in an exchange of statements of claim and defense in which the existence of an agreement is alleged by one party and not denied by another.

第4.7条　仲裁协议的定义和形式。第1.6条第A4款所界定的仲裁协议应为书面形式。如协议载于当事各方签署的文件中，或载于提供协议记录的换文、电传、电报或其他电信手段中，或载于当事一方声称存在协议但另一方没有否认的索赔和答辩书中，协议即为书面协议。

The reference in a contract to a document containing an arbitration clause constitutes an arbitration agreement provided that the contract is in writing and the reference is such as to make that clause part of the contract.

合同中提及载有仲裁条款的文件，构成仲裁协议，条件是该合同为书面形式，且该提及使其成为合同的一部分。

Article 4. 8. Arbitration Agreement and Substantive Claim Before Court.

第4.8条　仲裁协议和向法院提出的实质性索赔。

(a) A court before which an action is brought in a matter which is the subject of an arbitration agreement shall, if at least one party so requests not later than the pre-trial conference, or upon the request of both parties thereafter, refer the parties to arbitration unless it finds that the arbitration agreement is null and void，inoperative or incapable of being performed.

（a）对于仲裁协议所涉事项提起诉讼的法院，如果在预审前至少有一方要求，或在此后双方提出请求时，应将当事方提交仲裁，除非它认定仲裁协议无效、不生效或不能履行。

（b）Where an action referred to in the previous paragraph has been brought，arbitral proceedings may nevertheless be commenced or continued，and an award may be made，while the issue is pending before the court.

（b）如果前段所述诉讼已被提起，在未决期间，仍可启动或继续仲裁程序，并可作出裁决。

（c）Where the action is commenced by or against multiple parties，one or more of whom are parties to an arbitration agreement，the court shall refer to arbitration those parties who are bound by the arbitration agreement although the civil action may continue as to those who are not bound by such arbitration agreement.

（c）如果诉讼是由多方当事人提起或针对多方当事人提起的，其中一方或多方当事人是仲裁协议的当事人，法院应将受仲裁协议约束的当事人交付仲裁。

Article 4.9. Arbitration Agreement and Interim Measures by Court.
第 4.9 条　仲裁协议和法院的临时措施。

（a）It is not incompatible with an arbitration agreement for a party to request from a court，before the constitution of the arbitral tribunal or during arbitral proceedings，an interim measure of protection and for a court to grant such measure.

（a）一方当事人在组成仲裁庭之前或在仲裁程序期间请求法院采取临时保全措施以及法院准予采取这种措施，与仲裁协议并不抵触。

（b）To the extent that the arbitral tribunal has no power to act or is unable to act effectively，a request for interim measures of protection，or modification thereof as provided for，and in the manner indicated in, Article 4.17 (Power of Arbitral Tribunal to Order Interim Measures), may be made with the court.

(b) 在仲裁庭无权采取行动或不能采取有效行动的情况下,可向法院提出临时保护措施请求,或按照第4.17条(仲裁庭下令采取临时措施的权力)的规定和方式对其进行修改。

The rules on interim or provisional relief provided for in paragraph (c) of Article 4.17, of these Rules shall be observed. A party may bring a petition under this Article before the court in accordance with the Rules of Court or tre Special ADR Rules.

应遵守本规则第4.17条(c)款规定的临时或暂时之补救规则。一方当事人可以根据法院规则或替代性争议解决机制特别规则,根据本条向法院提起诉讼。

RULE 3 - Composition of Arbitral Tribunal
细则3——仲裁庭的组成

Article 4.10. Number of Arbitrators. The parties are free to determine the number of arbitrators. Failing such determination, the number of arbitrators shall be three (3).
第4.10条　仲裁员人数。当事各方可自由决定仲裁员人数。如果不能确定,仲裁员人数应为3名。

Article 4.11. Appointment of Arbitrators.
第4.11条　指定仲裁员。

(a) No person shall be precluded by reason of his/her nationality from acting as an arbitrator, unless otherwise agreed by the parties.

(a) 任何人不得因其国籍而不能担任仲裁员,除非当事人另有约定。

(b) The parties are free to agree on a procedure of appointing the arbitrator or arbitrators, subject to the provisions of paragraphs

(d) and (e) of this Article.

(b) 双方当事人可自由商定指定一名或多名仲裁员的程序,但须遵守本条(d)和(e)款的规定。

(c) Failing such agreement:

(c) 未达成此类协议:

> (i) in an arbitration with three (3) arbitrators, each party shall appoint one arbitrator, and the two (2) arbitrators thus appointed shall appoint the third arbitrator; if a party fails to appoint the arbitrator within thirty (30) days of receipt of a request to do so from the other party, or if the two(2) arbitrators fail to agree on the third arbitrator within thirty (30) days of their appointment, the appointment shall be made, upon request of a party, by the appointing authority;

> (i) 在三名仲裁员的仲裁中,每一方当事人应指定一名仲裁员,由此指定的两名仲裁员应指定第三名仲裁员;如果一方当事人未能在收到另一方当事人提出的 30 天内指定仲裁员,或两名仲裁员未能在指定后 30 天内就第三名仲裁员达成协议的,应指定机构根据一方当事人的请求进行指定;

> (ii) in an arbitration with a sole arbitrator, if the parties are unable to agree on the arbitrator, he/she shall be appointed, upon request of a party, by the appointing authority.

> (ii) 在独任仲裁员进行的仲裁中,如果双方当事人不能就仲裁员达成协议,应根据一方当事人的请求由指定机构指定。

(d) Where, under an appointment procedure agreed upon by the parties:

(d) 根据双方商定的指定程序:

> (i) a party fails to act as required under such procedure; or

> (i) 一方当事人未能按照这种程序的要求行事;或

> (ii) the parties, or two arbitrators, are unable to reach an agreement expected of them under such procedure; or

(ⅱ) 当事各方或两名仲裁员无法在这种程序下达成预期的协议；或

(ⅲ) a third party, including an institution, fails to perform any function entrusted to it under such procedure, any party may request the appointing authority to take the necessary measure to appoint an arbitrator, unless the agreement on the appointment procedure provides other means for securing the appointment.

(ⅲ) 第三方，包括机构在内的第三方未能履行此类程序赋予它的任何职能，任何一方当事人均可请求指定机构采取必要措施指定一名仲裁员，除非关于指定程序的协议提供了确保指定的其他手段。

(e) A decision on a matter entrusted by paragraphs (c) and (d) of this to the appointing authority shall be immediately executory and not be subject to a motion for reconsideration or appeal. The appointing authority shall have in appointing an arbitrator, due regard to any qualifications required of the arbitrator by the agreement of the parties and to such considerations as are likely to secure the appointment of an independent and impartial arbitrator and, in the case of a sole or third arbitrator, shall take into account as well the advisability of appointing an arbitrator of a nationality other than those of the parties.

(e) 关于(c)款和(d)款委托指定机构处理的事项的决定应立即执行，不受复议或上诉动议的影响。指定机构在指定仲裁员时，应适当考虑到各方当事人协议要求仲裁员具备的任何资格，以及可能确保指定独立和公正的仲裁员的各种考虑，对于独任或第三名仲裁员，还应考虑到指定一名非各方当事人国籍的仲裁员的可取性。

A party may bring a petition under this Article before the court in accordance with the Rules of Court or the Special ADR Rules.

一方当事人可根据法院规则或替代性争议解决机制特别规则，根据本条向法院提起诉讼。

Article 4.12. Grounds for Challenge.

第 4.12 条　提出质疑的理由。

(a) When a person is approached in connection with his/her possible appointment as an arbitrator，he/she shall disclose any circumstance likely to give rise to justifiable doubts as to his/her impartiality or independence. An arbitrator，from the time of his/her appointment and throughout the arbitral proceedings shall，without delay，disclose any such circumstance to the parties unless they have already been informed of them by him/her.

(a) 当一个人可能被任命为仲裁员时，他应披露任何可能引起对其公正性或独立性的合理怀疑的情况。仲裁员应自其被指定之时起并在整个仲裁程序中毫不拖延地向各方当事人披露任何此种情况，除非其已将此种情况通知各方当事人。

(b) An arbitrator may be challenged only if circumstances exist that give rise to justifiable doubts as to his/her impartiality or independence，or if he/she does not possess qualifications agreed to by the parties. A party may challenge an arbitrator appointed by him/her，or in whose appointment he/she has participated，only for reasons of which he/she becomes aware after the appointment has been made.

(b) 只有在存在对其公正性或独立性产生合理怀疑的情况下，或者如果仲裁员不具备当事各方同意的资格，才可对仲裁员提出质疑。一方当事人可以对其指定的仲裁员提出异议，或对其参与的指定仲裁员提出异议，但只能依据在指定后才知道的理由。

Article 4.13. Challenge Procedure.

第 4.13 条　质疑程序。

(a) The parties are free to agree on a procedure for challenging an arbitrator，subject to the provisions of this Article.

(a) 在不违反本条规定的情况下，当事各方可自由商定对仲裁员提出异议的程序。

（b） Failing such agreement，a party who intends to challenge an arbitrator shall，within fifteen（15）days after becoming aware of the constitution of the arbitral tribunal or after becoming aware of any circumstance referred to in paragraph（b）of Article 4.12（Grounds for Challenge），send a written statement of the reasons for the challenge to the arbitral tribunal. Unless the challenged arbitrator withdraws from his/her office or the other party agrees to the challenge，the arbitral tribunal shall decide on the challenge.

（b） 如果不能达成这样的协议，打算对仲裁员提出异议的一方当事人应在知悉仲裁庭的组成或知悉第 4.12 条（b）款中提及的任何情况后 15 天内，向仲裁庭提交一份书面陈述，说明提出异议的理由。除非被异议的仲裁员撤销其职务或另一方当事人同意该异议，仲裁庭应就该异议作出裁决。

（c） If a challenge under any procedure agreed upon by the parties or under the procedure of paragraph（b）of this Article is not successful，the challenging party may request the appointing authority，within thirty（30）days after having received notice of the decision rejecting the challenge，to decide on the challenge，which decision shall be immediately executory and not subject to motion for reconsideration or appeal. While such a request is pending，the arbitral tribunal，including the challenged arbitrator，may continue the arbitral proceedings and make an award.

（c） 如果根据当事各方商定的任何程序或根据本条（b）款的程序提出的异议未获成功，提出异议的一方当事人可在收到驳回异议的决定通知后 30 天内请求指定机构就该异议做出决定，该异议应立即执行，且不得提出复议或上诉。在此种请求待决期间，仲裁庭，包括被质疑的仲裁员，可继续进行仲裁程序并作出裁决。

A party may bring a petition under this Article before the court in accordance with the Rules of Court or the Special ADR Rules.

一方当事人可根据法院规则或替代性争议解决机制特别规则,根据本条向法院提起诉讼。

Article 4.14. Failure or Impossibility to Act.

第4.14条　未能或不可能履行职责。

(a) If an arbitrator becomes de jure or de facto unable to perform his/her functions or for other reasons fails to act without undue delay, his/her mandate terminates if he/she withdraws from his/her office or if the parties agree on the termination. Otherwise, if a controversy remains concerning any of these grounds, any party may request the appointing authority to decide on the termination of the mandate, which decision shall be immediately executory and not subject to motion for reconsideration or appeal.

(a) 如果仲裁员在法律上或事实上不能履行其职责,或由于其他原因不能及时采取行动,如果其辞去职务或当事方同意终止其职务,则其任期将终止。否则,如果对上述任何理由仍有争议,任何一方当事人均可请求指定机构就终止任务做出决定,该决定应立即执行,不得提出复议或提出上诉。

(b) If, under this Article or paragraph (b) of Article 4.13 (Challenge Procedure), an arbitrator withdraws from his/her office or a party agrees to the termination of the mandate of an arbitrator, this does not imply acceptance of the validity of any ground referred to in this Article or in paragraph (b) of Article 4.12 (Grounds for Challenge).

(b) 如果根据本条或第4.13条的(b)款,仲裁员撤回其职务或当事一方同意终止仲裁员的任期,这并不意味着接受本条或第4.12条的(b)款中提及的任何理由的有效性。

Article 4.15. Appointment of Substitute Arbitrator. Where the mandate of an arbitrator terminates under Articles 4.13（Challenge Procedure）and 4.14（Failure or Impossibility to Act）or because of his/her withdrawal from office for any other reason or because of the revocation of his/her mandate by agreement of the parties or in any other case of termination of his/her mandate，a substitute arbitrator shall be appointed according to the rules that were applicable to the appointment of the arbitrator being replaced.

第4.15条。指定替代仲裁员。如果仲裁员的授权根据第4.13条（质疑程序）和第4.14条（未能或不可能履行职责）或仲裁员因任何其他原因或其授权因当事各方同意而被撤销而终止，或在任何其他终止其授权的情况下，应根据适用于指定被替换仲裁员的规则指定替代仲裁员。

RULE 4 - Jurisdiction of Arbitral Tribunal
细则4——仲裁庭的管辖权

Article 4.16. Competence of Arbitral Tribunal to Rule on its Jurisdiction.

第4.16条　仲裁庭就其管辖权作出裁决的权限。

（a）The arbitral tribunal may rule on its own jurisdiction，including any objections with respect to the existence or validity of the arbitration agreement or any condition precedent to the filing of a request for arbitration. For that purpose，an arbitration clause，which forms part of a contract shall be treated as an agreement independent of the other terms of the contract. A decision by the arbitral tribunal that the contract is null and void shall not entail ipso jure the invalidity of the arbitration clause.

（a）仲裁庭可就其本身的管辖权作出裁决，包括就仲裁协议的存在或有效性提出任何异议，或就提出仲裁请求设定任何先决条件。为此目的，作为合同组成部分的仲裁条款应被视为独立于合同其他条款的协议。仲裁庭关于合同无效的裁决，并不必然导致仲裁条款的无效。

（b）A plea that the arbitral tribunal does not have jurisdiction shall be raised not later than the submission of the statement of defense（i.e., in an Answer or Motion to Dismiss）. A party is not precluded from raising such plea by the fact that he/she has appointed，or participated in the appointment of，an arbitrator.

（b）关于仲裁庭不具有管辖权的抗辩，应不迟于提交答辩书的时间，即答复或请求驳回。一方当事人已指定或参与指定一名仲裁员的事实并不妨碍其提出此种抗辩。

A plea that the arbitral tribunal is exceeding the scope of its authority shall be raised as soon as the matter alleged to be beyond the scope of its authority is raised during the arbitral proceedings. The arbitral tribunal may，in either case，admit a later plea if it considers the delay justified.

一经在仲裁程序中提出据称超出其权限的事项，即应提出关于仲裁庭正在超出其权限的抗辩。如果仲裁庭认为拖延是合理的，则在这两种情况下均可接受以后的抗辩。

（c）The arbitral tribunal may rule on a plea referred to in paragraph（b）of this Article either as a preliminary question or in an award on the merits. If the arbitral tribunal rules as a preliminary question that it has jurisdiction，any party may request，within thirty（30）days after having received notice of that ruling，the Regional Trial Court to decide the matter，which decision shall be immediately executory and not subject to motion for reconsideration or appeal. While such a request is pending，the arbitral tribunal may continue the arbitral proceedings and make an award.

（c）仲裁庭可就本条（b）款提及的抗辩作为初步问题或就案情实质作

出裁决。仲裁庭作为初步问题裁定其有管辖权的，任何一方当事人均可在收到该裁定通知后 30 天内请求区域审判法院裁定该事项，该裁定应立即执行，不得提出复议或上诉。在此种请求待决期间，仲裁庭可以继续进行仲裁程序并作出裁决。

Article 4. 17. Power of Arbitral Tribunal to Order Interim Measures.

第4.17条　仲裁庭下令采取临时措施的权力。

(a) Unless otherwise agreed by the parties, the arbitral tribunal may, at the request of a party, order any party to take such interim measures of protection as the arbitral tribunal may consider necessary in respect of the subject matter of the dispute following paragraph (c) of this Article. Such interim measures may include, but shall not be limited to, preliminary injunction directed against a party, appointment of receivers, or detention, preservation, inspection of property that is the subject of the dispute in arbitration.

(a) 除非各方当事人另有约定，仲裁庭可根据一方当事人的请求，命令任何一方当事人采取仲裁庭根据本条(c)款可能认为对争议标的必要的临时保全措施。这种临时措施可包括但不应限于针对当事一方的初步强制令、指定接管人，或对仲裁争议所涉财产进行扣留、保全、检查。

(b) After constitution of the arbitral tribunal, and during arbitral proceedings, a request for interim measures of protection, or modification thereof shall be made with the arbitral tribunal. The arbitral tribunal is deemed constituted when the sole arbitrator or the third arbitrator, who has been nominated, has accepted the nomination and written communication of said nomination and acceptance has been received by the party making the request.

(b) 在组成仲裁庭之后，以及在仲裁程序期间，应当向仲裁庭提出采取或修改临时保护措施的请求。如果提出请求的一方收到了独任仲裁员或第三名被提名的仲裁员接受该提名和接受的书面通知,即视为仲裁庭的组成。

(c) The following rules on interim or provisional relief shall be observed:

(c) 应遵守关于临时或暂时救济的下列规则:

(i) Any party may request that interim or provisional relief be granted against the adverse party.

(i) 任何一方均可请求对对方给予临时或暂时的救济。

(ii) Such relief may be granted:

(ii) 为以下目的可给予这种救济:

(aa) To prevent irreparable loss or injury;

(aa) 防止不可挽回的损失或伤害;

(bb) To provide security for the performance of an obligation;

(bb) 为履行义务提供担保;

(cc) To produce or preserve evidence; or

(cc) 提供或保存证据;或

(dd) To compel any other appropriate acts or omissions.

(dd) 迫使任何其他适当的作为或不作为。

(iii) The order granting provisional relief may be conditioned upon the provision of security or any act or omission specified in the order.

(iii) 给予临时救济的命令可以以提供该命令中规定的担保或任何作为或不作为为条件。

(iv) Interim or provisional relief is requested by written application transmitted by reasonable means to the arbitral tribunal and the party against whom relief is sought, describing in appropriate details of the precise relief, the party against whom the relief is

requested，the ground for the relief，and the
evidence supporting the request.

（iv）以合理方式向仲裁庭和寻求救济的当事人递交书
面申请,请求给予临时或暂时救济,并以适当细节
说明确切的救济、请求给予救济的当事人、救济理
由和支持请求的证据。

（v）The order either granting or denying an application
for interim relief shall be binding upon the parties.

（v）批准或拒绝临时救济申请的命令对双方当事人具有
约束力。

（vi）Either party may apply with the court for
assistance in implementing or enforcing an
interim measure ordered by an arbitral tribunal.

（vi）任何一方当事人均可向法院申请协助执行仲裁庭
下令采取的临时措施。

（vii）A party who does not comply with the order
shall be liable for all damages，resulting from
noncompliance，including all expenses，and
reasonable attorney's fees，paid in obtaining the
order's judicial enforcement.

（vii）不遵守命令的一方应负责赔偿因不遵守命令而造
成的一切损害,包括所有费用以及为获得命令的
司法执行而支付的合理律师费。

RULE 5 - Conduct of Arbitral Proceedings
细则 5——进行仲裁程序

Article 4. 18. Equal Treatment of Parties. The parties shall be
treated with equality and each party shall be given a full opportunity
of presenting his/her case.

第 4.18 条　平等对待当事人。应平等对待各方,各方应有充分机会陈述案情。

Article 4.19. Determination of Rules of Procedure.

第 4.19 条　确定议事规则。

(a) Subject to the provisions of this Chapter, the parties are free to agree on the procedure to be followed by the arbitral tribunal in conducting the proceedings.

(a) 在不违反本章规定的情况下,各方当事人可自由约定仲裁庭进行仲裁的程序。

(b) Failing such agreement, the arbitral tribunal may, subject to this Chapter, conduct the arbitration in such manner as it considers appropriate. Unless the arbitral tribunal considers it inappropriate, the UNCITRAL Arbitration Rules adopted by the UNCITRAL on 28 April 1976 and the UN General Assembly on 15 December 1976 shall apply subject to the following clarification: All references to the "Secretary-General of the Permanent Court of Arbitration at the Hague" shall be deemed to refer to the appointing authority.

(b) 在未达成此种协议的情况下,仲裁庭可在不违反本章规定的情况下,以其认为适当的方式进行仲裁。除非仲裁庭认为不适当,否则应适用由仲裁庭于 1976 年 4 月 28 日通过的仲裁规则和由联合国大会于 1976 年 12 月 15 日通过的仲裁规则,但须做出以下澄清:凡提及"海牙常设仲裁法院秘书长"的,均应视为指定机构。

(c) The power conferred upon the arbitral tribunal includes the power to determine the admissibility, relevance, materiality and weight of any evidence.

(c) 赋予仲裁庭的权力包括确定任何证据的可采性、相关性、实质性和重要性。

Article 4.20. Place of Arbitration.

第4.20条　仲裁地。

(a) The parties are free to agree on the place of arbitration. Failing such agreement, the place of arbitration shall be in Metro Manila unless the arbitral tribunal, having regard to the circumstances of the case, including the convenience, the parties, shall decide on a different place of arbitration.

(a) 当事人可以自由约定仲裁地。如果不能达成这种协议,仲裁地点应设在马尼拉市区,除非仲裁庭考虑到案件的情况,包括方便性,则当事人应当约定另一仲裁地。

(b) Notwithstanding the rule stated in paragraph (a) of this provision, the arbitral tribunal may, unless otherwise agreed by the parties, meet at any place it considers appropriate for consultation among its members, for hearing witnesses, experts or the parties, or for inspection of goods, other property or documents.

(b) 尽管本条(a)款规定了规则,仲裁庭仍可在其认为适当的任何地点开庭,以便在其成员之间进行协商,听取证人、鉴定人或当事人的意见,或检查货物、其他财产或文件。

Article 4.21. Commencement of Arbitral Proceedings. Unless otherwise agreed by the parties, the arbitral proceedings in respect of a particular dispute commence on the date on which a request for that dispute to be referred to arbitration is received by the respondent.

第4.21条　仲裁程序的启动。除非当事各方另有约定,关于某一特定争议的仲裁程序自被申请人收到将该争议提交仲裁的请求之日起开始。

Article 4.22. Language.

第 4.22 条 语言。

(a) The parties are free to agree on the language or languages to be used in the arbitral proceedings, Failing such agreement, the language to be used shall be English. This agreement, unless otherwise specified therein, shall apply to any written statement by a party, any hearing and any award, decision or other communication by the arbitral tribunal.

(a) 如果不能就仲裁程序中使用的一种或多种语言达成一致,则各方当事人可自由约定使用的语言应为英文。除另有规定外,本协议应适用于当事方的任何书面陈述、任何听讯以及仲裁庭的任何裁决、裁定或其他通信。

(b) The arbitral tribunal may order that any documentary evidence shall be accompanied by a translation into the language or languages agreed upon by the parties or determined by the arbitral tribunal in accordance with paragraph (a) of this Article.

(b) 仲裁庭可根据本条(a)款,命令将任何书面证据附有一份或多份翻译成各方当事人商定的或仲裁庭确定的一种或多种语言的译文。

Article 4.23. Statements of Claim and Defense.

第 4.23 条 索赔和答辩书。

(a) Within the period of time agreed by the parties or determined by the arbitral tribunal, the claimant shall state the facts supporting his/her/its claim, the points at issue and the relief or remedy sought, and the respondent shall state his/her/its defense in respect of these particulars, unless the parties have otherwise agreed as to the required elements of such statements. The parties may submit with their statements, all documents they consider to be relevant or may add a reference to the documents or other evidence they will submit.

（a）申请人应当在各方当事人约定或者仲裁庭确定的期限内，陈述支持其请求的事实、争议点、所寻求的救济，被申请人应当就这些细节陈述自己的答辩，除非各方当事人对这些陈述的必要内容另有约定。当事各方可将其认为相关的所有文件连同其陈述一并提交，或可在其将提交的文件或其他证据中添加一处出处。

（b）Unless otherwise agreed by the parties，either party may amend or supplement his/her claim or defense during the course of the arbitral proceedings，unless the arbitral tribunal considers it inappropriate to allow such amendment having regard to the delay in making it.

（b）除非各方当事人另有约定，任何一方当事人均可在仲裁程序进行过程中修改或补充其请求或答辩，除非仲裁庭认为考虑到延迟做出此种修改是不适当的。

Article 4.24 Hearing and Written Proceedings.

第4.24条　听证和书面诉讼。

（a）Subject to any contrary agreement by the parties，the arbitral tribunal shall decide whether to hold oral hearings for the presentation of evidence or for oral argument，or whether the proceedings shall be conducted on the basis of documents and other materials. However，unless the parties have agreed that no hearings shall be held，the arbitral tribunal shall hold such hearings at an appropriate stage of the proceedings，if so requested by a party.

（a）在当事各方达成任何相反协议的情况下，仲裁庭应决定是否为出示证据或进行口头辩论而举行口头听讯，或是否应根据文件和其他材料进行程序。但除非当事各方商定不举行听讯，仲裁庭应在程序的适当阶段，经当事一方请求，举行听讯。

（b）The parties shall be given sufficient advance notice of any hearing and of any meeting of the arbitral tribunal for the purposes of inspection of goods, other property or documents.

（b）为检查货物、其他财产或文件，应充分提前通知当事各方仲裁庭的任何听讯和任何会议。

（c）All statements, documents or other information supplied to the arbitral tribunal by one party shall be communicated to the other party. Also, an expert report or evidentiary document on which the arbitral tribunal may rely in making its decision shall be communicated to the parties.

（c）一方当事人向仲裁庭提供的所有陈述、文件或其他资料均应送交另一方当事人。此外，仲裁庭在做出决定时可依据的专家报告或证据文件应送交各方当事人。

Article 4.25. Default of a Party. Unless otherwise agreed by the parties, if, without showing sufficient cause,

第4.25条。一方违约。除非当事各方另有协议，如果没有充分理由，

（a）the claimant fails to communicate his statement of claim in accordance with paragraph（a）Article 4.23（Statement of Claim and Defense）, the arbitral tribunal shall terminate the proceedings;

（a）原告未能按照第4.23条（a）款（索赔和答辩书）提交其索赔书，仲裁庭应终止仲裁程序；

（b）the respondent fails to communicate his/her/its statement of defense in accordance with paragraph（a）Article 4.23（Statement of Claim and Defense）, the arbitral tribunal shall continue the proceedings without treating such failure in itself as an admission of the claimant's allegations;

（b）被告若未能做到第4.23条（a）款（索赔和答辩书），仲裁庭应继续进行仲裁程序，而不应将这种不作为本身视为承认申请人的指控；

（c）any party fails to appear at a hearing or to produce documentary evidence, the arbitral tribunal may continue the proceedings and make the award on the evidence before it.

(c) 任何一方当事人未出席听证或者未出示书面证据的,仲裁庭可以继续进行仲裁程序,并根据证据作出裁决。

Article 4. 26. Expert Appointed by the Arbitral Tribunal. Unless otherwise agreed by the parties, the arbitral tribunal,

第 4.26 条　仲裁庭指定的专家。除非当事人另有约定,仲裁庭,

(a) may appoint one or more experts to report to it on specific issues to be determined by the arbitral tribunal; or

(a) 可指定一名或多名专家就仲裁庭确定的具体问题向仲裁庭报告;或

(b) may require a party to give the expert any relevant information or to produce, or to provide access to, any relevant documents, goods or other property for his/her inspection.

(b) 可要求一方向专家提供任何相关信息,或提供或允许其查阅任何相关文件、货物或其他财产。

Unless otherwise agreed by the parties, if a party so requests or if the arbitral tribunal considers it necessary, the expert shall, after delivery of his/her written or oral report, participate in a hearing where the parties have the opportunity to put questions to him and to present expert witnesses in order to testify on the points at issue.

除非当事各方另有约定,如当事一方提出请求,或仲裁庭认为有必要,专家应在其做出书面或口头报告后,在当事各方有机会向其提出问题并提出专家证人以便就有关问题作证的情况下,参加听讯。

Article 4. 27. Court Assistance in Taking Evidence. The arbitral tribunal or a party with the approval of the arbitral tribunal may request from a court of the Philippines assistance in taking evidence. The court may execute the request within its competence and according to its rules on taking evidence. The arbitral tribunal shall have the power to require any person to attend a hearing as a witness. The arbitral tribunal shall have the power to subpoena witnesses and documents when the relevancy of the testimony and the materiality thereof has been demonstrated to it. The arbitral tribunal may also require the retirement of any witness during the testimony of any other witness. A party may bring a petition under this Section before the court in accordance with the Rules of Court or the Special ADR Rules.

第4.27条　法庭协助取证。经仲裁庭同意，仲裁庭或一方当事人可请求菲律宾法院协助取证。法院可在其权限范围内并根据其取证规则执行请求。仲裁庭有权要求任何人作为证人出席听讯。仲裁庭有权在证明证词的相关性及其实质性时传唤证人和文件。仲裁庭也可在任何其他证人作证期间要求任何证人退出。一方当事人可根据法院规则或替代性争议解决机制特别规则向法院提出本条规定的申诉。

Article 4.28. Rules Applicable to the Substance of Dispute.

第4.28条　适用于争议实质的规则。

(a) The arbitral tribunal shall decide the dispute in accordance with such rules of law as are chosen by the parties as applicable to the substance of the dispute. Any designation of the law or legal system of a given state shall be construed, unless otherwise expressed, as directly referring to the substantive law of that state and not to its conflict of laws rules.

(a) 仲裁庭应根据各方当事人选定的适用于争议实质内容的法律规则对争议作出裁决。除非另有表示，对某一特定国家法律或法律制度的任何指定，应解释为直接指该国的实体法，而不是该国的法律冲突规则。

(b) Failing any designation by the parties, the arbitral tribunal shall apply the law determined by the conflict of laws rules, which it considers applicable.

(b) 如果双方当事人未指定，仲裁庭应适用其认为适用的法律冲突规则所确定的法律。

(c) The arbitral tribunal shall decide ex aequo et bono or as amiable compositeur only if the parties have expressly authorized it to do so.

(c) 仲裁庭只有在当事方明确授权的情况下，才应根据公平公正或友好调解的原则作出裁决。

(d) In all cases, the arbitral tribunal shall decide in accordance with the terms of the contract and shall take into account the usages of the trade applicable to the transaction.

(d) 在所有情况下，仲裁庭应根据合同条款做出决定，并应考虑到适用于交易的行业惯例。

Article 4.29. Decision-Making by Panel of Arbitrators. In arbitral proceedings with more than one arbitrator, any decision of the arbitral tribunal shall be made, unless otherwise agreed by the parties, by a majority of all its members. However, questions of procedure may be decided by a presiding arbitrator, if so authorized by the parties or all members of the arbitral tribunal.

第4.29条。由仲裁员小组做出决定。在有一名以上仲裁员的仲裁程序中，仲裁庭的任何决定，除非各方当事人另有约定，应以仲裁庭全体仲裁员的过半数做出。但程序问题经当事各方或仲裁庭全体仲裁员授权，可由首席仲裁员作出裁决。

Article 4.30. Settlement. If, during arbitral proceedings, the parties settle the dispute, the arbitral tribunal shall terminate the proceedings and, if requested by the parties and not objected to by the arbitral tribunal, record the settlement in the form of an arbitral award on agreed terms. An award on agreed terms shall be made in accordance with the provisions of Article 4.31 (Form and Contents of Award), and shall state that it is an award. Such an award has the same status and effect as any other award on the merits of the case.

第4.30条。和解。如果在仲裁程序期间,当事各方解决了争议,仲裁庭应终止仲裁程序,并在当事各方提出请求且仲裁庭未表示反对的情况下,以商定条款的仲裁裁决形式记录和解。应根据第4.31条的规定(裁决的形式和内容)按商定条件作出裁决,并应说明其是裁决。这种裁决与关于案情的任何其他裁决具有同样的地位和效力。

Article 4.31. Form and Contents of Award.

第4.31条 裁决的形式和内容。

(a) The award shall be made in writing and shall be signed by the arbitrator or arbitrators. In arbitral proceedings with more than one arbitrator, the signatures of the majority of all members of the arbitral tribunal shall suffice, provided that the reason for any omitted signature is stated.

(a) 裁决应以书面作出,并应由仲裁员签署。在有一名以上仲裁员的仲裁程序中,只要说明任何省略签名的理由,仲裁庭全体成员的多数签名即可。

(b) The award shall state the reasons upon which it is based, unless the parties have agreed that no reasons are to be given or the award is an award on agreed terms under paragraph (a) of Article 4.20 (Place of Arbitration).

(b) 裁决应说明裁决所依据的理由,除非双方当事人同意不提出理由或裁决是根据第4.20条(a)款(仲裁地)商定的条件作出的。

(c) The award shall state its date and the place of arbitration as determined in accordance with paragraph (a) of this Article. The award shall be deemed to have been made at that place.

(c) 裁决应说明其日期和根据本条(a)款确定的仲裁地。裁决应视为在该地作出。

(d) After the award is made, a copy signed by the arbitrators in accordance with paragraph (a) of this Article shall be delivered to each party.

(d) 裁决作出后,由仲裁员根据本条(a)款签署的副本应送交各方当事人。

Article 4.32. Termination of Proceedings.

第4.32条　诉讼程序的终止。

(a) The arbitral proceedings are terminated by the final award or by an order of the arbitral tribunal in accordance with paragraph (b) of this Article.

(a) 根据本条第(b)款,仲裁程序由最后裁决或仲裁庭命令终止。

(b) The arbitral tribunal shall issue an order for the termination of the arbitral proceedings when:

(b) 在下列情况下,仲裁庭应发出终止仲裁程序的命令:

(i) The claimant withdraws his/her/its claim, unless the respondent objects thereto and the arbitral tribunal recognized a legitimate interest on his/her/its part in obtaining a final settlement of the dispute;

(i) 原告撤回其主张,除非被申请人对此表示反对,而且仲裁庭承认其在最后解决争议方面的合法权益;

(ii) The parties agree on the termination of the proceedings;

(ii) 当事各方同意终止诉讼程序;

(iii) The arbitral tribunal finds that the continuation of the procee-dings has for any other reason become unnecessary or impossible.

(iii) 仲裁庭认为,由于任何其他原因,程序的继续是没有必要或不可能的。

(c) The mandate of the arbitral tribunal ends with the termination of the arbitral proceedings, subject to the provisions of Articles 4.33 (Correction and Interpretation of Award, Additional

Award）and paragraph（d）of Article 4. 34（Application for Setting Aside an Exclusive Recourse against Arbitral Award）.

（c）仲裁庭的任务随着仲裁程序的终止而结束，但须遵守第 4.33 条（更正和解释裁决、补充裁决）和第 4.34 条（d）款（申请撤销对裁决的排他性追索）的规定。

（d）Notwithstanding the foregoing，the arbitral tribunal may，for special reasons，reserve in the final award or order，a hearing to quantify costs and determine which party shall bear the costs or the division thereof as may be determined to be equitable. Pending determination of this issue，the award shall not be deemed final for purposes of appeal，vacation，correction，or any post-award proceedings.

（d）尽管有上述规定，仲裁庭仍可出于特殊原因，在最后裁决或命令中保留一次听讯，以量化费用，并确定由哪一方承担费用或按确定的公平分摊费用。就上诉、休庭、更正或任何裁决后程序而言，裁决在裁定该问题之前，不应视为终局裁决。

Article 4.33. Correction and Interpretation of Award，Additional Award.

第 4.33 条　更正和解释裁决，补充裁决。

（a）Within thirty（30）days from receipt of the award，unless another period of time has been agreed upon by the parties：

（a）自收到裁决之日起 30 天内，除非当事各方商定另一段时间：

　（i）A party may，with notice to the other party，request the arbitral tribunal to correct in the award any errors in computation，any clerical or typographical errors or any errors of similar nature；

　（i）一方当事人可在通知另一方当事人后，请求仲裁庭更正裁决中的任何计算错误、任何文书或印刷错误或任何类似性质的错误；

　（ii）A party may，if so agreed by the parties and with notice to the other party，request the arbitral tribunal to give an interpretation of a specific point or part of the award.

（ii）一方当事人经双方当事人同意并通知另一方当事人后，可请求仲裁庭对裁决的某一具体内容或部分做出解释。

(b) If the arbitral tribunal considers the request to be justified，it shall make the correction or give the interpretation within thirty（30）days from receipt of the request. The interpretation shall form part of the award.

（b）仲裁庭认为该请求有正当理由的，应自收到请求之日起30天内做出更正或解释。解释应构成裁决的一部分。

(c) The arbitral tribunal may correct any error of the type referred to in paragraph（a）of this Article on its own initiative within thirty（30）days from the date of the award.

（c）仲裁庭可自裁决之日起30天内自行纠正本条（a）款所述的任何类型错误。

(d) Unless otherwise agreed by the parties，a party may，with notice to the other party，request，within thirty（30）days of receipt of the award，the arbitral tribunal to make an additional award as to claims presented in the arbitral procee-dings but omitted from the award. If the arbitral tribunal considers the request to be justified，it shall make the additional award within sixty（60）days.

（d）除非当事人另有约定，一方当事人可以在通知另一方当事人的情况下，请求仲裁庭在收到裁决后30天内就仲裁程序中提出但从裁决中删除的请求作出补充裁决。如果仲裁庭认为该请求有正当理由，则应在60天内作出补充裁决。

(e) The arbitral tribunal may extend，if necessary，the period of time within which it shall make a correction，interpretation or an additional award under paragraphs（a）and（b）of this Article.

（e）仲裁庭可在必要时延长其根据本条（a）款和（b）款做出更正、解释或作出补充裁决的期限。

(f) The provisions of Article 4.31 (Form and Contents of Award) shall apply to a correction or interpretation of the award or to an additional award.

(f) 第4.31条的规定(裁决的形式和内容)应适用于对裁决的更正或解释或补充裁决。

Article 4.34. Application for Setting Aside an Exclusive Recourse against Arbitral Award.

第4.34条　申请撤销对仲裁裁决的排他性追索权。

(a) Recourse to a court against an arbitral award may be made only by an application for setting aside in accordance with second and third paragraphs of this Article.

(a) 只有根据本条第(b)款和第(c)款提出撤销申请,才能将仲裁裁决诉诸法院。

(b) An arbitral award may be set aside by the Regional Trial Court only if:

(b) 只有在下列情况下,区域初审法院才可撤销仲裁裁决:

　(i) the party making the application furnishes proof that:

　(i) 提出申请的一方提供证据证明:

　　(aa) a party to the arbitration agreement was under some incapacity; or the said agreement is not valid under the law to which the parties have subjected it or, failing any indication thereon, under the law of the Philippines; or

　　(aa) 仲裁协议的一方当事人在某种程度上没有行为能力;或该协议根据双方当事人所适用的法律无效,或者,如果没有就此做出任何表示,根据菲律宾法律无效;或

　　(bb) the party making the application was not given proper notice of the appointment of an arbitrator or of the arbitral proceedings or was otherwise unable to present his case; or

(bb) 提出申请的一方当事人没有得到指定仲裁员或仲裁程序的适当通知，或无法陈述其理由；或

(cc) the award deals with a dispute not contemplated by or not falling within the terms of the submission to arbitration, or contains decisions on matters beyond the scope of the submission to arbitration, provided that, if the decisions on matters submitted to arbitration can be separated from those not so submitted, only the part of the award which contains decisions on matters not submitted to arbitration may be set aside; or

(cc) 裁决涉及提交仲裁的条款中没有考虑到或不属于其范围的争议，或载有关于超出提交仲裁范围的事项的决定，但条件是，关于提交仲裁的事项的决定可以与未提交仲裁的事项的决定分开，裁决中载有关于未提交仲裁的事项的决定的部分可以搁置；或

(dd) the composition of the arbitral tribunal or the arbitral procedure was not in accordance with the agreement of the parties, unless such agreement was in conflict with a provision of ADR Act from which the parties cannot derogate, or, failing such agreement, was not in accordance with ADR Act; or

(dd) 仲裁庭或仲裁程序的组成不符合当事各方的协议，除非此种协议与当事各方不能减损的《替代性争议解决法案》的规定相冲突，或者，如果没有此种协议，则不符合《替代性争议解决法案》；或

(ii) the Court finds that:

(ii) 法院认为：

(aa) the subject-matter of the dispute is not capable of settlement by arbitration under the law of the Philippines; or

(aa) 争议标的不能根据菲律宾法律通过仲裁解决;或

(bb) the award is in conflict with the public policy of the Philippines.

(bb) 该裁决与菲律宾的公共政策相冲突。

(c) An application for setting aside may not be made after three months have elapsed from the date on which the party making that application had received the award or, if a request had been made under Article 4.33 (Correction and Interpretation of Award, Additional Award) from the date on which that request has been disposed of by the Arbitral Tribunal.

(c) 提出申请的一方当事人收到裁决之日起 3 个月后不得提出撤销申请,如果根据第 4.33 条(更正和解释裁决、补充裁决)提出请求,则从仲裁庭处理该请求之日起不得提出附加裁决。

(d) The court, when asked to set aside an award, may, where appropriate and so requested by a party, suspend the setting aside proceedings for a period of time determined by it in order to give the arbitral tribunal an opportunity to resume the arbitral proceedings or to take such other action as in the arbitral tribunal's opinion will eliminate the grounds for setting aside.

(d) 法院在被要求撤销裁决时,可酌情并应一方当事人的请求,在其确定的期限内暂停撤销程序,以便使仲裁庭有机会恢复仲裁程序或采取仲裁庭意见中所述的其他行动,从而消除撤销的理由。

(e) A party may bring a petition under this Article before the court in accordance with the Special ADR Rules.

(e) 一方当事人可以根据替代性争议解决机制特别规则,根据本条款向法院提起诉讼。

RULE 6 - Recognition and Enforcement of Awards
细则 6——裁决的承认和执行

Article 4.35. Recognition and Enforcement.

第 4.35 条　承认和执行。

(a) A foreign arbitral award shall be recognized as binding and，upon petition in writing to the Regional Trial Court，shall be enforced subject to the provisions of this Article and of Article 4.36(Grounds for Refusing Recognition or Enforcement).

(a) 外国仲裁裁决应被承认具有约束力,在向区域初审法院提出书面请求后,应根据本条和第 4.36 条(拒绝承认或执行的理由)予以执行。

(b) The petition for recognition and enforcement of such arbitral awards shall be filed with the Regional Trial Court in accordance with the Special ADR Rules.

(b) 要求承认和执行此类仲裁裁决的请求,应根据替代性争议解决机制特别规则向区域初审法院提出。

(i) Convention Award-The New York Convention shall govern the recognition and enforcement of arbitral awards covered by said Convention.

(i) 公约裁决——《纽约公约》将管辖该公约所涵盖的仲裁裁决的承认和执行。

The petitioner shall establish that the country in which the foreign arbitration award was made is a party to the New York Convention.

申请人应当证明,作出外国仲裁裁决的国家是纽约公约的一方。

(ii) Non-Convention Award-The recognition and enforcement of foreign arbitral awards not covered by the New York Convention shall be done in accordance with procedural rules to be promulgated by the Supreme Court. The court may, on grounds of comity and reciprocity, recognize and enforce a non-convention award as a convention award.

（ii）非公约裁决——承认和执行未列入《纽约公约》的外国仲裁裁决，应根据最高法院颁布的程序规则进行。法院可基于礼让和互惠的理由，承认和执行非公约裁决作为公约裁决。

（c）The party relying on an award or applying for its enforcement shall file with the Regional Trial Court the original or duly authenticated copy of the award and the original arbitration agreement or a duly authenticated copy thereof. If the award or agreement is not made in an official language of the Philippines, the party shall supply a duly certified translation thereof into such language.

（c）依赖裁决或申请执行裁决的一方当事人，应当向区域审判法院提交裁决正本或经正式认证的裁决书副本以及仲裁协议正本或经正式认证的仲裁协议副本。如果裁决或协议并非以菲律宾的一种正式语言作出，该当事方应提供经正式核证的该语言的译文。

（d）A foreign arbitral award when confirmed by a court of a foreign country, shall be recognized and enforced as a foreign arbitral award and not as a judgment of a foreign court.

（d）外国仲裁裁决，经外国法院确认后，应承认并执行为外国仲裁裁决，而不是外国法院的判决。

（e）A foreign arbitral award when confirmed by the Regional Trial Court, shall be enforced in the same manner as final and executory decisions of courts of law of the Philippines.

（e）经区域初审法院确认的外国仲裁裁决，其执行方式应与菲律宾各国法院的最终执行裁决相同。

（f）If the Regional Trial Court has recognized the arbitral award but an application for （rejection and/or） suspension of enforcement of that award is subsequently made, the Regional Trial Court may, if it considers the application to be proper, vacate or suspend the decision to enforce that award and may also, on the application of the party claiming recognition or enforcement of that award, order the other party seeking rejection or suspension to provide appropriate security.

(f) 如果区域初审法院承认该仲裁裁决,但随后提出了执行该裁决的(拒绝和/或)中止的申请,区域初审法院如果认为该申请是适当的,可以撤销或中止执行该裁决的决定,也可以根据要求承认或执行该裁决的当事人的申请撤销或中止该裁决,命令寻求拒绝或中止的另一方提供适当的担保。

Article 4.36. Grounds for Refusing Recognition or Enforcement.
第4.36条 拒绝承认或执行的理由。

A. CONVENTION AWARD.
A. 公约裁决。

Recognition or enforcement of an arbitral award, made in a state, which is a party to the New York Convention, may be refused, at the request of the party against whom it is invoked, only if the party furnishes to the Regional Trial Court proof that:
在作为《纽约公约》当事方的一国作出的仲裁裁决的承认或执行,只有在该当事方向区域初审法院提供以下证据的情况下,才可应请求拒绝:

(a) The parties to the arbitration agreement were, under the law applicable to them, under some incapacity; or the said agreement is not valid under the law to which the parties have subjected it or, failing any indication thereon, under the law of the country where the award was made; or

(a) 根据对其适用的法律,仲裁协议的当事人在某种程度上是丧失行为能力的;或者根据当事各方所适用的法律,或者,如果没有就此进行任何指明,根据裁决地所在国的法律,该协议无效;或

(b) the party against whom the award is invoked was not given proper notice of the appointment of an arbitrator or of the arbitral proceedings or was otherwise unable to present his case; or

（b）未适当通知被援引裁决所针对的一方指定仲裁员或仲裁程序，或未能以其他方式陈述其理由；或

（c）the award deals with a dispute not contemplated by or not falling within the terms of the submission to arbitration，or it contains decisions on matters beyond the scope of the submission to arbitration，provided that，if the decisions on matters submitted to arbitration can be separated from those not so submitted，that part of the award which contains decisions on matters submitted to arbitration may be recognized and enforced; or

（c）裁决涉及提交仲裁的条款中没有考虑到或不属于其范围的争议，或者裁决中包含对超出提交仲裁范围的事项的决定，但条件是，如果提交仲裁的事项的决定可以与未提交的事项分开，则裁决中包含提交仲裁的事项的决定的部分可以得到承认和执行；或

（d）the composition of the arbitral tribunal or the arbitral procedure was not in accordance with the agreement of the parties or，failing such agreement，was not in accordance with the law of the country where the arbitration took place; or

（d）仲裁庭或仲裁程序的组成不符合当事各方的协议，或者，如果未能达成此种协议，则不符合仲裁发生地所在国的法律；或

（e）the award has not yet become binding on the parties or has been set aside or suspended by a court of the country in which，or under the law of which，that award was made.

（e）裁决尚未对当事各方具有约束力，或已被裁决地所在国或裁决地所在国的法院撤销或中止。

Recognition and enforcement of an arbitral award may also be refused if the Regional Trial Court where recognition and enforcement is sought finds that:

如果寻求承认和执行的区域审判法院认为存在下列情况,也可拒绝仲裁裁决的承认和执行:

(a) the subject-matter of the dispute is not capable of settlement by arbitration under the law of the Philippines; or

(a) 争端的事由不能根据菲律宾法律通过仲裁解决;或

(b) the recognition or enforcement of the award would be contrary to the public policy of the Philippines. A party to a foreign arbitration proceeding may oppose an application for recognition and enforcement of the arbitral award in accordance with the Special ADR Rules only on the grounds enumerated under paragraphs (a) and (c) of Article 4. 35 (Recognition and Enforcement). Any other ground raised shall be disregarded by the Regional Trial Court.

(b) 承认或执行裁决将违反菲律宾的公共政策。外国仲裁程序的一方当事人只有在根据第 4.35 条(a)款和(b)款(承认和执行)列举的理由的情况下,才可以根据替代性争议解决机制特别规则反对承认和执行仲裁裁决的申请。提出的任何其他理由应被区域审判法院无视。

B. NON-CONVENTION AWARD.

B. 非公约裁决。

(a) A foreign arbitral award rendered in a state which is not a party to the New York Convention will be recognized upon proof of the existence of comity and reciprocity and may be treated as a convention award. If not so treated and if no comity or reciprocity exists, the non-convention award cannot be recognized and/or enforced but may be deemed as presumptive evidence of a right as between the parties in accordance with Section 48 of Rule 39 of the Rules of Court.

(a) 在非《纽约公约》当事方的国家作出的外国仲裁裁决,在证明存在礼让和互惠的情况下将得到承认，并可作为公约裁决处理。如果未予如此处理，且不存在礼让或互惠，则不能承认和执行非公约裁决，但可根据《法院规则》第 39 条第 48 款将其视为当事人之间权利的推定证据。

（b）If the Regional Trial Court has recognized the arbitral award but a petition for suspension of enforcement of that award is subsequently made，the Regional Trial Court may，if it considers the petition to be proper，suspend the proceedings to enforce the award，and may also，on the application of the party claiming recognition or enforcement of that award，order the other party seeking suspension to provide appropriate security.

（b）如果区域审判法院承认仲裁裁决，但随后提出了中止执行该裁决的请求，区域审判法院如果认为该请求是适当的，可以中止执行该裁决的程序，还可以根据要求承认或执行该裁决的当事人的申请，命令寻求中止的另一方当事人提供适当的担保。

（c）If the petition for recognition or enforcement of the arbitral award is filed by a party and a counter-petition for the rejection of the arbitral award is filed by the other party，the Regional Trial Court may，if it considers the counter-petition to be proper but the objections thereto may be rectified or cured，remit the award to the arbitral tribunal for appropriate action and in the meantime suspend the recognition and enforcement proceedings and may also on the application of the petitioner order the counter-petitioner to provide appropriate security.

（c）如果一方当事人提出承认或执行仲裁裁决的请求，而另一方当事人提出驳回仲裁裁决的反请求，区域审判法院可以认为反请求是适当的，但反对意见可以纠正，将裁决发回仲裁庭采取适当行动，同时暂停承认和执行程序，还可根据申请人的申请命令反诉申请人提供适当担保。

Article 4. 37. Appeal from Court Decision on Arbitral Awards. A decision of the Regional Trial Court recognizing, enforcing, vacating or setting aside an arbitral award may be appealed to the Court of Appeals in accordance with the rules of procedure to be promulgated by the Supreme Court.

第 4.37 条　对法院仲裁裁决决定的上诉。区域审判法院承认、执行、撤销或撤销仲裁裁决的裁决，可根据最高法院颁布的程序规则向上诉法院提出上诉。

The losing party who appeals from the judgment of the court recognizing and enforcing an arbitral award shall be required by the Court of Appeals to post a counter-bond executed in favor of the prevailing party equal to the amount of the award in accordance with the Special ADR Rules.

对承认和执行仲裁裁决的法院判决提出上诉的败诉一方，上诉法院应要求其交付已执行的、对胜诉一方有利的反保证书，该反保证书金额应与根据替代性争议解决机制特别规则作出的裁决之金额相等。

Any stipulation by the parties that the arbitral tribunal's award or decision shall be final, and therefore not appealable, is valid. Such stipulation carries with it a waiver of the right to appeal from an arbitral award but without prejudice to judicial review by way of certiorari under Rule 65 of the Rules of Court.

当事各方关于仲裁庭的裁决或决定应为最终裁决因而不可上诉的任何规定均有效。这种规定意味着放弃对仲裁裁决提出上诉的权利，但不影响《法院规则》第 65 条规定的以调取案件的方式进行司法审查。

Article 4. 38. Venue and Jurisdiction. Proceedings for recognition and enforcement of an arbitration agreement or for vacation or setting aside of an arbitral award, and any application with a court for arbitration assistance and supervision, except appeal, shall be deemed as special proceedings and shall be filed with the Regional Trial Court where:

第4.38条　地点和管辖权。关于承认和执行仲裁协议、中止或撤销仲裁裁决的程序，以及向法院提出的任何仲裁协助和监督申请，除上诉外，应视为特别程序，并应提交以下地区的区域审判法院：

(a) the arbitration proceedings are conducted;

(a) 进行仲裁程序的地点；

(b) where the asset to be attached or levied upon, or the act to be enjoined is located;

(b) 被扣押或征税的资产或被禁止的行为所在地；

(c) where any of the parties to the dispute resides or has its place of business; or

(c) 争议任何一方当事人居住或拥有其营业地；或

(d) in the National Capital Judicial Region at the option of the applicant.

(d) 在国家首都司法区域可供申请人选择的区域审判法院。

Article 4.39. Notice of Proceedings to Parties. In a special proceeding for recognition and enforcement of an arbitral award, the court shall send notice to the parties at their address of record in the arbitration, or if any party cannot be served notice at such address, at such party's last known address. The notice shall be sent at least fifteen (15) days before the date set for the initial hearing of the application.

第4.39条　向当事人发出诉讼通知。在关于承认和执行仲裁裁决的特别程序中，法院应向各方当事人按仲裁记录中的地址发出通知，或者如果任何一方当事人不能在该地址收到通知的，则按该当事人最后为人所知的地址向其发出通知。通知须在首次聆讯日期前最少15天发出。

Article 4. 40. Legal Representation in International Commercial Arbitration. In international commercial arbitration conducted in the Philippines, a party may be represented by any person of his/her/its choice: Provided, that such representative, unless admitted to the practice of law in the Philippines, shall not be authorized to appear as counsel in any Philippine court or any other quasi-judicial body whether or not such appearance is in relation to the arbitration in which he/she appears.

第 4.40 条　国际商事仲裁中的法定代表人。在菲律宾进行的国际商事仲裁中,一方当事人可以由其选择的任何人作为其代表:条件是,该代表除非被允许在菲律宾执业,否则不得获准在任何菲律宾法院或任何其他准司法机构作为律师出庭,无论该出庭是否与其所参加的仲裁有关。

Article 4. 41. Confidentiality of Arbitration Proceedings. The arbitration proceedings, including the records, evidence and the arbitral award, shall be considered confidential and shall not be published except:

第 4.41 条　仲裁程序的机密性。仲裁程序,包括记录、证据和仲裁裁决,应视为机密,除下列情况外不得公布:

(a) with the consent of the parties; or

(a) 经当事人同意;或

(b) for the limited purpose of disclosing to the court relevant documents in cases where resort to the court is allowed herein. Provided, however, that the court in which the action or the appeal is pending may issue a protective order to prevent or prohibit disclosure of documents or information containing secret processes, developments, research and other information where it is shown that the applicant shall be materially prejudiced by an authorized disclosure thereof.

（b）在允许诉诸法院的案件中，为了向法院披露相关文件的有限目的。但如果经授权披露载有秘密程序、事态发展、研究和其他资料的文件或资料，证明申请者会受到实质损害，则诉讼或上诉待决的法院可发出保护令，防止或禁止披露这些文件或资料。

Article 4.42. Summary Nature of Proceedings before the Court. A petition for recognition and enforcement of awards brought before the court shall be heard and dealt with summarily in accordance with the Special ADR Rules.

第4.42条　法庭诉讼的简易性质。对向法院提出的承认和执行裁决的申请，应当按照替代性争议解决机制特别规则进行审理和即决处理。

Article 4.43. Death of a Party. Where a party dies after making a submission or a contract to arbitrate as prescribed in these Rules, the proceeding maybe begun or continued upon the application of, or notice to, his/her executor or administrator, or temporary administrator of his/her estate. In any such case, the court may issue an order extending the time within which notice of a motion to recognize or vacate an award must be served. Upon recognizing an award, where a party has died since it was filed or delivered, the court must enter judgment in the name of the original party; and the proceedings thereupon are the same as where a party dies after a verdict.

第4.43条　一方当事人死亡。当事人按照本规则规定提交仲裁文件或者订立仲裁合同后死亡的，可以在其遗嘱执行人、管理人或者财产临时管理人提出申请或者通知后开始或者继续进行仲裁。在任何这类情况下，法院可以发出命令，延长必须送达承认或撤销裁决的通知的时间。在承认裁决时，如果一方当事人自提交或交付裁决后死亡，法院必须以原始当事人的名义作出判决；而由此产生的诉讼程序与一方当事人在裁决后死亡的诉讼程序相同。

Article 4. 44. Multi-Party Arbitration. When a single arbitration involves more than two parties, the foregoing rules, to the extent possible, shall be used, subject to such modifications consistent with this Chapter as the arbitral tribunal shall deem appropriate to address possible complexities of a multi-party arbitration.

第 4.44 条　多方仲裁。一项仲裁涉及两个以上当事方的,应尽可能使用上述规则,但仲裁庭应根据本章做出其认为适当的修改,以处理多方当事人仲裁可能存在的复杂性。

Article 4. 45. Consolidation of Proceedings and Concurrent Hearings.

第 4.45 条　合并诉讼程序和同时举行听讯。

The parties and the arbitral tribunal may agree-

当事各方和仲裁庭可协议:

(a) that the arbitration proceedings shall be consolidated with other arbitration proceedings; or

(a) 将仲裁程序与其他仲裁程序合并;或

(b) that concurrent hearings shall be held, on such terms as may be agreed. Unless the parties agree to confer such power on the arbitral tribunal, the tribunal has no power to order consolidation of arbitration proceedings or concurrent hearings.

(b) 同时举行听讯,条件由双方商定。除非当事各方同意赋予仲裁庭这种权力,否则仲裁庭无权下令合并仲裁程序或同时进行审理。

Article 4.46. Costs.

第 4.46 条　费用。

(a) The arbitral tribunal shall fix the costs of arbitration in its award. The term "costs" include only:

(a) 仲裁庭应在其裁决中确定仲裁费用。"费用"一词仅包括:

（i）The fees of the arbitral tribunal to be stated separately as to each arbitrator and to be fixed by the tribunal itself in accordance with the paragraph（b）of this Article；

（i）仲裁庭给每一名仲裁员的费用，由仲裁庭根据本条(b)款自行确定；

（ii）The travel and other expenses incurred by the arbitrators；

（ii）仲裁员的旅费和其他费用；

（iii）The costs of expert advice and of other assistance required by the arbitral tribunal；

（iii）仲裁庭要求的专家咨询和其他协助的费用；

（iv）The travel and other expenses of witnesses to the extent such expenses are approved by the arbitral tribunal；

（iv）证人的旅费和其他费用，但以仲裁庭核准的数额为限；

（v）The costs for legal representation and assistance of the successful party if such costs were claimed during the arbitral proceedings，and only to the extent that the arbitral tribunal determines that the amount of such costs is reasonable；

（v）如果在仲裁程序期间提出法律代理和援助要求，则包括胜诉方的法律代理和援助费用，但仅限于仲裁庭确定此类费用的合理数额；

（vi）Any fees and expenses of the appointing authority.

（vi）指定机构的任何费用和开支。

（b）The fees of the arbitral tribunal shall be reasonable in amount，taking into account the amount in dispute，the complexity of the subject matter，the time spent by the arbitrators and any other relevant circumstances of the case.

（b）考虑到争议金额、标的复杂性、仲裁员花费的时间和案件的任何其他相关情况，仲裁庭的收费应当合理。

（c）If an appointing authority has been agreed upon by the parties and if such authority has issued a schedule of fees for arbitrators in international cases which it administers，the arbitral tribunal in fixing its fees shall take that schedule of fees into account to the extent that it considers appropriate in the circumstances of the case.

（c）如果指定机构已由各方当事人约定，且该指定机构已就其管理的国际案件发出仲裁员收费表，仲裁庭在确定其收费时，应在其认为适合该案件情形的范围内考虑到该收费表。

（d）If such appointing authority has not issued a schedule of fees for arbitrators in international cases，any party may，at any time request the appointing authority to furnish a statement setting forth the basis for establishing fees which is customarily followed in international cases in which the authority appoints arbitrators. If the appointing authority consents to provide such a statement，the arbitral tribunal，in fixing its fees，shall take such information into account to the extent that it considers appropriate in the circumstances of the case.

（d）该指定机构未发布国际案件仲裁员收费表的，任何一方当事人均可随时要求指定机构提供说明，说明在该机构指定仲裁员的国际案件中通常遵循的确定收费的依据。指定机构同意提供此种陈述的，仲裁庭在确定收费时，应当在其认为适合该案件情形的范围内考虑到这种信息。

（e）In cases referred to in the second and third sub-paragraphs of paragraph of this Article，when a party so requests and the appointing authority consents to perform the function，the arbitral tribunal shall fix its fees only after consultation with the appointing authority which may make any comment it deems appropriate to the arbitral tribunal concerning the fees.

（e）在本款第二项和第三项提到的情况下，如果当事一方提出请求并经指定机构同意履行该职能，仲裁庭只有在与指定机构协商后才确定其收费，指定机构可就收费问题向仲裁庭提出其认为适当的任何意见。

(f) Except as provided in the next sub-paragraph of this paragraph, the costs of arbitration shall, in principle, be borne by the unsuccessful party. However, the arbitral tribunal may apportion each of such costs between the parties if it determines that apportionment is reasonable, taking into account the circumstances of the case.

(f) 除本款下一项另有规定外,仲裁费用原则上应由败诉一方承担。但仲裁庭可根据案情,在其认定分摊合理的情况下,在各当事方之间分摊其中的每一项费用。

(g) With respect to the costs of legal representation and assistance referred to in paragraph (c) of paragraph (a)(iii) of this Article, the arbitral tribunal, taking into account the circumstances of the case, shall be free to determine which party shall bear such costs or may apportion such costs between the parties if it determines that appointment is reasonable.

(g) 关于本条(a)款(iii)项和(c)款提及的法律代理和协助的费用,仲裁庭应可自由确定应由哪一方承担此类费用,或在其认定指定合理的情况下可在各方当事人之间分摊此费用。

(h) When the arbitral tribunal issues an order for the termination of the arbitral proceedings or makes an award on agreed terms, it shall fix the costs of arbitration referred to in paragraphs (b), (c) and (d) of this Article in the context of that order or award.

(h) 仲裁庭下达终止仲裁程序的命令或根据商定的条件作出裁决时,仲裁庭应根据该命令或裁决确定本条(b)款、(c)款和(d)款提及的仲裁费用。

(i) The arbitral tribunal, on its establishment, may request each party to deposit an equal amount as an advance for the costs referred to in paragraphs (i), (ii) and (iii) of paragraph (a) of this Article.

(i) 仲裁庭在设立时,可要求每一方当事人交存一笔相等数额的款项,作为本条(a)款(i)(ii)(iii)项中提及的费用。

(j) During the course of the arbitral proceedings，the arbitral tribunal may request supplementary deposits from the parties.

(j) 在仲裁程序进行期间,仲裁庭可以要求各方当事人提供补充存款。

(k) If an appointing authority has been agreed upon by the parties and when a party so requests and the appointing authority consents to perform the function，the arbitral tribunal shall fix the amounts of any deposits or supplementary deposits only after consultation with the appointing authority which may make any comments to the arbitral tribunal which it deems appropriate concerning the amount of such deposits and supplementary deposits.

(k) 如果指定机构已得到各方当事人的约定,并且一方当事人提出请求并经指定机构同意履行该职能,仲裁庭只有在与指定机构协商后才可确定任何存款或补充存款的数额,指定机构可就此种存款和补充存款的数额向仲裁庭提出其认为适当的任何意见。

(l) If the required deposits are not paid in full within thirty（30）days after receipt of the request，the arbitral tribunal shall so inform the parties in order that the required payment may be made. If such payment is not made，the arbitral tribunal may order the suspension or termination of the arbitral proceedings.

(l) 如果在收到请求后30天内未全额支付所要求的押金,仲裁庭应将此通知各方当事人,以便支付所要求的款项。未支付此种款项的,仲裁庭可以下令中止或终止仲裁程序。

(m) After the award has been made，the arbitral tribunal shall render an accounting to the parties of the deposits received and return any unexpended balance to the parties.

(m) 在作出裁决后,仲裁庭应向各方当事人说明所收到的存款,并将任何未用余额退还各方当事人。

CHAPTER 5
DOMESTIC ARBITRATION
第五章 国内仲裁

RULE 1 - General Provisions
细则 1——总则

Article 5.1. Scope of Application.

第5.1条 适用范围。

(a) Domestic arbitration, which is not international as defined in paragraph C'8 of Article 1.6 shall continue to be governed by Republic Act No. 876, otherwise known as "The Arbitration Law", as amended by the ADR Act. Articles 8, 10, 11, 12, 13, 14, 18 and 19 and 29 to 32 of the Model Law and Sections 22 to 31 of the ADR Act are specifically applicable to domestic arbitration.

(a) 不属于第1.6条第C8款定义的国际仲裁,应继续受第876号共和国法(又称《仲裁法》)管辖,该法经《替代性争议解决法案》修正。《示范法》第8条、第10条、第11条、第12条、第13条、第14条、第18条、第19条和第29条至第32条以及《替代性争议解决法案》第22条至第31条特别适用于国内仲裁。

In the absence of a specific applicable provision, all other rules applicable to international commercial arbitration may be applied in a suppletory manner to domestic arbitration.

在没有具体适用规定的情况下,适用于国际商事仲裁的所有其他规则可以补充方式适用于国内仲裁。

(b) This Chapter shall apply to domestic arbitration whether the dispute is commercial, as defined in Section 21 of the ADR Act, or non-commercial, by an arbitrator who is a private individual appointed by the parties to hear and resolve their dispute by rendering an award; Provided that, although a construction dispute may be commercial, it shall continue to be governed by E. O. NO. 1 008, s. 1985 and the rules promulgated by the Construction Industry Arbitration Commission.

(b) 本章应适用于国内仲裁,无论该争议是《替代性争议解决法案》第21条所界定的商业争议,还是由当事各方指定的通过作出裁决来审理和解决其争议的私人仲裁员进行的非商业争议;但尽管建筑争议可能是商业争议,仍应继续受 E. O. 1008 号文件,以及建筑行业仲裁委员会颁布的规则的管辖。

(c) Two or more persons or parties may submit to arbitration by one or more arbitrators any controversy existing between them at the time of the submission and which may be the subject of an action; or the parties to any contract may in such contract agree to settle by arbitration a controversy thereafter arising between them. Such submission or contract shall be valid, enforceable and irrevocable, save upon such grounds as exist at law for the revocation of any contract.

(c) 两个或两个以上的人或当事人可以将提交材料时他们之间存在的任何争议提交一名或多名仲裁员仲裁,这些争议可能是诉讼的标的;或者任何合同的当事人可以在该合同中同意通过仲裁解决他们之间随后产生的争议。除非根据法律上存在的撤销任何合同的理由,此类提交或合同应有效、可强制执行且不可撤销。

Such submission or contract may include questions arising out of valuations, appraisals or other controversies which may be collateral, incidental, precedent or subsequent to any dispute between the parties.

这种提交或合同可能包括因估价或其他争议而产生的问题,这些问题可能是附带的、先例的或在当事方之间发生任何争端之后产生的。

A controversy cannot be arbitrated where one of the parties to the controversy is an infant, or a person judicially declared to be incompetent, unless the appropriate court having jurisdiction approved a petition for permission to submit such controversy to arbitration made by the general guardian or guardian ad litem of the infant or of the incompetent.

如果争议的一方当事人是婴儿,或被司法宣布为无行为能力的人,则不能对争议进行仲裁,除非具有管辖权的适当法院批准由婴儿或无行为能力人的总监护人或诉讼监护人提出的允许将此类争议提交仲裁的申请。

But where a person capable of entering into a submission or contract has knowingly entered into the same with a person incapable of so doing, the objection on the ground of incapacity can be taken only in behalf of the person so incapacitated.

但是,如果一个能够订立提交书或合同的人在知情的情况下与一个不能这样做的人订立了同样的文书,则以无行为能力为由提出的反对只能由代表无行为能力的人提出。

Article 5.2. Delivery and Receipt of Written Communications.

第5.2条　发送和接收书面通信。

(a) Except as otherwise agreed by the parties, a written communication from one party to the other or to the arbitrator or to an arbitration institution or from the arbitrator or arbitration institution to the parties shall be delivered to the addressee personally, by registered mail or by courier service. Such communication shall be deemed to have been received on the date it is delivered at the addressee's address of record, place of business, residence or last known address. The communication, as appropriate, shall be delivered to each party to the arbitration and to each arbitrator, and, in institutional arbitration, one copy to the administering institution.

(a) 除当事人另有约定外,一方与另一方或与仲裁员或仲裁机构或与仲裁员或仲裁机构或与仲裁员或仲裁机构的书面通信,应以挂号邮件或信使方式,送交收件人本人。该通知于送达收件人的记录地址、营业地点、住所或最后为人所知的地址之日被视为已收到。应酌情将来文送交仲裁各方和各仲裁员,在机构仲裁中,应向管理机构送交一份副本。

(b) During the arbitration proceedings, the arbitrator may order a mode of delivery and a rule for receipt of written communications different from that provided in paragraph (a) of this Article.

(b) 在仲裁程序期间,仲裁员可命令采用与本条(a)款规定不同的交付方式和接收书面通信的规则。

(c) If a party is represented by counselor a representative, written communications for that party shall be delivered to the address of record of such counselor representative.

(c) 如果一方由顾问来代表,应将该方的书面信函送交顾问代表的记录地址。

(d) Except as the parties may agree or the arbitrator may direct otherwise, a written communication may be delivered by electronic mail or facsimile transmission or by such other means that will provide a record of the sending and receipt thereof at the recipient's mailbox (electronic inbox). Such communication shall be deemed to have been received on the same date of its transmittal and receipt in the mailbox (electronic inbox).

(d) 除非双方当事人可能同意或仲裁员可能另有指示,否则书面通信可以通过电子邮件或传真传送,或以能在收件人的邮箱(电子收件箱)提供发送和接收的记录的方式传送。此类通信应视为在其发送和接收的同一天在邮箱(电子收件箱)收到。

Article 5.3. Waiver of Right to Object.

第5.3条 放弃反对的权利。

(a) A party shall be deemed to have waived his right to object to non-compliance with any non-mandatory provision of these Rules（from which the parties may derogate）or any requirement under the arbitration agreement when：

（a）一方当事人在下列情况下应被视为放弃了反对不遵守本规则任何非强制性规定的权利：

（i）he/she/it knows of such non-compliance；and

（i）其知道这种不遵守的行为；

（ii）proceeds with the arbitration without stating his/her/its objections to such non-compliance without undue delay or if a time-limit is provided therefor，within such period of time.

（ii）继续进行仲裁，且没有无故拖延却未说明，或在有时限时，未在时限内说明其对这种不遵守行为的反对意见。

（b）If an act is required or allowed to be done under this Chapter，unless the applicable rule or the agreement of the parties provides a different period for the act to be done，it shall be done within a period of thirty（30）days from the date when such act could have been done with legal effect.

（b）如果根据本章要求或允许采取某种行为，除非适用的规则或当事方的协议规定了采取该行为的不同期限，该行为应在可以采取该行为并具有法律效力之日起 30 天内进行。

Article 5.4. Extent of Court Intervention. In matters governed by this Chapter，no court shall intervene except in accordance with the Special ADR Rules.

第 5.4 条　法院干预的程度。对于本章规定的事项，除依照特别规则外，任何法院不得介入。

Article 5.5. Court or Other Authority for Certain Functions of Arbitration Assistance and Supervision. The functions referred to in paragraphs（c）and（d）of Article 5.10（Appointment of

Arbitrators）, paragraph （a） of Article 5.11 （Grounds for Challenge）, and paragraph （a） of Article 5.13 （Failure or Impossibility to Act）, shall be performed by the appointing authority, unless the latter shall fail or refuse to act within thirty （30） days from receipt of the request in which case, the applicant may renew the application with the court.

第5.5条　仲裁协助和监督的某些职能。指定机构应履行第5.10条（c）款和（d）款（指定仲裁员）、第5.11条（a）款（质疑理由）和第5.13条（a）款（法案的未能和不可能）提及的职能,除非后者在收到请求后30天内未能或拒绝采取行动,否则申请人可向法院重新提出申请。

RULE 2 - Arbitration Agreement
细则 2——仲裁协议

Article 5.6. Form of Arbitration Agreement. An arbitration agreement shall be in writing. An agreement is in writing if it is contained in a document signed by the parties or in an exchange of letters, telex, telegrams or other means of telecommunication which provide a record of the agreement, or in an exchange of statements of claim and defense in which the existence of an agreement is alleged by one party and not denied by the other. The reference in a contract to a document containing an arbitration clause constitutes an arbitration agreement provided that the contract is in writing and the reference is such as to make that clause part of the contract.

第5.6条　仲裁协议的形式。仲裁协议应当采用书面形式。如协议载于双方当事人签署的文件,或载于提供协议记录的换文、电传、电报或其他电信手段,或载于一方当事人声称存在协议且另一方当事人没有否认的索赔和答辩书的交换协议即为书面协议。合同中提及载有仲裁条款的文件,构成仲裁协议,条件是合同为书面形式,提及的内容使该条款成为合同的一部分。

Article 5. 7. Arbitration Agreement and Substantive Claim Before Court.

第 5.7 条　仲裁协议和向法院提出的实质性索赔。

(a) A party to an action may request the court before which it is pending to stay the action and to refer the dispute to arbitration in accordance with their arbitration agreement not later than the pre-trial conference. Thereafter，both parties may make a similar request with the court. The parties shall be referred to arbitration unless the court finds that the arbitration agreement is null and void，inoperative or incapable of being performed.

(a) 诉讼一方当事人可请求其正在审理的法院中止诉讼，并根据其仲裁协议，在预审会议前将争议提交仲裁。此后，双方可向法院提出类似请求。除非法院认定仲裁协议无效、不生效或不能履行，否则应将当事人交付仲裁。

(b) Where an action referred to in paragraph (a) of this Article has been brought，arbitral proceedings may nevertheless be commenced or continued，and an award may be made，while the issue is pending before the court.

(b) 在本条(a)款提及的一项诉讼已经提起而未决的情况下，仲裁程序仍可启动或继续进行，并可作出裁决。

(c) Where the action is commenced by or against multiple parties，one or more of whom are parties to an arbitration agreement，the court shall refer to arbitration those parties who are bound by the arbitration agreement although the civil action may continue as to those who are not bound by such arbitration agreement.

(c) 如果诉讼是由多方当事人提起或针对多方当事人（其中一方或多方当事人是仲裁协议的当事人）提起的，法院应将受仲裁协议约束的当事人交付仲裁。

Article 5.8. Arbitration Agreement and Interim Measures by Court.

第5.8条　仲裁协议和法院的临时措施。

(a) It is not incompatible with an arbitration agreement for a party to request from a court, before the constitution of the arbitral tribunal or during arbitral proceedings, an interim measure of protection and for a court to grant such measure.

(a) 一方当事人在组成仲裁庭之前或在仲裁程序期间请求法院采取临时保全措施以及法院准予采取这种措施,与仲裁协议并不抵触。

(b) After the constitution of the arbitral tribunal and during arbitral proceedings, a request for an interim measure of protection, or modification thereof, may be made with the arbitral tribunal or to the extent that the arbitral tribunal has no power to act or is unable to act effectively, the request may be made with the court.

(b) 在组成仲裁庭之后和仲裁程序进行期间,可以向仲裁庭提出临时保全措施的请求。或者在仲裁庭无权或无法有效采取行动的情况下,可以向法院提出请求。

(c) The following rules on interim or provisional relief shall be observed:

(c) 应遵守关于临时或暂时补救的下列规则:

(i) Any party may request that interim or provisional relief be granted against the adverse party.

(i) 任何一方均可请求由对方给予临时或暂时的救济。

(ii) Such relief may be granted:

(ii) 可给予如下救济:

(aa) To prevent irreparable loss or injury;

(aa) 防止不可挽回的损失或伤害;

(bb) To provide security for the performance of an obligation;

(bb) 为履行义务提供担保;

(cc) To produce or preserve evidence; or

(cc) 提供或保存证据;或

(dd) To compel any other appropriate act or omissions.

(dd) 迫使任何其他适当的作为或不作为。

(iii) The order granting provisional relief may be conditioned upon the provision of security or any act or omission specified in the order.

(iii) 给予临时救济的命令可以以提供该命令中规定的担保或任何作为或不作为为条件。

(iv) Interim or provisional relief is requested by written application transmitted by reasonable means to the arbitral tribunal and the party against whom relief is sought, describing in appropriate detail of the precise relief, the party against whom the relief is requested, the ground for the relief, and the evidence supporting the request.

(iv) 临时或暂时救济请求是通过书面申请以合理的方式转交仲裁庭和寻求救济的当事人,适当详细地说明确切的救济请求所针对的当事人、救济理由以及支持请求的证据。

(v) The order either granting or denying an application for interim relief shall be binding upon the parties.

(v) 批准或拒绝临时救济申请的命令对双方当事人具有约束力。

(vi) Either party may apply with the court for assistance in implementing or enforcing an interim measure ordered by an arbitral tribunal.

(vi) 任何一方当事人均可向法院申请协助执行仲裁庭下令采取的临时措施。

(vii) A party who does not comply with the order shall be liable for all damages, resulting from noncompliance, including all expenses, and reasonable attorney's fees, paid in obtaining the order's judicial enforcement.

（vii）不遵守命令的一方应负责赔偿因不遵守命令而造成的一切损害，包括所有费用以及为获得命令的司法执行而支付的合理律师费。

(d) Unless otherwise agreed by the parties, the arbitral tribunal may, at the request of a party, order any party to take such interim measures of protection as the arbitral tribunal may consider necessary in respect of the subject matter of the dispute following the Rules in this Article. Such interim measures may include but shall not be limited to preliminary injunction directed against a party, appointment of receivers or detention, preservation, inspection of property that is the subject of the dispute in arbitration. Either party may apply with the court for assistance in implementing or enforcing an interim measure ordered by an arbitral tribunal.

(d) 除非各方当事人另有约定，仲裁庭可根据一方当事人的请求，下令任何一方当事人根据本条规则就争议标的采取仲裁庭认为必要的临时保全措施。此类临时措施可包括但不应限于对一方当事人的初步强制令、指定接管人或拘留、保全、对作为仲裁争议标的的财产的检查。任何一方当事人均可向法院申请协助执行仲裁庭下令采取的临时措施。

RULE 3. Composition of Arbitral Tribunal
细则 3——仲裁庭的组成

Article 5. 9. Number of Arbitrators. The parties are free to determine the number of arbitrators. Failing such determination, the number of arbitrators shall be three (3).

第5.9条　仲裁员人数。当事各方可自由决定仲裁员人数。如果不能确定，仲裁员人数应为三名。

Article 5.10. Appointment of Arbitrators.

第5.10条　指定仲裁员。

（a）Any person appointed to serve as an arbitrator must be of legal age, in full enjoyment of his/her civil rights and knows how to read and write. No person appointed to serve as an arbitrator shall be related by blood or marriage within the sixth degree to either party to the controversy.

（a）任何被指定担任仲裁员的人必须达到法定年龄，充分享有其公民权利，并懂得读写。任何被指定担任仲裁员的人都不得与争议任何一方在第六级之内有血缘或婚姻关系。

No person shall serve as an arbitrator in any proceeding if he/she has or has had financial, fiduciary or other interest in the controversy or cause to be decided or in the result of the proceeding, or has any personal bias, which might prejudice the right of any party to a fair and impartial award. No party shall select as an arbitrator any person to act as his/her champion or to advocate his/her cause.

任何人如果在争议或诉讼结果中有经济、信托或其他利益，或有任何个人偏见，可能损害任何一方获得公平和公正裁决的权利，则不得担任任何程序的仲裁员。任何一方当事人均不得选择任何人担任其支持者。

（b）The parties are free to agree on a procedure of appointing the arbitrator or arbitrators. If, in the contract for arbitration or in the submission, a provision is made for a method of appointing an arbitrator or arbitrators, such method shall be followed.

（b）当事各方可自由商定指定仲裁员的程序。在仲裁合同或者提交的文件中，对指定一名或者多名仲裁员的方法作了规定的，应当遵守。

（c）Failing such agreement,

（c）如果没有这样的协议，

（i）in an arbitration with three（3）arbitrators, each party shall appoint one（1）arbitrator, and the two（2）arbitrators thus appointed shall appoint the third arbitrator; if a party fails to appoint the arbitrator within thirty （30） days of receipt of a request to do so from the other party，or if the two arbitrators fail to agree on the third arbitrator within thirty （30） days of their appointment，the appointment shall be made，upon request of a party，by the appointing authority；

(i) 在三名仲裁员的仲裁中，每一方当事人应指定一名仲裁员，由此指定的两名仲裁员应指定第三名仲裁员；如果一方当事人未能在 30 天内从另一方当事人或两名仲裁员未能在指定后 30 天内就第三名仲裁员达成协议的，应根据一方当事人的请求由指定机构指定；

(ii) in an arbitration with a sole arbitrator，if the parties are unable to agree on the arbitrator，he/she shall be appointed，upon request of a party，by the appointing authority.

(ii) 在与独任仲裁员进行的仲裁中，如果双方当事人不能就仲裁员达成一致意见，应根据一方当事人的请求由指定机构指定。

(d) Where，under an appointment procedure agreed upon by the parties，

(d) 根据双方商定的指定程序，

(i) a party fails to act or appoint an arbitrator as required under such procedure，or

(i) 一方当事人未能按照这种程序的要求采取行动或指定一名仲裁员，或

(ii) the parties，or two （2） arbitrators，are unable to appoint an arbitrator or reach an agreement expected of them under such procedure，or

(ii) 当事各方或两名仲裁员，不能指定一名仲裁员，也不能在此程序下达成一项协议，或

(iii) a third party，including an institution，fails to appoint an arbitrator or to perform any function entrusted to it under such procedure，or

（iii）包括机构在内的第三方未能指定仲裁员或履行此类程序赋予它的任何职能，或

（iv）The multiple claimants or the multiple respondents is/are unable to appoint its/their respective arbitrator，any party may request the appointing authority to appoint an arbitrator.

（iv）多个申请人或者被申请人不能指定其各自的仲裁员的，任何一方当事人都可以请求指定机构指定一名仲裁员。

In making the appointment，the appointing authority shall summon the parties and their respective counsel to appear before said authority on the date，time and place set by it，for the purpose of selecting and appointing a sole arbitrator. If a sole arbitrator is not appointed in such meeting，or the meeting does not take place because of the absence of either or both parties despite due notice，the appointing authority shall appoint the sole arbitrator.

指定机构在指定仲裁员时，应当传唤各方当事人及其各自的律师在指定机构确定的日期、时间和地点出庭，以便选择和指定独任仲裁员。如果在该会议上没有指定独任仲裁员，或者由于一方或双方未能出席而未能举行会议，尽管有适当的通知，指定机构应指定独任仲裁员。

（e）If the default appointment of an arbitrator is objected to by a party on whose behalf the default appointment is to be made，and the defaulting party requests the appointing authority for additional time to appoint his/her arbitrator，the appointing authority，having regard to the circumstances，may give the requesting party not more than thirty（30）days to make the appointment.

（e）如果默认指定的仲裁员遭到拟以其名义做出默认指定的一方当事人的反对，且该违约方当事人请求指定机构给予更多时间指定其仲裁员，指定机构可根据具体情况给予请求方不超过 30 天的指定。

If the objection of a party is based on the ground that the party did not fail to choose and appoint an arbitrator for the arbitral tribunal, there shall be attached to the objection the appointment of an arbitrator together with the latter's acceptance thereof and curriculum vitae. Otherwise, the appointing authority shall appoint the arbitrator for that party.

如果一方当事人的反对是基于该方当事人未能为仲裁庭选择和任命仲裁员的理由，则应在反对中附上一名仲裁员的任命以及仲裁员的接受情况和简历。否则，指定机构应为该当事人指定仲裁员。

(f) In making a default appointment, the appointing authority shall have regard to such considerations as are likely to secure the appointment of an independent and impartial arbitrator. In order to achieve speedy and impartial justice and to moderate the cost of arbitration, in choosing an arbitrator, the appointing authority shall give preference to a qualified person who has a place of residence or business in the same general locality as the agreed venue of the arbitration and who is likely to accept the arbitrator's fees agreed upon by the parties, or as fixed in accordance either with the internal guidelines or the Schedule of Fees approved by the administering institution or by the appointing authority.

(f) 在做出缺省指定时，指定机构应当考虑到可能确保指定一名独立和公正的仲裁员的各种因素。为了实现迅速和公正的司法并减少仲裁费用，在选择仲裁员时，指定机构应当优先考虑在与仲裁地点相同的地方拥有居住地或营业地点并可能接受各方当事人商定的仲裁员费用的合格人员，或根据内部准则或管理机构或指定机构核准的收费表确定。

(g) The appointing authority shall give notice in writing to the parties of the appointment made or its inability to comply with the Request for Appointment and the reasons why it is unable to

do so，in which later case，the procedure described under Article 5.
5（Court or Other Authority for Certain Functions of arbitration
Assistance and Supervision）shall apply.

（g）指定机构应当以书面形式通知各方当事人所做的指定或其不能遵
守指定请求以及不能这样做的原因，在后一种情况下，应当适用第
5.5条（法院或其他当局就某些仲裁协助和监督职能所规定的程
序）。

（h）　A decision on a matter entrusted by this Article to the
appointing authority shall be immediately executory and not
subject to appeal or motion for reconsideration. The
appointing authority shall be deemed to have been given by the
parties discretionary authority in making the appoint-ment but
in doing so，the appointing authority shall have due regard to
any qualification or disqualification of an arbitrator/s under
paragraph（a）of Article 5.10（Appointment of Arbitrators）
as well as any qualifications required of the arbitrator/s by the
agreement of the parties and to such considerations as are
likely to secure the appointment of an independent and
impartial arbitrator.

（h）关于本条委托指定机构处理的事项的决定应立即执行，不得提出
上诉或请求重新审议。指定机构应被视为由各方当事人赋予指定
的酌处权，但在这样做时，指定机构应适当考虑到根据第5.10条
（a）款（指定仲裁员）的任何资格或取消其资格，以及各方当事人协
议要求仲裁人具备的任何资格，并适当考虑到可能确保指定独立
和公正的仲裁员的各种考虑。

（i）The chairman of the arbitral tribunal shall be selected in
accordance with the agreement of the parties and/or the rules
agreed upon or，in default thereof，by the arbitrators
appointed.

（i）仲裁庭庭长应根据当事各方的协议和（或）商定的规则选出，否则

由指定的仲裁员选出。

(j) Any clause giving one of the parties the power to choose more arbitrators than the other is void. However，the rest of the agreement，if otherwise valid，shall be construed as permitting the appointment of one（1）arbitrator by all claimants and one（1）arbitrator by all respondents. The third arbitrator shall be appointed as provided above.

(j) 任何赋予一方当事人选择多于另一方仲裁员的权力的条款都是无效的。但协议的其余部分如在其他方面有效，应解释为允许所有申请人指定一名仲裁员，所有被申请人指定一名仲裁员。第三名仲裁员应按上述规定任命。

If all the claimants or all the respondents cannot decide among themselves on an arbitrator，the appointment shall be made for them by the appointing authority.

全体申请人或者被申请人不能自行决定仲裁员的，由指定机构指定。

(k) The appointing authority may adopt Guidelines for the making of a Request for Appointment.

(k) 指定机构可通过提出任命请求的准则。

(l) Except as otherwise provided in the Guidelines of the appointing authority，if any，a Request for Appointment shall include，as applicable，the following：

(l) 除指定机构的准则另有规定外，指定请求应酌情包括下列内容：

(i) the demand for arbitration；

(i) 要求仲裁；

(ii) the name/s and curricula vitae of the appointed arbitrator/s；

(ii) 被任命的仲裁员的姓名和履历；

(iii) the acceptance of his/herlits appointment of the appointed arbitrator/s；

(iii) 接受对指定仲裁人的任命；

(iv) any qualification or disqualification of the arbitrator as provided in the arbitration agreement;

（iv）仲裁协议中规定的仲裁员的任何资格或取消资格；

（v）an executive summary of the dispute which should indicate the nature of the dispute and the parties thereto;

（v）争端的执行摘要，其中应说明争端的性质和当事方；

（vi）principal office and officers of a corporate party;

（vi）公司一方的官员；

（vii）the person/s appearing as counsel for the party/ies; and

（vii）作为当事人的律师出现的人；以及

（viii）information about arbitrator's fees where there is an agreement between the parties with respect thereto.

（viii）如果当事各方就仲裁员的费用达成协议，则提供这方面的信息。

In institutional arbitration, the request shall include such further information or particulars as the administering institution shall require.

在机构仲裁中，请求应包括管理机构所要求的进一步资料或细节。

（m）A copy of the Request for Appointment shall be delivered to the adverse party. Proof of such delivery shall be included in, and shall form part of, the Request for Appointment filed with the appointing authority.

（m）应向对方提交一份任命请求。此种送达的证明应列入并构成向指定机构提交的任命请求书的一部分。

（n）A party upon whom a copy of the Request for Appointment is communicated may, within seven（7）days of its receipt, file with the appointing authority his/herlits objection/s to the Request or ask for an extension of time, not exceeding thirty（30）days from receipt of the request, to appoint an arbitrator or act in accordance with the procedure agreed upon or provided by these Rules.

（n）被送交指定请求书副本的一方当事人可在收到该请求书后 7 天内

向指定机构提出请求，或请求延长请求期限，但不得超过 30 天，或自收到请求之日起 30 天。

Within the aforementioned periods，the party seeking the extension shall provide the appointing authority and the adverse party with a copy of the appointment of his/her arbitrator，the latter's curriculum vitae，and the latter's acceptance of the appointment. In the event that the said party fails to appoint an arbitrator within said period，the appointing authority shall make the default appointment.

在上述期限内，寻求延期的一方当事人应当向指定机构和对方当事人提供其指定的仲裁员的副本、后者的简历以及后者接受指定的情况。该当事人未在上述期限内指定仲裁员的，指定机构应当做出缺省指定。

（o）An arbitrator，in accepting an appointment，shall include，in his/her acceptance letter，a statement that：

（o）仲裁员在接受指定时，应出具接受信，声明：

　　（i）he/she agrees to comply with the applicable law，the arbitration rules agreed upon by the parties，or in default thereof，these Rules，and the Code of Ethics for Arbitrators in Domestic Arbitration，if any；

　　（i）其同意遵守适用的法律、当事各方商定的仲裁规则，并遵守国内仲裁员的道德守则；

　　（ii）he/she accepts as compensation the arbitrator's fees agreed upon by the parties or as determined in accordance with the rules agreed upon by the parties，or in default thereof，these Rules；and

　　（ii）其接受当事各方商定的或根据当事各方商定的规则确定的仲裁员费用作为报酬，或在没有这些规则的情况下接受本规则；以及

　　（iii）he agrees to devote as much time and attention to the arbitration as the circumstances may require in order to achieve the objective of a speedy，effective and fair resolution of the dispute.

（iii）其同意在仲裁上投入尽可能多的时间和精力,以实现迅速、有效和公正解决争议的目标。

Article 5.11. Grounds for Challenge.

第5.11条　提出质疑的理由。

（a）When a person is approached in connection with his/her possible appointment as an arbitrator, he/she shall disclose any circumstance likely to give rise to justifiable doubts as to his/her impartiality, independence, qualifications and disqualifications. An arbitrator, from the time of his/her appointment and throughout the arbitral proceedings, shall, without delay, disclose any such circumstances to the parties unless they have already been informed of them by him/her.

（a）当一个人可能被任命为仲裁员时,其应披露可能对其公正性、独立性、资格和取消资格产生合理怀疑的任何情况。仲裁员自其被指定之时起及在整个仲裁程序中,应立即向各方当事人披露任何此类情况,除非其已将此类情况通知各方当事人。

A person, who is appointed as an arbitrator notwithstanding the disclosure made in accordance with this Article, shall reduce the disclosure to writing and provide a copy of such written disclosure to all parties in the arbitration.

被指定为仲裁员的人,尽管根据本条做出了披露,应将披露以书面形式记录,并向仲裁中的所有当事人提供书面披露的副本。

（b）An arbitrator may be challenged only if:

（b）只有在下列情况下才可对仲裁员提出异议:

（i）circumstances exist that give rise to justifiable doubts as to his/her impartiality or independence;

（i）存在的情况使人有理由怀疑其公正性或独立性;

（ii）he/she does not possess qualifications as provided for in this

Chapter or those agreed to by the parties;

（ii）其不具备本章规定的资格或当事人同意的资格；

（iii）he/she is disqualified to act as arbitration under these Rules;

（iii）根据这些规则，其没有资格担任仲裁；

（iv）he refuses to respond to questions by a party regarding the nature and extent of his professional dealings with a party or its counsel.

（iv）其拒绝回答一方当事人提出的关于其与一方当事人或其律师的职业交往的性质和程度的问题。

（c）If，after appointment but before or during hearing，a person appointed to serve as an arbitrator shall discover any circumstance likely to create a presumption of bias，or which he/she believes might disqualify him/her as an impartial arbitrator，the arbitrator shall immediately disclose such information to the parties. Thereafter，the parties may agree in writing：

（c）如果被指定担任仲裁员的人在任命后但在听证前或听证期间发现任何可能造成偏见推定的情况，或其认为有可能使其失去担任公正仲裁员的资格，仲裁员应立即向各方当事人披露此类信息。此后，各方可书面约定：

（i）to waive the presumptive disqualifying circumstances; or

（i）放弃假定的不符合资格的情况；或

（ii）to declare the office of such arbitrator vacant. Any such vacancy shall be filled in the same manner the original appointment was made.

（ii）宣布该仲裁员职位空缺。任何此种空缺应以原任命方式予以填补。

（d）After initial disclosure is made and in the course of the arbitration proceedings，when the arbitrator discovers circumstances that are likely to create a presumption of bias，he/she shall immediately disclose those circumstances to the parties. A written disclosure is not required where it is made during the arbitration and it appears in a written record of the arbitration proceedings.

（d）在初步披露后，在仲裁程序过程中，当仲裁员发现可能产生偏见推定的情况时，她应立即向当事人披露这些情况。在仲裁过程中做出的书面披露，无需在仲裁程序的书面记录中披露。

（e）An arbitrator who has or has had financial or professional dealings with a party to the arbitration or to the counsel of either party shall disclose in writing such fact to the parties，and shall，in good faith，promptly respond to questions from a party regarding the nature，extent and age of such financial or professional dealings.

（e）与仲裁一方当事人或任何一方当事人的律师有财务或专业往来的仲裁员，应以书面形式向当事人披露此类事实，并应本着诚意迅速回答一方当事人就此类财务或专业往来的性质、程度和年限提出的问题。

Article 5.12. Challenge Procedure.

第5.12条 质疑程序。

（a）The parties are free to agree on a procedure for challenging an arbitrator，subject to the provisions of paragraph（c）of this Article.

（a）当事各方可自由商定对仲裁员提出异议的程序，但须遵守本条（c）款的规定。

（b）Failing such agreement，a party who intends to challenge an arbitrator shall，within fifteen（15）days after becoming aware of the constitution of the arbitral tribunal or after becoming aware of any circumstance referred to in paragraph（b）of Article 5.11（Grounds for Challenge），send a written statement of the reasons for the challenge to the arbitral tribunal. Unless the challenged arbitrator withdraws from his/her office or the other party agrees to the challenge, the arbitral tribunal shall decide on the challenge.

(b) 如果不能达成这样的协议,打算对仲裁员提出异议的一方当事人应在了解仲裁庭组成或了解第 5.11 条(b)款(质疑理由)提及的任何情况后,于 15 天内向仲裁庭提交一份书面陈述,说明提出异议的理由。除非被异议的仲裁员撤销其职务或另一方当事人同意该异议,仲裁庭应就该异议作出裁决。

(c) If a challenge under any procedure agreed upon by the parties or under the procedure of paragraph (b) of this Article is not successful, the challenging party may request the appointing authority, within thirty (30) days after having received notice of the decision rejecting the challenge, to decide on the challenge, which decision shall be immediately executory and not subject to appeal or motion for reconsideration. While such a request is pending, the arbitral tribunal, including the challenged arbitrator, may continue the arbitral proceedings and make an award.

(c) 如果根据当事各方商定的任何程序或根据本条(b)款的程序提出的异议不成功,提出异议的一方当事人可在收到驳回该异议的决定通知后 30 天内请求指定机构就该异议做出决定,该异议应立即执行,且不得对该决定提出上诉或复议。在此种请求待决期间,仲裁庭,包括被质疑的仲裁员,可继续进行仲裁程序并作出裁决。

(d) If a request for inhibition is made, it shall be deemed as a challenge.

(d) 如果提出禁令请求,应将其视为异议。

(e) A party may challenge an arbitrator appointed by him/her/it, or in whose appointment he/she/it has participated, only for reasons of which he/she/it becomes aware after the appointment has been made.

（e）一方当事人只有在做出指定之后才能对其指定的仲裁员提出异议，或对其参与任命的仲裁员提出异议。

（f）The challenge shall be in writing and it shall state specific facts that provide the basis for the ground relied upon for the challenge. A challenge shall be made within fifteen（15）days from knowledge by a party of the existence of a ground for a challenge or within fifteen（15）days from the rejection by an arbitrator of a party's request for his/her inhibition.

（f）质疑应以书面提出，并应说明具体事实，为质疑所依据的理由提供依据。一方当事人在得知存在提出异议的理由后，应在 15 天内提出异议，或在仲裁员拒绝一方当事人关于禁止提出异议的请求后 15 天内提出异议。

（g）Within fifteen（15）days of receipt of the challenge，the challenged arbitrator shall decide whether he/she shall accept the challenge or reject it. If he/she accepts the challenge，he/she shall voluntarily withdraw as arbitrator. If he/she rejects it，he/she shall communicate，within the same period of time，his/her rejection of the challenge and state the facts and arguments relied upon for such rejection.

（g）在收到异议后 15 天内，被异议的仲裁员应决定是否接受该异议。如果他/她接受异议，他/她将自愿辞去仲裁员的职务。如果他/她拒绝，他/她应在同一时间内告知他/她对质疑的拒绝，并说明拒绝所依据的事实和论点。

（h）An arbitrator who does not accept the challenge shall be given an opportunity to be heard.

（h）不接受异议的仲裁员应获得陈述的机会。

（i）Notwithstanding the rejection of the challenge by the arbitrator，the parties may，within the same fifteen（15）day period，agree to the challenge.

（i）尽管仲裁员驳回了异议，但双方当事人可在同一期限内同意该异议。

(j) In default of an agreement of the parties to agree on the challenge thereby replacing the arbitrator，the arbitral tribunal shall decide on the challenge within thirty（30）days from receipt of the challenge.

(j) 如果当事各方不同意就异议达成协议，从而替换仲裁员，仲裁庭应在收到异议后 30 天内就异议作出裁决。

(k) If the challenge procedure as agreed upon by the parties or as provided in this Article is not successful，or a party or the arbitral tribunal shall decline to act，the challenging party may request the appointing authority in writing to decide on the challenge within thirty（30）days after having received notice of the decision rejecting the challenge. The appointing authority shall decide on the challenge within fifteen（15）days from receipt of the request. If the appointing authority shall fail to act on the challenge within thirty（30）days from the date of its receipt or within such further time as it may fix，with notice to the parties，the requesting party may renew the request with the court.

(k) 如果当事各方商定的质疑程序或本条规定的质疑程序不成功，或者当事一方或仲裁庭应拒绝采取行动，提出质疑的一方当事人可在收到驳回该质疑的决定的通知后 30 天内书面请求指定机构就该质疑做出决定。指定机构应在收到请求后 15 天内就质疑做出决定。指定机构自收到异议之日起 30 天内或在其可能确定的更长时间内未就该异议采取行动并通知各方当事人的，请求方当事人可以向法院重新提出请求。

The request made under this Article shall include the challenge，the reply or explanation of the challenged arbitrator and relevant communication，if any，from either party，or from the arbitral tribunal.

根据本条提出的请求应包括质疑、对被质疑仲裁员的答复或解释，以及任何一方当事人或仲裁庭的任何相关来文。

(l) Every communication required or agreement made under this Article in respect of a challenge shall be delivered，as appropriate，to the challenged arbitrator，to the parties，to the remaining members of the arbitral tribunal and to the institution administering the arbitration，if any.

(l) 根据本条就质疑提出的每一项通信或协议，均应酌情送交被质疑的仲裁员、当事各方、仲裁庭其余成员以及任何仲裁管理机构。

(m) A challenged arbitrator shall be replaced if：

(m) 在下列情况下，被质疑的仲裁员应予替换：

    (i) he/she withdraws as arbitrator，or

    (i) 其辞去仲裁员一职，或

    (ii) the parties agree in writing to declare the office of arbitrator vacant，or

    (ii) 双方当事人书面同意宣布仲裁员职位空缺，或

    (iii) the arbitral tribunal decides the challenge and declares the office of the challenged arbitrator vacant，or

    (iii) 仲裁庭裁定异议并宣布被质疑的仲裁员职位空缺，或

    (iv) the appointing authority decides the challenge and declares the office of the challenged arbitrator vacant，or

    (iv) 指定机构决定异议并宣布被质疑仲裁员的职位空缺，或

    (v) in default of the appointing authority，the court decides the challenge and declares the office of the challenged arbitrator vacant.

    (v) 在指定机构缺席的情况下，法院裁决异议并宣布被异议仲裁员的职位空缺。

(n) The decision of the parties，the arbitral tribunal，the appointing authority，or in proper cases，the court，to accept or reject a challenge is not subject to appeal or motion for reconsideration.

（n）各方当事人、仲裁庭、指定机构或在适当情况下法院接受或拒绝质疑的决定，不得上诉或请求复议。

（o）Until a decision is made to replace the arbitrator under this Article，the arbitration proceeding shall continue notwithstanding the challenge，and the challenged arbitrator shall continue to participate therein as an arbitrator. However，if the challenge incident is raised before the court，because the parties，the arbitral tribunal or appointing authority failed or refused to act within the period provided in paragraphs（j）and （k） of this Article，the arbitration proceeding shall be suspended until after the court shall have decided the incident. The arbitration shall be continued immediately after the court has delivered an order on the challenging incident. If the court agrees that the challenged arbitrator shall be replaced，the parties shall immediately replace the arbitrator concerned.

（o）在根据本条做出替换仲裁员的决定之前，尽管有异议，仲裁程序应继续进行，被质疑的仲裁员应继续作为仲裁员参与仲裁程序。但是，如果向法院提出质疑，由于当事各方、仲裁庭或指定机构未能或拒绝在本条（j）款和（k）款规定的期限内采取行动，仲裁程序应暂停，直至法院对该事件作出裁决。在法院就有争议的事件发出命令后，应立即继续进行仲裁。如果法院同意替换被质疑的仲裁员，当事各方应立即替换有关的仲裁员。

（p） The appointment of a substitute arbitrator shall be made pursuant to the procedure applicable to the appointment of the arbitrator being replaced.

（p）替代仲裁员的指定应根据被替换仲裁员的指定所适用的程序进行。

Article 5.13. Failure or Impossibility to Act.

第5.13条　未能或不能采取行动。

（a）If an arbitrator becomes de jure or de facto unable to perform his/her functions or for other reasons fails to act without undue delay，his/her mandate terminates if he/she withdraws from his/her office or if the parties agree on the termination. Otherwise，if a controversy remains concerning any of these grounds，any party may request the appointing authority to decide on the termination of the mandate，which decision shall be immediately executory and not subject to appeal or motion for reconsideration.

（a）如果仲裁员在法律上或事实上不能履行其职能，或由于其他原因不能及时采取行动，如果他/她撤销其职务或如果当事方同意终止其职务，则其任期终止。否则，如果对上述任何理由仍有争议，任何一方当事人均可请求指定机构就终止任务做出决定，该决定应立即执行，不得上诉或请求复议。

（b）If，under this Article or Article 5.12（Challenge Procedure），an arbitrator withdraws from his/her office or a party agrees to the termination of the mandate of an arbitrator，this does not imply acceptance of the validity of any ground referred to in this Article or in Article 5.12.

（b）如果根据该条或第 5.12 条（质疑程序），仲裁员撤回其职务或一方同意终止仲裁员的任期，这并不意味着接受该条或第 5.12 条提及的任何理由的有效性。

Article 5.14. Appointment of Substitute Arbitrator. Where the mandate of an arbitrator terminates under Articles 5.12（Challenge Procedure）or 5.13（Failure or Impossibility）or because of his withdrawal from office for any other reason or because of the revocation of his mandate by agreement of the parties or in any other case of termination of his/her mandate，a substitute arbitrator shall be appointed according to the rules applicable to the appointment of the arbitrator being replaced.

第 5.14 条　指定替代仲裁员。如果仲裁员的授权根据第 5.12 条（质疑程序）或 5.13 条（未能或不可能采取行动）或由于其他原因或由于当事各方协议撤销其授权或在任何其他情况下被终止授权，应根据被替换仲裁员的指定适用规则指定一名替代仲裁员。

RULE 4 - Jurisdiction of Arbitral Tribunal
细则 4——仲裁庭的管辖权

Article 5. 15. Competence of Arbitral Tribunal to Rule on its Jurisdiction.

第 5.15 条　仲裁庭就其管辖权作出裁决的权限。

(a) When a demand for arbitration made by a party to a dispute is objected to by the adverse party, the arbitral tribunal shall, in the first instance, resolve the objection when made on any of the following grounds：

(a) 当争端一方提出的仲裁要求遭到对方反对时，仲裁庭应以下列任何理由首先解决反对：

 (i) the arbitration agreement is inexistent, void, unenforceable or not binding upon a person for any reason, including the fact that the adverse party is not privy to said agreement；or

 (i) 仲裁协议不存在、无效、不可强制执行或因任何原因对某人没有约束力，包括对方不知悉该协议；或

 (ii) the dispute is not arbitrable or is outside the scope of the arbitration agreement；or

 (ii) 争议不可仲裁或不属于仲裁协议的范围；或

 (iii) the dispute is under the original and exclusive jurisdiction of a court or quasi-judicial body,

 (iii) 争端属于法院或准司法机构的原始和专属管辖权，

(b) If a party raises any of the grounds for objection, the same shall not preclude the appointment of the arbitrator/s as such issue is for the arbitral tribunal to decide. The participation of a party in the selection and appointment of an arbitrator and the filing of appropriate pleadings before the arbitral tribunal to question its jurisdiction shall not be construed as a submission to the jurisdiction of the arbitral tribunal or of a waiver of his/her/its right to assert such grounds to challenge the jurisdiction of the arbitral tribunal or the validity of the resulting award.

（b）当事人一方提出异议的，不排除仲裁庭对仲裁员的指定。一方当事人参与选择和指定仲裁员以及向仲裁庭提交适当书状以质疑其管辖权，不应被解释为向仲裁庭的管辖权提交材料，也不应被解释为放弃其主张这种理由以质疑仲裁庭管辖权或由此产生的裁决有效性的权利。

（c）The respondent in the arbitration may invoke any of such grounds to question before the court the existence，validity，or enforceability of the arbitration agreement，or the propriety of the arbitration，or the jurisdiction of the arbitrator and invoke the pendency of such action as ground for suspension of the arbitration proceeding. The arbitral tribunal，having regard to the circumstances of the case，and the need for the early and expeditious settlement of the dispute，in light of the facts and arguments raised to question its jurisdiction，may decide either to suspend the arbitration until the court has made a decision on the issue or continue with the arbitration.

（c）在仲裁中，被申请人可以援引任何此类理由向法院质疑仲裁协议的存在、有效性或可执行性，仲裁的适当性，或仲裁员的管辖权，并援引此类诉讼的未决作为中止仲裁程序的理由。仲裁庭考虑到案件的情况，并考虑到有必要根据对其管辖权提出质疑的事实和论点，早日迅速解决争议，可决定中止仲裁，直至法院就该问题作出裁决或继续进行仲裁。

（d）If a dispute is，under an arbitration agreement，to be submitted to arbitration，but before arbitration is commenced or while it is pending，a party files an action before the court which embodies or includes as a cause of action the dispute that is to be submitted to arbitration，the filing of such action shall not prevent the commencement of the arbitration or the continuation of the arbitration until the award is issued.

(d) 如果根据仲裁协议，争议须提交仲裁，但在仲裁开始前或仲裁待决期间，一方当事人向法院提起诉讼，将提交仲裁的争议作为诉讼事由，在裁决作出前，提起该诉讼不应妨碍仲裁的开始或仲裁的继续。

Article 5. 16. Power of Arbitral Tribunal to Order Interim Measures.

第 5.16 条 仲裁庭下令采取临时措施的权力。

(a) Unless otherwise agreed by the parties，the arbitral tribunal may，at the request of a party，order any party to take such interim measures of protection as the arbitral tribunal may consider necessary in respect of the subject matter of the dispute following the rules in this Article. Such interim measures may include，but shall not be limited to preliminary injunction directed against a party，appointment of receivers or detention，preservation，inspection of property that is the subject of the dispute in arbitration.

(a) 除非各方当事人另有约定，仲裁庭可根据一方当事人的请求，下令任何一方当事人根据本条规则就争议标的采取仲裁庭认为必要的临时保全措施。此类临时措施可包括但不应限于对一方当事人的初步禁令、指定接管人或拘留、保全、对作为仲裁争议标的的财产的检查。

(b) After the constitution of the arbitral tribunal，and during arbitral proceedings，a request for interim measures of protection, or modification thereof, shall be made with the arbitral tribunal. The arbitral tribunal is deemed constituted when the sole arbitrator or the third arbitrator, who has been nominated, has accepted the nomination and written communication of said nomination and acceptance has been received by the party making the request.

(b) 在组成仲裁庭之后,以及在仲裁程序期间,应当向仲裁庭提出采取或修改临时保护措施的请求。如果提出请求的一方收到了独任仲裁员或第三名被提名的仲裁员接受该提名和接受的书面通知,即视为仲裁庭的组成。

(c) The following rules on interim or provisional relief shall be observed:

(c) 应遵守关于临时或暂时补救的下列规则:

(i) Any party may request that provisional or interim relief be granted against the adverse party.

(i) 任何一方均可请求由对方给予临时或暂时救济。

(ii) Such relief may be granted:

(ii) 为以下目的可给予这种救济:

(aa) To prevent irreparable loss or injury;

(aa) 防止不可挽回的损失或伤害;

(bb) To provide security for the performance of an obligation;

(bb) 为履行义务提供担保;

(cc) To produce or preserve evidence; or

(cc) 提供或保存证据;或

(dd) To compel any other appropriate act or omissions.

(dd) 迫使任何其他适当的作为或不作为。

(iii) The order granting provisional relief may be conditioned upon the provision of security or any act or omission specified in the order.

(iii) 给予临时救济的命令可以以提供该命令中规定的担保或任何

作为或不作为为条件。

（iv） Interim or provisional relief is requested by written application transmitted by reasonable means to the arbitral tribunal and the party against whom relief is sought，describing in appropriate detail the precise relief，the party against whom the relief is requested，the ground for the relief and the evidence supporting the request.

（iv）临时或暂时救济请求应通过书面申请，以合理的方式转交仲裁庭和寻求救济的当事人，适当详细地说明确切的救济、请求救济的当事人、救济理由和支持请求的证据。

（v） The order either granting or denying an application for interim relief shall be binding upon the parties.

（v）批准或拒绝临时救济申请的命令对双方当事人具有约束力。

（vi） Either party may apply with the court for assistance in implementing or enforcing an interim measure ordered by an arbitral tribunal.

（vi）任何一方当事人均可向法院申请协助执行仲裁庭下令采取的临时措施。

（vii） A party who does not comply with the order shall be liable for all damages，resulting from noncompliance，including all expenses，and reasonable attorney's fees paid in obtaining the order's judicial enforcement.

（vii）不遵守命令的一方应对不遵守命令所造成的一切损害负责，包括所有费用，以及为获得命令的司法执行而支付的合理律师费。

RULE 5 - Conduct of Arbitral Proceedings
细则 5——仲裁程序的进行

Article 5.17. Equal Treatment of Parties. The parties shall be treated with equality and each party shall be given a full opportunity of presenting his/her/its case.

第5.17条　平等对待当事人。应平等对待各方,各方应有充分机会陈述案情。

Article 5.18. Determination of Rules of Procedure.

第5.18条　确定议事规则。

(a) Subject to the provisions of these Rules, the parties are free to agree on the procedure to be followed by the arbitral tribunal in conducting the proceedings.

(a) 在不违反本规则规定的情况下,各方当事人可自由约定仲裁庭进行的程序。

(b) Failing such agreement, the arbitral tribunal may, subject to the provision of the ADR Act, conduct the arbitration in such manner as it considers appropriate. The power conferred upon the arbitral tribunal includes the power to determine admissibility, relevance, materiality and weight of evidence.

(b) 如果不能达成这样的协议,仲裁庭可以在不违反《替代性争议解决法案》规定的情况下,以其认为适当的方式进行仲裁。赋予仲裁庭的权力包括确定证据的可采性、相关性、实质性和重要性。

Article 5.19. Place of Arbitration.

第5.19条　仲裁地。

(a) The parties are free to agree on the place of arbitration. Failing such agreement, the place of arbitration shall be in Metro Manila unless the arbitral tribunal, having regard to the circumstances of the case, including the convenience of the parties, shall decide on a different place of arbitration.

(a) 当事人可以自由约定仲裁地。如果不能达成协议,仲裁地点应设在马尼拉市区,除非仲裁庭考虑到案件的情况,包括当事人的方便,决定另一仲裁地点。

(b) The arbitral tribunal may, unless otherwise agreed by the parties, meet at any place it considers appropriate for consultation among its members, for hearing witnesses, experts or the parties, or for inspection of goods, other property or documents.

(b) 除非当事各方另有协议，仲裁庭可在其认为适当的任何地点举行会议，以便在其成员之间进行协商，听取证人、专家或当事各方的意见，或检查货物、其他财产或文件。

Article 5.20. Commencement of Arbitral Proceedings.

第5.20条　仲裁程序的启动。

(a) Where there is a prior arbitration agreement between the parties, arbitra-tion is deemed commenced as follows：

(a) 如果当事人之间事先有仲裁协议，则仲裁视为按下列方式开始：

(i) In institutional arbitration, arbitration is commenced in accordance with the arbitration rules of the institution agreed upon by the parties.

(i) 在机构仲裁中，根据当事人约定的机构仲裁规则启动仲裁。

(ii) In ad hoc arbitration, arbitration is commenced by the claimant upon delivering to the respondent a demand for arbitration. A demand may be in any form stating：

(ii) 在特别仲裁中，申请人在向被申请人提交仲裁请求时启动仲裁。索款可采取任何形式说明：

(aa) the name, address, and description of each of the parties；

(aa) 每一方的名称、地址和说明；

(bb) a description of the nature and circumstances of the dispute giving rise to the claim；

(bb) 关于引起索赔的争端的性质和情况的说明；

(cc) a statement of the relief sought, including the amount of the claim；

(cc) 关于所寻求的救济的说明，包括索赔额；

(dd) the relevant agreements, if any, including the arbitration agreement, a copy of which shall be attached; and

(dd) 如果有相关协议,包括仲裁协议,应附上一份副本;

(ee) appointment of arbitrators and/or demand to appoint.

(ee) 指定仲裁员和/或要求指定。

(b) If the arbitration agreement provides for the appointment of a sole arbitrator, the demand shall include an invitation of the claimant to the respondent to meet and agree upon such arbitrator at the place, time and date stated therein which shall not be less than thirty (30) days from receipt of the demand.

(b) 如果仲裁协议规定指定独任仲裁员,该请求应包括申请人邀请被申请人在其中规定的地点、时间和日期就该仲裁员进行会晤并达成协议,该日期不得少于收到请求后的 30 天。

(c) If the arbitration agreement provides for the establishment of an arbitral tribunal of three (3) arbitrators, the demand shall name the arbitrator appointed by the claimant. It shall include the curriculum vitae of the arbitrator appointed by the claimant and the latter's acceptance of the appointment.

(c) 如果仲裁协议规定设立一个由三名仲裁员组成的仲裁庭,则该要求应指定由申请人指定的仲裁员。其中应包括申请人指定的仲裁员的履历以及申请人接受任命的情况。

(d) Where there is no prior arbitration agreement, arbitration may be initiated by one party through a demand upon the other to submit their dispute to arbitration. Arbitration shall be deemed commenced upon the agreement by the other party to submit the dispute to arbitration.

(d) 没有仲裁协议的,一方当事人可以请求另一方当事人将争议交付仲裁。当事人一方约定将争议提交仲裁时,仲裁视为开始。

(e) The demand shall require the respondent to name his/her/its arbitrator within a period which shall not be less than fifteen (15) days from receipt of the demand. This period may be extended by agreement of the parties. Within said period, the respondent shall give a written notice to the claimant of the appointment of the respondent's arbitrator and attach to the notice the arbitrator's curriculum vitae and the latter's acceptance of the appointment.

(e) 请求应要求被申请人在收到请求后不少于15天的期限内指定其仲裁员。经双方同意,该期限可以延长。被申请人应当在上述期限内向申请人发出指定被申请人的仲裁员的书面通知,并在通知中附上仲裁员的简历和被申请人接受指定的情况。

Article 5.21. Language.
第5.21条　语言。

(a) The parties are free to agree on the language or languages to be used in the arbitral proceedings. Failing such agreement, the language to be used shall be English or Filipino. The language/s agreed, unless otherwise specified therein, shall be used in all hearings and all written statements, orders or other communication by the parties and the arbitral tribunal.

(a) 各方当事人可自由约定仲裁程序中使用的一种或多种语言。如果不能达成协议,应使用英语或菲律宾语。除另有规定外,当事各方和仲裁庭的所有听讯以及所有书面陈述、命令或其他通信均应使用所商定的语言。

(b) The arbitral tribunal may order that any documentary evidence shall be accompanied by a translation into the language or languages agreed upon by the parties in accordance with paragraph (a) of this Article.

(b) 仲裁庭可命令任何书面证据应附有根据本条(a)款所商定的一种或多种语言的译文。

Article 5.22. Statements of Claim and Defense.

第 5.22 条　索赔和答辩书。

(a) Within the period of time agreed by the parties or determined by the arbitral tribunal, the claimant shall state the facts supporting his/her claim, the points at issue and the relief or remedy sought, and the respondent shall state his/her defense in respect of these particulars, unless the parties may have otherwise agreed as to the required elements of such statements. The parties may submit with their statements all documents they consider to be relevant or may add a reference to the documents or other evidence they will submit.

(a) 在各方当事人约定或仲裁庭确定的期限内,申请人应陈述支持其主张的事实、有争议的论点和所寻求的救济,被申请人应就这些细节陈述答辩,除非各方当事人可能另有约定。当事各方可将其认为相关的所有文件连同其陈述一并提交,或可在其将提交的文件或其他证据中添加一处出处。

(b) Unless otherwise agreed by the parties, either party may amend or supplement his/her/its claim or defense during the course of the arbitral proceedings, unless the arbitral tribunal considers it inappropriate to allow such amendments having regard to the delay in making it.

(b) 除非各方当事人另有约定,任何一方当事人均可在仲裁程序进行过程中修改或补充其请求或答辩,除非仲裁庭认为考虑到会延迟诉讼不宜做出此种修改。

Article 5.23. Hearing and Written Proceedings.

第 5.23 条　听证和书面诉讼。

(a) In ad hoc arbitration, the procedure determined by the arbitrator, with the agreement of the parties, shall be followed. In institutional arbitration, the applicable rules of procedure of the arbitration institution shall be followed. In default of agreement of the parties, the arbitration procedure shall be as provided in this Chapter.

(a) 在特别仲裁中,应遵循仲裁员经双方同意确定的程序。在机构仲裁中,应当遵守仲裁机构适用的议事规则。当事人未约定的,按照本章规定办理。

(b) Within thirty (30) days from the appointment of the arbitrator or the constitution of an arbitral tribunal, the arbitral tribunal shall call the parties and their respective counsels to a pre-hearing conference to discuss the following matters:

(b) 在指定仲裁员或组成仲裁庭后 30 天内,仲裁庭应召集各方当事人及其各自的律师出席预审会议,讨论下列事项:

(i) The venue or place/s where the arbitration proceeding may be conducted in an office space, a business center, a function room or any suitable place agreed upon by the parties and the arbitral tribunal, which may vary per session/hearing/conference;

(i) 仲裁程序可以在一个办公场所、一个商业中心、一个会议室或当事各方与仲裁庭商定的任何适当地点进行的地点或地点,每届会议可有不同;

(ii) The manner of recording the proceedings;

(ii) 记录仲裁程序的方式;

(iii) The periods for the communication of the statement of claims, answer to the claims with or without counterclaims, and answer to the counterclaim/s and the form and contents of such pleadings;

(iii) 提交索赔书的期限、附有或不附有反诉的对索赔的答复、对反诉的答复以及这些书状的形式和内容;

(iv) The definition of the issues submitted to the arbitral tribunal for determination and the summary of the claims and counter-claims of the parties；

（iv）提交仲裁庭裁定的问题的定义以及当事各方的请求和反诉摘要；

（v）The manner by which evidence may be offered if an oral hearing is required，the submission of sworn written statements in lieu of oral testimony，the cross-examination and further examination of witnesses；

（v）在需要进行口头听证时提供证据的方式、提交宣誓的书面陈述以代替口头证词、盘问和进一步询问证人；

（vi）The delivery of certain types of communications such as pleadings，terms of reference，order granting interim relief，final award and the like that，if made by electronic or similar means，shall require further confirmation in the form of a hard copy or hard copies delivered personally or by registered post；

（vi）交付某些类型的通信，如书状、职权范围、准予临时救济的命令、最后裁决等，如果是以电子或类似方式作出的，则需要以亲自送交或以挂号邮递送交的硬盘拷贝形式进一步确认；

（vii）The issuance of a subpoena or a subpoena duces tecum by the arbitral tribunal to compel the production of evidence if either party shall or is likely to request it；

（vii）如果任何一方当事人应当或可能要求出示证据，仲裁庭签发传票或命令传票；

（viii）The manner by which expert testimony will be received if a party will or is likely to request the arbitral tribunal to appoint one or more experts，and in such case，the period for the submission to the arbitrator by the requesting party of the proposed terms of reference for the expert，the fees to be paid，the manner of payment to the expert and the deposit by the parties or of the requesting party of such amount necessary to cover all expenses associated with the referral of such issues to the expert before the expert is appointed;

(viii) 如果一方当事人将或可能请求仲裁庭指定一名或多名专家，接收专家证词的方式，以及在这种情况下，请求方当事人向仲裁员提交专家拟议职权范围的期限和应支付的费用，向专家支付款项的方式以及当事方或请求方为支付在专家任命之前将此类问题移交专家所需的一切费用而交存的款项；

(ix) The possibility of either party applying for an order granting interim relief either with the arbitral tribunal or with the court, and, in such case, the nature of the relief to be applied for;

(ix) 任何一方当事人可以向仲裁庭或法院申请准予临时救济的命令，在这种情况下，申请救济的性质；

(x) The possibility of a site or ocular inspection, the purpose of such inspection, and in such case, the date, place and time of the inspection and the manner of conducting it, and the sharing and deposit of any associated fees and expenses;

(x) 进行现场或目视检查的可能性，这种检查的目的，以及检查的日期、地点和时间及进行检查的方式，以及任何相关费用和开支的分担和存入；

(xi) The amount to be paid to the arbitral tribunal as fees and the associated costs, charges and expenses of arbitration and the manner and timing of such payments; and

(xi) 付给仲裁庭的费用和仲裁的相关费用、收费和开支以及支付方式和时间；以及

(xii) Such other relevant matters as the parties and the arbitral tribunal may consider necessary to provide for a speedy and efficient arbitration of the dispute.

(xii) 当事各方和仲裁庭可能认为必要的其他相关事项，以对争议进行迅速有效的仲裁。

(c) To the extent possible, the arbitral tribunal and the parties shall agree upon any such matters and in default of agreement, the arbitral tribunal shall have the discretion and authority to make the decision, although in making a decision, regard shall be given to the views expressed by both parties.

(c) 在可能的情况下,仲裁庭和当事各方应就任何此类事项达成协议,在未达成协议的情况下,仲裁庭应有做出决定的酌处权和权力,但在做出决定时,应考虑到当事双方发表的意见。

(d) The arbitral tribunal shall, in consultation with the parties, fix the date/s and the time of hearing, regard being given to the desirability of conducting and concluding an arbitration without undue delay.

(d) 仲裁庭应与当事各方协商,确定举行仲裁的日期和时间,同时考虑到在不无故拖延的情况下进行和结束仲裁的可取性。

(e) The hearing set shall not be postponed except with the conformity of the arbitrator and the parties and only for a good and sufficient cause. The arbitral tribunal may deny a request to postpone or to cancel a scheduled hearing on the ground that a party has requested or is intending to request from the court or from the arbitrator an order granting interim relief.

(e) 听证会不得推迟,除非仲裁员和双方当事人一致同意,而且只能是出于良好和充分的理由。仲裁庭可以一方当事人已请求或打算请求法院或仲裁员下达准予临时救济的命令为由,拒绝推迟或取消排定的审理。

(f) A party may, during the proceedings, represent himself/herself/itself or be represented or assisted by a representative as defined by these Rules.

(f) 一方当事人在诉讼程序期间可自行代表自己或由本规则所界定的代表代表或协助。

(g) The hearing may proceed in the absence of a party who fails to obtain an adjournment thereof or who, despite due notice, fails to be present, by himself/herself/itself or through a representative, at such hearing.

(g) 如果一方当事人未能获得延期，或尽管得到适当通知但未能亲自或通过一名代表出席，则可在缺席的情况下进行听讯。

(h) Only parties, their respective representatives, the witnesses and the administrative staff of the arbitral tribunal shall have the right to be present during the hearing, Any other person may be allowed by the arbitrator to be present if the parties, upon being informed of the presence of such person and the reason for his/her presence, interpose no objection thereto.

(h) 只有当事各方、其各自的代理人、证人和仲裁庭的行政工作人员才有权出席听讯，仲裁员可以允许任何其他人出席听讯，条件是当事各方在获悉该人在场和其出席的理由后对此没有提出异议。

(i) Issues raised during the arbitration proceeding relating to (a) the jurisdiction of the arbitral tribunal over one or more of the claims or counter-claims, or (b) the arbitrability of a particular claim or counter-claim, shall be resolved by the arbitral tribunal as threshold issues, if the parties so request, unless they are intertwined with factual issues that they cannot be resolved ahead of the hearing on the merits of the dispute.

(i) 在仲裁程序中提出的与仲裁法庭对一项或多项索赔或反诉的管辖权有关的问题，或与某一特定索赔或反诉的可仲裁性有关的问题，如果当事方提出请求，应由仲裁庭作为初步问题加以解决。除非他们与无法在审理争端案情之前解决的事实问题交织在一起。

(j) Each witness shall, before giving testimony, be required to take an oath/affirmation before the arbitral tribunal, to tell the whole truth and nothing but the truth during the hearing.

(j) 每位证人在作证前，都必须在仲裁庭面前做出确认，在审理过程中说出全部事实。

（k）The arbitral tribunal shall arrange for the transcription of the recorded testimony of each witness and require each party to share the cost of recording and transcription of the testimony of each witness.

（k）仲裁庭应安排对每一证人的证词进行记录，并要求每一方当事人分担对每一证人的证词进行记录的费用。

（l）Each party shall provide the other party with a copy of each statement or document submitted to the arbitral tribunal and shall have an opportunity to reply in writing to the other party's statements and proofs.

（l）一方当事人应当向另一方当事人提供提交仲裁庭的每一份陈述或文件的副本，并应当有机会对另一方当事人的陈述和证据做出书面答复。

（m）The arbitral tribunal may require the parties to produce such other documents or provide such information as in its judgment would be necessary for it to render a complete，fair and impartial award.

（m）仲裁庭可要求各方当事人出示其判决中所需的其他文件或提供此类信息，以作出完整、公正和无偏倚的裁决。

（n）The arbitral tribunal shall receive as evidence all exhibits submitted by a party properly marked and identified at the time of submission.

（n）仲裁庭应接受一方当事人提交的、在提交材料时做了适当标记和记号的所有证据。

（o）At the close of the hearing，the arbitral tribunal shall specifically inquire of all parties whether they have further proof or witnesses to present；upon receiving a negative reply，the arbitral tribunal shall declare the hearing closed.

（o）在审理结束时，仲裁庭应具体询问所有当事方是否有进一步的证据或证人出庭；在收到否定答复后，仲裁庭应宣布审理结束。

（p）After a hearing is declared closed，no further motion or

manifestation or submission may be allowed except for post-hearing briefs and reply briefs that the parties have agreed to submit within a fixed period after the hearing is declared closed, or when the arbitral tribunal, motu proprio or upon request of a party, allows the reopening of the hearing.

(p) 在宣布审理结束后,不得提出进一步的动议或表示或提交意见,但在宣布审理结束后的一段固定期间内当事人已同意提交的审理后案情摘要和答辩案情摘要除外,或仲裁庭自行决定或应一方当事人的请求允许重新审理。

(q) Decisions on interlocutory matters shall be made by the sole arbitrator or by the majority of the arbitral tribunal. The arbitral tribunal may authorize its chairman to issue or release, on behalf of the arbitral tribunal, its decision on interlocutory matters.

(q) 关于中间事项的裁决应由独任仲裁员或仲裁庭的多数作出。仲裁庭可以授权其主席代表仲裁庭就中间事项作出或解除其裁决。

(r) Except as provided in Section 17 (d) of the ADR Act, no arbitrator shall act as a mediator in any proceeding in which he/she is acting as arbitrator even if requested by the parties; and all negotiations towards settlement of the dispute must take place without the presence of the arbitrators.

(r) 除《替代性争议解决法案》第 17 条(d)款规定的情况外,任何仲裁员都不得在其担任仲裁员的任何程序中担任调解人,即使当事方提出要求;所有解决争端的谈判都必须在没有仲裁员在场的情况下进行。

(s) Before assuming the duties of his/her office, an arbitrator must be sworn by any officer authorized by law to administer an oath or be required to make an affirmation to faithfully and fairly hear and examine the matters in controversy and to make a just award according to the best of his/her ability and understanding. A copy of the arbitrator's oath or affirmation shall be furnished each party to the arbitration.

（s）在担任其职务之前，仲裁员必须由任何经法律授权进行宣誓的官员宣誓，或被要求做出确认，忠实和公正地听取和审查争议事项，并根据其能力和理解作出公正裁决。应当向仲裁各方当事人提供仲裁员宣誓或者确认的副本。

（t）Either party may object to the commencement or continuation of an arbitration proceeding unless the arbitrator takes an oath or affirmation as required in this Chapter. If the arbitrator shall refuse to take an oath or affirmation as required by law and this Rule，he/she shall be replaced. The failure to object to the absence of an oath or affirmation shall be deemed a waiver of such objection and the proceedings shall continue in due course and may not later be used as a ground to invalidate the proceedings.

（t）任何一方当事人均可对仲裁程序的开始或继续提出异议，除非仲裁员按照本章的要求做出宣誓或确认。如果仲裁员拒绝按照法律要求进行宣誓或确认，则应替换该仲裁员。未能对没有宣誓或确认提出异议，应视为放弃此种异议，诉讼程序应在适当时候继续进行，不得日后用作使诉讼无效的理由。

（u）The arbitral tribunal shall have the power to administer oaths to，or require affirmation from，all witnesses directing them to tell the truth，the whole truth and nothing but the truth in any testimony，oral or written，which they may give or offer in any arbitration hearing. The oath or affirmation shall be required of every witness before his/her testimony，oral or written，is heard or considered.

（u）仲裁庭应有权向所有证人宣誓或要求其确认，指示他们在任何仲裁听证会上可能做出或提供的任何口头或书面证词中陈述全部事实。在听取或考虑每位证人的口头或书面证词之前，应要求其进行宣誓或确认。

（v）The arbitral tribunal shall have the power to require any person to attend a hearing as a witness. It shall have the power to subpoena witnesses, to testify and/or produce documents when the relevancy and materiality thereof has been shown to the arbitral tribunal. The arbitral tribunal may also require the exclusion of any witness during the testimony of any other witness. Unless the parties otherwise agree, all the arbitrators appointed in any controversy must attend all the hearings and hear the evidence of the parties.

(v) 仲裁庭有权要求任何人作为证人出席听讯。仲裁庭有权传唤证人作证以及向仲裁庭证明其相关性和重要性的文件。仲裁庭也可要求在任何其他证人作证期间不得接纳任何证人。除非当事各方另有协议,在任何争议中指定的所有仲裁员必须出席所有审理并听取当事各方的证据。

Article 5. 24. Power of Arbitral Tribunal to Order Interim Measures.

第5.24条　仲裁庭下令采取临时措施的权力。

(a) Unless otherwise agreed by the parties, the arbitral tribunal may, at the request of a party and in accordance with the this Article, order any party to take such interim measures of protection as the arbitral tribunal may consider necessary in respect of the subject matter of the dispute or the procedure. Such interim measures may include, but shall not be limited, to preliminary injunction directed against a party, appointment of receivers or detention of property that is the subject of the dispute in arbitration or its preservation or inspection.

(a) 除非各方当事人另有约定,仲裁庭可根据一方当事人的请求并依照本条的规定,命令任何一方当事人就争议的主题事项或程序采取仲裁庭认为必要的临时保全措施。这种临时措施可包括但不限于针对当事一方的初步强制令、指定接管人或扣押作为仲裁争议标的的财产或对其进行保全或检查。

（b）After the constitution of the arbitral tribunal，and during the arbitration proceedings，a request for interim measures of protection，or modification thereof，may be made with the arbitral tribunal. The arbitral tribunal is deemed constituted when the sole arbitrator or the third arbitrator，who has been nominated，has accepted the nomination and written communication of said nomination and acceptance has been received by the party making the request.

（b）在组成仲裁庭之后，以及在仲裁程序期间，可以向仲裁庭提出采取或修改临时保护措施的请求。如果提出请求的一方收到了独任仲裁员或第三名被提名的仲裁员接受该提名和接受的书面通知，即视为仲裁庭的组成。

（c）The following rules on interim or provisional relief shall be observed：

（c）应遵守关于临时或暂时补救的下列规则：

　（i）Any party may request that provisional or interim relief be granted against the adverse party.

　（i）任何一方均可请求由对方给予临时或暂时救济。

　（ii）Such relief may be granted：

　（ii）为了以下目的，可给予这种救济：

　　（aa）To prevent irreparable loss or injury；

　　（aa）防止不可挽回的损失或伤害；

　　（bb）To provide security for the performance of an obligation；

　　（bb）为履行义务提供担保；

　　（cc）To produce or preserve evidence；or

　　（cc）提供或保存证据；或

　　（dd）To compel any other appropriate act or omissions.

　　（dd）迫使任何其他适当的作为或不作为。

(iii) The order granting provisional relief may be conditioned upon the provision of security or any act or omission specified in the order.

(iii) 给予临时救济的命令可以以提供该命令中规定的担保或任何作为或不作为为条件。

(iv) Interim provisional relief is requested by written application transmitted by reasonable means to the arbitral tribunal and the party against whom relief is sought，describing in appropriate detail of the precise relief，the party against whom the relief is requested，the ground for the relief，and the evidence supporting the request.

(iv) 临时救济请求应通过书面申请，以合理的方式转交仲裁庭和寻求救济的当事人，适当详细地说明确切的救济请求的当事人、请求救济的理由和支持请求的证据。

(v) The order either granting or denying an application for interim relief shall be binding upon the parties.

(v) 批准或拒绝临时补救申请的命令对双方当事人具有约束力。

(vi) Either party may apply with the court for assistance in implementing or enforcing an interim measure ordered by an arbitral tribunal.

(vi) 任何一方当事人均可向法院申请协助执行仲裁庭下令采取的临时措施。

(vii) A party who does not comply with the order shall be liable for all damages，resulting from noncompliance，including all expenses，and reasonably attorney's fees，paid in obtaining the order's judicial enforcement.

(vii) 不遵守命令的一方应负责赔偿因不遵守命令而造成的一切损害，包括为获得命令的司法执行而支付的所有费用和合理的律师费。

(d) The arbitral tribunal shall have the power at any time，before rendering the award，without prejudice to the rights of any party to petition the court to take measures to safeguard and/or conserve any matter which is the subject of the dispute in arbitration.

(d) 仲裁庭在作出裁决之前，应有权随时请求法院采取措施维护或保存在仲裁中引起争议的任何事项，但不损害任何一方当事人的权利。

Article 5.25. Default of a Party. Unless otherwise agreed by the parties，if，without showing sufficient cause，

第5.25条　一方违约。除非当事各方另有协议，如果没有充分理由，

(a) the claimant fails to communicate his/her/its statement of claim in accordance with paragraph（a）of Article 5.22（Statements of Claim and Defense），the arbitral tribunal shall terminate the proceedings；

(a) 原告未能根据第5.22条(a)款(关于索赔和答辩的说明)提交其索赔说明，仲裁庭应终止仲裁程序；

(b) the respondent fails to communicate his/her/its statement of defense in accordance with paragraph（a）of Article 5.22（Statements of Claim and Defense），the arbitral tribunal shall continue the proceedings without treating such failure in itself as an admission of the claimant's allegations；

(b) 被申请人未能根据第5.22条(a)款(声明和答辩)告知其答辩书，仲裁庭应继续进行仲裁程序，但其本身不应将这种不作为视为承认申请人的指控；

(c) any party fails to appear at a hearing or to produce documentary evidence，the arbitral tribunal may continue the proceedings and make the award based on the evidence before it.

(c) 任何一方当事人未出席庭审或未出示书面证据，仲裁庭均可继续进行程序并根据其收到的证据作出裁决。

Article 5.26. Expert Appointed by the Arbitral Tribunal.

第 5.26 条　仲裁庭指定的专家。

(a) Unless otherwise agreed by the parties, the arbitral tribunal,

(a) 除非当事人另有约定,仲裁庭,

> (i) may appoint one or more experts to report to it on specific issues to be determined by the arbitral tribunal; or

> (i) 可指定一名或多名专家就仲裁庭确定的具体问题向仲裁庭报告;或

> (ii) may require a party to give the expert any relevant information or to produce, or to provide access to, any relevant documents, goods or other property for his/her inspection.

> (ii) 可要求一方向专家提供任何相关信息,或提供或允许查阅任何相关文件、货物或其他财产,供其检查。

(b) Unless otherwise agreed by the parties, if a party so requests or if the arbitral tribunal considers it necessary, the expert shall, after delivery of his/her written or oral report, participate in a hearing where the parties have the opportunity to put questions to him/her and to present expert witnesses in order to testify on the points at issue.

(b) 除非当事各方另有约定,如当事一方提出请求,或仲裁庭认为有必要,专家应在做出书面或口头报告后,参加当事各方有机会向其提出问题并提出专家证人就有关问题作证的听讯。

> (c) Upon agreement of the parties, the finding of the expert engaged by the arbitral tribunal on the matter/s referred to him shall be binding upon the parties and the arbitral tribunal.

(c) 经各方当事人同意,仲裁庭就提交给他的事项所聘请的专家的结论对各方当事人和仲裁庭具有约束力。

Article 5. 27. Court Assistance in Taking Evidence and Other Matters.

第 5.27 条　法庭协助取证及其他事宜。

(a) The arbitral tribunal or a party, with the approval of the arbitral tribunal may request from a court，assistance in taking evidence such as the issuance of subpoena adtestificandum and subpoena duces tecum，deposition taking，site or ocular inspection，and physical examination of properties. The court may grant the request within its competence and according to its rules on taking evidence.

（a）经仲裁庭批准，仲裁庭或一方当事人可请求法院协助取证，如发出传票、取证、现场或目视检查和财产实物检查。法院可在其权限范围内并根据其取证规则批准请求。

（b）The arbitral tribunal or a party to the dispute interested in enforcing an order of the arbitral tribunal may request from a competent court，assistance in enforcing orders of the arbitral tribunal，including but not limited，to the following：

（b）执行仲裁庭命令的仲裁法庭或争端当事方可请求主管法院协助执行仲裁庭的命令，包括但不限于下列命令：

（i）Interim or provisional relief；

（i）临时救济；

（ii）Protective orders with respect to confidentiality；

（ii）关于保密的保护令；

（iii）Orders of the arbitral tribunal pertaining to the subject matter of the dispute that may affect third persons and/or their properties；and/or

（iii）仲裁庭关于可能影响第三人及其财产的有关争议标的的命令；以及/或

（iv）Examination of debtors.

（iv）对债务人的审查。

Article 5.28. Rules Applicable to the Substance of Dispute.

第 5.28 条　适用于争议实质的规则。

（a）The arbitral tribunal shall decide the dispute in accordance with such law as is chosen by the parties. In the absence of such agreement，Philippine law shall apply.

（a）仲裁庭应根据各方当事人选定的法律对争议作出裁决。如果没有这样的协议，则适用菲律宾法律。

（b）The arbitral tribunal may grant any remedy or relief which it deems just and equitable and within the scope of the agreement of the parties，which shall include，but not be limited to，the specific performance of a contract.

（b）仲裁庭可以在当事人协议的范围内，给予其认为公正和公平的任何补救或救济，其中应包括但不限于合同的具体履行。

（c）In all cases, the arbitral tribunal shall decide in accordance with the terms of the contract and shall take into account the usages of the trade applicable to the transaction.

（c）在所有情况下，仲裁庭应根据合同条款做出决定，并应考虑到适用于交易的行业惯例。

Article 5.29. Decision Making by the Arbitral Tribunal.
第5.29条　仲裁庭的裁决。

（a）In arbitration proceedings with more than one arbitrator, any decision of the arbitral tribunal shall be made，unless otherwise agreed by the parties，by a majority of all its members. However，questions of procedure may be decided by the chairman of the arbitral tribunal，if so authorized by the parties or all members of the arbitral tribunal.

（a）在有一名以上仲裁员的仲裁程序中，仲裁庭的任何决定，除非各方当事人另有约定，均应由仲裁庭全体仲裁员的过半数做出。但程序问题经各方当事人或仲裁庭全体仲裁员授权，可由仲裁庭庭长决定。

（b）Unless otherwise agreed upon by the parties, the arbitral tribunal shall render its written award within thirty （30） days after the closing of the hearings and/or submission of the parties' respective briefs or if the oral hearings shall have been waived，within thirty（30）days after the arbitral tribunal shall have declared such proceedings in lieu of hearing closed. This period may be further extended by mutual consent of the parties.

（b）除非各方当事人另有约定,仲裁庭应在审理结束后 30 天内作出书面裁决,并提交或提交各方当事人各自的书状,或者如果已放弃口头审理,则应在仲裁庭宣布此种程序以代替非公开审理后 30 天内作出书面裁决。经双方同意,该期限可进一步延长。

Article 5.30. Settlement.

第 5.30 条　和解。

（a）If，during arbitral proceedings, the parties settle the dispute，the arbitral tribunal shall terminate the proceedings and，if requested by the parties and not objected to by the arbitral tribunal，record the settlement in the form of an arbitral award on agreed terms，consent award or award based on compromise.

（a）如果在仲裁程序期间,当事各方解决了争议,仲裁庭应终止仲裁程序,如果当事各方提出请求,且仲裁庭未表示反对,则应记录以协议条款、同意裁决或基于妥协的裁决形式作出的仲裁裁决。

（b）An award as rendered above shall be made in accordance with the provisions of Article 5.31（Form and Contents of Award）and shall state that it is an award. Such an award has the same status and effect as any other award on the merits of the case.

（b）上述裁决应根据第 5.31 条(裁决的形式和内容)作出,并应说明这是裁决。这种裁决与关于案情的任何其他裁决具有同样的地位和效力。

Article 5.31. Form and Contents of Award.

第 5.31 条　裁决的形式和内容。

（a）The award shall be made in writing and shall be signed by the arbitral tribunal. In arbitration proceedings with more than one arbitrator, the signatures of the majority of all members of the arbitral tribunal shall suffice, provided that the reason for any omitted signature is stated.

（a）裁决应以书面形式作出，并应由仲裁庭签署。在有一名以上仲裁员的仲裁程序中，只要说明任何省略签名的理由，仲裁庭全体成员的多数签名即可。

（b）The award shall state the reasons upon which it is based, unless the parties have agreed that no reasons are to be given or the award is an award on agreed terms, consent award or award based on compromise under Article 5.30 (Settlement).

（b）裁决应说明裁决所依据的理由，除非当事各方同意不提出理由，或裁决是根据商定的条件、同意裁决或根据第 5.30 条（和解裁决）的和解作出的裁决。

（c）The award shall state its date and the place of arbitration as determined in accordance with paragraph (a) of Article 5.19 (Place of Arbitration). The award shall be deemed to have been made at that place.

（c）裁决应说明其日期和根据第 5.19 条（a）款（仲裁地）确定的仲裁地。裁决应视为在该地作出。

（d）After the award is made, a copy signed by the arbitrators in accordance with paragraph (a) of this Article shall be delivered to each party.

（d）裁决作出后，由仲裁员根据本条（a）款签署的副本应送交各方当事人。

（e）The award of the arbitral tribunal need not be acknowledged, sworn to under oath, or affirmed by the arbitral tribunal unless so required in writing by the parties. If despite such requirement, the arbitral tribunal shall fail to do as required, the parties may, within thirty days from receipt of said award, request the arbitral tribunal to supply the omission. The failure of the parties to make an objection or make such request within the said period shall be deemed a waiver of such requirement and may no longer be raised as a ground to invalidate the award.

（e）仲裁庭的裁决无须得到承认、宣誓或经仲裁庭确认，除非各方当事人以书面形式要求如此。尽管有这种要求，仲裁庭仍应不按要求行事的，各方当事人可在收到该裁决之日起 30 天内请求仲裁庭按要求行事。当事人未在上述期限内提出异议或者请求的，视为放弃该要求，不得再作为裁决无效的理由。

Article 5.32. Termination of Proceedings.

第 5.32 条　诉讼程序的终止。

（a）The arbitration proceedings are terminated by the final award or by an order of the arbitral tribunal in accordance with paragraph（b）of this Article.

（a）根据本条（b）规定，仲裁程序由最后裁决或仲裁庭命令终止。

（b）The arbitral tribunal shall issue an order for the termination of the arbitration proceedings when：

（b）在下列情况下，仲裁庭应发出终止仲裁程序的命令：

（i）The claimant withdraws his claim, unless the respondent objects thereto for the purpose of prosecuting his counterclaims in the same proceedings or the arbitral tribunal recognizes a legitimate interest on his part in obtaining a final settlement of the dispute；or

（i）申请人撤回请求除非被申请人为在同一程序中对其反诉，或仲裁庭承认其在争取最后解决争议方面的合法利益；或

(ii) The parties agree on the termination of the proceedings; or

(ii) 当事各方同意终止程序;或

(iii) The arbitral tribunal finds that the continuation of the proceedings has for any other reason become unnecessary or impossible; or

(iii) 仲裁庭认为,由于任何其他原因,程序的继续已变得不必要或不可能;或

(iv) The required deposits are not paid in full in accordance with paragraph (d) of Article 5.46 (Fees and Costs).

(iv) 所需费用没有按照第5.46条(d)款(收费和费用)全额支付。

(c) The mandate of the arbitral tribunal ends with the termination of the arbitration proceedings, subject to the provisions of Article 5.33 (Correction and Interpretation of Award, Additional Award) and Article 5.34 (Application for Setting Aside an Exclusive Recourse Against Arbitral Award).

(c) 仲裁庭的任务授权随着仲裁程序的终止而结束,但须遵守第5.33条(更正和解释裁决,补充裁决)和第5.34条(申请撤销对仲裁裁决的排他性追索)。

(d) Except as otherwise provided in the arbitration agreement, no motion for reconsideration, correction and interpretation of award or additional award shall be made with the arbitral tribunal. The arbitral tribunal, by releasing its final award, loses jurisdiction over the dispute and the parties to the arbitration. However, where it is shown that the arbitral tribunal failed to resolve an issue submitted to him for determination, a verified motion to complete a final award may be made within thirty (30) days from its receipt.

(d) 除仲裁协议另有规定外,不得向仲裁庭提出重新审议、更正和解释裁决或补充裁决的动议。仲裁庭通过公布其最后裁决,丧失对争议和仲裁各方的管辖权。但如果证明仲裁庭未能解决提交其裁定

的问题,则可在收到后 30 天内提出经核实的完成最后裁决的动议。

(e) Notwithstanding the foregoing, the arbitral tribunal may, for special reasons, reserve in the final award or order, a hearing to quantify costs and determine which party shall bear the costs or apportionment thereof as may be determined to be equitable. Pending determination of this issue, the award shall not be deemed final for purposes of appeal, vacation, correction, or any post-award proceedings.

(e) 尽管有上述规定,仲裁庭仍可出于特殊原因,在最后裁决或命令中保留一次听讯,以量化费用并确定由哪一方承担费用或按确定的公平分摊费用。就上诉、休庭、更正或任何裁决后程序而言,裁决在裁定该问题之前,不应视为终局裁决。

Article 5.33. Correction and Interpretation of Award, Additional Award.

第 5.33 条　更正和解释裁决,补充裁决。

(a) Within thirty (30) days from receipt of the award, unless another period of time has been agreed upon by the parties:

(a) 自收到裁决之日起 30 天内,除非当事各方商定另一段时间:

(i) A party may, with notice to the other party, the arbitral tribunal to correct in the award any errors in computation, any clerical or typographical errors or any errors of similar nature.

(i) 一方当事人可以在通知另一方当事人的情况下,更正裁决中计算上的任何错误、任何文书或印刷错误或任何类似性质的错误。

(ii) If so agreed by the parties, a party, with notice to the other party, may request the arbitral tribunal to give an interpretation of a specific point or part of the award. If the arbitral tribunal considers the request to be justified, it shall make the correction or give the interpretation within thirty （30） days from receipt of the request. The interpretation shall form part of the award.

(ii) 当事人约定的,一方当事人在通知另一方当事人的情况下,可以请求仲裁庭对裁决的某一具体内容或部分做出解释。仲裁庭认为请求有正当理由的,应当自收到请求之日起 30 天内做出更正或者做出解释。解释应构成裁决的一部分。

(b) The arbitral tribunal may correct any error of the type referred to in paragraph （a） of this Article on its own initiative within thirty（30）days of the date of the award.

(b) 仲裁庭可在裁决之日起 30 天内自行纠正本条(a)款所述的任何错误。

(c) Unless otherwise agreed by the parties, a party may, with notice to the other party, may request, within thirty （30） days of receipt of the award, the arbitral tribunal to make an additional award as to claims presented in the arbitral proceedings but omitted from the award. If the arbitral tribunal considers the request to be justified, it shall make the additional award within sixty（60）days.

(c) 除非当事人另有约定,一方当事人可以在通知另一方当事人后,请求仲裁庭在收到裁决后 30 天内就仲裁程序中提出但从裁决中删除的请求作出补充裁决。如果仲裁庭认为该请求有正当理由,则应在 60 天内作出补充裁决。

(d) The arbitral tribunal may extend, if necessary, the period of time within which it shall make a correction, interpretation or an additional award under paragraphs （a） and （c） of this Article.

(d) 仲裁庭可在必要时延长其根据本条(a)款和(c)款做出更正、解释或作出附加裁决的期限。

(e) The provisions of Article 5.31 （Form and Contents of Award） shall apply to a correction or interpretation of the award or to an additional award.

（e）第 5.31 条的规定（裁决的形式和内容）应适用于对裁决的更正或解释或附加裁决。

Article 5.34. Application for Setting Aside an Exclusive Recourse against Arbitral Award. The court，when asked to set aside an award，may，where appropriate and so requested by a party，suspend the setting aside proceedings for a period of time determined by it in order to give the arbitral tribunal an opportunity to resume the arbitral proceedings or to take such other action as in the arbitral tribunal's opinion will eliminate the grounds for setting aside an award.

第 5.34 条　申请撤销对仲裁裁决的排他性追索权。法院在被要求撤销裁决时，可酌情并应一方当事人的请求，在其确定的一段时间内暂停撤销程序，以便仲裁庭有机会恢复仲裁程序或采取仲裁庭认为将消除撤销裁决的理由的其他行动。

Article 5.35. Grounds to Vacate an Arbitral Award.

第 5.35 条　撤销仲裁裁决的理由。

（a）The arbitral award may be questioned，vacated or set aside by the appropriate court in accordance with the Special ADR Rules only on the following grounds：

（a）只有在以下理由的情况下，有关法院才可根据《替代性争议解决法案》对仲裁裁决提出质疑或撤销：

（i）The arbitral award was procured by corruption，fraud or other undue means; or

（i）仲裁裁决是通过腐败、欺诈或其他不当手段取得的；或

（ii）There was evident partiality or corruption in the arbitral tribunal or any of its members; or

（ii）在仲裁庭或其任何成员中存在明显的偏袒或腐败；或

(iii) The arbitral tribunal was guilty of misconduct or any form of misbehavior that has materially prejudiced the rights of any party such as refusing to postpone the hearing upon sufficient cause shown or to hear evidence pertinent and material to the controversy; or

(iii) 仲裁庭犯有不当行为或任何形式的不当行为,这些不当行为实质上损害了任何一方当事人的权利,例如,有充分理由拒绝推迟审理,或拒绝听取与争议有关的证据和材料;或

(iv) One or more of the arbitrators was disqualified to act as such under this Chapter and willfully refrained from disclosing such disqualification; or

(iv) 一名或多名仲裁员根据本章被取消担任仲裁员的资格,并故意不披露此类信息;或

(v) The arbitral tribunal exceeded its powers, or so imperfectly executed them, such that a complete, final and definite award upon the subject matter submitted to it was not made. Any other ground raised to question, vacate or set aside the arbitral award shall be disregarded by the court.

(v) 仲裁庭超越了其权限,或者不能完美地执行这些权限,因此没有就提交给它的争议标的作出完整、最终和确定的裁决。提出质疑、撤销或撤销仲裁裁决的任何其他理由,法院应不予考虑。

(b) Where a petition to vacate or set aside an award is filed, the petitioner may simultaneously, or the oppositor may in the alternative, petition the court to remit the case to the same arbitral tribunal for the purpose of making a new or revised final and definite award or to direct a new hearing before the same or new arbitral tribunal, the members of which shall be chosen in the manner originally provided in the arbitration agreement or submission. In the latter case, any provision limiting the time in which the arbitral tribunal may make a decision shall be deemed applicable to the new arbitral tribunal and to commence from the date of the court's order.

（b）如果提出撤销裁决的请求，申请人可以同时请求法院将案件移交同一仲裁庭，以便作出新的或经修订的最后和确定的裁决，或指导同一仲裁庭或新仲裁庭进行新的审理，其成员应按仲裁协议或提交书最初规定的方式选出。在后一种情况下，任何限制仲裁庭作出裁决的时间的规定应被视为适用于新的仲裁庭，并自法院下达命令之日起生效。

（c）Where a party files a petition with the court to vacate or set aside an award by reason of omission/s that do not affect the merits of the case and may be cured or remedied, the adverse party may oppose that petition and instead request the court to suspend the vacation or setting aside proceedings for a period of time to give the arbitral tribunal an opportunity to cure or remedy the award or resume the arbitration proceedings or take such other action as will eliminate the grounds for vacation or setting aside.

（c）如果一方当事人以不影响案情并可能得到救济的理由提出要求撤销或撤销裁决的请求，对方当事人可以反对该请求，而请求法院在一段时间内暂停撤销程序，使仲裁庭有机会纠正或补救裁决或恢复仲裁程序，或采取其他行动，消除撤销的理由。

RULE 6 - Recognition and Enforcement of Awards
细则 6——承认和执行裁决

Article 5. 36. Confirmation of Award. The party moving for an order confirming, modifying, correcting, or vacating an award, shall, at the time that such motion is filed with the court for the entry of judgment thereon, also file the original or verified copy of the award, the arbitration or settlement agreement, and such papers as may be required by the Special ADR Rules.

第5.36条   裁决确认。请求命令确认、修改、纠正或撤销裁决的当事人，应当在向法院提出该项请求以便作出判决时，还应当提交裁决、仲裁或和解协议的原件或经核实的副本，以及替代性争议解决法案特别规则可能要求的文件。

Article 5. 37. Judgment. Upon the grant of an order confirming, modifying or correcting an award, judgment may be entered in conformity therewith in the court where said application was filed. Costs of the application and the proceedings subsequent thereto may be awarded by the court in its discretion. If awarded, the amount thereof must be included in the judgment. Judgment will be enforced like court judgments.

第5.37条   判决。在发布命令确认、修改或纠正裁决后，判决可在提出申请的法院作出。申请费用和随后的诉讼程序可由法院酌情裁定。如果裁定，其数额必须包括在判决中。判决将像法院判决一样执行。

Article 5.38. Appeal. A decision of the court confirming, vacating, setting aside, modifying or correcting an arbitral award may be appealed to the Court of Appeals in accordance with Special ADR Rules. The losing party who appeals from the judgment of the Court confirming an arbitral award shall be required by the Court of Appeals to post a counter-bond executed in favor of the prevailing party equal to the amount of the award in accordance with the Special ADR Rules.

第5.38条   上诉。对法院确认、撤销、撤销、修改或纠正仲裁裁决的判决，可根据特别规则向上诉法院提出上诉。对法院确认仲裁裁决的判决提出上诉的败诉一方，上诉法院应要求其按照特别的仲裁规则出具以胜诉一方为受益人的反保证书，保证金额相当于裁决金额。

Article 5. 39. Venue and Jurisdiction. Proceedings for recognition and enforcement of an arbitration agreement or for vacation or setting aside of an arbitral award, and any application with a court for arbitration assistance and supervision, except appeal, shall be deemed as special proceedings and shall be filed with the court.

第 5.39 条 地点和管辖权。关于承认和执行仲裁协议、撤销仲裁裁决的程序,以及向法院提出的任何仲裁协助和监督申请,除上诉外,应视为特别程序,并应提交以下地区的法院。

(a) where the arbitration proceedings are conducted;

(a) 进行仲裁程序的地方;

(b) where the asset to be attached or levied upon, or the act to be enjoined is located;

(b) 被扣押或征税的资产或被禁止的行为所在地;

(c) where any of the parties to the dispute resides or has its place of business; or

(c) 争议任何一方当事人居住或拥有其营业地;或

(d) in the National Capital Judicial Region at the option of the applicant.

(d) 在国家首都司法区域内申请人选择的地区。

Article 5. 40. Notice of Proceedings to Parties. In a special proceeding for recognition and enforcement of an arbitral award, the court shall send notice to the parties at their address of record in the arbitration, or if any party cannot be served notice at such address, at such party's last known address. The notice shall be sent at least fifteen (15) days before the date set for the initial hearing of the application.

第 5.40 条 向当事人发出诉讼通知。在关于承认和执行仲裁裁决的特别程序中,法院应向仲裁记录所在地的各方当事人发出通知,或者任何一方当事人不能在该地址接收的,以该当事人最后为人所知的地址向当事人发出通知。通知须在首次聆讯日期前最少 15 天发出。

Article 5.41. Legal Representation in Domestic Arbitration.
第 5.41 条 在国内仲裁中的法律代理。

(a) In domestic arbitration conducted in the Philippines, a party may be represented by any person of his/her/its choice: Provided, that such representative, unless admitted to the practice of law in the Philippines, shall not be authorized to appear as counsel in any Philippine Court, or any other quasi-judicial body whether or not such appearance is in relation to the arbitration in which he/she appears.

(a) 在菲律宾进行的国内仲裁中,一方当事人可以由其选择的任何人作为其代表:条件是,该代表除非被允许在菲律宾从事法律实践,否则不得获准作为律师出席任何菲律宾法院或任何其他准司法机构,无论这种出席是否与他(她)出席的仲裁有关。

(b) No arbitrator shall act as a mediator in any proceeding in which he/she is acting as arbitrator and all negotiations towards settlement of the dispute must take place without the presence of the arbitrators.

(b) 任何仲裁员均不得在其担任仲裁员的程序中担任调解人,所有解决争端的谈判都必须在仲裁员不在场的情况下进行。

Article 5.42. Confidentiality of Arbitration Proceedings. The arbitration proceedings, including the records, evidence and the arbitral award and other confidential information, shall be considered privileged and confidential and shall not be published except—

第 5.42 条 仲裁程序的机密性。仲裁程序,包括记录、证据和仲裁裁决及其他机密资料,应视为保密和保密,除下列情况外不得公布:

(a) with the consent of the parties; or

（a）经当事方同意；或

（b）for the limited purpose of disclosing to the court relevant documents in cases where resort to the court is allowed herein.

（b）在允许诉诸法院的案件中，为了向法院披露相关文件的有限目的。

Provided，however，that the court in which the action or the appeal is pending may issue a protective order to prevent or prohibit disclosure of documents or information containing secret processes，developments，research and other information where it is shown that the applicant shall be materially prejudiced by an authorized disclosure thereof.

但如果经授权披露载有秘密程序、事态发展、研究和其他资料的文件或资料，证明申请者应受到实质损害，则诉讼或上诉待决的法院可发出保护令，防止或禁止披露这些文件或资料。

Article 5.43. Death of a Party. Where a party dies after making a submission or a contract to arbitrate as prescribed in these Rules，the proceeding may be begun or continued upon the application of，or notice to，his/her executor or administrator，or temporary administrator of his/her estate. In any such case，the court may issue an order extending the time within which notice of a motion to recognize or vacate an award must be served. Upon recognizing an award，where a party has died since it was filed or delivered，the court must enter judgment in the name of the original party；and the proceedings thereupon are the same as where a party dies after a verdict.

第5.43条　一方当事人死亡。当事人根据本规则的规定提交仲裁文件或订立仲裁合同后死亡的，经其遗嘱执行人或管理人或其财产的临时管理人申请或通知，可以启动或继续进行仲裁。在任何这类情况下，法院可以发出命令，延长必须送达承认或撤销裁决的通知的时间。在承认裁决时，如果一方当事人自提交或交付裁决以来死亡，法院必须以原始当事人的名义作出判决;而由此产生的诉讼程序与一方当事人在判决后死亡的诉讼程序相同。

Article 5.44. Multi-Party Arbitration.

第5.44条 多方仲裁。

(a) When a single arbitration involves more than two parties, these Rules, to the extent possible, shall be used subject to such modifications consistent with Articles 5.17 (Equal Treatment of Parties) and 5.18 (Determination of Rules of Procedure) as the arbitral tribunal shall deem appropriate to address possible complexities of a multi-party arbitration.

(a) 当一项仲裁涉及两个以上当事方时,应尽可能使用本规则,但须按照第5.17条(对当事方的平等待遇)和第5.18条(确定程序规则)处理多方仲裁可能存在的复杂性。

(b) When a claimant includes persons who are not parties to or otherwise bound by the arbitration agreement, directly or by reference, between him/her and the respondent as additional claimants or additional respondents, the respondent shall be deemed to have consented to the inclusion of the additional claimants or the additional respondents unless not later than the date of communicating his/her answer to the request for arbitration, either by motion or by a special defense in his answer, he objects, on jurisdictional grounds, to the inclusion of such additional claimants or additional respondents. The additional respondents shall be deemed to have consented to their inclusion in the arbitration unless, not later than the date of communicating their answer to the request for arbitration, either by motion or a special defense in their answer, they object, on jurisdictional grounds, to their inclusion.

(b) 如果申请人包括其本人与被申请人之间作为附加申请人或附加被

申请人的非仲裁协议的当事人或以其他方式直接或通过提及方式受仲裁协议约束的人,除非被申请人不迟于其对仲裁请求做出答复之日,被申请人应被视为同意列入附加申请人或附加被申请人,他在答复中以动议或特别辩护的方式,根据管辖权理由反对列入这种额外的原告或其他被告。其他被申请人应被视为同意将其列入仲裁,除非至迟于对仲裁请求做出答复之日,在答复中以动议或特别答辩方式表示反对将其列入仲裁。

Article 5.45. Consolidation of Proceedings and Concurrent Hearings.

第 5.45 条　合并诉讼程序和同时举行听讯。

The parties may agree that—

当事各方可同意:

(a) the arbitration proceedings shall be consolidated with other arbitration proceedings; or

(a) 仲裁程序应与其他仲裁程序合并;或

(b) that concurrent hearings shall be held, on such terms as may be agreed.

(b) 同时举行听讯,条件由双方商定。

Unless the parties agree to confer such power on the arbitral tribunal, the tribunal has no power to order consolidation of arbitration proceedings or concurrent hearings.

除非当事各方同意赋予仲裁庭这种权力,否则仲裁庭无权下令合并仲裁程序或同时进行审理。

Article 5.46. Fees and Costs.

第 5.46 条　费用。

(a) The fees of the arbitrators shall be agreed upon by the parties and the arbitrator/s in writing prior to the arbitration.

(a) 仲裁员的费用应由双方当事人和仲裁方在仲裁前书面约定。

In default of agreement of the parties as to the amount and manner of payment of arbitrator's fees, the arbitrator's fees shall be determined in accordance with the applicable internal rules of the regular arbitration institution under whose rules the arbitration is conducted; or in ad hoc arbitration, the Schedule of Fees approved by the IBP, if any, or in default thereof, the Schedule of Fees that may be approved by the OADR.

在当事各方未就支付仲裁员费用的数额和方式达成协议的情况下,应根据进行仲裁的常设仲裁机构的适用内部规则确定仲裁员的费用;或在特别仲裁中,应根据菲律宾综合律师协会会长核准的费用表,如果没有,应根据由替代性争议解决机制办公处批准的费用表。

(b) In addition to arbitrator's fees, the parties shall be responsible for the payment of the administrative fees of an arbitration institution administering an arbitration and cost of arbitration. The latter shall include, as appropriate, the fees of an expert appointed by the arbitral tribunal, the expenses for conducting a site inspection, the use of a room where arbitration proceedings shall be or have been conducted, and expenses for the recording and transcription of the arbitration proceedings.

(b) 除仲裁员费用外,当事人还应当负责支付仲裁管理机构的行政费和仲裁费用。后者应酌情包括仲裁庭指定的专家的费用、进行现场检查的费用、使用正在进行或已经进行仲裁程序的房间的费用,以及记录仲裁程序的费用。

(c) The arbitral tribunal shall fix the costs of arbitration in its award. The term "costs" include only:

(c) 仲裁庭应在其裁决中确定仲裁费用。"费用"一词仅包括:

(i) The fees of the arbitral tribunal to be stated separately as to each arbitrator and to be fixed by the arbitral tribunal itself in accordance with this Article;

(i) 仲裁庭对每名仲裁员的收费,由仲裁庭根据本条自行确定;

(ii) The travel and other expenses incurred by the arbitrators;

(ii) 仲裁员的旅费和其他费用;

(iii) The costs of expert advice and of other assistance required by the arbitral tribunal，such as site inspection and expenses for the recording and transcription of the arbitration proceedings；

(iii) 仲裁庭要求的专家意见和其他协助的费用，如现场检查费用以及仲裁程序的记录费用；

(iv) The travel and other expenses of witnesses to the extent such expenses are approved by the arbitral tribunal；

(iv) 证人的旅费和其他费用，但以仲裁庭核准的数额为限；

(v) The costs for legal representation and assistance of the successful party if such costs were claimed during the arbitral proceedings，and only to the extent that the arbitral tribunal determines that the amount of such costs is reasonable；

(v) 如果在仲裁程序期间提出法律代理和援助要求，则包括胜诉方的法律代理和援助费用，但仅限于仲裁庭确定此类费用的合理数额；

(vi) Any fees and expenses of the appointing authority.

(vi) 指定机构的任何费用和开支。

(d) The fees of the arbitral tribunal shall be reasonable in amount，taking into account the amount in dispute，the complexity of the subject matter，the time spent by the arbitrators and any other relevant circumstances of the case.

(d) 考虑到争议金额、主题事项的复杂性、仲裁员花费的时间和案件的任何其他相关情况，仲裁庭的收费应合理。

If an appointing authority has been agreed upon by the parties and if such appointing authority has issued a schedule of fees for arbitrators in domestic cases which it administers，the arbitral tribunal，in fixing its fees shall take that schedule of fees into account to the extent that it considers appropriate in the circumstances of the case.

如果指定机构已由各方当事人约定，且该指定机构已就其管理的国内案件发出仲裁员收费表，仲裁庭在确定其收费表时，应在其认为适合该案件情形的范围内考虑到该收费表。

If such appointing authority has not issued a schedule of fees for arbitrators in international cases，any party may，at any time request the appointing authority to furnish a statement setting forth the basis for establishing fees which is customarily followed in international cases in which the authority appoints arbitrators. If the appointing authority consents to provide such a statement，the arbitral tribunal，in fixing its fees shall take such information into account to the extent that it considers appropriate in the circumstances of the case.

该指定机构未发布国际案件仲裁员收费表的，任何一方当事人均可随时要求指定机构提供说明，说明在该机构指定仲裁员的国际案件中通常遵循的确定收费的依据。指定机构同意提供此种陈述的，仲裁庭在确定收费时，应当在其认为适合该案件情形的范围内考虑到这种信息。

In cases referred to in paragraph（d）of this Article，when a party so requests and the appointing authority consents to perform the function，the arbitral tribunal shall fix its fees only after consultation with the appointing authority which may make any comment it deems appropriate to the arbitral tribunal concerning the fees.

在本条（d）款所述情况下，当一方当事人提出请求并经指定机构同意履行该职能时，仲裁庭只有在与指定机构协商后才确定其收费，指定机构可就收费问题向仲裁庭提出其认为适当的任何意见。

（e） Except as provided in the next paragraph，the costs of arbitration shall，in principle，be borne by the unsuccessful party. However，the arbitral tribunal may apportion each of such costs between the parties if it determines that apportionment is reasonable，taking into account the circumstances of the case.

（e）　除下一款另有规定外，仲裁费用原则上应由败诉一方承担。但仲裁庭可根据案情，在其认定分摊合理的情况下，在各当事方之间分摊其中的每一项费用。

With respect to the costs of legal representation and assistance referred to in paragraph（c）（v）of this Article，the arbitral tribunal，taking into account the circumstances of the case，shall be free to determine which party shall bear such costs or may apportion such costs between the parties if it determines that appointment is reasonable.

关于本条(c)款(v)项提及的法律代理和协助费用，仲裁庭应可根据案件的具体情况，自行确定应由哪一方承担此种费用，或在仲裁庭认定指定的当事人之间分摊此种费用。

When the arbitral tribunal issues an order for the termination of the arbitral proceedings or makes an award on agreed terms，it shall fix the costs of arbitration referred to in paragraph（a）of this Article in the context of that order or award.

仲裁庭下达终止仲裁程序的命令或根据商定的条件作出裁决时，应当根据该命令或裁决确定本条(a)款所述的仲裁费用。

Except as otherwise agreed by the parties，no additional fees may be charged by the arbitral tribunal for interpretation or correction or completion of its award under these Rules.

除当事人另有约定外，仲裁庭不得在解释、更正或完成本规则所规定的裁决方面收取额外费用。

（f）　The arbitral tribunal，on its establishment，may request each party to deposit an equal amount as an advance for the costs referred to in paragraphs（i），（ii）and（iii）of paragraph（c）of this Article.

（f）仲裁庭设立时，可根据本条(c)款(i)(ii)(iii)项，要求每一当事方预付同等数额的费用。

During the course of the arbitral proceedings，the arbitral tribunal may request supplementary deposits from the parties.

在仲裁程序进行期间，仲裁庭可以要求各方当事人提供补充存款。

If an appointing authority has been agreed upon by the parties，and when a party so requests and the appointing authority consents to perform the function，the arbitral tribunal shall fix the amounts of any deposits or supplementary deposits only after consultation with the appointing authority which may make any comments to the arbitral tribunal which it deems appropriate concerning the amount of such deposits and supplementary deposits.

当事人约定指定机构的，经一方当事人请求并经指定机构同意履行该项职能的，仲裁庭只有在与指定机构协商后，方可确定任何存款或补充存款的数额，指定机构可就此种存款和补充存款的数额向仲裁庭提出其认为适当的任何意见。

If the required deposits are not paid in full within thirty（30）days after receipt of the request，the arbitral tribunal shall so inform the parties in order that one of them may make the required payment within such a period or reasonable extension thereof as may be determined by the arbitral tribunal. If such payment is not made，the arbitral tribunal may order the termination of the arbitral proceedings.

如果在收到请求后30天内未全额支付所要求的押金，仲裁庭应将此通知各方当事人，以便其中一方当事人可在仲裁庭确定的期限内或合理延长期限内支付所要求的款项。如果没有付款，仲裁庭可以命令终止仲裁程序。

After the award has been made，the arbitral tribunal shall render an accounting to the parties of the deposits received and return any unexpended balance to the parties.

在作出裁决后，仲裁庭应向各方当事人说明所收到的存款，并将任何未用余额退还各方当事人。

CHAPTER 6
ARBITRATION OF CONSTRUCTION DISPUTES
第六章　建筑争议的仲裁

The Construction Industry Arbitration Commission（CIAC），which has original and exclusive jurisdiction over arbitration of construction disputes pursuant to Executive Order NO. 1 008，s. 1985，otherwise known as the "Construction Industry Arbitration Law"，shall promulgate the Implementing Rules and Regulations governing arbitration of construction disputes，incorporating therein the pertinent provisions of the ADR Act.

建筑行业仲裁委员会根据第 008 号行政命令(S. 1985)(又称《建筑行业仲裁法》)对建筑争议的仲裁拥有原始和专属管辖权,该仲裁委员会应颁布建筑争议仲裁的实施细则和条例,并将《替代性争议解决法案》的相关规定纳入其中。

CHAPTER 7
OTHER ADR FORMS
第七章　其他替代性争议解决机制形式

RULE 1 - General Provisions
细则 1——总则

Article 7.1. Scope of Application and General Principles. Except as otherwise agreed，this Chapter shall apply and supply the deficiency in the agreement of the parties for matters involving the following forms of ADR：

第 7.1 条　适用范围和一般原则。除另有约定外,本章应适用并补充当事人协议中涉及以下替代性争议解决机制中形式的缺陷:

(a) early neutral evaluation；

（a）早期中立评价；

（b）neutral evaluation；

（b）中立评价；

（c）mini-trial；

（c）微型审判；

（d）mediation-arbitration；

（d）仲裁；

（e）a combination thereof；or

（e）他们的组合；或

（f）any other ADR form.

（f）任何其他替代性争议解决机制。

Article 7.2. Applicability of the Rules on Mediation. If the other ADR form/process is more akin to mediation (i. e., the neutral third-person merely assists the parties in reaching a voluntary agreement), Chapter 3 governing Mediation shall have suppletory application to the extent that it is not in conflict with the agreement of the parties or this Chapter.

第7.2条　调解规则的适用。如果另一个替代性争议解决机制更接近于调解，即中立的第三人只是协助当事方达成自愿协议，则涉及调解的第三章在与当事方的协议或本章没有冲突的情况下应具有补充性适用。

Article 7.3. Applicability of the Rules on Arbitration. If the other ADR form/process is more akin to arbitration (i. e., the neutral third-person has the power to make a binding resolution of the dispute), Chapter 5 governing Domestic Arbitration shall have suppletory application to the extent that it is not in conflict with the agreement of the parties or this Chapter.

第7.3条　仲裁规则的适用。如果另一个替代性争议解决机制更类似于仲裁,即中立的第三人有权对争议做出有约束力的解决,则涉及国内仲裁的第五章在与当事人协议或本章不冲突的情况下应具有补充性适用。

Article 7.4. Referral. If a dispute is already before a court, either party may, before and during pre-trial, file a motion for the court to refer the parties to other ADR forms/processes. However, at any time during court proceedings, even after pre-trial, the parties may jointly move for suspension/dismissal of the action pursuant to Article 2030 of the Civil Code of the Philippines.

第7.4条　转介。如果争议已提交法院,任何一方均可在预审前和预审期间提出动议,要求法院将当事人提交其他替代性争议解决程序。然而,在法庭诉讼期间的任何时候,即使在预审之后,当事各方均可根据《菲律宾民法》第2030条提出联合动议,要求中止诉讼。

Article 7.5. Submission of Settlement Agreement. Either party may submit to the court before which the case is pending any settlement agreement following a neutral or an early neutral evaluation, mini-trial or mediation-arbitration.

第7.5条　提交和解协议。任何一方当事人均可在进行中立或早期中立评价、微型审判或调解仲裁后,将案件提交给正在等待任何和解协议的法院。

RULE 2 - Neutral or Early Neutral Evaluation
细则2——中立或早期中立评价

Article 7.6. Neutral or Early Neutral Evaluation.

第7.6条　中立或早期中立评价。

(a) The neutral or early neutral evaluation shall be governed by the rules and procedure agreed upon by the parties. In the absence of said agreement，this Rule shall apply.

(a) 中立或早期中立评价应遵守各方当事人商定的规则和程序。如无上述协议，应适用本规则。

(b) If the parties cannot agree on；or fail to provide for：

(b) 如果当事方不能就下列事项达成协议；或未能做出规定：

(i) The desired qualification of the neutral third person；

(i) 中立第三人的理想资格；

(ii) The manner of his/her selection；

(ii) 他/她的选择方式；

(iii) The appointing authority（not IBP）who shall have the authority to make the appointment of a neutral third person；or

(iii) 应有权指定中立的第三人的指定机构（而不是菲律宾综合律师协会会长）；或

(iv) if despite agreement on the foregoing and the lapse of the period of time stipulated for the appointment，the parties are unable to select a neutral third person or appointing authority，then，either party may request the default appointing authority，as defined under paragraph C1 of Article（Definition of Terms），to make the appointment taking into consideration the nature of the dispute and the experience and expertise of the neutral third person.

(iv) 如果双方当事人就上述问题达成一致意见，且约定的指定期限已过，但双方当事人仍不能选择中立的第三人或指定机构，则任何一方当事人均可请求按照解释细则 C1（术语的定义）来指定机构，在任命时考虑到争议的性质以及中立第三人的经验和专长。

(c) The parties shall submit and exchange position papers containing the issues and statement of the relevant facts and appending supporting documents and affidavits of witnesses to assist the neutral third person in evaluating or assessing the dispute.

（c）双方应提交和交换立场文件，其中载有问题和有关事实的陈述，并附上证人的证明文件和宣誓证词，以协助中立的第三人评价或评估争议。

（d）The neutral third person may request either party to address additional issues that he/she may consider necessary for a complete evaluation/assessment of the dispute.

（d）中立的第三人可要求任何一方解决其认为对争议进行全面评估所必需的其他问题。

（e）The neutral third person may structure the evaluation process in any manner he/she deems appropriate. In the course thereof，the neutral third person may identify areas of agreement，clarify the issues，define those that are contentious，and encourage the parties to agree on a definition of issues and stipulate on facts or admit the genuineness and due execution of documents.

（e）中立的第三人可以其认为适当的任何方式组织评价过程。在此过程中，中立的第三人可确定协议领域，澄清问题，界定有争议的问题，并鼓励当事各方商定问题的定义，规定事实或承认文件的真实性和应有的执行。

（f）The neutral third person shall issue a written evaluation or assessment within thirty（30）days from the conclusion of the evaluation process. The opinion shall be non-binding and shall set forth how the neutral third person would have ruled had the matter been subject to a binding process. The evaluation or assessment shall indicate the relative strengths and weaknesses of the positions of the parties，the basis for the evaluation or assessment，and an estimate，when feasible，of the amount for which a party may be liable to the other if the dispute were made subject to a binding process.

（f）中立的第三人应在评估过程结束后30天内发出书面评估。该意见不具约束力,并应规定中立的第三人在该事项须经过具有约束力的程序时将如何作出裁决。评价或评估应表明各方立场的相对优势和弱点、评估的依据,以及在可行的情况下,在争端经过具有约束力的程序后,一方可能对另一方负有责任的概数。

(g) There shall be no ex-parte communication between the neutral third person and any party to the dispute without the consent of all the parties.

(g) 中立的第三人与争端的任何一方之间未经所有各方同意,不得进行单方面联系。

(h) All papers and written presentations communicated to the neutral third person, including any paper prepared by a party to be communicated to the neutral third person or to the other party as part of the dispute resolution process, and the neutral third person's written non-binding assessment or evaluation, shall be treated as confidential.

(h) 所有提交给中立第三人的文件和书面陈述,包括一方当事人准备作为争议解决程序的一部分提交给中立第三人或另一方当事人的任何文件,以及中立第三人的不具约束力的书面评估或评价,均应视为机密。

RULE 3 - Mini-Trial
细则 3——微型审判

Article 7.7. Mini-Trial.
第 7.7 条 微型审判。

(a) A mini-trial shall be governed by the rules and procedure agreed upon by the parties. In the absence of said agreement, this Rule shall apply.

(a) 微型审判应遵守双方当事人商定的规则和程序。如无上述协议,应适用本规则。

（b）A mini-trial shall be conducted either as：

（b）应作为以下两种方式之一进行微型审判：

   （i）a separate dispute resolution process；or

   （i）一个单独的争端解决程序；或

   （ii）a continuation of mediation，neutral or early neutral evaluation or any other ADR process.

   （ii）继续调解、中立或早期中立评价或任何其他替代性争议解决机制

（c）The parties may agree that a mini-trial be conducted with or without the presence and participation of a neutral third person. If a neutral third person is agreed upon and chosen，he/she shall preside over the mini-trial. The parties may agree to appoint one or more（but equal in number per party）senior executive/s，on its behalf，to sit as mini-trial panel members.

（c）当事各方可同意在中立第三人在场或不在场的情况下进行微型审判。如果同意和选择中立的第三人，其将主持微型审判。当事人可以同意指定一人或多人担任审判小组成员，但每个当事人的人数相等。

（d）The senior executive/s chosen to sit as mini-trial panel members must be duly authorized to negotiate and settle the dispute with the other party. The appointment of a mini-trial panel member/s shall be communicated to the other party. This appointment shall constitute a representation to the other party that the mini-trial panel member/s has/have the authority to enter into a settlement agreement binding upon the principal without any further action or ratification by the latter.

（d）被选为微型审判小组成员的高级行政人员必须有权与对方谈判和解决争端。任命一名微型审判小组成员应通知对方。这项任命应构成向另一方代表，即微型审判小组成员有权达成对委托人具有约束力的和解协议，而无需委托人采取进一步行动或批准。

（e）Each party shall submit a brief executive summary of the dispute in sufficient copies as to provide one copy to each mini-trial panel member and to the adverse party. The summary shall identify the specific factual or legal issue or issues. Each party may attach to the summary a more exhaustive recital of the facts of the dispute and the applicable law and jurisprudence.

（e）每一当事方应提交足够副本的争端执行摘要，以便向每一位微型审判小组成员和对方当事人提供一份副本。摘要应指明具体事实或法律问题。每一当事方可在摘要中更详尽地叙述争端的事实以及适用的法律和判例。

（f）At the date, time and place agreed upon, the parties shall appear before the mini-trial panel member/so The lawyer of each party and/or authorized representative shall present his/her case starting with the claimant followed by the respondent. The lawyer and/or representative of each party may thereafter offer rebuttal or sur-rebuttal arguments.

（f）在约定的日期、时间和地点，各方当事人应当在微型审判小组成员面前出庭，这样，各方的律师和/或授权代表应当首先陈述案情，然后由被告陈述案情。当事人的律师、代理人或者代理人可以提出反驳或者对立观点。

Unless the parties agree on a shorter or longer period, the presentation-in-chief shall be made, without interruption, for one hour and the rebuttal or sur-rebuttal shall be thirty（30）minutes. At the end of each presentation, rebuttal or sur-rebuttal, the mini-trial panel member/s may ask clarificatory questions from any of the presentors.

除非当事各方商定一个较短或较长的期限，否则本方陈述不得中断，陈述时间为 1 个小时，反驳或推翻答辩的时间为 30 分钟。在每次陈述、反驳或超反驳结束时，微型审判小组成员可以向任何陈述人提出澄清问题。

（g）After the mini-trial, the mini-trial panel members shall negotiate a settlement of the dispute by themselves. In cases where a neutral third person is appointed, the neutral third person shall assist the parties/mini-trial panel members in settling the dispute and, unless otherwise agreed by the parties, the proceedings shall be governed by Chapter 3 on Mediation.

（g）微型审判后，微型审判小组成员应自行协商解决争议。在指定中立第三人的情况下，中立第三人应协助当事方调解争端。

RULE 4 - Mediation-Arbitration
细则 4——仲裁

Article 7.8. Mediation-Arbitration.

第7.8条　仲裁。

（a）A Mediation-Arbitration shall be governed by the rules and procedure agreed upon by the parties. In the absence of said agreement，Chapter 3 on Mediation shall first apply and thereafter，Chapter 5 on Domestic Arbitration.

（a）仲裁应遵守当事人约定的规则和程序。在没有上述协议的情况下，关于调解的第三章应首先适用，然后适用关于国内仲裁的第五章。

（b）No person shall, having been engaged and having acted as mediator of a dispute between the parties，following a failed mediation，act as arbitrator of the same dispute，unless the parties，in a written agreement，expressly authorize the mediator to hear and decide the case as an arbitrator.

（b）在调解失败后，当事方之间争端的调解人，不得担任同一争端的仲裁员，除非当事方在书面协议中明确授权调解人作为仲裁员审理案件并作出裁决。

（c）The mediator who becomes an arbitrator pursuant to this Rule shall make an appropriate disclosure to the parties as if the arbitration proceeding had commenced and will proceed as a new dispute resolution process，and shall，before entering upon his/her duties，execute the appropriate oath or affirmation of office as arbitrator in accordance with these Rules.

(c) 根据本条规则成为仲裁员的调解员应向各方当事人适当披露,如同仲裁程序已经启动,并将作为新的争议解决程序进行,并应在其履行职责之前,根据本规则履行作为仲裁员的适当宣誓或职务确认。

RULE 5 - Costs and Fees
细则 5——费用和收费

Article 7.9. Costs and Fees.
第 7.9 条　费用和收费。

(a) Before entering his/her duties as ADR Provider, he/she shall agree with the parties on the cost of the ADR procedure, the fees to be paid and manner of payment for his/her services.

(a) 在履行其作为替代性争议解决机制的从业者的职责之前,其应就替代性争议解决机制程序的费用、应支付的费用以及其服务的支付方式与当事人达成一致。

(b) In the absence of such agreement, the fees for the services of the ADR provider/practitioner shall be determined as follows:

(b) 在没有此类协议的情况下,替代性争议解决机制从业者的服务费应按以下方式确定:

(i) If the ADR procedure is conducted under the rules and/or administered by an institution regularly providing ADR services to the general public, the fees of the ADR professional shall be determined in accordance with schedule of fees approved by such institution, if any;

(i) 如果替代性争议解决机制是根据规则进行的,或由一个经常向公众提供替代性争议解决服务的机构管理,替代性争议解决专业人员的费用应根据该机构批准的任何费用表确定;

(ii) In ad hoc ADR, the fees shall be determined in accordance with the schedule of fees approved by the OADR;

(ii) 费用应根据替代性争议解决机制办公处批准的费用表确定;

(iii) In the absence of a schedule of fees approved by the ADR institution or by the OADR，the fees shall be determined by the ADR institution or the OADR，as the case may be，on the basis of quantum meruit，taking into consideration，among others，the length and complexity of the process，the amount in dispute and the professional standing of the ADR professional.

（iii）在没有得到替代性争议解决机构或替代性争议解决机制办公处批准的费用表的情况下，费用应由替代性争议解决机构或替代性争议解决机制办公处确定，视情况而定，按劳计酬，除其他外，考虑过程的长度和复杂性、争议金额和替代性争议解决专业人员的专业地位。

（c）A contingency fee arrangement shall not be allowed. The amount that may be allowed to an ADR professional may not be made dependent upon the success of his/her effort in helping the parties to settle their dispute.

（c）不允许以风险代理方式收费。允许替代性争议解决机制专业人员获得的金额不取决于其是否成功帮助当事人解决争议。

CHAPTER 8
MISCELLANEOUS PROVISIONS
第八章　杂项条款

Article 8.1. Amendments. These Rules or any portion hereof may be amended by the Secretary of Justice.

第8.1条　修正。本细则或本细则的任何部分，可由司法部长修正。

Article 8.2. Separability Clause. If any part，article or provision of these Rules are declared invalid or unconstitutional，the other parts hereof not affected thereby shall remain valid.

第 8.2 条　条款的可分割性。如果本细则的任何部分、条款或规定被宣布无效或违宪,本细则不受影响的其他部分将继续有效。

Article 8. 3. Funding. The heads of departments and agencies concerned, especially the Department of Justice, insofar as the funding requirements of the OADR is concerned, shall immediately include in their annual appropriation the funding necessary to implement programs and extend services required by the ADR Act and these Rules.

第 8.3 条　资金。各有关部门及机构的首长,特别是律政司的首长,根据替代性争议解决机制办公处的资金需求,应立即在其年度拨款中列入执行《替代性争议解决法案》及本细则所要求的计划及提供服务所需的资金。

Article 8. 4. Transitory Provisions. Considering the procedural character of the ADR Act and these Rules, the provisions of these Rules shall be applicable to all pending arbitration, mediation or other ADR forms covered by the ADR Act if the parties agree.

第 8.4 条　过渡性规定。考虑到《替代性争议解决法案》和本规则的程序性质,如果双方同意,本规则的规定应适用于《替代性争议解决法案》所涵盖的所有未决仲裁、调解或其他替代性争议解决形式。

Article 8.5. Effectivity Clause. These Rules shall take effect fifteen (15) days after the completion of its publication in at least two (2) national newspapers of general circulation.

第 8.5 条　有效性条款。本规则在至少两份国内通用报纸上发表后15 天生效。

APPROVED.

核准。

December 4,2009

2009 年 12 月 4 日

AGNES VST DEVANADERA

Acting Secretary

代理部长

Deportment of Justice

司法部

ATD‐09‐0003970

Committee for the Formulation of the Implementing Rules and Regulations of the Alternative Dispute Resolution Act of 2004：

2004 年《替代性争议解决法实施细则与条例》拟订委员会

Undersecretary Jose Vicente B. Salazar

副部长 Jose Vicente B. Salazar

Department of Justice

司法部

Undersecretary Zenaida N. Maglaya

副部长 Zenaida N. Maglaya

Department of Trade and Industry

贸易与工业部

Director Nelda D. Leda

主任 Nelda D. Leda

Department of the Interior and Local Government

内政和地方政府部

Atty. Victor P. Lazatin

Representative of the President of the Integrated Bar of the Philippines

菲律宾综合律师协会主席代表

Atty. Custodio O. Parlade

Arbitration Profession

仲裁专业人员

Atty. Alfredo F. Tadiar

Professor Annabelle T. Abaya

Annabelle T. Abaya 教授

Mediation Profession

调解专业人员

Atty. Mario E. Valderrama

ADR Organization

替代性争议解决机制组织

OTHER PARTICIPANTS IN THE FORMULATION OF THE IMPLEMENTING

参与制定实施办法的其他与会者

RULES AND REGULATIONS:

规章制度:

DEPARTMENT OF JUSTICE

司法部

Chief State Counsel Ricardo V. Paras III

首席政府律师 Ricardo V. Paras III

Assistant Chief State Counsel Ruben F. Fondevilla

助理首席国家顾问 Ruben F. Fondevilla

Retired Assistant Chief State Prosecutor Nilo C. Mariano

退休助理首席国家检察官 Nilo C. Mariano

Senior State Counsel Marlyn L. Angeles

高级政府律师 Marlyn L. Angeles

State Counsel Bernadette C. Ongoco

政府律师 Bernadette C. Ongoco

State Counsel Leilani R. Fajardo

政府律师 Leilani R. Fajardo

Ms. Suerte 1. Gamiao

Mr. Jose Mario B. Uy

DEPARTMENT OF TRADE AND INDUSTRY

贸易与工业部

Director Victorio Mario A. Dimagiba

Victorio Mario A. Dimagiba 主任

OFFICE OF THE PRESIDENT OF THE INTEGRATED BAR OF THE

PHILIPPINES

Atty. Patricia Tysman-Clemente

菲律宾综合律师协会主席办公室

MEDIATION PROFESSION

调解专业人员

Former Prosecutor Dominador Bornasal，Jr. 前检察官 Dominador Bornasal，Jr.

第四节 文莱商事仲裁法英汉对照

CONSTITUTION OF BRUNEI DARUSSALAM

《文莱达鲁萨兰国宪法》

（Order under Article 83〈3〉）

根据第 83(3)条

ARBITRATION ORDER，2009

2009 年《仲裁法》

ARRANGEMENT OF SECTIONS

章节安排

PART I

PRELIMINARY

第一部分 序言

1. Short title，commencement and long title

    简称、生效、全称

2. Interpretation

    解释

3. Application of Order
   适用

PART II

ARBITRATION AGREEMENT
第二部分　仲裁协议

4. Arbitration agreement
   仲裁协议

5. Arbitration agreement not to be discharged by death of party
   不由当事人死亡解除的仲裁协议

PART III

STAY OF LEGAL PROCEEDINGS
第三部分　中止法律诉讼

6. Stay of legal proceedings
   中止法律诉讼

7. Court's powers on stay of proceedings
   法院中止诉讼的权力

8. Reference of interpleader issue to arbitration
   确认竞合权利仲裁

PART IV

COMMENCEMENT OF ARBITRATION PROCEEDINGS
第四部分　仲裁程序的开始

9. Commencement of arbitration proceedings
   仲裁程序的开始

10. Powers of Court to extend time for beginning of arbitration proceedings
    法庭延迟仲裁程序开始的权力

11. Application of Chapter 14
    第十四章的适用

PART V

ARBITRAL TRIBUNAL

第五部分 仲裁庭

12. Number of arbitrators

    仲裁员数量

13. Appointment of arbitrators

    仲裁员指定

14. Grounds for challenge

    申请仲裁员回避

15. Challenge procedure

    申请回避程序

16. Failure or impossibility to act

    不作为或履行不能

17. Arbitrator ceasing to hold office

    仲裁员离任

18. Appointment of substitute arbitrator

    指定替补仲裁员

19. Decision by panel of arbitrators

    仲裁小组决定

20. Liability of arbitrator

    仲裁员的责任

PART VI

JURISDICTION OF ARBITRAL TRIBUNAL

第六部分 仲裁庭的管辖权

21. Separability of arbitration clause and competence of arbitral tribunal to rule on its own jurisdiction

    仲裁条款可分性与仲裁庭独立管辖权

PART VII
ARBITRAL PROCEEDINGS
第七部分 仲裁程序

22. General duties of arbitral tribunal
    仲裁庭的一般职责

23. Determination of rules of procedure
    程序规则的确定

24. Statements of claim and defence
    仲裁申请书和答辩状

25. Hearings and written proceedings
    开庭审理和书面审理

26. Consolidation of proceedings and concurrent hearings
    合并诉讼与同时审理

27. Power to appoint experts
    任命专家的权力

28. General powers exercisable by arbitral tribunal
    仲裁庭行使的一般权力

29. Powers of arbitral tribunal in case of party's default
    仲裁庭在当事人违约时的权力

30. Witnesses may be summoned by subpoena
    传票传唤证人

31. Court's powers exercisable in support of arbitration proceedings
    法院支持仲裁程序行使的权力

PART VIII
AWARD
第八部分 裁决

32. Law applicable to substance of dispute
    适用于争议实体的规则

33. Awards made on different issues

针对不同问题的裁决

34. Remedies

    救济

35. Interest

    权益

36. Extension of time for making award

    延长裁决

37. Award by consent

    合意裁决

38. Form and contents of award

    裁决的形式和内容

39. Costs of arbitration

    仲裁费用

40. Fees of arbitrator

    仲裁员的费用

41. Power to withhold award in case of non-payment

    针对未付款的裁决保留权

42. Court may charge property with payment of solicitor's costs in arbitration

    法院可在仲裁中收取财产以支付律师费用

43. Correction or interpretation of award and additional award

    裁决书的更正与解释，补充裁决

44. Effect of award

    裁决的效力

PART IX
POWERS OF COURT IN RELATION TO AWARD
第九部分　法院对裁决的权力

45. Determination of preliminary point of law

    法律的初步确定

PART X
GENERAL
第十部分　总则

58. Application to references under statutory powers

   法定权力适用的参考

59. Immunity of arbitral institutions

   仲裁机构的豁免权

60. Service of notices

   通知的送达

61. Reckoning periods of time

   时间的计算

62. Appointment of mediator

   调解员的任命

63. Power of arbitrator to act as mediator

   仲裁员担任调解员的权力

64. Government to be bound

   责任机构

65. Transitional provisions

   暂行条文

66. Enabling power

   权力行使

67. Repeal

   废除

In the exercise of the power conferred by Article 83（3） of the Constitution of Brunei Darussalam，His Majesty the Sultan and Yang Di-Pertuan hereby makes the following Order-

根据《文莱达鲁萨兰国宪法》第 83 条第（3）款赋予的权力，苏丹陛下杨迪佩尔图安兹立本法如下：

PART I
PRELIMINARY
第一部分　序言

Short title，commencement and long title

简称、生效、全称

1. (1) This Order may be cited as the Arbitration Order, 2009 and shall commence on a day to be appointed by the Attorney General, with the approval of His Majesty the Sultan and Yang Di-Pertuan, by notification in the Gazette.

   (1) 本法简称 2009 年《仲裁法》，经苏丹陛下杨迪佩尔图安批准，自总检察长指定之日起生效，并见于公报。

   (2) The long title of this Order is "An Order to provide for arbitration in civil matters and for matters relating thereto".

   (2) 本法全称《针对民事及相关问题仲裁的法令》。

Interpretation

解释

2. (1) In this Order, unless the context otherwise requires-

   (1) 本法中，除非上下文另有要求：

   " appointing authority " means the appointing authority designated under sections 13(8) or (9);

   "指定机构"是指第 13 条第(8)款或第(9)款中的特定机构；

   " arbitral tribunal " means a sole arbitrator, a panel of arbitrators or an arbitral institution;

   "仲裁庭"是指一名独任仲裁员、一组仲裁员或仲裁机构；

   "arbitration agreement " has the meaning given to it by section 4(1);

   "仲裁协议"是指第 4 条第(1)款所述协议；

   "award" means a decision of the arbitral tribunal on the substance of the dispute and includes any interim, interlocutory or partial award, but excludes any order or direction made under section 28;

   "裁决"是指仲裁庭对争议实质的决定，包括任何临时、中间或部分裁决，但不包括第 28 条中提到的任何命令或指示；

"Court" means the High Court；

"法院"是指高级法院；

"court"，for the purposes of sections 6，7，8，11(1)，55，56 and 57 means the High Court，an Intermediate Court，a Court of a Magistrate or any other court in which the proceedings referred to in those sections are instituted or heard；

在第 6 条、第 7 条、第 8 条、第 11 条第(1)款、第 55 条、第 56 条和第 57 条中，"法院"指高级法院、中级法院、裁判法院或任何其他法院,诉讼方式为提起或审理。

"party" means a party to an arbitration agreement or，in any case where an arbitration does not involve all of the parties to the arbitration agreement，means a party to the arbitration；

"当事人"是指仲裁协议的当事一方,或仲裁未涉及仲裁协议各方时,指其中参与仲裁的当事一方。

"place of the arbitration" means the juridical seat of the arbitration designated by —

"仲裁地"是指由下列人员指定的仲裁法人所在地:

(a) the parties to the arbitration agreement；

(a) 仲裁协议的当事人;

(b) any arbitral or other institution or person authorised by the parties for that purpose；or

(b) 为此目的而由当事人授权的任何仲裁机构或其他机构;或

(c) the arbitral tribunal as authorised by the parties，

(c) 当事人授权的仲裁庭,

or determined，in the absence of any such designation，having regard to the arbitration agreement and all the relevant circumstances；

或者在没有任何此类指定的情况下,根据仲裁协议和所有相关情况决定。

"Registrar of the Supreme Court" has the same meaning as in section 2 of the Supreme Court Act（Chapter 5）；

"最高法院书记处"的含义与《最高法院法》第五章第 2 条相同；

"Rules of Court" means the Rules of Court made by the Chief Justice under this Order.

"法院规则"是指首席大法官根据本法令制定的法院规则。

（2）Where any provision in this Order allows the parties to determine any issue，the parties may authorise a third party，including an arbitral institution，to make that determination.

（2）若本法条文允许当事人对问题做决定，当事人可授权包括仲裁机构在内的第三方做决定。

（3）Where any provision in this Order refers to the fact that the parties have agreed or that they may agree or in any other way refers to an agreement of the parties，such agreement includes any arbitration rules incorporated in that agreement.

（3）若本法条文提到当事人已经达成协议、可能达成协议，或以任何其他形式提到当事人的协议，这种协议包括该协议中所提到的任何仲裁规则。

（4）Where any provision in this Order refers to a claim，it shall also apply to a cross-claim or counter-claim，and where such provision refers to a defence，it shall also apply to a defence to any such cross-claim or counter-claim.

（4）若本法条文提到诉讼的，也应适用交叉诉讼或反诉；若本法条文提到抗诉的，也应适用此交叉诉讼或反诉中的抗诉。

Application of Order

适用

3. This Order shall apply to any arbitration where the place of arbitration is Brunei Darussalam and where Part II of the International Arbitration Order，2009 does not apply to that arbitration.

3. 本法适用仲裁地为文莱达鲁萨兰国的任何仲裁，以及 2009 年的《国际仲裁法》的第二部分不适用的仲裁。

PART II
ARBITRATION AGREEMENT
第二部分 仲裁协议

Arbitration agreement

仲裁协议

4.（1）In this Order，"arbitration agreement" means an agreement by the parties to submit to arbitration all or certain disputes which have arisen or which may arise between them，whether contractual or not.

（1）在本法中，"仲裁协议"是指各方当事人同意将所有或个别争议提交仲裁解决，该协议是否已在合同中规定不影响仲裁协议的成立。

（2） An arbitration agreement may be in the form of an arbitration clause in a contract or in the form of a separate agreement.

（2）仲裁协议可以是合同中的仲裁条款，也可以是独立的仲裁协议。

（3）An arbitration agreement shall，except as provided for in subsection（4），be in writing，being contained in —

（a）a document signed by the parties；or

（b） an exchange of letters，telex，telefacsimile or other means of communication which provide a record of the agreement.

（3）除第（4）款另有规定外，仲裁协议应以书面形式载于双方签署的文件，或通过信件、电话、传真或其他通信方式进行交换，以记录协议。

（4）Where in any artitral or legal proceedings, a party asserts the existence of an arbitration agreement in a pleading, statement of case or any other document in circumstances in which the assertion calls for a reply and the assertion is not denied, there shall be deemed to be an effective arbitration agreement as between the parties to the proceedings.

（4）在书面或法律诉讼中，当事人主张在仲裁请求书、案件陈述书或其他任何文件中仲裁协议存在仲裁协议，在要求答复而不能被拒绝的情况下，应视为诉讼当事人之间的有效协议。

（5）A reference in a bill of lading to a charterparty or other document containing an arbitration clause shall constitute an arbitration agreement if the reference is such as to make that clause part of the bill of lading.

（5）提单中提及的租船合同或其他含仲裁条款的文件，若提及该条款是提单的一部分，即构成仲裁协议。

Arbitration agreement not to he discharged by death of party
不由当事人死亡解除的仲裁协议

5.（1）An arbitration agreement shall not be discharged by the death of any party to the agreement but shall continue to be enforceable by or against the personal representative of the deceased party.

（1）仲裁协议不得因协议任何一方的死亡解除，而应由死者的遗产代理人继续执行。

（2）The authority of an arbitrator shall not be revoked by the death of any party by whom he was appointed.

（2）仲裁员的权力不因被任命的任何一方的死亡而撤销。

（3）Nothing in this section shall be taken to affect the operation of any written law or rule of law by virtue of which any right of action is extinguished by the death of a person.

（3）本条不得影响任何债权因自然人死亡而消灭的成文法或法治的运作。

PART III
STAY OF LEGAL PROCEEDINGS
第三部分　中止法律诉讼

Stay of legal proceedings

中止法律诉讼

6.（1）Where any party to an arbitration agreement institutes any proceedings in any court against any other party to the agreement in respect of any matter which is the subject of the agreement，any party to the agreement may，at any time after entering an appearance and before delivering any pleading or taking any other step in the proceedings，apply to that court to stay the proceedings so far as they relate to that matter.

（1）仲裁协议的任何一方就协议内容中的任何问题对协议另一方向法院提起诉讼的，可在应诉后、提出诉讼请求前或采取其他措施前，向法院申请在涉及该事项的情况下中止诉讼。

（2）The court to which an application has been made in accordance with subsection（1）may，if it is satisfied that —

　　（a）there is no sufficient reason why the matter should not be referred in accordance with the arbitration agreement; and

　　（b）the applicant was，at the time when the proceedings were commenced，and still remains ready and willing to do all things necessary to the proper conduct of the arbitration,

make an order, upon such terms as it thinks fit, staying the proceedings so far as they relate to that matter.

（2）根据第（1）款提出申请的法院，如认为没有充分理由不按照仲裁协议提交事项，或申请人在诉讼开始时准备好并愿意为正确进行仲裁而做所有必要的事情，则可根据其认为合适的条件做出命令，中止诉讼，直到诉讼涉及该事项。

（3）Where a court makes an order under subsection（2），it may, for the purpose of preserving the rights of parties，make such interim or supplementary orders as it thinks fit in relation to any property which is or forms part of the subject of the dispute to which the order under that subsection relates.

（3）凡法院根据第（2）款做出命令，为维护当事人的权利，则可根据该款做出的命令所涉及的争议，就其属于或构成该主体的任何财产做出其认为适当的临时命令或补充命令。

（4）Where no party to the proceedings has taken any further step in the proceedings for a period of not less than 2 years after an order staying the proceedings has been made，the court may，on its own motion，make an order discontinuing the proceedings without prejudice to the right of any of the parties to apply for the discontinued proceedings to be reinstated.

（4）在中止诉讼的决定做出后，如诉讼当事人未对诉讼采取进一步措施持续不超过 2 年，则法院可主动停止诉讼程序，不妨碍当事人申请恢复已中止的诉讼。

（5）For the purposes of this section，a reference to a party includes a reference to any person claiming through or under such party.

（5）就本条而言，凡提及当事人时，包括提及该方主张的任何人。

Court's powers on stay of proceedings

法院中止诉讼的权力

7. (1) Where a court stays proceedings under section 6, the court may, if in those proceedings property has been arrested or bail or other security has been given to prevent or obtain release from arrest, order that —

(a) the property arrested be retained as security for the satisfaction of any award made on the arbitration; or

(b) the stay be conditional on the provision of equivalent security for the satisfaction of any such award.

(1) 在依第 6 条中止诉讼程序的过程中,如财产已被法院扣押,或者已提供阻止或获取解押的保释金或其他担保,法院可下令保留所押财产以作为履行仲裁裁决的担保,或以备付履行该裁决的等值担保为条件中止诉讼。

(2) Subject to the Rules of Court and to any necessary modification, the same law and practice shall apply in relation to property retained in pursuance of an order under this section as would apply if it were held for the purposes of proceedings in the court which made the order.

(2) 以服从法院规则及其任何必要的修订为准,法院依本条做出有关保留财产事项的命令的适用法律和措施,应与以诉讼为目的的相同。

Reference of interpleader issue to arbitration

确认竞合权利仲裁

8. Where in proceedings before any court relief by way of interpleader is granted and any issue between the claimants is one in respect of which there is an arbitration agreement between them, the court granting the relief may direct the issue

between the claimants to be determined in accordance with the agreement.

凡法庭准许在诉讼程序中采用确认竞合权利救济方式，且申诉人之间的争议事项是其仲裁协议中的相关事项，法庭可指示按仲裁协议来决定申述人之间的争议事项。

PART IV
COMMENCEMENT OF ARBITRATION PROCEEDINGS
第四部分 仲裁程序的开始

Commencement of arbitration proceedings

仲裁程序的开始

9. Unless otherwise agreed by the parties, the arbitration proceedings in respect of a particular dispute shall commence on the date on which a request for that dispute to be referred to arbitration is received by the respondent.

除非当事各方另有协议，特定争议的仲裁程序，于应诉人收到将该争议提交仲裁的请求之日开始。

Powers of Court to extend time for beginning of arbitration proceedings

法庭延迟仲裁程序开始的权力

10. (1) Where the terms of an arbitration agreement to refer future disputes to arbitration provide that a claim to which the arbitration agreement applies shall be barred unless —

将未来争议提交仲裁的仲裁协议条款规定，适用仲裁协议的请求权应予以禁止，除非：

(a) some step has been taken to begin other dispute resolution procedures which must be exhausted before arbitration proceedings can be begun;

（a）已经采取了一些措施开始其他争端解决程序，这些程序在仲裁程序开始前必须先用尽；

（b）notice to appoint an arbitrator is given；

（b）已给出指定任命仲裁员的通知；

（c）an arbitrator is appointed; or

（c）仲裁员已被指定；或

（d）some other step is taken to commence arbitration proceedings，

（d）已采取其他步骤开始仲裁程序，

within a time fixed by the agreement and a dispute to which the agreement applies has arisen，the Court may，if it is of the opinion that in the circumstances of the case undue hardship would otherwise be caused，extend the time for such period and on such terms as it thinks fit.

在协议所规定的时间内，以及本协议适用的争议发生时，如果法院认为不延迟仲裁程序可能会造成不必要的困难，法院可根据合适的条款延迟该程序。

（2）An order of extension of time made by the Court under subsection（1）—

（a）may be made only after any available arbitral process for obtaining an extension of time has been exhausted；

（b）may be made notwithstanding that the time so fixed has expired; and

（c）shall not affect the operation of sections 9 and 11 and any other written law relating to the limitation of actions.

（2）法院根据第（1）款做出的延迟命令只有在任何可用的延长时间的仲裁程序已经用尽之后才能做出，规定的期限已经届满后可以做出，且不得影响第 9 条和第 11 条法律，也不得影响与诉讼时效相关的任何其他成文法。

Application of Chapter 14

第十四章的适用

11. (1) The Limitation Act (Chapter 14) shall apply to arbitration proceedings as it applies to proceedings before any court and a reference in that Act to the commencement of any action shall be construed as a reference to the commencement of arbitration proceedings.

(1)《时效法》(第 14 章)适用于仲裁程序,如同该法令在法院适于诉讼程序,其有关诉讼程序开始的说明可解释为对仲裁程序开始的说明。

(2) The Court may order that in computing the time prescribed by the Limitation Act for the commencement of proceedings (including arbitration proceedings) in respect of a dispute which was the subject-matter of —

(2) 对于下列裁决所涉及的标的之争议,法院在按《时效法》计算诉讼程序(包括仲裁程序)的开始时间时可下令:

(a) an award which the Court orders to be set aside or declares to be of no effect; or

(a) 法院命令撤销或宣告无效的裁决;或

(b) the affected part of an award which the Court orders to be set aside in part or declares to be in part of no effect,

(b) 法院命令部分撤销或宣告部分无效的裁决中受影响的部分。

the period between the commencement of the arbitration and the date of the order referred to in paragraphs (a) or (b) shall be excluded.

从仲裁开始日至下列(a)或(b)项命令作出日之间时段不计在内。

(3) Notwithstanding any term in an arbitration agreement to the effect that no cause of action shall accrue in respect of any matter required by the agreement to be referred until

an award is made under the agreement，the cause of action shall，for the purpose of the Limitation Act，be deemed to have accrued in respect of any such matter at the time when it would have accrued but for that term in the agreement.

（3）仲裁协议可规定在依协议作出裁决之前，其中任何事项均不存在诉由。若非有此规定，有关上述事项出现争议之时本应计作诉由发生时间。尽管如此，为了《时效法》目的，该争议发生时间应被视为诉由已发生时间。

PART V
ARBITRAL TRIBUNAL
第五部分　仲裁庭

Number of arbitrators

仲裁员数量

12.（1）The parties are free to determine the number of arbitrators.

（1）当事双方可自由决定仲裁员数量。

（2）Failing such determination，there shall be a single arbitrator.

（2）如果无法决定，应有一个仲裁员。

Appointment of arbitrators

仲裁员指定

13.（1）Unless otherwise agreed by the parties，no person shall be precluded by reason of his nationality from acting as an arbitrator.

（1）除非当事人另有约定，任何人不得因其国籍而无法担任仲裁员。

（2）The parties are free to agree on a procedure for appointing the arbitrator or arbitrators.

（2）当事人可以自由地就仲裁员或仲裁员的任命程序达成一致。

（3）Where the parties fail to agree on a procedure for appointing the arbitrator or arbitrators ——

（3）若当事人无法就指定仲裁员达成一致，则：

（a）in an arbitration with 3 arbitrators, each party shall appoint one arbitrator, and the parties shall by agreement appoint the third arbitrator; or

（a）在三名仲裁员进行的仲裁中，每方应指定一名仲裁员，双方应经协议指定第三名仲裁员；或

（b）in an arbitration with a sole arbitrator, if the parties are unable to agree on the arbitrator, the arbitrator shall be appointed, upon the request of a party, by the appointing authority.

（b）在独任仲裁员的仲裁中，如果双方当事人不能商定仲裁员人选，则经一方当事人请求，应由指定机构任命仲裁员。

（4）Where subsection（3）（a）applies ——

（4）第（3）款（a）项适用以下情况：

（a）if a party fails to appoint an arbitrator within 30 days of the receipt of the first request to do so from the other party; or

（a）一方在收到另一方提出的第一项请求后 30 天内未指定仲裁员的；或

（b）if the 2 parties fail to agree on the appointment of the third arbitrator within 30 days of the receipt of the first request by either party to do so,

（b）双方未能在收到任何一方提出的第一项请求之日起 30 天内就第三名仲裁员的任命达成一致的，则

the appointment shall be made, upon the request of a party, by the appointing authority.

根据一方的要求，应由指定机构任命仲裁员。

（5）If, under an appointment procedure agreed upon by the

parties —

（5）在各方当事人就仲裁员指定程序达成合意的情况下，如果：

（a）a party fails to act as required under such procedure；

（a）一方当事人没能按照约定指定仲裁员；

（b）the parties are unable to reach an agreement expected of them under such procedure；or

（b）各方当事人没能在约定的程序下达成合意；或

（c）a third party，including an arbitral institution，fails to perform any function entrusted to it under such procedure，

（c）第三方（包括仲裁机构）没能履行其所受委托的作用，

any party may apply to the appointing authority to take the necessary action unless the agreement on the appointment procedure provides other means for securing the appointment.

任意一方当事人都可以请求指定机构采取必要措施，除非其先前约定的程序规定了其他救济方式。

（6）Where a party makes a request or makes an application to the appointing authority under subsections（3），（4）or（5），the appointing authority shall，in appointing an arbitrator，have regard to the following —

（6）如一方根据第（3）款、第（4）款或第（5）款向指定当局提出请求或申请，指派当局在任命仲裁员时应考虑到下列事项：

（a）the nature of the subject-matter of the arbitration；

（a）仲裁标的的性质；

（b）the availability of any arbitrator；

（b）有无仲裁员；

（c）the identities of the parties to the arbitration；

（c）仲裁当事人的身份；

（d）any suggestion made by any of the parties regarding the

appointment of any arbitrator;

（d）双方就任命仲裁员所达成的约定；

（e）any qualifications required of the arbitrator by the arbitration agreement; and

（e）仲裁协议对仲裁员资格的要求；

（f）such considerations as are likely to secure the appointment of an independent and impartial arbitrator.

（f）上诉因素可确保任命独立和公正的仲裁员。

（7）No appointment by the appointing authority shall be challenged except in accordance with this Order.

（7）除非依据本法，指定当局的任何任命均不受质疑。

（8）For the purposes of this Order, the appointing authority shall be the President of the Arbitration Association Brunei Darussalam.

（8）为实施本法，指定当局为文莱达鲁萨兰国仲裁协会主席。

（9）The Chief Justice may, if he thinks fit, by notification published in the Gazette appoint any other person to exercise the powers of the appointing authority under this section.

（9）首席大法官如认为适当，可借公报刊登通知，委任他人行使本款所规定的任命权。

Grounds for challenge

申请仲裁员回避

14.（1）Where any person is approached in connection with his possible appointment as an arbitrator, he shall disclose any circumstance likely to give rise to justifiable doubts as to his impartiality or independence.

（1）可能被指定为仲裁员的人，应在与此指定有关的洽谈中披露可能对其公正性和独立性产生有正当理由怀疑的任何情况。

(2) An arbitrator shall，from the time of his appointment and throughout the arbitration proceedings，disclose without delay any such circumstance as is referred to in subsection (1) to the parties，unless they have already been so informed by him.

(2) 仲裁员应自其被指定之时起，并在整个仲裁程序期间，毫无延迟地向各方当事人披露第(1)款中的任何情况，除非此种情况已由其告知各方当事人。

(3) Subject to subsection(4)，an arbitrator may be challenged only if —

(3) 除第(4)款另有规定外，只有在下列情况才能申请仲裁员回避：

(a) circumstances exist that give rise to justifiable doubts as to his impartiality or independence；or

(a) 存在对仲裁员公正性或独立性有合理怀疑的情况；或

(b) he does not possess the qualifications agreed to by the parties.

(b) 仲裁员不被双方当事人同意。

(4) A party who has appointed or participated in the appointment of any arbitrator may challenge such arbitrator only if he becomes aware of any of the grounds of challenge set out in subsection (3) as may be applicable to the arbitrator after he has been appointed.

(4) 指定或参与任命仲裁员的当事人，只有在得知第(3)款所列关于申请仲裁员回避的理由适用该仲裁员后，才可以申请该仲裁员回避。

Challenge procedure

申请回避程序

15.（1）Subject to subsection（3）, the parties may agree on a procedure for challenging an arbitrator.

（1）除第（3）款另有规定外,双方当事人可就申请仲裁员回避的程序达成协议。

（2）If the parties have not agreed on a procedure for challenge, a party who intends to challenge an arbitrator shall —

（2）如果双方当事人没有就申请回避程序达成一致,则有意申请仲裁员回避的一方应:

（a）within 15 days after becoming aware of the constitution of the arbitral tribunal; or

（a）在知悉仲裁庭的组成之日起 15 日内;或

（b）after becoming aware of any circumstance referred to in section 14（3）, send a written statement of the grounds for the challenge to the arbitral tribunal.

（b）在知悉第 14 条第（3）款所述的情况后,向仲裁庭提出申请回避的书面理由。

（3）The arbitral tribunal shall, unless the challenged arbitrator withdraws from his office or the other party agrees to the challenge, decide on the challenge.

（3）除非被申请回避的仲裁员辞职或对方当事人同意回避申请,则仲裁庭应对申请作出决定。

（4）If a challenge before the arbitral tribunal is unsuccessful, the aggrieved party may, within 30 days after receiving notice of the decision rejecting the challenge, apply to the Court to decide on the challenge and the Court may make such order as it thinks fit.

（4）如果申请回避失败,受损害一方应在接到驳回上诉决定通知后 30 天内向法院申请裁定。法院可作出其认为合适的裁定。

（5）No appeal shall lie against the decision of the Court under subsection（4）.

（5）根据第（4）款，不得对法院所作裁定上诉。

（6）While an application to the Court under subsection（4）is pending，the arbitral tribunal，including the challenged arbitrator，may continue the arbitration proceedings and make an award.

（6）根据第（4）款向法院提出的申请待决时，仲裁庭（包括被申请回避的仲裁员）可继续进行仲裁程序并作出裁决。

Failure or impossibility to act

不作为或履行不能

16.（1）A party may request the Court to remove an arbitrator —

（a）who is physically or mentally incapable of conducting the proceedings or where there are justifiable doubts as to his capacity to do so; or

（b）who has refused or failed —

（i）to properly conduct the proceedings; or

（ii）to use all reasonable despatch in conducting the proceedings or making an award，and where substantial injustice has been or will be caused to that party.

（1）当仲裁员身体上或精神上不能进行诉讼，或其能力受到正当怀疑的；拒绝、无法正确进行程序或拒绝、无法用所有合理的方式进行程序、作出判决，并且已经或将会对一方造成重大不公正的，该方可请求法院更换仲裁员。

（2）If there is an arbitral or other institution or person vested by the parties with power to remove an arbitrator，the Court shall not exercise its power of removal unless it is satisfied that the applicant has first exhausted any available recourse to that institution or person.

（2）如果仲裁机构、其他机构或人员有权更换仲裁员，法院不得更换仲裁员,除非法院确信申请人已经用尽了对该机构或人的任何可用方法。

(3) While an application to the Court under this section is pending, the arbitral tribunal, including the arbitrator concerned, may continue the arbitration proceedings and make an award.

(3) 根据本款向法院提出的申请尚待审理时,仲裁庭(包括有关仲裁员)仍可继续进行仲裁程序并作出裁决。

(4) Where the Court removes an arbitrator, the Court may make such order as it thinks fit with respect to his entitlement, if any, to fees or expenses, or the repayment of any fees or expenses already paid.

(4) 凡法院撤销仲裁员的,法院可就其有权享有的费用或开支,或已付的任何费用或开支做出其认为适当的决定。

(5) The arbitrator concerned is entitled to appear and be heard by the Court before it makes any order under this section.

(5) 在法院根据本条做出任何命令之前,有关仲裁员有权出庭。

(6) No appeal shall lie against the decision of the Court made under subsection (4).

(6) 不得对法院根据第(4)款所作裁定上诉。

Arbitrator ceasing to hold office

仲裁员离任

17. (1) The authority of an arbitrator shall cease upon his death.

(1) 仲裁员的权力在其死后即告终止。

(2) An arbitrator shall cease to hold office if —

(2) 仲裁员在下列情况下不得继续任职:

(a) he withdraws from office under section 15(3);

(a) 根据第 15 条第(3)款离任;

(b) an order is made under section 15(4) for the termination of his mandate or his removal；

(b) 根据第 15 条第(4)款命令终止其职务或被罢免；

(c) he is removed by the Court under section 16 or by an institution referred to in section 16(2)；or

(c) 根据第 16 条被法院免职或被第 16 条第(2)款所述机构免职；或

(d) the parties agree on the termination of his mandate.

(d) 当事人同意终止程序。

(3) The withdrawal of an arbitrator or the termination of an arbitrator's mandate by the parties shall not imply acceptance of the validity of any ground referred to in sections 14(3) or 16(1).

(3) 撤销仲裁员或当事人授权终止仲裁员的委任，不等同于接受第 14 条第(3)款或 16 条第(1)款所述的任何理由的有效性。

Appointment of substitute arbitrator

指定替补仲裁员

18. (1) Where an arbitrator ceases to hold office，the parties may agree —

(1) 仲裁员离任的，双方当事人可以约定：

(a) whether and if so how the vacancy is to be filled；

(a) 是否填补空缺；

(b) whether and if so to what extent the previous proceedings should stand；and

(b) 先前的程序进展情况；以及

(c) what effect (if any) his ceasing to hold office has on any appointment made by him，whether alone or jointly.

(c) 仲裁员的离任对该仲裁员或仲裁小组的委任所产生的影响。

（2）If or to the extent that there is no such agreement，the following subsections shall apply.

（2）若无此种协议，则应适用下列款项。

（3）Section 13 shall apply in relation to the filling of the vacancy as in relation to an original appointment.

（3）第 13 条适用于与原委任相关的空缺填补。

（4）The arbitral tribunal（when reconstituted）shall determine whether and if so to what extent the previous proceedings should stand.

（4）仲裁庭（在重新组成时）应确定先前的程序应进行至何种程度。

（5）The reconstitution of the arbitral tribunal shall not affect any right of a party to challenge the previous proceedings on any ground which had arisen before the arbitrator ceased to hold office.

（5）仲裁庭的重组不得影响当事人对仲裁员离任前发生的任何程序提出质疑的权利。

（6）The ceasing to hold office by the arbitrator shall not affect any appointment by him，whether alone or jointly，of another arbitrator，in particular any appointment of a presiding arbitrator.

（6）仲裁员的离任不得影响其单独或共同任命的另一名仲裁员，特别是首席仲裁员。

Decision by panel of arbitrators

仲裁小组决定

19.（1）In arbitration proceedings with more than one arbitrator，any decision of the arbitral tribunal shall be made，unless otherwise agreed by the parties，by all or a majority of all its members.

（1）在有一组仲裁员的仲裁中，除非当事人另有约定，仲裁庭的任
何决定应由多数仲裁员做出。

（2）Any question of procedure may be decided by a presiding
arbitrator if so authorised by the parties or all members of
the arbitral tribunal.

（2）出现程序问题时，经各方当事人或仲裁庭全体成员授权，首席
仲裁员可单独做出决定。

Liability of arbitrator

仲裁员的责任

20. An arbitrator shall not be liable for —

仲裁员不必为下述行为承担责任：

（a）negligence in respect of anything done or omitted to be done
in the capacity of the arbitrator; or

（a）在履行职责时的过失或疏忽；或

（b）any mistake of law, fact or procedure made in the course of
arbitration proceedings or in the making of an arbitral
award.

（b）在仲裁过程中或在作出裁决过程中的任何法律上、事实上或
程序上的错误。

PART VI

JURISDICTION OF ARBITRAL TRIBUNAL
第六部分　　仲裁庭的管辖权

Separability of arbitration clause and competence of arbitral tribunal
to rule on its own jurisdiction

仲裁条款可分性与仲裁庭独立管辖权

21.（1）The arbitral tribunal may rule on its own jurisdiction,
including any objections to the existence or validity of the

arbitration agreement.

（1）仲裁庭有权力对其自身管辖权作出裁定，包括对与仲裁协议的存在或效力有关的任何异议作出裁定。

（2）For the purpose of subsection（1），an arbitration clause which forms part of a contract shall be treated as an agreement independent of the other terms of the contract.

（2）第（1）款中作为合同组成部分的仲裁条款应当被视为独立于合同其他条款的一项协议。

（3）A decision by the arbitral tribunal that the contract is void shall not entail *ipso jure*（as a matter of law）the invalidity of the arbitration clause.

（3）仲裁庭有关合同无效的决定不会自动导致仲裁条款的无效。

（4）A plea that the arbitral tribunal does not have jurisdiction shall he raised not later than the submission of the statement of defence.

（4）认为仲裁庭不具有管辖权的，应当在辩方提交答辩之前提出。

（5）A party shall not be precluded from raising the plea that the arbitral tribunal does not have jurisdiction by the fact that he has appointed，or participated in the appointment of，an arbitrator.

（5）一方当事人已指定或参与指定一名仲裁员，不妨碍其提出管辖权异议的权利。

（6）A plea that the arbitral tribunal is exceeding the scope of its authority shall be raised as soon as the matter alleged to be beyond the scope of its authority is raised during the arbitration proceedings.

（6）关于仲裁庭超越权限的请求，应在仲裁程序过程中越权行为发生后立即提出。

（7）Notwithstanding any delay in raising a plea referred to in subsections（4）or（6），the arbitral tribunal may admit such plea if it considers the delay to be justified in the circumstances.

（7）若第（4）款或第（6）款所述的请求未及时提出，但仲裁庭认为此类情况下的延迟是合理的，可接受该请求。

（8）The arbitral tribunal may rule on a plea referred to in this section either as a preliminary question or in an award on the merits.

（8）对于本款述及的请求，仲裁庭既可作为初裁问题作出裁定，也可在实体裁决书中作出裁定。

（9）If the arbitral tribunal rules on a plea as a preliminary question that it has jurisdiction，any party may，within 30 days after having received notice of that ruling，apply to the Court to decide the matter.

（9）如果仲裁庭将请求视为其管辖权内的初裁问题，则任何一方可在收到通知后的 30 日内向法院申请作出裁决。

（10）The leave of the Court is required for any appeal from a decision of that Court under this section.

（10）对法院根据本节做出的任何决定的上诉都需要该法院许可。

（11）While an application under subsection（9）is pending，the arbitral tribunal may continue the arbitration proceedings and make an award.

（11）根据第（9）款提出的申请待决时，仲裁庭可继续进行仲裁程序并作出裁决。

PART VII
ARBITRAL PROCEEDINGS
第七部分　仲裁程序

General duties of arbitral tribunal

仲裁庭的一般职责

22. The arbitral tribunal shall act fairly and impartially and shall give each party a reasonable opportunity of presenting his case.

仲裁庭应当公平公正地行事,并给予双方合理的陈述案情的机会。

Determination of rules of procedure
程序规则的确定

23.（1）Subject to the provisions of this Order，the parties may agree on the procedure to be followed by the arbitral tribunal in conducting the proceedings.

（1）根据本法的规定,当事各方可以就仲裁庭进行仲裁所应遵循的程序达成协议。

（2）Failing such agreement，the arbitral tribunal may，subject to the provisions of this Order，conduct the arbitration in such manner as it considers appropriate.

（2）如未能达成一致,仲裁庭可根据本法选择适当的仲裁程序。

（3）The power conferred on the arbitral tribunal under subsection includes the power to determine the admissibility，relevance，materiality and weight of any evidence.

（3）授予仲裁庭的权力包括确定任何证据的可采性、相关性、实质性和重要性。

Statements of claim and defence
仲裁申请书和答辩状

24.（1）Within the period of time agreed by the parties or，failing such agreement，as determined by the arbitral tribunal，the claimant shall state —

（1）在双方当事人协议的期限内,或仲裁庭认定协议不成立时,申请人应当就下列事项做出声明:

（a）the facts supporting his claim;

（a）支持其主张的事实;

（b）the points at issue; and

（b）争议点;以及

（c）the relief or remedy sought，

（c）申请人寻求的救济或补偿，

and the respondent shall state his defence in respect of the particulars set out in this subsection，unless the parties have otherwise agreed to the required elements of such statements.

除非双方当事人另有约定，被告方应就本款所列事项做出辩护。

（2）The parties may submit to the arbitral tribunal with their statements，all documents they consider to be relevant and other documents which refer to such documents，or other evidence.

（2）双方当事人可以向仲裁庭提交陈述及当事人认为的有关文件和相关其他文件或其他证据。

（3）Except as otherwise agreed by the parties，either party may amend or supplement his claim or defence during the course of the arbitration proceedings，unless the arbitral tribunal considers it inappropriate to allow such amendment，having regard to the delay in making the amendment.

（3）除非各方当事人另有协议，在仲裁程序进行中，任何一方当事人均可以修改或补充其申请书或答辩状，除非仲裁庭考虑到提出已迟而认为不宜允许提出这种改动。

Hearings and written proceedings

开庭审理和书面审理

25.（1）Subject to any contrary agreement by the parties，the arbitral tribunal shall determine if proceedings are to be conducted by oral hearing for the presentation of evidence or oral argument or on the basis of documents and other materials.

（1）在当事人有反向协议的情况下，仲裁庭应决定是否采用口头审理呈现证据，或根据文件和其他材料进行口头辩论。

（2）Unless the parties have agreed that no hearings shall be held，the arbitral tribunal shall，upon the request of a party，hold such hearings at an appropriate stage of the proceedings.

（2）双方当事人未约定不开庭审理的，仲裁庭应当根据当事人的请求，在开庭的适当阶段举行听证。

（3）The parties shall be given sufficient notice in advance of any hearing and of any meeting of the arbitral tribunal for the purposes of inspection of documents，goods or other property.

（3）开庭审理，及仲裁庭为检查文件、货物或其他财产召开会议的，均应充分提前通知当事人。

（4）All statements，documents or other information supplied to the arbitral tribunal by one party shall be communicated to the other party.

（4）一方当事人向仲裁庭提交的一切陈述、文件或其他信息均应送交另一方当事人。

（5）Any expert report or evidentiary document on which the arbitral tribunal may rely in making its decision shall be communicated to the parties.

（5）仲裁庭可能据以作出裁决的任何具有证据性质的专家报告或其他文件也应送交各方当事人。

Consolidation of proceedings and concurrent hearings

合并诉讼与同时审理

26.（1）The parties may agree —

（1）双方当事人可达成如下协议：

（a）that the arbitration proceedings shall be consolidated with other arbitration proceedings；or （a）本仲裁程序应与其他仲裁程序合并；或

（b）that concurrent hearings shall be held，on such terms as may be agreed.

（b）同时举行听证。

（2）Unless the parties agree to confer such power on the arbitral tribunal，the tribunal has no power to order consolidation of arbitration proceedings or concurrent hearings.

（2）除非双方同意授予仲裁庭此种权力，否则仲裁庭无权命令合并仲裁程序或同时举行听证。

Power to appoint experts

任命专家的权力

27.（1）Unless otherwise agreed by the parties，the arbitral tribunal may —

（1）除非双方当事人另有约定，仲裁庭：

（a）appoint one or more experts to report to it on specific issues to be determined by the tribunal；and

（a）可以指定一名或数名专家就仲裁庭确定的具体问题向仲裁庭提出报告；

（b）require a party to give the expert any relevant information or to produce，or to provide access to，any relevant documents，goods or other property for his inspection.

（b）可要求一方当事人向专家提供任何有关资料，提供相关文件、货物或其他财产或提供上述物件的取得途径，以供专家检查。

（2）Unless otherwise agreed by the parties，if a party so requests or if the arbitral tribunal considers it necessary，the expert shall，after delivery of his written or oral report，participate in a hearing where the parties have the opportunity to question him and to present other expert witnesses in order to testify on the points at issue.

（2）除非当事人另有约定，经一方当事人请求或仲裁庭认为必要，专家在提出他的书面或口头报告后，应参加开庭，以便让当事人向他提问并派专家证人就争论焦点作证。

General powers exercisable by arbitral tribunal

仲裁庭行使的一般权力

28.（1）The parties may agree on the powers which may be exercised by the arbitral tribunal for the purposes of and in relation to the arbitration proceedings.

（1）双方当事人需同意仲裁庭为达到仲裁目的、与仲裁程序达成一致而行使的权力。

（2）Without prejudice to the powers conferred on the arbitral tribunal by the parties under subsection（1），the tribunal shall have powers to make orders or give directions to any party for —

（2）在不影响双方当事人根据第（1）款赋予仲裁庭权力的情况下，仲裁庭有权向任何一方做出下列命令或指示：

（a）security for costs；

（a）仲裁费用担保；

（b）discovery of documents and interrogatories；

（b）文件开示和质询；

（c）giving of evidence by affidavit；

（c）提供证据并宣誓；

（d）a party or witness to he examined on oath，and may for that purpose administer any necessary oath；

（d）经宣誓审查的当事人或证人，并可为此目的进行必要的宣誓；

（e）the preservation and interim custody of any evidence

for the purposes of the proceedings;

（e）为仲裁保存和临时保管证据;

（f）samples to be taken from, or any observation to be made of or experiment conducted upon, any property which is or forms part of the subject-matter of the dispute; and

（f）从属于或构成争议标的物的财产取得样本,或对其进行观察、实验;以及

（g）the preservation, interim custody or sale of any property which is or forms part of the subject-matter of the dispute.

（g）保存、临时保管或出售任何属于或构成争议标的物的财产。

（3）The power of the arbitral tribunal to order a claimant to provide security for costs as referred to in subsection（2）（a）shall not be exercised by reason only that the claimant is —

（3）如果原告满足下列条件之一,仲裁庭不得命令原告为第（2）款（a）项所述费用提供担保:

（a）an individual ordinarily resident outside Brunei Darus-salam; or

（a）通常居住在文莱达鲁萨兰国境外的个人;或

（b）a corporation or an association incorporated or formed under the law of a country or territory outside Brunei Darussalam, or whose central management and control is exercised outside Brunei Darussalam.

（b）根据文莱达鲁萨兰国境外的国家或地区的法律成立或组建的公司或协会,或中央管理、控制权在文莱达鲁萨兰国境外行使的公司或协会。

（4）All orders or directions made or given by an arbitral tribunal in the course of an arbitration shall, by leave of the Court, be enforceable in the same manner as if they were orders made by the Court and，where leave is so given，judgment may be entered in terms of the order or direction.

（4）仲裁庭在仲裁过程中做出或提出的所有命令或指示，应经法院许可，其执行方式与法院判决相同。如有许可，可根据命令或指示作出裁决。

Powers of arbitral tribunal in case of party's default

仲裁庭在当事人违约时的权力

29.（1）The parties may agree on the powers which may be exercised by the arbitral tribunal in the case of a party's failure to take any necessary action for the proper and expeditious conduct of the proceedings.

（1）双方当事人可以约定仲裁庭可行使的职权，以防一方当事人未能正当和迅速地按照程序采取必要的行动。

（2）Unless otherwise agreed by the parties，if，without showing sufficient cause —

（2）除非双方当事人另有约定，如在不提出充分理由的情况下：

(a) the claimant fails to communicate his statement of claim in accordance with section 24，the arbitral tribunal may terminate the proceedings；

（a）申诉人不按第 24 条的规定提交仲裁申请书，则仲裁庭应终止程序；

(b) the respondent fails to communicate his statement of defence in accordance with section 24，the arbitral tribunal may continue the proceedings without treating such failure in itself as an admission of the claimant's allegations；and

（b）被申请人未按照第 24 条规定递交对仲裁通知的答复或答辩状，不表明充分理由的，仲裁庭应下令继续进行仲裁程

序。不递交答复或答辩书之事本身不应视为承认申请人的主张；以及

(c) any party fails to appear at a hearing or to produce any documentary evidence, the arbitral tribunal may continue the proceedings and make the award on the evidence before it.

(c) 任何一方当事人不出庭或不提供书证,仲裁庭仍可继续进行仲裁程序并根据已有证据作出裁决。

(3) If the arbitral tribunal is satisfied that there has been inordinate and inexcusable delay on the part of the claimant in pursuing his claim, and the delay —

(3) 如果仲裁庭认为申请人有下列过度拖延追索的情况的,可以作出驳回申索的裁决:

(a) gives rise, or is likely to give rise, to a substantial risk that it is not possible to have a fair resolution of the issues in that claim; or

(a) 引起或可能引起重大风险,即无法公正地解决该诉讼中的问题;或

(b) has caused, or is likely to cause, serious prejudice to the respondent, the tribunal may make an award dismissing the claim.

(b) 已经或可能导致对被告的严重损害。

Witnesses may be summoned by subpoena

传票传唤证人

30. (1) Any party to an arbitration agreement may take out a subpoena to testify or to produce documents.

(1) 仲裁协议的任何一方可以拿出传票作证或出示文件。

(2) The Court may order that a subpoena to testify or to produce documents shall be issued to compel the attendance

before an arbitral tribunal of a witness wherever he may be within Brunei Darussalam.

（2）无论证人位于文莱达鲁萨兰国何处，法庭可发出传票或出示文件强制证人出庭作证。

（3）The Court may also issue an order under section 32（1）of the Prisons Act（Chapter 51）to bring up a prisoner for examination before an arbitral tribunal.

（3）法院也可根据《监狱法》（第五十一章）第 32 条第（1）款发出命令，将囚犯提交仲裁庭审理。

（4）No person shall be compelled under any such subpoena to produce any document which he could not be compelled to produce on the trial of an action.

（4）对于庭审中不可被强制出示的文件，不得通过传票强制任何人出示。

Court's powers exercisable in support of arbitration proceedings
法院支持仲裁程序行使的权力

31.（1）The Court shall have the following powers for the purpose of and in relation to an arbitration to which this Order applies —

（1）就本法所适用的仲裁而言，法院具有以下权力：

（a）the same power to make orders in respect of any matter set out in section 28 as it has for the purpose of and in relation to an action or matter in the Court；

（a）根据第 28 条做出命令，效力与法院处理诉讼时等同；

（b）securing the amount in dispute；

（b）担保争议金额；

（c）ensuring that any award which may be made in the arbitral proceedings is not rendered ineffectual by the dissipation of assets by a party；and （c）确保仲裁程序中可能作出的裁决不因一方当事人的资产耗尽而无效；以及

（d）an interim injunction or any other interim measure.

（d）临时禁令或任何其他临时措施。

（2）An order of the Court under this section shall cease to have effect in whole or in part if the arbitral tribunal or any such arbitral or other institution or person having power to act in relation to the subject-matter of that order makes an order to which the order of the Court relates.

（2）如果仲裁庭或任何有权针对该争议采取行动的仲裁机构或其他机构或个人做出命令，法院根据本条发出的命令将不再具有效力。

（3）The Court，in exercising any power under this section，shall have regard to —

（a）any application made before the arbitral tribunal；or

（b）any order made by the arbitral tribunal，in respect of the same issue.

（3）在根据本条行使权力时，法院应就同一问题考虑当事人对仲裁庭提出的申请或仲裁庭做出的命令。

（4）Provision may be made by Rules of Court for conferring on the Registrar of the Supreme Court all or any of the jurisdiction conferred by this Order on the Court.

（4）根据法院规则，可向最高法院书记处授予本法赋予法院的全部管辖权。

PART VIII
AWARD
第八部分　裁决

Law applicable to substance of dispute

适用于实体争议的规则

32.（1）The arbitral tribunal shall decide the dispute in accordance with the law chosen by the parties as applicable to the substance of the dispute.

（1）仲裁庭应按照双方当事人选定的适用于争议实体的法律解决争议。

（2）If or to the extent that the parties have not chosen the law applicable to the substance of their dispute，the arbitral tribunal shall apply the law determined by the conflict of laws rules.

（2）如果当事人未选择适用于其争议点的法律，仲裁庭应适用冲突法规则所确定的法律。

（3）The arbitral tribunal may decide the dispute，if the parties so agree，in accordance with such other considerations as are agreed by them or determined by the tribunal.

（3）如果当事人同意，仲裁庭可根据当事人或法庭确定的其他考虑事项来解决争议。

Awards made on different issues

针对不同问题的裁决

33.（1）Unless otherwise agreed by the parties，the arbitral tribunal may make more than one award at different times during the proceedings on different aspects of the matters to be determined.

（1）除非当事人另有约定，仲裁庭可以在诉讼期间的不同阶段对待决事项作出不同的裁决。

（2）The arbitral tribunal may，in particular，make an award relating to

（a）an issue affecting the whole claim；or

（b）a part only of the claim，counter-claim or cross-claim，which is submitted to the tribunal for decision.

（2）针对一些问题，尤其是影响整个诉讼的问题或诉讼、反诉或交叉诉讼的部分问题，仲裁庭可裁决提交法院决定。

（3）If the arbitral tribunal makes an award under this section, it shall specify in its award the issue, or claim or part of a claim, which is the subject-matter of the award.

（3）仲裁庭根据本款作出裁决的，应在裁决书中具体说明仲裁裁决的争议点及全部或部分主张。

Remedies

救济

34.（1）The parties may agree on the powers exercisable by the arbitral tribunal as regards remedies.

（1）双方当事人可就仲裁庭可行使的救济达成一致。

（2）Unless otherwise agreed by the parties, the arbitral tribunal may award any remedy or relief that could have been ordered by the Court if the dispute had been the subject of civil proceedings in that Court.

（2）除非当事人另有约定，仲裁庭可对法院在该争议中民事诉讼标的的任何补救或救济措施进行裁决。

Interest

权益

35.（1）The arbitral tribunal may award interest, including interest on a compound basis, on the whole or any part of any sum that —

（1）在裁决或付款日期前，仲裁庭可对以下任何一笔款项的全部或部分利息，包括复利作出判决：

（a）is awarded to any party; or

（a）判给任何一方；或

（b）is in issue in the arbitral proceedings but is paid before the date of the award, for the whole or any part of the period up to the date of the award or payment, whichever is applicable.

(b) 在仲裁程序中有争议,但在裁决之日之前支付。

(2) A sum directed to be paid by an award shall, unless the award otherwise directs, carry interest as from the date of the award and at the same rate as a judgment debt.

(2) 除裁决另有指示外,指示由裁决支付的款项应自裁决之日起以与判定债务相同的利率计息。

Extension of time for making award
延长裁决

36. (1) Where the time for making an award is limited by the arbitration agreement, the Court may by order, unless otherwise agreed by the parties, extend that time.

(1) 裁决时间受仲裁协议限制的,除当事人另有约定外,法院可责令延期。

(2) An application for an order under this section may be made —

(2) 根据本条可申请:

(a) upon notice to the parties, by the arbitral tribunal; or

(a) 由仲裁庭通知当事人;或

(b) upon notice to the arbitral tribunal and the other parties, by any party to the proceedings.

(b) 由仲裁庭和其他当事人通知诉讼的任何一方。

(3) An application under this section shall not be made unless all available tribunal processes for application of extension of time have been exhausted.

(3) 除非适用于延长裁决的所有法庭程序已用尽,否则不应提出延长裁决申请。

(4) The Court shall not make an order under this section unless it is satisfied that substantial injustice would otherwise be done.

(4) 除非法院认为不延长裁决会造成重大不公正,否则不得延长裁决。

(5) The Court may extend the time for such period and on such terms as it thinks fit, and may do so whether or not the time previously fixed by or under the arbitration agreement or by a previous order has expired.

(5) 无论先前根据仲裁协议或以前的命令所确定的时间是否已经过期,法庭可按其认为合适的条款延长裁决。

(6) The leave of the Court shall be required for any appeal from a decision of the Court under this section.

(6) 对本条所做任何决定的上诉均须经法院许可。

Award by consent

合意裁决

37. (1) If, during arbitration proceedings, the parties settle the dispute, the arbitral tribunal shall terminate the proceedings and, if requested by the parties and not objected to by the arbitral tribunal, record the settlement in the form of an arbitral award on agreed terms.

(1) 仲裁过程中,各方当事人和解的,仲裁庭应当终结程序。如果当事人申请且仲裁庭接受,则应记录此项和解协议并按照和解协议条款作出仲裁裁决。

(2) An arbitral award on agreed terms —

(2) 合意的仲裁裁决应符合下列条件:

(a) shall be made in accordance with section 38;

(a) 按照第 38 条作出;

(b) shall state that it is an award; and

（b）说明这是一项裁决；以及

（c）shall have the same status and effect as any other award on the merits of the case.

（c）与任何其他就争议实体作出的仲裁裁决具有同等效力并得以执行。

（3）An award on agreed terms may，with the leave of the Court，be enforced in the same manner as a judgment or order to the same effect，and where leave is so given，judgment may be entered in terms of the award.

（3）合意裁决可以在法院许可的情况下执行，与判决或命令的方式相同。在得到允许的情况下，可以根据裁决书作出判决。

Form and contents of award

裁决的形式和内容

38.（1）The award shall be made in writing and shall be signed —

（a）in the case of a single arbitrator，by the arbitrator himself；or

（b）in the case of 2 or more arbitrators，by all the arbitrators or the majority of the arbitrators provided that the reason for any omitted signature of any arbitrator is stated.

（1）仲裁庭的裁决应采取书面形式，由各仲裁员签字。如仲裁庭由一名以上仲裁员组成，有多数仲裁员签字即可，但应说明少数仲裁员未签字的原因。

（2）The award shall state the reasons upon which it is based，unless the parties have agreed that no grounds are to be stated or the award is an award on agreed terms under section 37.

（2）仲裁庭应说明裁决所依据的理由，除非各方当事人约定无须说明理由，或该裁决为根据第 37 条按照和解协议条款作出的仲裁裁决。

（3）The date of the award and place of arbitration shall be stated in the award.

（3）裁决的日期和仲裁地点应在裁决中注明。

（4）The award shall be deemed to have been made at the place of arbitration.

（4）仲裁裁决应视为在仲裁地作出。

（5）After the award is made，a copy of the award signed by the arbitrators in accordance with subsection（1）shall be delivered to each party.

（5）仲裁裁决作出后，经仲裁员签字的仲裁裁决副本应送达至各方当事人。

Costs of arbitration
仲裁费用

39.（1）Any costs directed by an award to be paid shall，unless the award otherwise directs，be taxed by the Registrar of the Supreme Court.

（1）除非裁决另有指示，否则仲裁费用应由最高法院书记处征收。

（2）Subject to subsection（3），any provision in an arbitration agreement to the effect that the parties or any party shall in any event pay their or his own costs of the reference or award or any part thereof shall be void；and this Order shall，in the case of an arbitration agreement containing any such provision，have effect as if there were no such provision.

（2）在符合第（3）款的情况下，仲裁协议中规定当事各方或任何一方在任何情况下支付其自己的费用或其任何部分的条款或其任何部分均无效；如果仲裁协议中含有此类规定，本法即使无此规定也具有效力。

（3）Subsection （2） shall not apply where a provision in an arbitration agreement to the effect that the parties or any party shall in any event pay their or his own costs is part of an agreement to submit to arbitration a dispute which has arisen before the making of such agreement.

（3）第（2）款不适用于仲裁协议中规定双方或一方当事人承担自身费用作为提请仲裁的条件，且争议在仲裁协议达成前已产生的条款。

（4）If no provision is made by an award with respect to the costs of the reference，any party to the reference may，within 14 days of the delivery of the award or such further time as the arbitral tribunal may allow，apply to the arbitral tribunal for an order directing by and to whom such costs shall be paid.

（4）如果在裁决中没有就裁判费用作出规定，裁判文书的任何一方可以在裁决书交付后 14 天内或仲裁庭允许的更长时间内，向仲裁庭申请就费用支付做出指示。

（5）The arbitral tribunal shall，after giving the parties a reasonable opportunity to be heard，amend its award by adding thereto such directions as it thinks fit with respect to the payment of the costs of the reference.

（5）仲裁庭应在给予当事人合理的听证机会后修改其裁决，并在裁决中增加其认为适当的指示以支付裁决的费用。

Fees of arbitrator

仲裁员的费用

40.（1）The parties are jointly and severally liable to pay to the arbitrators such reasonable fees and expenses as are appropriate in the circumstances.

（1）当事人共同分别负责向仲裁员支付合理费用和开支。

(2) Unless the fees of the arbitral tribunal have been fixed by written agreement or such agreement has provided for determination of the fees by a person or institution agreed to by the parties, any party to the arbitration may require that such fees be taxed by the Registrar of the Supreme Court.

(2) 除非仲裁庭的费用已通过书面协议确定，或协议规定由双方当事人约定的人或机构确定费用，仲裁的任何一方可以要求这些费用由最高法院书记处收取。

Power to withhold award in case of non-payment

针对未付款的裁决保留权

41. (1) The arbitral tribunal may refuse to deliver an award to the parties if the parties have not made full payment of the fees and expenses of the arbitrators.

(1) 当事人未完全支付仲裁员的费用和开支的，仲裁庭可以拒绝向当事人交付仲裁裁决。

(2) Where subsection (1) applies, a party to the arbitration proceedings may, upon notice to the other parties and the arbitral tribunal, apply to the Court which may order that —

(2) 当第(1)款适用时，仲裁程序的当事人可在通知其他当事人及仲裁庭后向法院提出申请如下：

(a) the arbitral tribunal shall deliver the award upon payment into Court by the applicant of those fees and expenses, or such lesser amount as the Court may specify;

(a) 仲裁庭应根据申请人的费用和开支或法院规定的较小数额向法院提交裁决书；

(b) the amount of those fees and expenses demanded shall be taxed by the Registrar of the Supreme Court; and

(b) 所需费用和开支须由最高法院书记处征收；

(c) out of the money paid into Court，the arbitral tribunal shall be paid such fees and expenses as may be found to be properly payable and the balance of such money（if any）shall be paid to the applicant.

(c) 在支付给法院的款项中，应向仲裁庭支付适当费用和支出，并将该款项的余额（如有）付还给申请人。

(3) A taxation of fees under this section shall be reviewed in the same manner as a taxation of costs.

(3) 根据本条征收的费用，应按照费用征税的方式进行审查。

(4) The arbitrator shall be entitled to appear and be heard on any taxation or review of taxation under this section.

(4) 仲裁员有权就本条规定的税收或税务审查出庭听取意见。

(5) For the purpose of this section，the amount of fees and expenses properly payable is the amount the applicant is liable to pay under section 40 or under any agreement relating to the payment of fees and expenses of the arbitrators.

(5) 就本条而言，适当缴付的费用及开支金额是指申请人须根据第 40 条或有关支付仲裁员费用及开支的协议而须缴付的款额。

(6) No application to the Court may be made unless the Court is satisfied that the applicant has first exhausted any available arbitral process for appeal or review of the amount of the fees or expenses of the arbitrators.

(6) 除非法院采信当事人已用尽任何可用的仲裁程序上诉或审查仲裁员的费用或开支，否则当事人不得向法院提出申请。

(7) This section shall apply to any arbitral or other institution or person vested with powers by the parties in relation to the delivery of the award by the tribunal and any reference to the fees and expenses of the arbitrators shall be construed

as including the fees and expenses of that institution or person.

（7）本条适用于任何被当事人赋予权力的、与仲裁裁决送达相关的仲裁机构、其他机构或个人，对仲裁员费用和开支的任何解释都应包括该机构或个人的费用和开支。

（8）The leave of the Court shall be required for any appeal from a decision of the Court under this section.

（8）对本条所做任何决定的上诉均须经法院许可。

Court may charge property with payment of solicitor's costs in arbitration

法院可在仲裁中收取财产以支付律师费用

42. Section 58(1) of the Legal Profession Act（Chapter 132）shall apply as if an arbitration were a proceeding in the Court，and the Court may make declarations and orders accordingly.

《法律职业法》（第一百三十二章）第 58 条第（1）款适用仲裁，并赋予仲裁等同诉讼的地位，法院可据此做出声明和发出命令。

Correction or interpretation of award and additional award

裁决书的更正与解释以及补充裁决

43.（1）A party may，within 30 days of the receipt of the award，unless another period of time has been agreed upon by the parties —

（1）除非双方当事人对期间另有约定，在收到裁决书后的 30 天内：

（a）upon notice to the other parties，request the arbitral tribunal to correct in the award any error in computation，any clerical or typographical error，or any other error of a similar nature；and （a）任何一方当事人在通知另一方当事人后可以请求仲裁庭改正裁决中出现的任何计算、书写、打印错误或任何类似性质的错误；以及

（b）upon notice to the other parties, request the arbitral tribunal to give an interpretation of a specific point or part of the award, if such request is also agreed to by the other parties.

（b）一方可在通知另一方并取得同意后要求仲裁庭就裁决的某一点或部分裁决做出解释。

（2）If the arbitral tribunal considers the request in subsection (1) to be justified, the tribunal shall make such correction or give such interpretation within 30 days of the receipt of the request and such interpretation shall form part of the award.

（2）如果仲裁庭认为第（1）款中的请求是正当的，仲裁庭应在收到请求后 30 天内做出更正或做出解释，此解释应构成裁决的一部分。

（3）The arbitral tribunal may correct any error of the type referred to in subsection (1)(a) or give an interpretation referred to in subsection (1)(b), on its own initiative, within 30 days of the date of the award.

（3）仲裁庭可以在裁决之日起 30 日内，自行纠正第（1）款（a）项所述类型的错误或根据第（1）款（b）项对裁决做出解释。

（4）Unless otherwise agreed by the parties, a party may, within 30 days of receipt of the award and upon notice to the other party, request the arbitral tribunal to make an additional award as to claims presented during the arbitration proceedings but omitted from the award.

（4）除非双方当事人另有约定，一方当事人可在收到裁决书之日起 30 天内，通知另一方当事人，请求仲裁庭对仲裁时提出的、

但在裁决中被遗漏的主张作出补充裁决。

(5) If the arbitral tribunal considers the request in subsection (4) to be justified, the tribunal shall make the additional award within 60 days of the receipt of such request.

(5) 仲裁庭认为要求合理的,应在收到要求后60天之内作出补充裁决。

(6) The arbitral tribunal may, if necessary, extend the period of time within which it shall make a correction, interpretation or an additional award under this section.

(6) 如有必要,仲裁庭可延长其做出更正、解释或作出补充裁决的时间。

(7) Section 38 shall apply to an award in respect of which a correction or interpretation has been made under this section and to an additional award.

(7) 第38条适用于根据本条作出更正或解释的裁决及额外裁决。

Effect of award
裁决的效力

44. (1) An award made by the arbitral tribunal pursuant to an arbitration agreement shall be final and binding on the parties and on any person claiming through or under them and may be relied upon by any of the parties by way of defence, set-off or otherwise in any proceedings in any court of competent jurisdiction.

(1) 仲裁庭根据仲裁协议作出的裁决是终局的,对双方当事人以及任何通过或根据双方当事人进行主张的人均有约束力,任何当事人均可通过抗辩、抵销或其他方式向有管辖权的法院提起诉讼。

(2) Except as provided in section 43, upon an award being made, including an award made in accordance with section

33，the arbitral tribunal shall not vary，amend，correct，review，add to or revoke the award.

（2）除第43条规定外,在作出裁决包括根据第33条作出裁决时,仲裁庭不得更改、修正、纠正、复审、补充或撤销裁决。

（3）For the purposes of subsection（2），an award is made when it has been signed and delivered in accordance with section 38.

（3）根据第38条签署和交付时,即作出第（2）款所称裁决。

（4）This section shall not affect the right of a person to challenge the award by any available arbitral process of appeal or review or in accordance with the provisions of this Order.

（4）本节不影响任何人根据可上诉的仲裁程序、复审或依照本命令对裁决提出质疑的权利。

PART IX
POWERS OF COURT IN RELATION TO AWARD
第九部分　法院对裁决的权力

Determination of preliminary point of law
法律的初步确定

45.（1）Unless otherwise agreed by the parties，the Court may，on the application of a party to the arbitration proceedings who has given notice to the other parties，determine any question of law arising in the course of the proceedings which the Court is satisfied substantially affects the rights of one or more of the parties.

（1）除非当事人另有约定,法院可根据一方的申请,决定裁决过程中产生的严重影响一方或多方权利的法律问题。

（2）The Court shall not consider an application under this section unless —

（2）法院不得考虑根据本条提出的申请，除非

（a）it is made with the agreement of all parties to the proceedings; or

（a）其是在各方当事人同意的情况下提出的；或

（b）it is made with the permission of the arbitral tribunal and the Court is satisfied that —

（b）经仲裁庭许可，法院确信：

（i）the determination of the question is likely to produce substantial savings in costs; and

（i）该申请的确定可能大大节省成本
该申请是各方当事人同意作出的；以及

（ii）the application is made without delay.

（ii）该申请是及时提出的

（3）The application shall identify the question of law to be determined and, except where made with the agreement of all parties to the proceedings, shall state the grounds on which it is said that the question should be decided by the Court.

（3）申请应说明待确定的法律问题，除非该申请在诉讼各方同意的情况下做出，否则应说明由法院确定该问题的理由。

（4）Unless otherwise agreed by the parties, the arbitral tribunal may continue the arbitral proceedings and make an award while an application to the Court under this section is pending.

（4）除非当事各方另有协议，本款所述的向法院提出的申请待决时，仲裁庭可以继续进行仲裁程序并作出裁决。

（5）Except with the leave of the Court, no appeal shall lie from a decision of the Court on whether the conditions in subsection（2）are met.

（5）除非得到法院许可，不得以是否符合第（2）款的条件为由向法院上诉。

（6）The decision of the Court on a question of law shall be a judgment of the Court for the purposes of an appeal to the Court of Appeal.

（6）法院对法律问题的决定应是与上诉有关的法院判决。

（7）The Court may give leave to appeal against the decision of the Court in subsection（6）only if it considers that the question of law before it is one of general importance，or is one which for some other special reason should be considered by the Court of Appeal.

（7）只有在法院认为申请首先是法律问题而非一般问题，也不应由上诉法院来考虑其他特殊原因时，法院才可根据第（6）款许可该申请。

Enforcement of award

裁决的执行

46.（1）An award made by the arbitral tribunal pursuant to an arbitration agreement may，with leave of the Court，be enforced in the same manner as a judgment or order of the Court to the same effect.

（1）仲裁庭根据仲裁协议作出的裁决，可在法院许可的情况下，以与法院作出判决或提出命令相同的方式执行。

（2）Where leave of the Court is so granted，judgment may be entered in the terms of the award.

（2）如果法院给予了这样的许可，则可以根据裁决的条款作出判决。

（3）Notwithstanding section 3，subsection（1）shall apply to an award irrespective of whether the place of arbitration is Brunei Darussalam or elsewhere.

（3）尽管有第 3 条的规定，第（1）款应适用于不论仲裁地是否位于文莱达鲁萨兰国的裁决。

No judicial review of award

不对裁决进行司法审查

47. The Court shall not have jurisdiction to confirm，vary，set aside or remit an award on an arbitration agreement except where so provided in this Order.

除本法规定的情况外，法院无权对仲裁协议进行确认、变更、撤销或移交。

Court may set aside award

法院可撤销裁决

48. (1) An award may be set aside by the Court —

(1) 仲裁裁决只有在下列情况下才可以被法院撤销：

（a）if the party who applies to the Court to set aside the award proves to the satisfaction of the Court that —

（a）如果向法院申请撤销裁决的一方证明：

（i）a party to the arbitration agreement was under some incapacity；

（i）仲裁协议一方当事人存在不完全民事行为能力的情况；

（ii）the arbitration agreement is not valid under the law to which the parties have subjected it or，failing any indication thereon，under the laws of Brunei Darussalam；

（ii）仲裁协议根据当事各方所依据的法律无效，或者无法根据文莱达鲁萨兰国法律说明；

（iii）the party making the application was not given proper notice of the appointment of an arbitrator or of the arbitration proceedings or was otherwise unable to present his case；

（iii）未将有关指定仲裁员或仲裁程序的事情适当地通知提出申请的当事一方，或该方因其他理由未能陈述

其案情；或

(iv) the award deals with a dispute not contemplated by or not falling within the terms of the submission to arbitration, or contains decisions on matters beyond the scope of the submission to arbitration, except that, if the decisions on matters submitted to arbitration can be separated from those not so submitted, only that part of the award which contains decisions on matters not submitted to arbitration may be set aside;

(iv) 该裁决涉及的是提交仲裁之外的争议，如果提交仲裁的决定可以从未提交仲裁的部分中区分出来，那么只有未提交仲裁的那部分裁决可以被撤销；

(v) the composition of the arbitral tribunal or the arbitral procedure is not in accordance with the agreement of the parties, unless such agreement is contrary to any provisions of this Order from which the parties cannot derogate or, in the absence of such agreement, is contrary to the provisions of this Order;

(v) 仲裁庭的组成或仲裁程序与当事各方的协议不一致，除非这种协议与当事各方不能背离的本法的规定相抵触，或当事各方并无此种协议，则与本法不符；或

(vi) the making of the award was induced or affected by fraud or corruption; or

(vi) 裁决由欺诈或腐败引起或被其影响；或

(vii) a breach of the rules of natural justice occurred in connection with the making of the award by which the rights of any party have been prejudiced; or

(vii) 违背了自然正义的规则，使一方的权利受到了损害；或

(b) if the Court finds that —

（b）如经法院认定：

（i）the subject-matter of the dispute is not capable of settlement by arbitration under this Order; or

（i）该争议的标的不能通过仲裁解决；或

（ii）the award is contrary to public policy.

（ii）裁决有悖公共政策。

（2）An application for setting aside an award may not be made after the expiry of 3 months from the date on which the party making the application had received the award, or if a request has been made under section 43, from the date on which that request had been disposed of by the arbitral tribunal.

（2）提出申请的当事一方自收到裁决书之日起，3 个月后不得申请撤销；如根据第 43 条提出了请求，则从该请求被仲裁庭处理完毕之日起 3 个月后不得申请撤销。

（3）When a party applies to the Court to set aside an award under this section, the Court may, where appropriate and so requested by a party, suspend the proceedings for setting aside the award, for such period of time as it may determine, to allow the arbitral tribunal to resume the arbitration proceedings or take such other action as may eliminate the grounds for setting aside the award.

（3）一方当事人根据本条向法院申请撤销裁决时，法院可酌情按照当事人提出的要求中止程序，暂停裁决，并在确定的时间内允许仲裁庭恢复仲裁程序或采取其他恢复裁决的行动。

Appeal against award

对裁决进行上诉

49.（1）A party to arbitration proceedings may, upon notice to the other parties and to the arbitral tribunal, appeal to the Court on a question of law arising out of an award made in the proceedings.

（1）仲裁程序的一方当事人可以在通知其他当事人和仲裁庭的情况下，就法律程序中的裁决所引起的法律问题向法院提出上诉。

（2）Notwithstanding subsection（1），the parties may agree to exclude the jurisdiction of the Court under this section and an agreement to dispense with reasons for the arbitral tribunal's award shall be treated as an agreement to exclude the jurisdiction of the Court under this section.

（2）尽管有第（1）款的规定，当事各方可根据本节达成一致，排除法院的管辖权，并且免除仲裁庭裁决理由的协议应被视为按照本条规定排除法院管辖权的协议。

（3）An appeal shall not be brought under this section except —

（3）除以下情况外，不得上诉：

（a）with the agreement of all the other parties to the proceedings; or

（a）经所有当事方同意；或

（b）with the leave of the Court.

（b）经法庭许可。

（4）The right to appeal under this section shall be subject to the restrictions in section 50.

（4）根据本条提出上诉的权利受第 50 条的限制。

（5）Leave to appeal shall be given only if the Court is satisfied that —

（5）法院只有在采信下列情况时才可做出上诉许可：

（a）the determination of the question will substantially affect the rights of one or more of the parties;

（a）问题的确定将严重影响一方或多方的权利；

（b）the question is one which the arbitral tribunal was asked to determine;

（b）该问题是仲裁庭被要求确定的问题；

（c）on the basis of the findings of fact in the award —

（c）根据裁决事实认定符合下列情况：

　　（i）the decision of the arbitral tribunal on the question is obviously wrong; or

　　（i）仲裁庭对这个问题的裁决有明显错误；或

　　（ii）the question is one of general public importance and the decision of the arbitral tribunal is at least open to serious doubt; and

　　（ii）该问题受到公众普遍关注，且裁决可能引起严重的怀疑；以及

（d）despite the agreement of the parties to resolve the matter by arbitration，it is just and proper in all the circumstances for the Court to determine the question.

（d）尽管各方同意通过仲裁解决该问题，但法院对该问题的决定公正且合理。

（6）An application for leave to appeal under this section shall identify the question of law to be determined and state the grounds on which it is alleged that leave to appeal should be granted.

（6）根据本条申请上诉许可应说明待确定的法律问题及上诉理由。

（7）The leave of the Court shall be required for any appeal from a decision of the Court under this section to grant or refuse leave to appeal.

（7）对本条所做任何决定的上诉均须经法院许可。

（8）On an appeal under this section，the Court may by order —

（8）对根据本条提出的上诉，法院可命令如下：

（a）confirm the award;

（a）确认裁决；

（b）vary the award;

（b）更改裁决；

（c）remit the award to the arbitral tribunal, in whole or in part, for reconsideration in the light of the Court's determination; or

（c）由法院决定将裁决全部或部分交给仲裁庭复议；或

（d）set aside the award in whole or in part.

（d）撤销全部或部分裁决。

（9）The Court shall not exercise its power to set aside an award, in whole or in part, unless it is satisfied that it would be inappropriate to remit the matters in question to the arbitral tribunal for reconsideration.

（9）除非法院认定不宜将有关事项交由仲裁庭复议，法院不得撤销全部或部分裁决。

（10）The decision of the Court on an appeal under this section shall be treated as a judgment of the Court for the purposes of an appeal to the Court of Appeal.

（10）法院根据本款对上诉所做决定，应视为可向上诉法院提出上诉的判决。

（11）The Court may give leave to appeal against the decision of the Court in subsection（10）only if it considers that the question of law before it is one of general importance, or is one which for some other special reason should be considered by the Court of Appeal.

（11）只有在法院认为申请首先是法律问题而非一般问题，也不应由上诉法院来考虑其他特殊原因时，法院才可根据第（10）款许可该申请。

Supplementary provisions to appeal under section 49

根据第 49 条提出上诉的补充条文

50.（1）This section shall apply to an application or appeal under section 49.

（1）本条适用于根据第 49 条提出的申请或上诉。

（2） An application or appeal may not be brought if the applicant or appellant has not first exhausted —

（2）如果申请人或上诉人没有用尽下列方式，则不得申请或上诉：

（a） any available arbitral process of appeal or review; and

（a）任何可用的上诉或审查仲裁程序；以及

（b） any available recourse under section 43.

（b）根据第 43 条的任何可用追索权。

（3） Any application or appeal shall be brought within 28 days of the date of the award or，if there has been any arbitral process of appeal or review，of the date when the applicant or appellant was notified of the result of that process.

（3）任何申请或上诉均应在裁决之日起 28 天内提出，或在上诉或复审过程中申请人或上诉人被告知结果之日起 28 天内提出。

（4） If on an application or appeal it appears to the Court that the award —

（4）如果在申请或上诉中，法院认为裁决具有下列情形的：

（a） does not contain the arbitral tribunal's reasons; or

（a）不包含仲裁庭的理由；或

（b） does not set out the arbitral tribunal's reasons in sufficient detail to enable the Court to properly consider the application or appeal，

（b）未详细列出仲裁庭的理由，以便法院能够适当考虑申请或上诉的，

the Court may order the arbitral tribunal to state the reasons for its award in sufficient detail for that purpose.

法院可命令仲裁庭详细说明其裁决理由。

（5） Where the Court makes an order under subsection （4），it

may make such further order as it thinks fit with respect to any additional costs of the arbitration resulting from its order.

（5）法院根据第（4）款做出命令时，可就其命令所产生的额外费用按适当方式做出进一步命令。

（6）The Court may order the applicant or appellant to provide security for the costs of the application or appeal，and may direct that the application or appeal be dismissed if the order is not complied with.

（6）法院可命令申请人或上诉人为申请或上诉的费用提供担保，并指示如果该命令未得到遵守，申请或上诉将被驳回。

（7）The power to order security for costs shall not be exercised by reason only that the applicant or appellant is —

（7）申请人或上诉人满足下列情形的，法院不得命令其提供担保：

 （a）an individual ordinarily resident outside Brunei Darussalam; or

 （a）通常居住在文莱达鲁萨兰国境外的个人；或

 （b）a corporation or association incorporated or formed under the law of a country or territory outside Brunei Darussalam or whose central management and control is exercised outside Brunei Darussalam.

 （b）根据文莱达鲁萨兰国境外的国家或地区的法律成立或组建的公司或协会，或中央管理、控制权在文莱达鲁萨兰国境外行使的公司或协会。

（8）The Court may order that any money payable under the award shall be brought into Court or otherwise secured pending the determination of the application or appeal，and may direct that the application or appeal be dismissed if the order is not complied with.

（8）法院可命令申请人或上诉人向法院缴纳应付款项或以其他

方式担保，否则法院将暂缓对申请或上诉做出决定，并可指示申请人或上诉人如果该命令未得到遵守，则驳回其申请或上诉。

（9）The Court may grant leave to appeal subject to conditions to the same or similar effect as an order under subsections（6）or（8）and this shall not affect the general discretion of the Court to grant leave subject to conditions.

（9）法庭可在符合条件的情况下许可上诉，其效力与根据第（6）款或第（8）款做出的命令相同或类似，不影响法院做出许可的一般酌情权。

Effect of order of Court upon appeal against award
法院裁定上诉对裁决的效力

51.（1）Where the Court makes an order under section 49 with respect to an award，subsections（2），（3）and（4）shall apply.

（1）法院根据第 49 条就裁决做出的命令适用第（2）款、第（3）款和第（4）款。

（2）Where the award is varied by the Court，the variation shall have effect as part of the arbitral tribunal is award.

（2）裁决由法院做出变更的，仲裁庭的一部分裁决即为变更。

（3）Where the award is remitted to the arbitral tribunal，in whole or in part，for reconsideration，the tribunal shall make a fresh award in respect of the matters remitted within 3 months of the date of the order for remission or such longer or shorter period as the Court may direct.

（3）全部或部分裁决转交仲裁庭复议的，仲裁庭应当自命令之日起 3 个月内重新汇出的事项重新作出裁决，法院可指示更长或更短的期限。

（4）Where the award is set aside or declared to be of no effect， in whole or in part, the Court may also order that any provision that an award is a condition precedent to the bringing of legal proceedings in respect of a matter to which the arbitration agreement applies, shall be of no effect as regards the subject-matter of the award or, as the case may be, the relevant part of the award.

(4) 如裁定被撤销或宣布全部或部分无效,法院可裁定裁决中的规定主体或部分无效。

Application for leave of Court etc.

申请法院许可

52. (1) An application for the leave of the Court to appeal or an application referred to in sections 21(10),36(6) or 49(3)(b) or (7) shall be made in such manner as may be prescribed in the Rules of Court.

(1) 法院的上诉申请或第 21 条第(10)款、第 36 条第(6)款、49 条第(3)款(b)项或第(7)款所述的申请,须按法院规则所规定的方式提出。

(2) The Court shall determine an application for leave to appeal without a hearing unless it appears to the Court that a hearing is required.

(2) 除非法院认为需要听证,否则法院应决定不开庭审理上诉申请。

(3) For the purposes of this section —

(3) 就本节而言:

(a) an application for leave of the Court may be heard and determined by a Judge in Chambers; and

(a) 内庭法官可听取和裁定申请;以及

(b) the Court of Appeal shall have the like powers and jurisdiction on the hearing of such applications as the

High Court or any Judge in Chambers has on the hearing of such applications.

(b) 上诉法院在举行上述听证时，具有类似高等法院或内庭法官的权力及管辖权。

PART X
GENERAL
第十部分　总则

Notice and other requirements in connection with legal proceedings
关于法律诉讼的通知和其他要求

53. (1) References in this Order to an application，appeal or other step in relation to legal proceedings being taken upon notice to the other parties to the arbitration proceedings，or to the arbitral tribunal， are references to such notice of the originating process as is required by the Rules of Court.

(1) 本法中涉及到的有关申请、上诉或其他方式的对仲裁的其他当事人或仲裁庭发出的通知，均为法院规则所规定的通知。

(2) Subject to any provision made by the Rules of Court，a requirement to give notice to the arbitral tribunal of legal proceedings shall be construed —

(2) 在不违反法院规则规定的情况下，要求向仲裁庭通知法律程序的规定应做出如下解释：

(a) if there is more than one arbitrator，as a requirement to give notice to each of them；and

(a) 如果有一名以上的仲裁员，要求通知每名仲裁员；以及

(b) if the arbitral tribunal is not fully constituted，as a requirement to give notice to any arbitrator who has been appointed.

(b) 如果仲裁庭未完全组成，要求通知已被任命的仲裁员。

(3) References in this Order to making an application or appeal

to the Court within a specified period are references to the issue within that period of the appropriate originating process in accordance with the Rules of Court.

（3）本法所述的在特定时期内向法院提出申请或上诉，是指根据法院规则在发起程序的适当时期内提起的问题。

（4）Where any provision of this Order requires an application or appeal to be made to the Court within a specified time, the Rules of Court relating to the reckoning of periods, the extending or abridging of periods, and the consequences of not taking a step within the period prescribed by the Rules of Court, shall apply in relation to that requirement.

（4）凡本法要求在规定的时间内向法院提出申请或上诉，法院规则关于期限的计算、延长或缩短以及不按期提出要求的规定，应适用于该申请或上诉。

（5）Provision may be made by the Rules of Court amending the provisions of this Order —

（5）法院规则可以修改本法规定如下：

（a）with respect to the time within which any application or appeal to the Court must be made；

（a）须向法院提出申请或上诉的时间；

（b）so as to keep any provision made by this Order in relation to arbitral proceedings in step with the corresponding provision of the Rules of Court applying in relation to proceedings in the Court； or

（b）按照与法院诉讼程序有关的法院规则的相应规定，保持本法关于仲裁程序的规定；或

（c）so as to keep any provision made by this Order in relation to legal proceedings in step with the corresponding provision of the Rules of Court applying generally in relation to proceedings in the Court.

  (c) 按照与法院诉讼程序有关的一般规则的相应规定,保持本
    法关于诉讼程序的规定。

(6) Nothing in this section shall affect the generality of the
  power of the Judges of the Supreme Court to make Rules of
  Court under section 12(1) of the Supreme Court Act
  (Chapter 5).

(6) 本条的任何规定均不影响最高法院法官根据《最高法院法》
  (第五章)第 12 条第(1)款制定法院规则的一般权力。

Powers of Registrar
书记官长的权力

54. Provision may be made by the Rules of Court for conferring on
the Registrar of the Supreme Court all or any of the jurisdiction
conferred by this Order on the Court.

根据法院规则,可授予最高法院书记官长本法赋予法院的全部或
任何管辖权。

Rules of Court
法院规则

55. The Chief Justice may,with the approval of His Majesty the
Sultan and Yang Di-Pertuan,make Rules of Court for
regulating the practice and procedure of any court in respect of
any matter under this Order.

经苏丹陛下杨迪佩尔图安同意,首席大法官可根据本法所述事宜
制定规则,以规范法院的行为和程序。

Proceedings to be heard otherwise than in open court
公开审理外的其他程序

56. Proceedings under this Order in any court shall,on the
application of any party to the proceedings,be heard otherwise

than in open court.

根据本法进行的诉讼,可经诉讼一方申请不公开审判。

Restrictions on reporting of proceedings heard otherwise than in open court

对公开审理外的程序进行报告的限制

57.（1）This section shall apply to proceedings under this Order in any court heard otherwise than in open court.

（1）本条适用于根据本法进行的公开审理外的程序。

（2）A court hearing any proceedings to which this section applies shall, on the application of any party to the proceedings, give directions as to whether any and, if so, what information relating to the proceedings may be published.

（2）法院审理本条所适用的程序时,在诉讼一方的申请下,应指示其是否可以公布有关诉讼资料。

（3）A court shall not give a direction under subsection（2）permitting information to be published unless —

（3）法院不得根据第（2）款发出指示,准许资料公布,除非有下列情况:

（a）all parties to the proceedings agree that such information may be published; or

（a）诉讼各当事方同意公布该资料;或

（b）the court is satisfied that the information, if published in accordance with such directions as it may give, would not reveal any matter, including the identity of any party to the proceedings, that any party to the proceedings reasonably wishes to remain confidential.

（b）法庭信纳,如该资料按照指示公布,不会透露任何事宜,包括诉讼任何一方希望保密的身份。

（4）Notwithstanding subsection（3）, where a court gives

grounds of decision for a judgment in respect of proceedings to which this section applies and considers that judgment to be of major legal interest, the court shall direct that reports of the judgment may be published in law reports and professional publications but, if any party to the proceedings reasonably wishes to conceal any matter, including the fact that he was such a party, the court shall —

(4) 尽管有第(3)款的规定,如法庭对相关判决给出理由,并认为判决大体符合法律权益,法庭应指示在法律报道和专业出版物中公开判决报告。但如果判决一方有正当理由希望不公开,包括不公开其作为判决一方的事实,法院应:

(a) give directions as to the action that shall be taken to conceal that matter in those reports; and

(a) 就报告中应采取的不公开行为发出指示;

(b) if it considers that a report published in accordance with directions given under paragraph (a) would be likely to reveal that matter, direct that no report shall be published until after the end of such period, not exceeding 10 years, as it considers appropriate.

(b) 如法院认为根据(a)项所做指示发表的报告可能会披露该事项,应指示该期间结束后不得发表任何报告,但以不超过 10 年为宜。

Application to references under statutory powers
法定权力适用的参考

58. This Order shall apply in relation to every arbitration under any other written law (other than the International Arbitration Order, 2009), as if the arbitration were commenced pursuant to an arbitration agreement, except in so far as this Order is

inconsistent with that other written law.

本法适用于根据任何其他成文法展开的仲裁（2009 年的《国际仲裁法》除外），如同根据仲裁协议展开仲裁一样，除非本法与其他成文法不一致。

Immunity of arbitral institutions

仲裁机构的豁免权

59. (1) The appointing authority, or an arbitral or other institution or person designated or requested by the parties to appoint or nominate an arbitrator, shall not be liable for anything done or omitted in the discharge or purported discharge of that function unless the act or omission is shown to have been in bad faith.

(1) 指定机构或由当事方指定或要求指定仲裁员的其他机构或个人，对于履行该职能时做的事不承担责任，除非存在恶意作为或恶意不作为。

(2) The appointing authority, or an arbitral or other institution or person by whom an arbitrator is appointed or nominated, shall not be liable, by reason only of having appointed or nominated him, for anything done or omitted by the arbitrator, his employees or agents in the discharge or purported discharge of his functions as arbitrator.

(2) 指定了仲裁员的指定机构、仲裁机构、其他机构或个人，不得仅因为指定了该仲裁员而对该仲裁员的作为或不作为承担责任。

(3) This section shall apply to an employee or agent of the appointing authority or of an arbitral or other institution or person as it applies to the appointing authority, institution or person himself.

(3) 本条适用于指定机关、仲裁机构、其他机构或个人的雇员或代理人，如同本条适用于指定机关、机构或个人本身。

Service of notices

通知的送达

60.（1）The parties may agree on the manner of service of any notice or other document required or authorised to be given or served in pursuance of the arbitration agreement or for the purposes of the arbitration proceedings.

（1）当事人可以按照仲裁协议或者仲裁程序的要求,约定通知或者其他文件的送达方式。

（2）If or to the extent that there is no such agreement as is referred to in subsection（1）, subsections（3）and（4）shall apply.

（2）若无第（1）款所述的协议,则应适用第（3）款和第（4）款。

（3）A notice or other document may be served on a person by any effective means.

（3）通知或其他文件可以通过任何有效方式送达。

（4）If a notice or other document is addressed，prepaid and delivered by post —

（4）如果通知或文件满足以下情况:

（a）to the addressee's usual or last known place of residence or，if he is or has been carrying on a trade，profession or business，his usual or last known place of business; or

（a）如收件人从事贸易、职业或商务活动,送达至该收件人常用居住地、最近居住地或最近商务活动所在地;或

（b）if the addressee is a body corporate，to the body corporate's registered office，

（b）如收件人是法人团体,送达至该法人团体的注册办事处,

it shall be treated as effectively served.

则应视为有效送达。

（5）This section shall not apply to the service of documents for the purposes of legal proceedings, for which provision is made by the Rules of Court.

（5）根据法院规则规定，本条不适用于法律程序文件的送达。

（6）References in this Part to a notice or other document include any form of communication in writing and references to giving or serving a notice or other document shall be construed accordingly.

（6）本部分所述通知或其他文件包括任何形式的书面通讯，据此解释通知书或其他文件的送达。

Reckoning periods of time

时间的计算

61. （1）The parties may agree on the method of reckoning periods of time for the purposes of —

（1）双方当事人可以就以下事项约定时间的计算方法：

（a）any provision agreed by them; or

（a）当事人同意的条款；或

（b）any provision of this Order having effect in default of such agreement.

（b）本法违约时仍有效的条款。

（2）If or to the extent that the parties have not agreed on the method of reckoning time, periods of time shall be reckoned in accordance with this section.

（2）如当事人未对时间的计算达成协议，则根据本条计算时间。

（3）Where the act is required to be done within a specified period after or from a specified date, the period shall begin immediately after that date.

（3）要求在指定日期之后或在指定日期完成该行为的，该期限应在该日期之后立即开始。

（4）Where an act is required to be done within or not less than a specified period before a specified date, the period shall end immediately before that date.

（4）要求在指定日期之前或不晚于指定日期采取行为的，该期限应在该日期之前终止。

（5）Where the act is required to be done, a specified number of clear days after a specified date, at least that number of days shall intervene between the day on which the act is done and that date.

（5）如果要求采取行为，指定日期后的指定天数从采取行为之日起开始计算。

（6）Where the period in question, being a period of 7 days or less, would include a Friday, Sunday or a public holiday, that day shall be excluded.

（6）如期限为 7 日或以下，包含一个星期五、星期天或公共假日，则应排除该日。

Appointment of mediator

调解员的任命

62.（1）In any case where an agreement provides for the appointment of a mediator by a person who is not one of the parties and that person refuses to make the appointment or does not make the appointment within the time specified in the agreement or, if no time is so specified, within a reasonable time of being requested by any party to the agreement to make the appointment, the President of the Arbitration Association of Brunei Darussalam may, on the application of any party to the agreement, appoint a mediator who shall have the like powers to act in the mediation proceedings as if he had been appointed in accordance with the terms of the agreement.

（1）如果协议规定由非当事人的人员任命调解员，而且该人在协议规定的时间内拒绝任命或未能任命，如果没有规定时间，在协议一方要求任命的合理时间内，文莱达鲁萨兰国仲裁协会主席可根据协议一方的申请指定一名调解员，其行使调解的权力等同协议赋予调解员的权力。

（2）The Chief Justice may，if he thinks fit，by notification published in the Gazette，appoint any other person to exercise the power of appointment under subsection（1）.

（2）首席法官如认为适当，可借宪报刊登通知，赋予其他人根据第（1）款行使委任的权力。

（3）Where an arbitration agreement provides for the appointment of a mediator and further provides that the person so appointed shall act as an arbitrator in the event of the mediation proceedings failing to produce a settlement acceptable to the parties —

（3）仲裁协议规定了调解员的任命，并进一步规定，在未能达成当事人可接受的调解时，被指定的人应担任仲裁员。

（a）no objection shall be taken to the appointment of such person as an arbitrator，or to his conduct of the arbitral proceedings，solely on the ground that he had acted previously as a mediator in connection with some or all of the matters referred to arbitra-tion；and

（a）不应仅以该人以前作为调解员就仲裁中的一些或全部事项行事而反对该仲裁员的任命或他的行为；以及

（b）if such person declines to act as an arbitrator，any other person appointed as an arbitrator shall not be required first to act as a mediator unless a contrary intention appears in the arbitration agreement.

（b）如该人拒绝担任仲裁员，则任何被指定为仲裁员的其他人不得首先担任调解员,除非仲裁协议中有相反规定。

(4) Unless a contrary intention appears therein, an agreement which provides for the appointment of a mediator shall be deemed to contain a provision that in the event of the mediation proceedings failing to produce a settlement acceptable to the parties within 4 months, or such longer period as the parties may agree to, of the date of the appointment of the mediator or, where he is appointed by name in the agreement, of the receipt by him of written notification of the existence of a dispute, the mediation proceedings shall thereupon terminate.

(4) 除非有相反规定,任命调解员的协议应规定,如在 4 个月内或可能更长的期限内各方未能就调解员的任命时间、书面接受任命问题达成一致,则应终止调解程序。

Power of arbitrator to act as mediator

仲裁员担任调解员的权力

63. (1) If all parties to any arbitral proceedings consent in writing and for so long as no party has withdrawn his consent in writing, an arbitrator may act as a mediator.

(1) 如果仲裁程序的各方当事人以书面形式同意,只要没有一方书面撤回其同意,仲裁员可以担任调解员。

(2) An arbitrator acting as a mediator —

　(a) may communicate with the parties to the arbitral proceedings collectively or separately; and

　(b) shall treat information obtained by him from a party to the arbitration proceedings as confidential, unless that party otherwise agrees or unless subsection (3) applies.

(2) 担任调解员的仲裁员可集体或单独地与仲裁程序的当事人进行沟通,应将从一方当事人获得的仲裁程序资料保密,除非当事人同意或第（3）款适用。

（3）Where confidential information is obtained by an arbitrator from a party to the arbitration proceedings during mediation proceedings and those proceedings terminate without the parties reaching agreement in settlement of their dispute，the arbitrator shall before resuming the arbitration proceedings disclose to all other parties to the arbitration proceedings as much of that information as he considers material to the arbitration proceedings.

（3）仲裁员在仲裁程序中获得保密信息，且仲裁程序终止时当事人未能达成协议解决争议的，仲裁员应当在恢复仲裁程序之前向仲裁程序的所有其他当事人尽可能多地提供他认为对仲裁程序具有重要意义的资料。

（4）No objection shall be taken to the conduct of arbitration proceedings by a person solely on the ground that he had acted previously as a mediator in accordance with this section.

（4）任何人不得仅因以前根据本条担任过调解员而进行仲裁。

（5）For the purposes of this section and section 62 —

（5）就本条及第 62 条而言：

（a）any reference to a mediator shall include a reference to any person who acts as a conciliator；

（a）调解员应包含任何调解人员；

（b）any reference to mediation proceedings shall include a reference to conciliation proceedings.

（b）调解程序应包含任一调解程序。

Government to be bound

责任机构

64. This Order shall apply to any arbitration to which the

Government is a party.

本法适用于政府为一方当事人的仲裁。

Transitional provisions

暂行条文

65.（1）This Order shall apply to arbitration proceedings commenced on or after the commencement of this Order but the parties may in writing agree that this Order shall apply to any arbitration proceedings commenced before that date.

（1）本法适用于在本法生效之日或之后开始的仲裁程序,但当事人可就本法适用于该日期之前开始的仲裁程序达成书面协议。

（2）Notwithstanding the repeal of the Arbitration Act（Chapter 173）, where the arbitration proceedings were commenced before the commencement of this Order, the law governing the arbitration agreement and the arbitration shall be the law which would have applied if this Order had not been made.

（2）尽管原《仲裁法》（第一百七十三章）被废止,在本法生效前开始仲裁程序的,其相关仲裁协议和仲裁应适用本法尚未制定时的法律。

（3）Where an arbitration agreement made or entered into before the commencement of this Order provides for the appointment of an umpire or an arbitral tribunal comprising 2 arbitrators, the law to the extent that it governs the appointment, role and function of the umpire shall be the law which would have applied if this Order had not been made.

（3）本法生效前订立的仲裁协议,规定委任仲裁员或由两名仲裁员组成仲裁庭的,适用其仲裁员的任命、作用和职能的法律应为本法尚未制定时的法律。

（4）For the purposes of this section, arbitration proceedings are to be taken as having commenced on the date of the receipt by the respondent of a request for the dispute to be referred to arbitration or，where the parties have agreed in writing that any other date is to be taken as the date of commencement of the arbitration proceedings，then on that date.

（4）本条中仲裁程序自被申请人收到将争议提交仲裁的请求之日起开始，或者自双方书面同意仲裁程序启动的其他日期起。

Enabling power

权力行使

66. His Majesty the Sultan and Yang Di-Pertuan may by order make such provisions as may appear to him to be necessary or expedient

苏丹陛下杨迪佩尔图安可下令做出他认为必要或适宜的规定

（a）for giving effect to the provisions of this Order；

（a）执行本命令的规定；

（b）for the purpose of bringing the provisions of any other written law（other than the Constitution of Brunei Darussalam）into accord with the provisions of this Order or with any Rules of Court.

（b）使其他成文法（除《文莱达鲁萨兰国宪法》）符合本法或法院规则的规定。

Repeal

废除

67. Subject to section the Arbitration Act（Chapter 173）is repealed.

兹废除原《仲裁法》（第一百七十三章）。

Made this 6th. day of Syaaban，1430 Hijriah corresponding to the 28th. day of July，2009 at Our Istana Nurul Iman，Bandar Seri Begawan，Brunei Darussalam.

伊斯兰历 1430 年，即公元 2009 年 7 月 28 日

于文莱达鲁萨兰国斯里巴加湾市努洛伊曼皇宫

HIS MAJESTY

THE SULTAN AND YANG DI-PERTUAN

BRUNEI DARUSSALAM

文莱达鲁萨兰国

苏丹陛下

杨迪佩尔图安

第五节　柬埔寨商事仲裁法英汉对照

KINGDOM OF CAMBODIA

柬埔寨王国

NATION RELIGION KING

国家·宗教·国王

THE COMMERCIAL ARBITRATION LAW OF THE KINGDOM OF CAMBODIA

《柬埔寨王国商事仲裁法》

Adopted by The NATIONAL ASSEMBLY

经国会通过

Phnom Penh，March 6th，2006

2006 年 3 月 6 日，于金边

THE COMMERCIAL ARBITRATION LAW OF THE KINGDOM OF CAMBODIA

《柬埔寨王国商事仲裁法》

CHAPTER I
GENERAL PROVISIONS
第一章 总则

Article 1：Purpose and Scope of Application
第 1 条 申请目的和范围

The purpose of this law is to facilitate the impartial and prompt resolution of commercial disputes in accordance with the wishes of the parties，to safeguard the legal rights and interests of the parties，and to promote the sound development of the economy.

本法的宗旨是：根据当事人的意愿，促进商事纠纷的公正、及时解决，维护当事人的合法权益，促进经济的健康发展。

This Law shall not affect any other law of the Kingdom of Cambodia by virtue of which certain dispute may be submitted to arbitration or other dispute resolution procedures，or by virtue of which certain disputes may not be submitted to arbitration.

本法不影响柬埔寨王国的任何其他法律，某些争议可以提交仲裁或其他争端解决程序，某些争议不能提交仲裁。

Article 2：Definitions and Rules of Interpretation
第 2 条 术语的定义及规则的解释

For purposes of this Law：

本法中：

(a)"Arbitration" means any arbitration whether or not administered by a permanent arbitral institution；

(a)"仲裁"是指任何仲裁，无论其是否由永久性仲裁机构管理；

(b)"Arbitral tribunal" means a sole arbitrator or a panel of arbitrators；

(b)"仲裁庭"是指一名独任仲裁员或一组仲裁员（仲裁庭）；

(c)"Court" means a body or organ of the judicial system of a state；

(c)"法院"是指国家司法体系的相应机关；

（d）"Arbitration agreement" is an agreement by the parties to submit to arbitration all or certain disputes which have arisen or which may arise between them in respect of a defined legal relationship, whether contractual or not.

（d）"仲裁协议"是指各方当事人同意将所有或个别争议提交仲裁解决,该协议是否已在合同中规定不影响仲裁协议的成立。

（e）Where a provision of this law, except Article 36 of this Law, leaves the parties free to determine a certain issue, such freedom includes the right of the parties to authorize a third party, including an institution, to make that determination;

（e）本法条文(除第 36 条)赋予双方当事人决定某一事项的自由,包括双方授权第三方(包括机构)做决定的自由。

（f）Where a provision of this Law refers to the fact that the parties have agreed, or that they may agree, or in any other way refers to an agreement of the parties, such agreement includes any rules referred to in that agreement;

（f）如果本法条文提到当事人已经达成协议、可能达成协议,或以任何其他形式提到当事人的协议,这种协议包括该协议中所提到的任何仲裁规则;

（g）Where a provision of this Law, other than in Articles 33(a) and 40(a), refers to a claim, it also applies to a counter-claim, and where it refers to a defense, it also applies to a defense to such counter-claim;

（g）本法条文,除第 33 条第(1)款和第 40 条第(1)款,所指请求同样适用于反诉;所指抗辩也同样适用于对反诉的抗辩。

（h）An arbitration is "international" if

（h）如有下列情况,则仲裁为"国际仲裁":

　　（i）the parties to an arbitration agreement have their places of business in different States at the time of the conclusion of that agreement; or （i）仲裁协议各方当事人在订立协议时营业地在不同国家；或

（ii）one of the following places is situated outside the state in which the parties have their places of business：

（ii）下列地点之一位于各方营业地所在的国家外：

-the place of arbitration，if determined in，or pursuant to，the arbitration agreement；

在仲裁协议中确定或依据仲裁协议确定的仲裁地点；

-any place where a substantial part of the obligations of the commercial relationship is to be performed or the place with which the subject matter of the dispute is most closely connected；or

履行商业关系主要义务或与争议标的所在地联系最密切的地方；

（iii）The parties have expressly agreed that the subject matter of the arbitration agreement relates to more than one country.

（iii）当事人明确同意仲裁协议的标的涉及多个国家。

（iv）For the purposes of this paragraph（h）：

（iv）本款中：

-if a party has more than one place of business，the place of business is that which has the closest relationship to the arbitration agreement；

如果当事人有一个以上的营业地点，则营业地点为与仲裁协议关系最为密切的营业地点；

-if a party does not have a place of business，reference is to be made to his habitual residence.

如果当事人没有营业地点，以其惯常住所地为准。

（i）The term "commercial" should be given a wide interpretation so as to cover matters arising from all relationships of a commercial nature，whether contractual or not relationships of a commercial nature include，but are not limited to，the following transactions：any trade transaction for the supply or exchange of good or services；distribution agreement；commercial representation or agency；factoring；leasing；construction of works；consulting；engineering；licensing；investment；financing；banking；insurance；exploitation agreement or concession；joint venture and other forms of industrial or business co-operation；and carriage of goods or passenger by air，sea，rail or road.

（i）"商业"一词应采广义解释，包括从商业关系中产生的事项，无论是合同的还是非商业性质的，包括但不限于以下交易：商品或服务的供应或交换；分销协议；商业代表或代理；保理；租赁；工程建设；咨询；工程；许可；投资；融资；银行；保险；开发协议或特许权；工商合作合资等形式；以及空运、海运、铁路或公路运输货物或旅客。

Article 3：Receipt of Written Communications
第 3 条　收到书面信件

Unless otherwise agreed by the parties：

除非当事人另有约定：

（1）any written communication is deemed to have been received if it is delivered to the addressee personally，or if it is delivered at his place of business，habitual residence or mailing address；if none of these can be found after making a reasonable inquiry，a written communication is deemed to have been received if it is sent to the addressee's last-known place of business，habitual residence or at the last known address of the addressee；

（1）任何书面信件，如经当面递交收件人，或投递到收件的营业地点、惯常住所或通信地址，或经合理查询仍不能找一上述任一地点而以挂号信或能提供做过投递企图的记录的其他任何方式投递到收件人最后一个为人所知的营业地点、惯常住所或通信地址，即应视为已经收到；

（2）The provisions of Article 3 of this Law do not apply to

communications in Court proceedings.

(2) 本法第 3 条的规定不适用于法院程序中的通讯送达。

Article 4: Waiver of Right to Object
第 4 条　放弃提出异议的权利

A party who knows that any provision of this Law from which parties may derogate，or any requirement under the arbitration agreement，has not been complied with，and yet proceeds with the arbitration without stating his objection to such non-compliance without undue delay or，if a time limit is provided therefore，within such period of time，shall be deemed to have waived his right to object.

如果一方当事人知道本法中当事各方可以背离的任何规定,或仲裁协议规定的任何要求未得到遵守,但仍继续进行仲裁而没有迟延,或在订有时限的情况下没有在此时限内对此种不遵守的情形提出异议,则应视为已放弃提出异议的权利。

Article 5: Extent of Court Intervention
第 5 条　法院介入程度

In matters governed by this Law，no Court shall intervene except where so provided in this Law.

由本法调整的问题,法院应毫不干预,除非本法有此规定。

Article 6: Court or other Authority for Certain Functions of Arbitration Assistance Supervision
第 6 条　法院或其他机构行使仲裁协助监督职能

The functions referred to in Articles 19(3)，19(4)，and 19(5)；21(3)；22；and 24(3) of this law shall be performed by the Court (Commercial，or Appeal，or Supreme) or National Arbitration Center.

本法第 19 条第(3)款、第 19 条第(4)款、第 19 条第(5)款、第 21 条第
(3)款、第 22 条和第 24 条第(3)款所指的职能,由法院(商事法院、上诉
法院、最高法院)或国家仲裁中心执行。

CHAPTER II
ARBITRATION AGREEMENT
第二章　仲裁协议

Article 7: Definition and Form of Arbitration Agreement
第 7 条　仲裁协议的定义和形式

Arbitration agreement includes an arbitration clause in a contract or
a separate submission agreement.

仲裁协议包括合同中的仲裁条款或单独的提交协议。

The arbitration agreement shall be in writing. An agreement is in
writing if it is contained in a document signed by the parties or in an
exchange of letters, or other means of electronic telecommunication
which provide a record of the agreement, or in an exchange of
statements of claim and defense in which the existence of an agreed
is alleged by one party and not denied by another. The reference in
a contract to a document containing an arbitration clause constitutes
an arbitration agreement, provided that the contract is in writing
and the reference is such as to make the clause part of the contract.

仲裁协议应以书面形式订立。如果协议载于双方当事人签署的文件,
载于信件交换或其他能记录协议的电子通信手段,载于一方声称存在
而另一方无异议的主张和辩护声明,即构成书面协议。如果合同中提
及的包含仲裁条款的文件能明确构成合同的一部分,则该仲裁条款构
成书面形式的仲裁协议。

Article 8: Arbitration Agreement and Substantive Claim before Court
第 8 条　仲裁协议和庭前实质性请求

A Court before which an action is brought in a matter which is the subject of an arbitration agreement shall，if a party so requests not later than when submitting his first statement on the substance of the dispute，refer the parties to arbitration unless it finds that the agreement is null and void，inoperative or incapable of being performed.

如果向法院提起的诉讼的争议是仲裁协议的标的，且一方当事人在不迟于就争议实体提出第一次申述时要求仲裁，法院应终止程序并让当事各方付诸仲裁，除非法院认为仲裁协议无效、失效或不能执行。

Where an action referred to in paragraph（1）of this Article has been brought，arbitral proceedings may nevertheless be commenced or continued and the court shall refer the issue to the arbitration，while it is pending before the arbitration.

当一个涉及本条第(1)款的案件被提起诉讼，在争议处于待决状态时，仲裁程序仍然可以被启动或继续，也可以作出仲裁裁决。

Article 9：Arbitration Agreement and Interim Measures by Court
第9条　仲裁协议和法院临时措施

It is not incompatible with an arbitration agreement for a party to request，before or during arbitral proceedings from a Court an interim measure of protection and for a Court to grant such measure.

一方当事人在仲裁程序启动之前或进行过程当中请求法院采取临时措施，以及法院批准采取措施的行为，都不会被认定为与仲裁协议相矛盾。

CHAPTER III
NATIONAL CENTER OF COMMERCIAL ARBITRATION
第三章　国家商事仲裁中心

Article 10：National Arbitration Center
第10条　国家仲裁中心

An independent National Arbitration Center（"NAC"）shall be

established under the auspices of Ministry of Commerce. The objectives of the National Arbitration Center are：

由商务部主持设立独立的国家仲裁中心（"NAC"）。国家仲裁中心的宗旨是：

（1）to promote settlement of commercial disputes by means of arbitration in Cambodia；

（1）通过仲裁促进解决柬埔寨的商事纠纷；

（2）to create the necessary infrastructure and rules for the administration of arbitration cases in the Kingdom of Cambodia，where an express agreement of disputing parties to refer disputes to National Arbitration Center；

（2）为管理柬埔寨仲裁案件创造必要的基础设施和规则，争议双方将争议提交国家仲裁中心，达成明确协议；

（3）to ensure that high quality standards of arbitration are maintained in the Kingdom of Cambodia. This objective includes setting standards for the qualification of arbitrators.

（3）确保柬埔寨保持高质量的仲裁标准，包括制定仲裁员资格标准。

Article 11：Arbitrators

第 11 条　仲裁员

The Khmer natural person or foreigner who is arbitrator shall register with the National Arbitration Center. The National Arbitration Center shall have an obligation to determine the arbitrators' qualification and shall make the public announcement of arbitrators' list yearly. The list is not absolute；the parties are free to choose the arbitrator outside that list.

柬埔寨自然人或外籍人员担任仲裁员，应在国际仲裁中心登记。国家仲裁中心有义务决定仲裁员资格，每年公布仲裁员名单。名单不是绝对的，当事人可自由选择名单之外的仲裁员。

Article 12: Qualification of Members of Arbitrators
第 12 条　仲裁员资格

The natural person and legal entity to be permitted as a member of the National Arbitration Center are:

被批准为国家仲裁中心成员的自然人和法人可以是:

-an Arbitrator who has registered his/her name with the National Arbitration Center;

已在国家仲裁中心登记姓名的仲裁员;

-the Chamber of Commerce;

商会;

-the Bar of the Kingdom of Cambodia; and

柬埔寨王国的律师;

-the Association that comprises of businessman, industrialist, merchant and services provider.

由商人、实业家、商贩和服务人员组成的协会。

The application to be a member of the National Arbitration Center shall be determined by the Executive Board of the National Arbitration Center that comprises not more than seven (7) members. The term of each member is three (3) years and may re-elect for one more term.

申请成为国家仲裁中心成员的,由不超过七名成员的国家仲裁中心执行委员会决定。每名成员任期三年,可连任一届。

Article 13: The Chamber of Commerce and Chamber of Professionals
第 13 条　商会和职业协会

The Chamber of Commerce may establish an Arbitration Center in Phnom Penh. The Association that comprises of businessman, industrialist, merchant and services provider may establish its own arbitral institution for disputes arising among its members; and between its members and third party.

商会可在金边设立仲裁中心。由商人、实业家、商贩和服务人员组成的协会可以建立自己的仲裁机构,以解决其成员之间以及其成员与第三方之间的争端。

Article 14: Management of National Arbitration Center

第 14 条　国家仲裁中心的管理

The National Arbitration Center shall be governed by:

国家仲裁中心的由如下部门管理:

-a General Assembly; and

大会;

-an Executive Office.

行政办公室。

The General Assembly shall have *inter alia* functions and duties:

大会应履行下列职责:

-to meet one or twice per year at the request of the Chairman of the National Arbitration Center or at the request of the majority members of Executive Board;

应国家仲裁中心主席或执委会多数成员的要求,每年举行一到二次会议;

-to elect the Executive Board;

选举执行委员会;

-to inspect the annual report of Executive Board;

检查执行局的年度报告;

-to approve the financial budget of National Arbitration Center;

批准国家仲裁中心的财务预算;

-to determine the fees and costs of arbitration;

确定仲裁的费用和开支;

-to approve the amendment of rules and regulations that related to the operation of National Arbitration Center and functioning of arbitration; and

批准与国家仲裁中心运作和仲裁功能相关的规章制度的修改;以及

-to fulfill other functions and duties that determined in the Sub-Decree of the organization and functioning of National Arbitration Center.

履行《国家仲裁中心组织和运作条例》规定的其他职责。

Article 15: The General Assembly
第 15 条　大会

The General Assembly shall be attended by the members who are natural persons and a representative of each legal entity.

大会由自然人和各法人代表出席。

Article 16: Composition of Executive Board
第 16 条　执行委员会的组成

The Composition of Executive Board that manages the National Arbitration Center shall be elected among its members by the General Assembly. The Chairman of Executive Board shall be the Chairman of the National Arbitration Center.

管理国家仲裁中心的执行委员会应由大会成员选举产生。执行委员会主席为国家仲裁中心主席。

Article 17: Organization and Functioning of National Arbitration Center
第 17 条　国家仲裁中心的组织与运作

The organization and functioning of National Arbitration Center shall be determined by implementing Sub-Decree.

国家仲裁中心的组织和运作由执行分则决定。

CHAPTER IV
COMPOSITION OF ARBITRAL TRIBUNAL
第四章　仲裁庭的组成

Article 18: Number of Arbitrators
第 18 条　仲裁员数量

The parties are free to determine the number of arbitrators. The number of arbitrators shall be odd number.

当事双方可自由决定仲裁员数量，但必须为奇数。

Failing such determination，the number of arbitrators shall be three（3）.

如当事人未确定，则仲裁员的人数应为三名。

Article 19：Appointment of Arbitrators
第 19 条　仲裁员任命

The appointment of arbitrator shall determine as follows：

仲裁员的任命规定如下：

（1）no person shall be precluded by reason of his nationality from acting as an arbitrator，unless otherwise agreed by the parties.

（1）任命仲裁员时，不得以国籍为由将任何人排除在外，但各方当事人另有规定除外。

（2）the parties are free to agree on a procedure for appointing the arbitrator or arbitrators，subject to the provisions of paragraphs （4）and（5）of this Article.

（2）各方当事人有权在符合本条第（4）款、第（5）款规定的前提下，对任命仲裁员的程序自行达成一致。

（3）failing such agreement，

（3）未能达成一致时：

　　（a）in an arbitration with three arbitrators，each party shall appoint one arbitrator，and the two arbitrators thus appointed shall appoint the third arbitrator；if a party fails to appoint the arbitrator within thirty days of receipt of a request to do so from the other party，or if the two arbitrators fail to agree on the third arbitrator within thirty days of their appointment，the appointment shall be made，upon request of a party，by the Court（Commercial，or Appeal，or Supreme）or National Arbitration Center as specified in Article 6 of this Law；

(a) 在三名仲裁员进行的仲裁中,每方应指定一名仲裁员,两名仲裁员指定第三名仲裁员。如果一方未能在收到另一方请求指定仲裁员的通知后 30 天内指定仲裁员,或两名仲裁员无法在 30 天内就第三名仲裁员的任命达成一致,则应由法院(商事法院、上诉法院或最高法院)或国家仲裁中心根据本法第 6 条指定仲裁员。

(b) in an arbitration with a sole arbitrator, if the parties are unable to agree on the arbitrator, he shall be appointed, upon request of a party, by the Court (Commercial, or Appeal, or Supreme) or National Arbitration Center as specified in Article 6 of this Law.

(b) 在独任仲裁员的仲裁中,如果双方当事人不能就仲裁人达成协议,应当经一方当事人要求,由法院(商事法院、上诉法院或最高法院)或国家仲裁中心根据本法第 6 条指定仲裁员。

(4) Where, under an appointment procedure agreed upon by the parties, either party may request to the Court (Commercial, or Appeal, or Supreme) or National Arbitration Center as specified in Article 6 of this Law to take a necessary measure for any of the following:

(4) 凡当事人约定仲裁员任命程序的,一方可请求法院(商事法院、上诉法院或最高法院)或国家仲裁中心根据本法第 6 条,针对下列情况采取必要措施:

(a) a party fails to act as required under such procedure, or

(a) 一方当事人未能按照约定指定仲裁员,或

(b) the parties, or two (2) arbitrators, are unable to reach an agreement expected of them under such procedure, or

(b) 各方当事人,或两名仲裁员没能在约定的程序下达成合意,或

(c) A third party, including an institution, fails to perform any function entrusted to it under such procedure. This article shall not apply, unless the agreement on the appointment procedure provides other means for securing the appointment.

　　　　(c) 第三方(包括仲裁机构)没能履行其所受委托的作用。除非双方约定了指定仲裁员的其他手段，否则本条不适用。

(5) A decision on a matter entrusted by paragraph（3）or（4）of this Article to the Court（Commercial，or Appeal，or Supreme）or National Arbitration Center as specified in Article 6 of this Law shall be subject to no appeal. The Court（Commercial，or Appeal，or Supreme）or National Arbitration Center as specified in Article 6 of this Law，in appointing an arbitrator，shall have due regard to any qualifications required of the arbitrator by the agreement of the parties and to such considerations as are likely to secure the appointment of an independent and impartial arbitrator. In the case of a sole or third arbitrator in an international arbitration，the Court（Commercial，or Appeal，or Supreme）or National Arbitration Center as specified in Article 6 of this Law shall take into account as well the advisability of appointing an arbitrator of a nationality other than those of the parties as specified in Article 19（1）of this Law.

(5) 根据本法第 6 条的规定，对法院(商事法院、上诉法院或最高法院)或国家仲裁中心依据本条第(3)款和第(4)款做出的决定，不得上诉。根据本法第 6 条，法院(商事法院、上诉法院或最高法院)或国家仲裁中心任命仲裁员时，应充分考虑各方当事人约定的仲裁员的资格，以确保仲裁的独立和公正。对于国际仲裁中的独任仲裁员或第三位仲裁员，本法第 6 条中的法院(商事法院、上诉法院或最高法院)或国家仲裁中心应考虑仲裁员的国籍，以及本法第 19 条第(1)款的规定。

Article 20：Ground for Challenge

第 20 条　申请仲裁员回避

When a person is approached in connection with his possible appointment as an arbitrator，he shall disclose any circumstances likely to give rise to justifiable doubts as to his impartiality or independence. An arbitrator, from the time of his appointment and throughout the arbitral proceedings, shall without delay disclose any such circumstances to the parties, unless they have already been informed of them by him.

可能被指定为仲裁员的人,应在与此指定有关的洽谈中披露可能对其公正性和独立性产生有正当理由怀疑的任何情况。仲裁员从被指定之时起以至整个仲裁程序过程中,应不迟延地向各方当事人陈述此类情况,除非此前他已将此类情事告诉各方当事人。

An arbitrator may be challenged only if circumstances exists that give rise to justifiable doubts as to his impartiality or independence, or if he does not possess qualifications agreed to by the parties. A party may challenge an arbitrator appointed by him, or in whose appointment he has participated, only for reasons of which he becomes aware after the appointment has been made.

如果存在可能对任何仲裁员的公正性或独立性产生有正当理由怀疑的情况,或者仲裁员或该仲裁员不具有各方当事人要求的资格,均可要求该仲裁员回避。只有是任命做出之后才意识到的原因,一方当事人才可以申请其指定的或其参与指定的仲裁员回避。

Article 21: Challenge Procedure
第 21 条　申请回避程序

To challenge the arbitrator, the parties shall comply with the following procedures:

申请仲裁员回避时,当事人应遵守下列程序:

(1) the parties are free to agree on a procedure for challenging an arbitrator, subject to the provisions of paragraph (3) of this Article.

(1) 在本条第(3)款规定下,各方当事人有权就申请仲裁员回避的程序达成合意。

(2) failing such agreement，a party who intends to challenge an arbitrator shall，within fifteen (15) days after becoming aware of the constitution of the arbitral tribunal or after becoming aware of any circumstance referred to in Article 20(2) of this Law，send a written statement of the reasons for the challenge to the arbitral tribunal and the other party or parties. Unless the challenged arbitrator withdraws from his office or the other party agrees to the challenge，the arbitral tribunal shall decide on the challenge.

(2) 如果没有商定,拟要求仲裁员回避的一方当事人应在他得知仲裁庭组成或得知第 20 条第(2)款所列的任何情事起 15 天内以书面形式向仲裁庭阐明回避的理由。除非被申请回避的仲裁员辞职或对方当事人同意回避申请,则仲裁庭应对申请做出决定。

(3) if a challenge under any procedure agreed upon by the parties or under the procedure of paragraph (2) of this Article is not successful，the challenging party may request，within thirty days after having received notice of the decision rejecting the challenge，the Court (Commercial，or Appeal，or Supreme) or National Arbitration Center as specified in Article 6 of this Law to decide on the challenge，which decision shall be subject to no appeal；while such a request is pending，the arbitral tribunal，including the challenged arbitrator，may continue the arbitral proceedings and make an award.

(3) 如果某一回避申请在合意的程序规定下或在本条第(2)款的程序规定下不成功,申请回避的一方当事人可以在收到拒绝回避通知的 30 天内请求本法第 6 条所述法院(商事法院、上诉法院或最高法院)或国家仲裁中心做出决定,且该决定不得上诉。当该请求待决时,仲裁庭(包括被申请回避的仲裁员)可继续进行仲裁并作出裁决。

Article 22: Failure or Impossibility to Act
第 22 条　不作为或履行不能

If an arbitrator becomes *De Jure* or *De Facto* unable to perform his functions, or for other reasons fails to act without undue delay, his mandate terminates if he withdraws from his office or if the parties agree on the termination. Otherwise, if a controversy remains concerning any of these grounds, any party may request the Court (Commercial, or Appeal, or Supreme) or National Arbitration Center as specified in Article 6 of this Law to decide on the termination of the mandate, which decision shall be subject to no appeal.

如果仲裁员无法履行职责或由于其他原因不能在规定时间内履行职责,如果该仲裁员辞职或各方当事人同意对其终结委托,则他的委托应当终结。如果仍有争议,一方可按本法第 6 条请求法院(商事法院、上诉法院或最高法院)或国家仲裁中心决定终止仲裁员的职务,且不得对该决定上诉。

If, under this Article or Article 21(2), an arbitrator withdraws from his office or a party agrees to the termination of the mandate of an arbitrator, this does not imply acceptance of the validity of any ground referred to in this Article or Article 20(2).

如果在本条或第 21 条第(2)款规定下,仲裁员辞职或一方当事人同意对该仲裁员的终结委托,这不意味着对本条或第 20 条第(2)款正当性的接受。

Article 23: Appointment of Substitute Arbitrator
第 23 条　任命替补仲裁员

Where the mandate of an arbitrator terminates under Article 21 or 22 of this law, a substitute arbitrator shall be appointed according to Article 19 of this law.

仲裁员根据本法第 21 条或第 22 条终止职务的,依照本法第 19 条的规定替补仲裁员。

CHAPTER V
JURISDICTION OF ARBITRAL TRIBUNAL
第五章 仲裁庭管辖权

Article 24: Competence of Arbitral Tribunal To Rule on Its Jurisdiction
第 24 条 仲裁庭管辖权限

The jurisdiction of Arbitral Tribunal shall determine as follows:

仲裁庭管辖权如下:

(1) The arbitral tribunal may rule on its own jurisdiction, including any objections with respect to the existence or validity of the arbitration agreement. For that purpose, an arbitration clause that forms part of a contract shall be treated as an agreement independent of the other terms of the contract. A decision by the arbitral tribunal that the contract is null and void shall not entail *Ipso Jure* the invalidity of the arbitration clause.

(1) 仲裁庭可以对它自己的管辖权,包括对仲裁协议的存在或效力的任何异议做出决定。为此目的,构成合同一部分的仲裁条款,应视为独立于合同中其他条款的一项协议。仲裁庭作出合同无效的裁定,不应自动造成仲裁条款无效。

(2) A plea that the arbitral tribunal does not have jurisdiction shall be raised not later than the submission of the statement of defense. A party is not precluded from raising such a plea by the fact that he has appointed, or participated in the appointment of, an arbitrator, A plea that the arbitral tribunal is exceeding the scope of its authority shall be raised as-soon as the matter alleged to be beyond the scope of its authority is raised during the arbitral proceedings. The arbitral tribunal may, in either case, admit a later plea if it considers the delay justified.

（2）对仲裁庭的管辖权异议，应在不迟于辩方陈述提交时提出。一方当事人不得因他指定或参加仲裁员的任命而提出抗辩，不得在仲裁程序中提出仲裁庭超过其职权范围的抗辩。仲裁庭如认为延迟是正当的，可在上述任一情形中准许延迟提出抗辩。

（3）The arbitral tribunal may rule on a plea referred to in paragraph （2）of this Article either as a preliminary question or in an award on the merits. If the arbitral tribunal rules as a preliminary question that it has jurisdiction，any party may request，within thirty days after having received notice of that ruling，the Court specified in Article 6 to decide the matter，which decision shall be subject to no appeal；while such a request is pending，the arbitral tribunal may continue the arbitral proceedings and make an award.

（3）对于第（2）款所述抗辩，仲裁庭既可作为先决问题作出裁定，也可在实体裁决书中作出裁定。如果仲裁庭将其作为其有管辖权的先决问题裁定，一方可在收到通知后 30 天内请求第 6 条所述法院裁定此项事宜，不得对该裁定上诉；请求待决时，仲裁庭可以继续进行仲裁程序并作出裁决。

Article 25：Power of Arbitral Panel to Order Interim Measures
第 25 条　仲裁庭命令采取临时措施的权利

Unless otherwise agreed by the parties，the arbitral panel may，at the request of a party，order any party to take such interim measure of protection as the arbitral panel may consider necessary in respect of the subject matter of the dispute. The arbitral panel may require any party to provide appropriate security in connection with such measure.

经一方当事人请求，仲裁庭在认为与仲裁有必要联系的情况下，可准予临时措施。仲裁庭可要求申请临时措施的一方提供与临时措施相适应的保证。

CHAPTER VI
CONDUCT OF ARBITRAL PROCEEDINGS
第六章　仲裁程序的进行

Article 26: Equal Treatment of Parties
第 26 条　对各方当事人平等对待

The parties shall be with equality and each party shall be given a full opportunity to present his case, including representation by any party of his choice.

应平等对待各方当事人,并给予各方当事人充分陈述案情,包括各方选择的机会。

Article 27: Determination of Rules of Procedure
第 27 条　程序规则的确定

The parties are free to agree or disagree on the procedure to be followed by the arbitral tribunal in conducting the proceedings.

双方可以自由同意或反对仲裁庭进行的程序。

Failing such agreement, the arbitral tribunal may, subject to the provisions of this Law, conduct the arbitration in such manner as it considers appropriate. The power conferred upon the arbitral tribunal includes the power to determine the admissibility, relevance, materiality and weight of any evidence.

如未达成一致,仲裁庭可以在本法的规定的限制下,按照它认为适当的方式进行仲裁。授予仲裁庭的权力包括确定任何证据的可采性、相关性、实质性和重要性。

Article 28: Place of Arbitration
第 28 条　仲裁地

The parties are free to agree on the place of arbitration. Failing such agreement, the place of arbitration shall be determined by the arbitral tribunal having regard to the circumstances of the case, including the agreement of the parties.

当事各方可以自由地就仲裁地点达成协议。未达成上述约定,仲裁地应由仲裁庭根据各方便利的案件情况加以确定。

Notwithstanding the provisions of paragraph（1）of this Article, the arbitral tribunal may, unless otherwise agreed by the parties, meet at any place it considers appropriate for consultation among its members, for hearing witnesses, experts, or the parties, or to conduct inspection to equipment, property or other documents.

虽有本条第(1)款的规定,除非当事各方另有协议,仲裁庭可以在它认为适当的任何地点集合,以便在它的成员间进行磋商,听取证人、专家或当事各方的意见或检查设备、财产或其他文件。

Article 29: Commencement of Arbitral Proceedings
第 29 条　仲裁程序的开始

Unless otherwise agreed by the parties, the arbitral proceedings in respect of a particular dispute commence on the date on which a request for that dispute to be referred to arbitration is received by the respondent.

除非当事各方另有协议,特定争议的仲裁程序,于应诉人收到将该争议提交仲裁的请求之日开始。

Article 30: Language
第 30 条　语言

The parties are free to agree on the language or languages to be used in the arbitral proceedings. Failing such agreement, the arbitral tribunal shall determine the language or languages to be used in the proceedings.

各方当事人有权自由确定仲裁程序中所使用的一种或数种语言。如无约定,仲裁庭应确定程序中使用的一种或数种语言。

The arbitral tribunal may order that any documentary evidence shall be accompanied by a translation into the language or languages agreed upon by the parties or determined by the arbitral tribunal.

仲裁庭可下达指令,任何证据文件均应附具各方当事人所约定的或仲裁庭所确定的一种或数种语言的译文。

Article 31: Statements of Claim and Defense
第 31 条 仲裁申请书和答辩状

Within the period of time agreed by the parties of determined by the arbitral panel, the claimant shall state the facts supporting his claim, the points at issue and the relief of remedy sought, and the respondent shall state his defense in respect of these particulars, unless the parties have otherwise agreed as to the required elements of such statements. The parties may submit with their statements all documents they consider to be relevant or may add a reference to the documents or other evidence they will submit.

除非各方当事人另有约定,在各方约定或仲裁庭确定的期间内,申请人应说明支持本仲裁请求的事实陈述、争议点和寻求的救济或损害赔偿,被申请人也应在其答辩状中说明前述事项。当事人可提交申诉书和答辩书及他们认为与案件有关的全部文件,也可以附注说明他们将来提交的文件和其他证据。

Unless otherwise agreed by the parties, either party may amend or supplement his claim or defense during the course of the arbitral proceedings, unless the arbitral panel considers it inappropriate to allow such amendment, having regard to the delay in making it.

除非各方当事人另有协议,在仲裁程序进行中,任何一方当事人均可以修改或补充其申诉书或答辩书,除非仲裁庭考虑到提出已迟而认为不宜允许提出这种改动。

Article 32: Hearings and Written Proceedings

第 32 条 开庭审理和书面程序

Subject to any contrary agreement by the parties, the arbitral tribunal shall decide whether to hold oral hearings for the presentation of evidence or for oral argument, or whether the proceedings shall be conducted on the basis of documents and other materials. However, unless the parties have agreed that no hearings shall be held, the arbitral tribunal shall hold such hearings at an appropriate stage of the proceedings, if so requested by a party.

在不违反当事人任何协议的前提下,由仲裁庭决定进行口头审理以让当事人提供证据或口头辩论,还是仅以文件及其他材料为基础进行审理。然而,除非当事人约定不进行口头审理。否则只要一方当事人要求,仲裁庭应在仲裁程序的适当阶段开庭审理。

The parties shall be given sufficient advance notice of any hearing and of any meeting of the arbitral tribunal for the purposes of inspection of materials, goods, other property or documents.

任何开庭及仲裁庭为检查材料、货物、其他财产或文件而进行的任何会议,均应充分提前通知当事人。

All statements, documents or other information supplied to the arbitral tribunal by one party shall be communicated to the other party. Also, any expert report or evidentiary document on which the arbitral tribunal may rely in making its decision shall be communicated to the parties.

一方当事人向仲裁庭提交的一切陈述、文件或其他信息均应送交另一方当事人。仲裁庭可能据以作出裁决的任何具有证据性质的专家报告或其他文件也应送交各方当事人。

Article 33: Default of a Party

第 33 条 一方当事人不履行责任

Unless otherwise agreed by the parties, if, without showing

sufficient cause，

除非当事人另有约定，如在不提出充分理由的情况下：

(1) the claimant fails to communicate his statement of claim in accordance with Article 31(1) of this Law，the arbitral panel shall terminate the proceedings.

(1) 申诉人不按第 31 条第(1)款的规定提交仲裁申请书，则仲裁庭应终止程序；

(2) the respondent fails to communicate his statement of defense in accordance with Article 31(1) of this Law，the arbitral panel shall continue the proceedings without treating such failure in itself as an admission of the claimant's allegations；

(2) 被诉人不按照第 31 条第(2)款的规定提交答辩书，仲裁庭应继续进行程序，但不把这种不提交答辩行为本身视为对申诉人请求的承认；

(3) Any party fails to appear at a hearing，or fails to produce documentary evidence，the arbitral panel may continue the proceedings and make the award on the evidence before it.

(3) 任何一方当事人不出庭或不提供书证，仲裁庭仍可继续进行仲裁程序并根据已有证据作出裁决。

Article 34：Expert Appointed by Arbitral Tribunal
第 34 条　仲裁庭指定的专家

Unless otherwise agreed by the parties，the arbitral tribunal，

除非双方当事人另有约定，仲裁庭：

(1) may appoint one or more experts to report to it on specific issues to be determined by the arbitral tribunal；

(1) 可以指定一名或数名专家就仲裁庭确定的具体问题向仲裁庭提出报告；

(2) may require a party to give the expert any relevant information，or to produce，or to provide access to，any relevant documents，goods or other property for his inspection.

(2) 可以要求当事人向专家提供或出示与案件有关的任何信息，或向专家提供让其查看与案件有关的文件、物品或其他财产的机会。

Unless otherwise agreed by the parties, if a party so requests, or if the arbitral tribunal considers it necessary, the expert shall, after delivery of his written or oral report, participate in a hearing, at which the parties have the opportunity to put questions to him and to present expert witnesses to testify on the points at issue.

除非双方当事人另有约定，专家应在书面或口头报告提交后，如果一方当事人请求并且仲裁庭认为确有必要，专家可在开庭时听询，各方当事人应有机会出庭并质询专家。任何一方当事人均可在此次开庭时委派专家证人出庭，就争议点作证。

Article 35: Court Assistance in Taking Evidence
第 35 条　法院协助取证

The arbitral tribunal, or a party with the approval of the arbitral tribunal, may request from a competent Court (Commercial, or Appeal, or Supreme) assistance in taking evidence. The Court (Commercial, or Appeal, or Supreme) may execute the request within its competence and according to its rules on taking evidence.

仲裁庭或经仲裁庭允许的一方当事人可以请求法院（商事法院、上诉法院或最高法院）协助取证。法院（商事法院、上诉法院或最高法院）可以在其权限范围内依照规则执行该请求。

CHAPTER VII
MAKING OF AWARD AND TERMINATION OF PROCEEDINGS
第七章　仲裁裁决的作出和程序的终止
Article 36: Rules Applicable to Substance of Dispute
第 36 条　适用于实体争议的规则

The Arbitral Tribunal shall apply applicable rules during the arbitration proceedings：

仲裁庭应在仲裁程序中适用下列规则：

(1) The parties shall be free to agree upon the rules of law to be applied by arbitral tribunal to the merits of the dispute. Any designation of the law or legal system of a given state shall be construed，unless otherwise expressed，as directly referring to the substantive law of that state and not to its conflict of laws rules.

(1) 各方当事人可以自由地就仲裁庭适用于争议的法律规则达成一致。任何关于所选特定国家的法律或法律体系，应被认为是直接指向其实体法而非冲突规则。

(2) Failing such an agreement by the parties，the arbitral tribunal shall apply the law that it considers appropriate.

(2) 当事人未达成协议的，仲裁庭应当适用其认为适当的法律。

(3) The arbitral tribunal shall decide *ex aegu et bono* or as amiable compositeur only if the parties have expressly authorized it to do so.

(3) 只有在双方明确授权的情况下，仲裁庭才可按公平合理的原则作为友好调剂人裁决。

(4) In all cases，the arbitral tribunal shall take into account all the provisions of the arbitration agreement and also the usages of the trade and customs applicable to the transaction.

(4) 在所有案件中，仲裁庭均应根据合同条款作出裁决，还应当考虑交易适用的贸易惯例。

Article 37：Decision Making by Panel of Arbitrators
第 37 条　仲裁小组决定

In arbitral proceedings with more than one arbitrator，any decision of the arbitral tribunal may be made by a majority of all its members.

裁员不止一名的，仲裁庭的任何裁决或判决均应以仲裁员的多数作出。

Article 38: Settlement
第 38 条　和解

Upon request by both parties, prior to commencement of formal arbitration proceedings, the arbitral tribunal may confer with the parties for the purpose of exploring whether the possibility exists of a voluntary settlement of the parties' dispute:

在双方要求下，在正式仲裁程序开始之前，仲裁庭可以与当事人进行协商，以探讨是否存在自愿解决双方争议的可能性：

(1) if the parties determines that it does, the arbitral tribunal shall assist the parties in any manner it deems appropriate.

(1) 当事人认为存在和解可能性的，仲裁庭应按照其认为适当的方式协助当事人。

(2) If the parties settle the dispute prior to commencement of the formal arbitral proceedings, or in the course thereof, the arbitral tribunal shall terminate the proceedings and, if requested by the parties, may record the settlement in the form of an arbitral award on agreed terms.

(2) 当事人在正式仲裁程序开始前或在仲裁过程中解决争议的，仲裁庭应终止程序，经当事人要求，可以根据双方当事人的约定制作裁决书。

(3) An award on agreed terms shall be made in accordance with the provisions of Article 39 of this Law, and shall state that it is an award. Such an award has the same status and effect as any other award on the merits of the case.

(3) 按和解条件作出的仲裁裁决应按照第 39 条的规定作出并应说明它是一项仲裁裁决。这一协议与实体裁决书具有同等效力。

Article 39: Form and Content of Award

第 39 条　裁决书的形式和内容

The arbitral tribunal form and content of award shall contain as follows:

仲裁庭的裁决形式和内容应包括如下：

(1) The award shall be made in writing and shall be signed by the arbitrator or arbitrators. In arbitral proceedings with more than one arbitrator, the signatures of the majority of all members of the arbitral tribunal shall suffice, provided that the reason for any omitted signature is stated.

(1) 所有仲裁裁决均应以书面形式作出并由独任仲裁员或多位仲裁员签名。在有一组仲裁员的仲裁程序中，仲裁庭多数成员的签字即可，但须说明没有其余仲裁员签字的原因。

(2) The award shall state the reasons upon which it is based, unless the parties have agreed that no reasons are to be given or the award is an award on agreed terms under Article 38 of this law.

(2) 仲裁庭应说明裁决所依据的理由，除非各方当事人约定无需说明理由，或该裁决为根据第 38 条按照和解协议条款作出的仲裁裁决。

(3) The award shall allocate among the parties the costs of the arbitration, including the arbitrator(s) fee(s) and incidental expenses, in the manner agreed by the parties, or in the absence of such agreement, as the arbitrators deem appropriate. If the parties have so agreed, or the arbitrators deem it appropriate, the award may also provide for recovery by the prevailing party of reasonable counsel fees.

(3) 仲裁裁决应以当事人约定的方式或仲裁员认为适当的方式，将包括仲裁员费用和附带费用在内的仲裁费用分摊给当事人。如果当事人同意或仲裁员认为适当，也可以由胜诉方承担合理的律师费。

(4) The award shall state its date and the place of arbitration as

determined in accordance with Article 28(1) of this law. The award shall be deemed to have been made at that place.

（4）仲裁裁决应说明日期和按第 28 条第（1）款规定所确定的仲裁地点。仲裁裁决应视为在该地点作出。

（5）After the award is made，a copy signed by the arbitrators in accordance with paragraph (1) of this Article shall be delivered to each party.

（5）仲裁裁决作出后，根据本条第（1）款，经仲裁员签字的仲裁裁决副本应送达各方当事人。

Article 40：Termination of Proceedings
第 40 条　终止程序

The arbitral Proceedings are terminated by the final award，an agreed settlement，or by an order of the arbitral tribunal in accordance with Paragraph (2) of this Article.

仲裁程序于最终裁决书作出后或于仲裁庭根据本条第（2）款下达指令后终止。

The arbitral tribunal shall issue an order for the termination of the arbitral Proceedings when：

仲裁庭应在下列情况下做出终止仲裁程序的决定：

（1）the claimant withdraws his claim，unless the respondent objects thereto and the arbitral tribunal recognizes a legitimate interest on his part in obtaining a final settlement of the dispute；

（1）申请人放弃请求，但被申请人拒绝且仲裁庭认为采取和解方式对被申请人有合法利益；

（2）the parties agree on the termination of the proceedings；

（2）当事人协议终止程序；

（3）the arbitral tribunal finds that the continuation of the proceedings has，for any other reason，become unnecessary or impossible.

(3) 仲裁庭认定,由于某些原因已无必要或可能继续程序。

The mandate of the arbitral tribunal terminates with the termination of the arbitral proceedings, subject to the provisions of Articles 41 and 42(4) of this Law.

根据第 41 条和第 42 条第(4)款,仲裁程序终止,仲裁庭授权终止。

Article 41: Correction and Interpretation of Award; Additional Award

第 41 条　裁决书的更正与解释;补充裁决

The correction and interpretation of award shall determine as follows:

裁决书的更正和解释应确定如下:

(1) Within thirty (30) days of the receipt of the award, unless another period of time has been agreed upon by the parties

(1) 除非当事人约定了另一期限,在收到仲裁裁决之日起 30 天内:

   (a) with notice to the other party, a party may request the arbitral tribunal to correct in the award any errors in computation, any clerical or typographical errors, or any other errors of a similar nature.

   (a) 任何一方当事人在通知另一方当事人后可以请求仲裁庭改正裁决中出现的任何计算、书写、打印错误或任何类似性质的错误;

   (b) with notice to the other party, a party may request the arbitral tribunal to give an interpretation or amplification of a specific point or part of the award. If the arbitral tribunal considers the request justified, it shall provide the interpretation or amplification within thirty days of receipt of the request. The interpretation or amplification shall form part of the award;

   (b) 一方当事人可在通知另一方方当事人后,请求仲裁庭对裁决书的具体一点或部分做出解释或扩大。仲裁庭认为请求有正当理由的,应当在收到请求的 30 天内做出解释。解释应构成裁决书的一部分。

（2） Within no later than thirty（30） days after the issuance of award by the arbitral tribunal，the arbitration may correct the errors stated in paragraph 1（a） of this Article at its own initiatives.

（2） 在裁决发布后 30 天内，仲裁庭可以自行更正本条第（1）款（a）项所述的错误。

（3） unless otherwise agreed by the parties，within no later than thirty（30）days after receiving an award as to the claims，the party who has notified another party may request for additional awards presented in the arbitral proceeding but omitted from the award. If the arbitral tribunal considers the request justified，it shall make the additional award within thirty（30） days of receipt of the request.

（3） 除当事人另有约定外，在收到裁决书之日起 30 天内，已经通知另一方的当事人可以要求仲裁庭对裁决过程中涉及的，但在裁决书中遗漏的事宜作出补充裁决。如果仲裁庭认为请求合理，它应在收到请求后 30 天内作出补充裁决。

（4） if it is required and by notifying the parties，the arbitral tribunal may extend the period of time with which it shall make a correction，interpretation，amplification，or additional award under paragraph （1） and （3） of this Article.

（4） 如有必要，仲裁庭可将其根据本条第（1）款和第（3）款延长更正、解释、扩大或补充裁决的期限，并通知当事人。

（5） The provisions of Article 39 of this Law shall apply to a correction，interpretation or amplification，or an addition to the award.

（5） 第 39 条的规定应适用于裁决书的更正、解释、扩大以及补充裁决。

CHAPTER VIII
RECOURSE, RECOGNITION, AND ENFORCEMENT
OF ARBITRAL AWARD
第八章 仲裁裁决的追索、承认与执行
SECTION I RECOURSE INSTITUTION, RECOGNITION, AND ENFORCEMENT OF ARBITRAL AWARD
第一节 仲裁裁决的追索制度、承认与执行

Article 42: Application for Setting Aside as Exclusive Recourse Against Arbitral Award

第 42 条 申请撤销作为对仲裁裁决异议的唯一手段

The jurisdiction over recourse, recognition, and enforcement of arbitral award shall rest with the Appellate Court of the Kingdom of Cambodia.

仲裁裁决的追索、认可和执行归柬埔寨王国上诉法院管辖。

Article 43: Conclusive Jurisdiction

第 43 条 确定的管辖权

The Supreme Court of Cambodia shall be the final jurisdiction to try counter claim of the party who is not satisfying with the decision of the Appellate Court within fifteen (15) days.

柬埔寨最高法院应在上诉法院裁决作出 15 天内，对不满上诉法院裁决的当事人的反诉作最终裁定。

SECTION II RECOURSE AGAINST ARBITRAL AWARDS
第二节 对仲裁裁决的追索

Article 44: Application for Setting Aside as Exclusive Recourse Against Arbitral Award

第 44 条 申请撤销作为对仲裁裁决异议的唯一手段

The party may file an application for setting aside as exclusive recourse against arbitral award as follows:

当事人可以申请撤销作为对仲裁裁决异议的唯一手段：

（1）Recourse to a Court against an arbitral award may be made only by an application for setting aside in accordance with paragraphs（2）and（3）of this Article.

（1）只有按照本条第（2）款和第（3）款的规定申请撤销，才可以就仲裁裁决向法院追诉。

（2）An arbitral award may be set aside by the Appeal Court and Supreme Court only if：

（2）仲裁裁决只有在下列情况下才可以被上诉法院和最高法院撤销：

　（a）the party making the application furnishes proof that：

　（a）提出申请的当事一方提出证据证明：

　　（i）a party to the arbitration agreement referred to in Article 7 of this Law was under some incapacity；or the said agreement is not valid under the law to which the parties have subjected it or，failing，any indication by the parties，under the law of the Kingdom of Cambodia；or

　　（i）第 7 条所指仲裁协议的一方当事人在任何程度上无行为能力，或者根据当事人约定的适用于仲裁协议的法律，如双方未约定则根据柬埔寨的法律仲裁协议无效；或

　　（ii）the party making the application was not given proper notice of the appointment of an arbitrator(s) or of the arbitral proceedings，or was otherwise unable effectively present his case；or

　　（ii）未将有关指定仲裁员或仲裁程序的事情适当地通知提出申请的当事一方，或该方因其他理由未能陈述其案情；

　　（iii）the award deals with a dispute not contemplated by or not falling within the terms of the arbitration agreement，or contains decisions on matters beyond the scope of the arbitration agreement，provided that，if the decisions on matters submitted to arbitration can be separated from those not so submitted，only that part of the award which contains decisions on matters not submitted to arbitration may be set aside；or

(iii) 裁决处理了不是提交仲裁的条款所考虑的或不是其范围以内的争议，或裁决包括有对提交仲裁以外的事项做出的决定，但如果对提交仲裁的事项所做的决定与对未提交仲裁的事项所做出的决定能分开的话，只可以撤销包括有对未提交仲裁的事项做出决定的那一部分裁决；或

(iv) the composition of the arbitral tribunal or the arbitral procedure was not in accordance with the agreement of the parties，unless such agreement was in conflict with a provision of this Law from which the parties cannot derogate，or，failing such agreement，was not in accordance with this Law；or

(iv) 仲裁庭的组成或仲裁程序与当事各方的协议不一致，除非这种协议与当事各方不能背离的本法的规定相抵触，或当事各方并无此种协议，则与本法不符；或

(b) the Appeal Court and Supreme Court finds that

(b) 上诉法院和最高法院认定：

(i) the subject matter of the dispute is，not capable of settlement by arbitration under the law of the Kingdom of Cambodia；or

(i) 根据柬埔寨的法律，争议不能成为仲裁解决的对象；或

(ii) The recognition of the award would be contrary to public policy of the Kingdom of Cambodia

(ii) 承认和执行该仲裁裁决与柬埔寨的公共政策相抵触。

(3) An application for setting aside may not be made after thirty (30) days have elapsed from the date on which the party making that application had received the award or，if a request had been made under Article 41 of this article within thirty (30)

days, from the date on which that request had been disposed of by the arbitral tribunal.

（3）提出申请的当事一方自收到裁决书之日起，30 天内不得申请撤销；如根据第 41 条提出了请求，则从该请求被仲裁庭处理完毕之日起 30 天后不得申请撤销。

（4）The Appeal Court and Supreme Court, when asked to set aside an award, may, where appropriate and so requested by a party, suspend the setting aside proceedings for a period of time determined by the Appeal Court and Supreme Court, in order to give the arbitral tribunal an opportunity to resume the arbitral proceedings or to take such other action as in the arbitral tribunal's opinion will eliminate the grounds for setting aside.

（4）上诉法院和最高法院被请求撤销裁决时，如果适当而且当事一方也要求暂时停止进行撤销程序，则可以在上诉法院和最高法院确定的一段期间内暂时停止进行，以便给予仲裁庭机会重新进行仲裁程序或采取仲裁庭认为能够消除请求撤销裁决的理由的其他行动。

SECTION III RECOGNITION AND ENFORCEMENT OF AWARDS
第三节 仲裁裁决的承认和执行

Article 45: Recognition and Enforcement

第 45 条 仲裁裁决的承认和执行

An arbitral award, irrespective of the country in which it was made, shall be recognized as binding and, upon application in writing to the competent court, shall be enforced subject to the provisions of this Article and Article 44 of this Law.

仲裁裁决不论在哪一国家作出，均应承认具有约束力；向有管辖权的法院提出书面申请，即应予以执行，但应考虑到本法中本条及第 44 条的规定。

The party relying on and award or applying for its enforcement shall supply the duty authenticated original award or a duly certified copy thereof，and the original arbitration agreement referred to in Article 7 of this Law or a duly certified copy thereof. If the award or agreement is not made in Khmer，the party shall supply a duly certified translation thereof into Khmer.

援用裁决或申请予以执行的当事一方，应提供裁决书正本或经正式认证的裁决书副本，以及第 7 条所指的仲裁协议正本或经正式认证的仲裁协议副本。如果仲裁裁决或协议是以外语表述，则申请执行方应提供这些文件经过认证的高棉语译本。

Article 46：Grounds for Refusing Recognition or Enforcement
第 46 条　拒绝承认或执行的理由

Recognition or enforcement of an arbitral award，irrespective of the country in which it was made，may be refused only：

不论裁决是在哪一国家作出的，只有在下列情况下才能拒绝承认或执行：

（1）At the request the party against whom it is invoked，if that party furnishes to the Appeal Court where recognition or enforcement is sought proof that：

（1）经被申请承认和执行人的请求，如果该方当事人向被要求承认或执行的上诉法院举证证明：

（a）A party to the arbitration agreement referred to in Article 7 was under some incapacity；or the said agreement is not valid under the law to which the parties have subjected it or，failing，any indication by the parties，under the law of the Kingdom of Cambodia；or

（a）第 7 条所指仲裁协议的一方当事人在任何程度上无行为能力，或者根据当事人约定的适用于仲裁协议的法律，如双方未约定则根据柬埔寨的法律仲裁协议无效；或

（b）the party making the application was not given proper notice of the appointment of an arbitrator（s）or of the arbitral proceedings，or was otherwise unable effectively present his case; or

(b) 未将有关指定仲裁员或仲裁程序的事情适当地通知提出申请的当事一方,或该方因其他理由未能有效陈述其案情;或

(c) the award deals with a dispute not contemplated by or not falling within the terms of the arbitration agreement, or contains decisions on matters beyond the scope of the arbitration agreement, provided that, if the decisions on matters submitted to arbitration can be separated from those not so submitted, only that part of the award which contains decisions on matters not submitted to arbitration may be set aside; or

(c) 裁决处理了不是提交仲裁的条款所考虑的或不是其范围以内的争议,或裁决包括有对提交仲裁以外的事项做出的决定,但如果对提交仲裁的事项所做的决定与对未提交仲裁的事项所做出的决定能分开的话,只可以撤销包括有对未提交仲裁的事项做出决定的那一部分裁决;或

(d) The composition of the arbitral panel or the arbitral procedure was not in accordance with the agreement of the parties or, failing such agreement, was not in accordance with the law of the where the arbitration took place; or

(d) 仲裁庭的组成或仲裁程序与当事各方的协议不一致,或并无这种协议,则与仲裁地的法律不符;或

(e) The award has not yet become binding on the parties in the country in which, or under the law of which, that award was made, or the award has been set aside or suspended by a court in the country which the award was made; or

(e) 裁决尚未在裁决所在国对当事人产生约束力,或裁决已由裁决所在国的法院予以撤销或中止;或

(2) the Appeal Court finds that

(2) 法院认定:

(a) the subject matter of the dispute is, not capable of

settlement by arbitration under the law of the Kingdom of Cambodia; or

（a）根据柬埔寨的法律,争议不能成为仲裁解决的对象;或

（b）The recognition of the award would be contrary to public policy of the Kingdom of Cambodia.

（b）承认该仲裁裁决与柬埔寨的公共政策相抵触。

If an application for setting aside or suspension of an award has been to a court referred to in paragraph （1）（e） of this Article, the court where recognition or enforcement is sought may, if it consider it proper, adjourn its decision and may also, on the application of the party claiming recognition of the award, order the party to provide appropriate security.

如已向本条第(1)款(e)项所指的法院申请撤销或中止裁决,被请求承认或执行的法院如认为适当,可以暂停做出决定,而且如经要求承认或执行裁决的当事一方提出申请,还可以命令当事他方提供适当的担保。

CHAPTER IX
FINAL PROVISIONS
第九章　最后条款

Article 47: Abrogation
第 47 条　废除

Any provisions in commercial arbitration sector that are contrary to this Law shall be abrogated.

对任何违反本法的商事仲裁规定,应予以废除。

This Law is enacted by the National Assembly of the Kingdom of Cambodia on the 6th of March 2006 at its 4th Session of the 3rd Legislature.

本法于 2006 年 3 月 6 日由柬埔寨王国国民议会第三届立法会第四次

会议通过。

Signed and Sealed at Phnom Penh March 7th，2006

2006 年 3 月 7 日在金边签署并盖章

First Vice President

第一副总统

Samdech HENG SAMRIN

韩桑林亲王殿下

第六节　老挝商事仲裁法英汉对照

LAO PEOPLE'S DEMOCRATIC REPUBLIC

老挝人民民主共和国

PEACE INDEPENDENCE DEMOCRACY UNITY PROSPERITY

和平·独立·民主·团结·繁荣

President's Office

主席办公室

No. 44/PO

第 44/PO 号主席令

DECREE of the PRESIDENT of the LAO PEOPLE'S DEMOC-
RATIC REPUBLIC

老挝人民民主共和国主席令

On the Promulgation of the Law on Resolution of Economic Disputes

颁布《经济纠纷解决法》

Pursuant to the Chapter 6，Article 67，point 1 of the Constitution of
the Lao People's Democratic Republic which provides for the
promulgation of the Constitution and of laws adopted by the
National Assembly；

根据《老挝人民民主共和国宪法》第六章第 67 条第 1 款对颁布《宪法》
和国会通过的法律所做规定；

Pursuant to Resolution No. 27/NA，dated 20 May 2005，of the National Assembly of the Lao People's Democratic Republic regarding the adoption of the Law on Resolution of Economic Disputes；and

根据 2005 年 5 月 20 日老挝人民民主共和国国会关于通过《经济纠纷解决法》的第 27/NA 号决议；

Pursuant to Proposal No. 06/NASC，dated 23 May 2005，of the National Assembly Standing Committee.

根据 2005 年 5 月 23 日国会常务委员会第 06/NASC 号提案。

The President of the Lao People's Democratic Republic Decrees That：

老挝人民民主共和国主席令：

Article 1. The Law on Resolution of Economic Disputes is hereby promulgated.

第 1 条　特此公布《经济纠纷解决法》。

Article 2. This decree shall enter into force on the date it is signed.

第 2 条　本法令自签署之日起生效。

Vientiane，25 May 2005

2005 年 5 月 25 日于万象

The President of the Lao People's Democratic Republic

老挝人民民主共和国主席

[Seal and Signature]

[盖章签名]

Khamtai SIPHANDONE

坎代·西潘敦

National Assembly

老挝国会

No. 02/NA

第 02/NA 号

19 May 2005

2005 年 5 月 19 日

LAW ON RESOLUTION OF ECONOMIC DISPUTES
《经济纠纷解决法》

Part I
General Provisions
第一部分　总则

Article 1. Purpose
第1条　宗旨

The Law on Resolution of Economic Disputes determines the principles, regulations and measures regarding the resolution of economic disputes by mediators or arbitrators in order to ensure that economic disputes are solved fairly and speedily in order to promote the production and expansion of business, and to contribute to a civilized and just national socio-economic development plan.

《经济纠纷解决法》确定了调解员、仲裁员解决经济纠纷的原则、规定和措施,确保经济纠纷得到公平、快捷的解决,从而促进生产,扩大经营,推动文明、公正的国家社会经济发展计划。

Article 2. Economic Disputes
第2条　经济纠纷

Economic disputes are conflicts which takes place in relation to production and business operations between organisations and other organisations, organisations and individuals, and individuals and other individuals[,] both domestic and foreign.

经济纠纷是指发生在国内外法人之间、法人与自然人之间,以及自然人之间的生产和经营活动的冲突。

Article 3. Resolution of Economic Disputes
第3条　经济纠纷的解决

Economic disputes shall be resolved by amicable settlement between the parties to the dispute, mediation or by arbitration.

经济纠纷应当由各方当事人通过调解或仲裁手段友好解决。

Resolution of economic disputes shall be handled in compliance with this law, other laws and regulations of the Lao PDR and rules for the resolution of economic disputes selected by the parties to the dispute in accordance with agreements and treaties which the Lao PDR has signed or is a party to.

经济纠纷的解决应依照本法、老挝人民民主共和国的其他法律和法规，以及各方当事人根据协议和条约所选的，且老挝人民民主共和国签署或加入的解决经济纠纷的规则。

Article 4. Conditions for Economic Dispute Resolution
第 4 条　经济纠纷解决的条件

The resolution of a dispute must be conducted according to the following conditions:

纠纷的解决须满足下列条件：

The dispute shall be an economic dispute;

纠纷应为经济纠纷；

The submission of the dispute for resolution shall be agreed upon by the parties;

解决纠纷的提交应由双方当事人商定；

The economic dispute shall not be a dispute on which the people's court is in the process of adjudicating or has already issued a final judgment;

经济纠纷不应是人民法院正在进行审判或者已经下达终审的纠纷；

The resolution of the economic dispute shall be consistent with the actual situation, and shall not violate rules relating to the resolution of economic disputes, or laws and regulations pertaining to stability, peace and social order.

经济纠纷的解决应符合实际情况，不得违反经济纠纷解决相关的规定，不得违反安定、和平、社会秩序相关的法律和法规。

Article 5. Impartiality in the Resolution of Economic Disputes
第 5 条　经济纠纷解决的公正性

In the resolution of economic disputes, mediators or arbitrators must be impartial in the performance of their duties, follow the laws and regulations and act without interference from other persons or organisations.

在解决经济纠纷时，调解员或仲裁员在履行职责时应保持公正，遵守法律和法规，其行为不得受他人或其他组织干预。

Article 6. Equality between the Parties to the Dispute
第 6 条　争议双方地位平等

In the resolution of economic disputes, the parties have equal rights, and the parties may participate in the resolution by themselves or through a representative.

在解决经济纠纷时，双方享有平等的权利，可自行参与或派代表参与。

Article 7. Confidentiality
第 7 条　保密

In the resolution of economic disputes, mediators or arbitrators, the parties and other participants must maintain confidentiality of all information and documents used in the resolution or arbitration [and] shall not disclose them to third parties.

在解决经济纠纷时，调解人或仲裁员、当事人和其他参与者应对决议或仲裁中使用的所有信息和文件保密，不得泄露给第三方。

Article 8. Language Used
第 8 条　使用的语言

In the resolution of economic disputes in the Lao PDR, the Lao language must be used. A participant to the resolution of a dispute who does now the Lao language has the right to use his own language or other languages through translation.

在解决老挝经济纠纷时,应使用老挝语。不懂老挝语的参与者有权通过翻译使用其本国语或其他语言。

Article 9. International Relations
第 9 条 国际关系

The State promotes international relations and cooperation in the resolution of economic disputes by coordination, exchange of experience, upgrading of knowledge and capacity building of the staff of economic dispute resolution organisations, in accordance with agreements and treaties which the Lao Peoples' Democratic Republic has signed or is a party to, in order to ensure the efficiency of economic dispute resolution.

国家提倡国际关系与合作在协调、交流经验解决经济纠纷的作用,增进经济纠纷解决机构中工作人员的知识和能力建设,依照老挝人民民主共和国签署或加入的协议和条约,保证经济纠纷的有效解决。

Part II
Organisation of Economic Dispute Resolution
第二部分 经济纠纷解决机构

Article 10. Status and Role
第 10 条 地位和作用

The organisation of economic dispute resolution refers to an organisation attached to the justice sector which has the role to manage and facilitate economic dispute resolution to ensure a just, speedy and fair resolution.

经济纠纷解决机构是指隶属于司法部的机构,其作用是管理和促进经济纠纷的解决,从而确保纠纷得到公正、快捷和公平的解决。

Article 11. Organisational Structure

第 11 条　组织结构

The organisational structure which handles economic dispute resolution consists of 2 levels:

经济纠纷解决机构的组织结构包含两个层面：

Central level;

中央层面；

Provincial level.

地方层面。

At the central level, there is an Office of Economic Dispute Resolution abbreviated as "OEDR". Such office is equivalent to a department and is part of the Ministry of Justice.

在中央层面，设有经济纠纷解决司，简称"调解司"。调解司相当于一个部门，隶属于司法部。

At the provincial level, where necessary, there is a Unit of Economic Dispute Resolution abbreviated as "UEDR". The chief of a UEDR has a title equivalent to a deputy chief of a provincial division and is part of the justice division.

在地方层面，必要时设有经济纠纷解决委，简称"调解委"。调解委的长官头衔相当于副省级官员，调解委隶属于司法分支部门。

Regulations concerning the organisation and function of the OEDR and UEDR are determined separately.

调解司和调解委的组织和职能分开规定。

Article 12. Staff Structure

第 12 条　员工结构

The OEDR has a director general, a deputy director general, and technical and administrative staff.

调解司设司长一名，副司长一名，技术和行政人员若干。

Each UEDR has a director，a deputy director，and technical and administrative staff.

各调解委设委员长一名,副委员长一名,技术和行政人员若干。

Article 13. Rights of the OEDR
第 13 条 调解司的权利

The OEDR has the following rights：

调解司享有下列权利：

1. To properly，speedily and fairly administer and support the resolution of economic disputes throughout the country；

1. 妥善、迅速、公正地管理和支持全国经济纠纷的解决；

2. To receive economic dispute resolution petitions，and to examine and handover such petitions to the mediator or arbitrator for resolution if such petitions fulfil the conditions；

2. 受理审查经济纠纷解决请求,如果请求符合条件,则交给调解员或仲裁员解决；

3. To demand information and evidence from the parties；

3. 要求各方当事人提供信息和证据；

4. To propose to the Minister of Justice the appointment of mediators or arbitrators to the list of mediators and arbitrators of the OEDR，and to propose the discharge of mediators or arbitrators who do not perform properly；

4. 提请司法部长根据调解司提供名单任命调解员或仲裁员,并提请司法部长免除未能正确履职的调解员或仲裁员的职务；

5. To appoint a mediator or arbitrator for the resolution of a dispute；

5. 为解决某一纠纷指定调解员或仲裁员；

6. To exercise such other rights as provided in the laws and regulations.

6. 行使法律和法规规定的其他权利。

As far as a UEDR is concerned，it has the same rights as the OEDR except the rights stipulated in point 4 of this article.

除本条第 4 款规定的权利外，调解委与调解司享有相同的权利。

Article 14. Duties of the OEDR
第 14 条　调解司的职责

1. To coordinate with the parties and relevant organisations in order to facilitate the mediators and arbitrators in the resolution of economic disputes；

1. 协调当事人和有关组织，协助调解员和仲裁员解决经济纠纷；

2. To monitor and record the result of the enforcement of mediation settlement agreements，settlement agreements of the parties and arbitral awards；

2. 监督并记录调解协议、当事人和解协议和仲裁裁决的执行结果；

3. To devise and print documents and regulations regarding economic dispute resolution；

3. 拟定和印制解决经济纠纷的相关文件和规定；

4. To study and improve laws and regulations regarding economic dispute resolution for submission to the higher authority for consideration；

4. 研究和完善解决经济纠纷的有关法律法规，提交上级机关审议；

5. To study and submit proposals to the Ministry of Justice relating to the training and the upgrading of the technical skills of OEDR and UEDR staff；

5. 对培训与提高调解司和调解委人员的技术技能进行研究，并将建议提交司法部；

6. To disseminate laws and regulations and economic dispute resolution activities；

6. 宣传法律法规和经济纠纷解决措施；

7. To liaise and cooperate internationally in the area of economic

dispute resolution；

7. 在经济纠纷解决领域进行国际联络和合作；

8. To prepare reports，evaluate and report on economic dispute resolution to the Ministry of Justice；

8. 编写报告，评估经济纠纷解决情况并呈报司法部；

9. To perform such other duties as provided in the laws and regulations.

9. 履行法律、法规规定的其他职责。

As far as a UEDR is concerned，it has the same duties as the OEDR，except points 3 and 7 of this article.

除本条第 3 款和第 7 款规定的职责外，调解委与调解司履行相同的职责。

Article 15．Types of Economic Dispute Resolution
第 15 条　经济纠纷解决类型

There are 2 types of economic dispute resolution：resolution of dispute by mediators and by arbitrators.

经济纠纷解决类型有两种：通过调解员解决，以及通过仲裁员解决。

Article 16．Mediators and Arbitrators
第 16 条　调解员和仲裁员

Mediators and arbitrators are individuals from organisations，and State and private business units，or foreign individuals who volunteer to act as such，and are appointed by the Minister of Justice based upon selection and proposal by the OEDR.

调解员和仲裁员是来自组织、国家和私营企业单位的个人或志愿担任该职务的外国人，由司法部长根据调解司的选择和提议任命。

Article 17．Criteria of Mediators and Arbitrators
第 17 条　担任调解员和仲裁员的标准

Mediators and arbitrators must meet the following criteria：

调解员和仲裁员应达到下列标准：

1. Have a good personality, good ethics and honesty;

1. 品行端正，道德高尚，诚实守信；

2. Have technical knowledge supported by a proper certificate;

2. 具备专业证书支持的技术知识；

3. Have a minimum of 5 years of practical experience in their respective fields of study;

3. 在各自的研究领域具备至少 5 年的实践经验；

4. Have never been sentenced to imprisonment;

4. 从未被判处监禁；

5. Be in good health.

5. 身体健康。

Part III

Procedure of an Economic Dispute Resolution

第三部分　经济纠纷解决程序

Chapter 1

Petition

第一章　申请

Article 18. Contents of the Petition

第 18 条　申请内容

A petition shall be made in writing and shall include the following key contents:

申请应以书面形式提出，并应包括下列主要内容：

1. The name and surname, age, occupation, nationality, address and location of the petitioner, his representative and the other party;

1. 申请人、申请人代表和被申请人的姓名、年龄、职业、国籍和地址；

2. The purpose, grounds and value of the dispute;

2. 纠纷的目的、事由和金额；

3. The agreement of the parties to bring the dispute to be resolved by the OEDR or a UEDR（if any）；

3. 双方当事人将争议提交调解司或调解委的协议；

4. The name and surname，age，occupation，nationality and address of witnesses.

4. 证人的姓名、年龄、职业、国籍和地址；

The petition regarding the economic dispute resolution must be affixed with a tax stamp in accordance with regulations and filed with the OEDR or UEDR where it is most convenient to the petitioner.

经济纠纷解决申请书应依法附税票，并就近提交调解司或调解委。

Article 19. Acceptance of Petition
第 19 条　接受申请

The OEDR or UEDR will accept a petition regarding an economic dispute for resolution only if the parties have agreed in their contract to submit their dispute to the OEDR or UEDR.

只有经双方同意提交的解决经济纠纷的申请，调解司或调解委才可接受。

In the event that the parties have not agreed in their contract to use the OEDR or UEDR，the parties may decide to use the OEDR or UEDR when the dispute arises.

如果双方在协议中未能达成一致，双方可在纠纷产生时决定将其提交仲裁司或仲裁委。

Upon acceptance of the petition，the OEDR or UEDR must check the petition to decide whether to accept it or not. If the OEDR or UEDR does not accept the petition，it must notify the petitioner of the reasons for rejecting the petition within ten days from the date of receipt of the petition.

收到申请后,仲裁司或仲裁委应审查申请并决定是否受理。如果仲裁司或仲裁委不受理申请,则应在收到申请之日起 10 日内通知申请人驳回申请的理由。

In the event that the petition is accepted，the OEDR or UEDR must invite the parties to carry out the resolution process. If one or both do not appear without a valid reason or in the event that the petition does not fulfil the requirements stipulated in articles 4 and 18 of this law，such petition will not be considered.

受理申请后,仲裁司或仲裁委应请各方当事人参与程序。一方或双方无正当理由不出席的,或申请书不符合本法第 4 条和第 18 条规定的,则不予考虑申请。

Article 20. Selection of Types of Dispute Resolution
第 20 条　纠纷解决类型的选择

Once the OEDR or UEDR has accepted a petition for economic dispute resolution，it shall invite the parties to discuss and decide whether to use mediation or arbitration.

调解司或调解委接受解决经济纠纷的请求后,应当请双方当事人讨论决定使用调解或仲裁。

Chapter 2
Mediation
第二章　调解

Article 21. Appointment of Mediators
第 21 条　调解员的任命

Mediators must always be appointed in an odd number. There may be one or more mediators depending on the agreement of the parties.

调解员人数必须始终为奇数。根据双方协议,可有一个或多个调解员。

In the event that the parties agree to have one mediator, the OEDR or UEDR shall provide a list of at least three mediators to each party for selection. The parties shall agree to one mediator from the list. If the parties cannot decide on the selection of a mediator within fifteen days, the OEDR or UEDR will select a mediator based on knowledge, competence, experience and integrity.

如果双方同意有一名调解员,则调解司或调解委应向每方提供至少三名调解员的名单以供选择。双方当事人应一致同意名单上的一名调解员。如果当事人未能在 15 天内就调解员的选择达成一致,调解司或调解委将根据知识、能力、经验和信誉选择调解员。

In the event that the parties agree to have three mediators, the OEDR or UEDR shall provide a list of at least five mediators to each party so that each party can select one mediator. Thereafter the mediators from both parties shall select a third mediator from the list who will be the chairman of the mediation committee.

如果双方同意有三名调解员,调解司或调解委应向每方提供至少五名调解员的名单,以供每方选择一名调解员。此后双方调解员应从名单中选出第三名调解员担任调解委员会主席。

In the event that one or both parties are unable to select a mediator or are unable to make a selection within fifteen days from the date the OEDR or UEDR has provided the list, or if the two mediators who were selected are unable to select a third mediator or are unable to make a selection within fifteen days from the date they have been selected, the OEDR or UEDR will select [the third mediator].

如果一方或双方在调解司或调解委提供名单之日起 15 天内无法选出调解员,或者被选中的两位调解人在其当选之日起 15 天内无法选出调解员,调解司或调解委可选择第三名调解员。

In the event that the parties agree to have more than three mediators, the principles stipulated in the above paragraph (s) apply.

如果双方同意有三名以上的调解人，则适用上述规定的原则。

In all cases, the appointment of mediators must first be approved in writing by the mediators and the parties.

在所有情况下，调解员的任命须首先得到调解员和双方当事人的书面批准。

The OEDR or UEDR shall appoint the mediators within seven days from the date of receipt of the list of mediators which the parties wish to have appointed.

调解司或调解委应在收到当事人希望指定的调解人名单之日起 7 天内任命调解人。

Article 22. Disqualification and Recusal of a Mediator
第 22 条　调解员资格的取消

The parties have the right to object to a mediator, and the mediator himself has the right to disqualify himself if he is a relative or has an interest in or a dispute with one of the parties.

当事人有权向调解员提出异议，调解员本人有权以其作为当事人一方的亲属或与当事人一方有利害关系或争议的原因取消自己的调解员资格。

In the event that an appointed mediator disqualifies himself or has been objected to or is unable to perform his duties, a new mediator shall be selected and appointed. The procedure for selecting a new mediator is as provided in Article 21 of this law.

被指定的调解员不具有资格、被拒绝或不能履行职务的，应当选定新的调解员。新调解员的选择按照本法第 21 条。

Article 23. Conduct of Mediation
第 23 条　调解的进行

The mediation must be conducted within fifteen days from the date of appointment of the mediators. Mediation must be conducted in the presence of the parties or their authorized representatives.

调解应在调解员任命之日起 15 天内进行。调解应在当事人或当事人代表在场的情况下进行。

Each of the parties has the right to present the issues，data and evidence regarding the dispute to the mediators and to the other party at any time during the mediation.

一方有权在调解过程中随时向调解员和另一方提供争议相关的问题、数据和证据。

The mediators have the right to propose a solution to the parties at any time during the mediation.

调解员有权在调解过程中随时向当事人提出解决方案。

The mediation must be recorded in writing. The record of the mediation must contain the key contents as provided in Article 26 of this law.

调解必须以书面形式记录。调解记录应包含本法第 26 条规定的主要内容。

Article 24. End of Mediation
第 24 条　调解结束

Mediation will come to an end upon the occurrence of the following circumstances：

发生下列情况时，调解即告结束：

1. The parties are able to come to an agreement；

1. 双方当事人能达成协议；

2. One of the parties or both parties do not appear at the mediation without a reason；

2. 一方或双方当事人无故缺席调解；

3. The parties are unable to come to an agreement.

3. 双方当事人无法达成协议。

Article 25. The Parties are Unable to Reach an Agreement

第 25 条　双方当事人无法达成协议

In the event that the parties are unable to reach an agreement, the parties may decide to bring the dispute to the OEDR or UEDR for arbitration. A mediator who was involved in the mediation of a dispute cannot perform as arbitrator in the same dispute.

如果双方无法达成一致,可决定将纠纷提交调解司或调解委仲裁。参与调解纠纷的调解员不得在同一纠纷中担任仲裁员。

In the event that the parties do not wish to use the OEDR or UEDR for arbitration, they may bring their dispute to the people's courts.

如果双方当事人不愿通过调解司或调解委进行仲裁,则可将纠纷提交人民法院。

Article 26. Memorandum of Mediation

第 26 条　调解书

A memorandum of mediation shall have the following key contents:

调解书应具备下列主要内容:

1. The day, time, month, year, name, reference number of dispute and venue of mediation;

1. 调解的日期、时间、月份、年份、名称、编号和地点;

2. The name and surname of the mediator(s) and the memorandum-taker;

2. 调解员和登记员姓名;

3. The name and surname, age, occupation, nationality and address of the parties or representatives of the parties;

3. 当事人或当事人代表的姓名、年龄、职业、国籍和地址;

4. Key matters relating to the economic dispute;

4. 与经济纠纷有关的关键事项;

5. The settlement of the parties and proposals and matters presented by the parties;

5. 当事人的调解方案及其提出的意见和问题；

6. Each party's responsibilities in relation to service charges and other fees；

6. 各方当事人应承担的服务费用及其他费用；

7. The method of enforcement of the mediation settlement；

7. 调解的执行方式；

8. The signatures of the parties or their representatives，signatures of mediator(s) and the memorandum-taker，and the signature of the director general of the OEDR or the director of the UEDR where the mediation took place.

8. 各方当事人或其代表的签名、调解员和登记员的签名、调解司司长或调解地调解委委员长的签名。

Chapter 3

Arbitration

第三章　仲裁

Article 27. Appointment of Arbitration Panel

第 27 条　仲裁庭的任命

The arbitration panel must always have an odd number of arbitrators which may be three or more depending on the agreement of the parties.

仲裁庭人数应为奇数，根据当事人的协议，可以是三人或三人以上。

The selection of arbitrators must be in accordance with Article 21 of this law.

仲裁员的选择应符合本法第 21 条的规定。

Article 28. Disqualification and Recusal of an Arbitrator

第 28 条　仲裁员资格的取消

The disqualification and recusal of an arbitrator must be in accordance with Article 22 of this law.

仲裁员资格的取消应符合本法第 22 条的规定。

Article 29. Collection of Evidence
第 29 条 收集证据

In preparing for an arbitration, the arbitration panel must examine the petition, collect information and evidence, and hear the statements of involved witnesses.

在准备仲裁时,仲裁庭应审查申请书,收集信息和证据,并听取相关证人的陈述。

If necessary, the arbitration panel must collect information, evidence at site, and invite experts, involved witnesses to provide clarification or related documents to it.

如有必要,仲裁庭应现场收集信息和证据,并邀请专家和相关证人提供证词或相关文件。

Once the arbitration panel has collected complete information and evidence, the parties must be invited and be given one final opportunity to provide explanation and reasons, [and to] bring witnesses and evidence.

仲裁庭收集到完整的信息和证据后应邀请当事人,给予当事人最后的机会提供解释和理由,并提供证人和证据。

Article 30. Duration of Arbitration
第 30 条 仲裁期限

Generally, arbitration shall be completed within three months from the date the OEDR or UEDR accepted the petition. In the case of complicated disputes, the arbitration shall not exceed six months. In the case of particularly highly complicated disputes, the arbitration shall not exceed twelve months from the date of receipt of the petition.

一般来说,仲裁应在调解司或调解委受理申请之日起 3 个月内完成。

如遇复杂纠纷,仲裁不得超过 6 个月。在特别复杂的纠纷中,仲裁不得超过自收到申请之日起 12 个月。

In the event that the arbitration cannot be completed within the specified timeframe, the OEDR or UEDR shall notify the parties of the reason for the delay.

如果仲裁不能在规定时间内完成,调解司或调解委应通知双方当事人延误的原因。

Article 31. Measures to Protect the Interests of the Parties
第 31 条　保护当事人利益的措施

During the arbitration, the parties have the right to demand that the arbitration panel request the people's court to issue an order to seize, confiscate or take other measures to protect their interests. If such demand is reasonable, the arbitration panel will request the people's court to issue an order or take measures to protect the interests of the parties.

仲裁期间,当事人有权要求仲裁庭提请人民法院下达扣押、没收或者采取其他保全措施的命令。如果要求合理,仲裁庭可提请人民法院下达命令或采取措施,以保护当事人的利益。

The people's court must examine the request within fifteen days from the date of receipt of such request.

人民法院应当自收到请求之日起 15 天内审查请求。

Article 32. Right to Resolve the Dispute by the Parties
第 32 条　当事人解决纠纷的权利

After the arbitration panel has accepted the dispute of the parties, the parties still have the right to come to a settlement before an arbitral award is given. The settlement of the parties shall be made in writing and must be signed by the parties, the arbitration panel and the director general of the OEDR or the director of the UEDR where such arbitration takes place.

仲裁庭受理当事人的争议后,当事人仍有权在仲裁裁决作出前达成和解。当事人的和解应以书面形式做出,应有当事人、仲裁庭成员和调解司司长或仲裁地调解委委员长的签名。

The settlement of the parties prior to an arbitral award has the same force as an arbitral award.

仲裁裁决作出前,双方的和解与仲裁裁决具有同等效力。

Article 33. Timeframe for Issuing an Arbitral Award
第 33 条　颁发仲裁裁决的期限

An arbitral award must be issued not later than fifteen days from the date of completion of collection of information and evidence.

仲裁裁决必须在完成资料和证据收集之日起 15 天内发出。

Article 34. Principles Used in Arbitration
第 34 条　仲裁原则

The arbitral award must be within the scope of the petition of the parties. In the event that the arbitration panel cannot reach a unanimous decision, the award will be given based on a majority vote.

仲裁裁决应在当事人申请的范围内。如果仲裁庭无法做出一致决定,则应以多数表决为准。

The arbitral award must be read out in the presence of the parties and shall be effective from the date it is issued.

仲裁裁决应在当事人面前宣读,自发布之日起生效。

If, upon invitation, one of the parties does not appear without a reason, the arbitration panel will read out the award without the presence of such party and send such arbitral award to each party. The arbitral award will become effective from the date the parties have received such award.

如果一方当事人无故缺席，仲裁庭可在该方缺席的情况下宣读仲裁裁决，并将仲裁裁决送达各方当事人。仲裁裁决自送达当事人之日起生效。

Article 35. Contents of an Arbitral Award
第35条 仲裁裁决的内容

An arbitral award shall have the following key contents：

仲裁裁决应具备下列主要内容：

1. The day，time，month，year，name，reference number of dispute and venue of arbitration；

1. 仲裁的日期、时间、月份、年份、名称、编号和调解地点；

2. The name and surname of the arbitrators and the memorandum-taker；

2. 仲裁员和登记员姓名；

3. The name and surname，age，occupation，nationality and address of the parties or representatives of the parties；

3. 当事人或当事人代表的姓名、年龄、职业、国籍和地址；

4. The decision and grounds of the arbitration panel；

4. 仲裁庭的决定及理由；

5. The arbitral award and measures to enforce such award；

5. 仲裁裁决结果和执行措施；

6. Each party's responsibility in relation to service charges and other fees；

6. 各方当事人应承担的服务费用及其他费用；

7. The signatures of all arbitrator(s)，of the memorandum-taker and signature of the director general of the OEDR or the director of the UEDR where the arbitration took place.

7. 仲裁员和登记员的签名、调解司司长或仲裁地调解委委员长的签名。

Article 36. Amendment of an Arbitral Award

第36条　修改仲裁裁决

An arbitral award may be amended pursuant to the request of one or both parties as long as the mistake relates to calculation or printing errors which do not affect the substance of the arbitral award. The request to amend the arbitral award must be submitted to the OEDR or UEDR that issued the award within fifteen days from the date the parties become aware.

仲裁裁决可根据一方或双方的要求进行修改，只要错误涉及计算或印刷错误，而不影响仲裁裁决的实质内容。修改仲裁裁决的请求应在双方知悉之日起15天内提交给发布裁决的调解司或调解委。

The examination of the request to amend the arbitral award must be completed within fifteen days from the date of receipt of the request.

对修改仲裁裁决请求的审查必须在收到请求之日起15天内完成。

Part IV

Implementation of the Results of Economic Dispute Resolution

第四部分　经济纠纷解决结果的执行

Article 37. Results of Economic Dispute Resolution

第37条　经济纠纷解决结果

The results of economic dispute resolution consist of:

经济纠纷解决的结果包括：

1. Mediation settlement agreements;

1. 调解协议；

2. Settlement agreements before the issuance of arbitral awards;

2. 仲裁裁决发布前的和解协议；

3. Arbitral awards.

3. 仲裁裁决书。

Article 38. Obligations of the Parties

第 38 条 当事人义务

The parties have the obligation to implement the results of economic dispute resolution within fifteen days from the date the decision was issued or from the date the parties became aware of the arbitral award in the event that the parties were not present at the arbitration.

在决定发布之日起 15 天内，或在当事人未出席仲裁情况下，得知仲裁裁决之日起 15 天内，当事人有义务执行经济纠纷解决结果。

Article 39. Rights of the Disadvantaged Party

第 39 条 处于不利地位的当事人的权利

The party which is in a disadvantaged situation because of the non-implementation of the result of any economic dispute resolution has the right to request the people's court to issue a final judgment in order to ensure that the result of economic dispute resolution is enforced.

因经济纠纷解决结果未能执行而处于不利地位的当事人，有权请求人民法院作出终审判决，以确保经济纠纷解决的结果得到执行。

Article 40. Confirmation by the People's Court

第 40 条 人民法院确认

Upon receipt of the parties' request, the people's court must issue a final judgment not later than thirty days from the date of receipt of the request. The court will only verify whether the dispute resolution procedure was in compliance with existing regulations on economic dispute resolution and verify compliance with laws and regulations pertaining to stability, peace and social order. If the verification confirms compliance, the people's court will confirm the decision, which will then become enforceable. The parties do not have the right to appeal unless the confirmation of the people's court was a confirmation of a wrong settlement or the confirmation by the people's court is inconsistent with the settlement agreement between the parties or the arbitral award.

收到当事人的请求后,人民法院应当在收到请求之日起 30 天内作出终审判决。法院只会核查纠纷解决程序是否符合现行的经济纠纷解决条例,并核查是否遵守有关稳定、和平和社会秩序的法律法规。如经核查确认合规,人民法院将确认决定,然后执行。除非人民法院的确认是对错误的和解的确认,或者人民法院的确认不符合当事人之间的和解协议或仲裁裁决,双方无权上诉。

In the event that the people's court finds that the result of economic dispute resolution has violated the laws and regulations stipulated in the above paragraph, the court will not confirm the resolution. The parties have the right to request the OEDR or UEDR to re-examine the dispute or to file a claim in the people's court for adjudication.

人民法院认定经济纠纷解决结果违反前款法律法规的,法院不予确认。当事人有权要求调解司或调解委重新审理纠纷,或者向人民法院申请判决。

Article 41. Enforcement of Arbitral Awards of Foreign or International Economic Dispute Resolution Organisations

第 41 条　执行外国或国际经济纠纷解决机构的仲裁裁决

Upon receipt of an arbitral award of a foreign or international economic dispute resolution organisation, the OEDR must examine such award. If it is found that the arbitral award is within the scope of the rights and duties of the Lao PDR as a party to international treaties relating to economic dispute resolution and such award is consistent with the laws of the Lao PDR, the OEDR shall call on the parties to guide implementation.

在收到外国或国际经济纠纷解决组织的仲裁裁决后,调解司应审查该裁决。如果仲裁裁决在老挝作为经济纠纷解决国际条约当事人的权利和义务范围内,且符合老挝法律,调解司应敦促各方执行。

In the event that one of the parties does not implement the award, the OEDR must inform the other party. The party which is in a disadvantaged situation has the right to request the people's court of the Lao PDR to issue a final judgment to ensure that the arbitral award is enforced.

如果其中一方不执行裁决,调解司应通知另一方。处于不利地位的当事人有权请求老挝人民法院作出终审判决,以确保仲裁裁决的执行。

If it is found that the arbitral award of the foreign or international economic dispute resolution organisation conflicts with the laws of the Lao PDR, the OEDR shall reject and return the arbitral award together with the reasons for rejection to such organisation.

如果发现外国或国际经济纠纷解决机构的仲裁裁决与老挝法律冲突,调解司应拒绝该裁决,并将裁决和拒绝原因反馈回该组织。

Part V

Expenses Relating to Economic Dispute Resolution

第五部分 经济纠纷解决相关费用

Article 42. Expenses Relating to Economic Dispute Resolution

第 42 条 经济纠纷解决相关费用

Expenses relating to economic dispute resolution consist of:

经济纠纷解决相关费用包括:

1. The service charge for economic dispute resolution;

1. 经济纠纷解决服务费;

2. The fee.

2. 国家收费。

Article 43. Service Charge for Economic Dispute Resolution

第 43 条 经济纠纷解决服务费

The service charge refers to an expense incurred in relation to mediation or arbitration such as: honorarium of mediators or arbitrators, payment to experts and witnesses and other expenses relating to economic dispute resolution activities.

服务费指涉及调解或仲裁的费用,如调解员或仲裁员的酬金,向专家和证人支付的费用,以及与经济纠纷解决活动有关的其他费用。

In order to facilitate economic dispute resolution, one or both parties shall make a deposit for services with the OEDR or UEDR in a certain amount as specified in the regulations. In the event that such deposit is not sufficient, an additional amount must be deposited. In the event that the deposit exceeds the required amount, the balance must be returned to the person making the deposit.

为便于解决经济纠纷,一方或双方应按规定向调解司或调解委缴纳一定金额的保证金。保证金多退少补。

In the event that the resolution of an economic dispute ends without a settlement or arbitral award because the parties did not appear, the parties do not have the right to demand the return of the deposit made by them with the OEDR or UEDR and spent on the service. The party that did not appear on the invitation of the OEDR or UEDR without giving a reason must be responsible.

如因当事人未出席而无法达成和解或仲裁裁决,当事人无权要求调解司或调解委退还保证金。收到调解司或调解委邀请而无故缺席的一方应对此承担责任。

Details regarding expenditures relating to services are determined separately.

有关服务的支出详情另行确定。

Article 44. Fee
第 44 条　国家收费

The fee refers to an obligation of the user of economic dispute resolution which should be paid to the State budget.

国家收费是经济纠纷解决措施使用者应支付国家预算的义务。

The collection of the fee must be as follows：

费用收取如下：

For a dispute with a value under twenty million Kip，the fee is two hundred thousand Kip；

对于价值低于 2000 万(含 2000 万)基普的纠纷,费用为 20 万基普；

For a dispute with a value between twenty million and one Kip to forty million Kip，the fee is four hundred thousand Kip；

对于价值在 2000 万到 4000 万(含 4000 万)基普之间的纠纷,费用为 40 万基普；

For a dispute with a value between forty million and one Kip to seventy million Kip，the fee is six hundred thousand Kip；

对于价值在 4000 万到 7000 万(含 7000 万)基普之间的纠纷,费用为 60 万基普；

For a dispute with a value between seventy million and one Kip to one hundred million Kip，the fee is eight hundred thousand Kip；

对于价值在 7000 万到 1 亿(含 1 亿)基普之间的纠纷,费用为 80 万基普；

For a dispute with a value higher than one hundred million Kip，the fee is one million Kip.

对于价值超过 1 亿基普的纠纷,费用为 100 万基普。

If the fee is in a foreign currency，the fee has to be converted into Kip currency according to the State bank exchange rate on that day.

如果费用是外币,则应根据当天的国家银行汇率转换为基普。

The payment of the fee by the parties must be made after the completion of economic dispute resolution by the OEDR or UEDR.

各方应在调解司或调解委解决经济纠纷后支付费用。

In the case of arbitration，as a rule，the party which loses the case shall pay the fee but the arbitration panel may determine that both parties pay the fee jointly as appropriate.

一般情况下,在仲裁案件中失败的当事人应承担费用,但仲裁庭可以决定双方当事人共同承担费用。

Part VI

Administration and Inspections of Economic Dispute Resolution
第六部分　经济纠纷解决的管理和检查

Article 45. Organisation Responsible for the Administration of Economic Dispute Resolution

第 45 条　负责经济纠纷解决管理的组织

The organisation responsible for the administration of economic dispute resolution consists of：

负责经济纠纷解决管理的组织包括：

The Ministry of Justice；

司法部；

Justice offices in the provinces, cities and special zones.

各省、市、特区的司法机关。

Article 46. Rights and Duties of the Ministry of Justice

第 46 条　司法部的权利和义务

In administering economic dispute resolution, the Ministry of Justice has the following rights and duties：

在管理经济纠纷解决方面,司法部有下列权利和义务：

1. To study and prepare strategic plans, programs, laws and regulations regarding economic dispute resolution for submission to the government for consideration and approval；

1. 研究制定解决经济纠纷的战略计划、方案、法律、法规,提交政府审议批准；

2. To issue decisions, orders, instructions and notifications regarding economic dispute resolution；

2. 发布关于解决经济纠纷的决定、命令、指示和通知；

3. To supervise and administer economic dispute resolution according to a vertical line of reporting by collaborating with relevant sectors and local administrations；

3. 与有关部门和地方管理机构合作，按照垂直报告的形式监督管理经济纠纷解决；

4. To administer the organisation and budget，and to inspect the performance，of the OEDR；

4. 管理组织和预算，并考评调解司的绩效；

5. To amend，suspend，cancel and nullify orders，notifications or other legal acts issued by the OEDR and UEDR or to propose to other relevant organisations that they cancel legal acts of other sectors that conflict with the laws and regulations relating to economic dispute resolution；

5. 修改、暂停、取消和撤销由调解司和调解委发布的命令、通知或其他法律行为，或向其他相关组织提出取消与解决经济纠纷相关的法律法规抵触的法律行为；

6. To train and upgrade the knowledge，competence，behaviour，ethics，technical skills and working methods of staff，mediators and arbitrators of the OEDR and UEDR；

6. 培养与提升调解司和调解委工作人员、调解员和仲裁员的知识、能力、行为、道德、技能和工作方法；

7. To propose to the Prime Minister to appoint，remove or transfer the director general of the OEDR in coordination with relevant sectors；

7. 提请总理与相关部门协调，任命、免除或调动调解司司长；

8. To appoint，remove or transfer the deputy director general of the OEDR and the deputy director of a UEDR in coordination with relevant sectors；

8. 与相关部门协调，任命、免除或调动调解司副司长和调解委副委员长；

9. To appoint or remove mediators or arbitrators based on the recommendation of the OEDR；

9. 根据调解司的建议任命或免除调解员或仲裁员；

10. To provide policies to staff who have outstanding achievements and apply disciplinary measures against those who have committed wrongful acts in economic dispute resolution in coordination with relevant sectors；

10. 与相关部门协调，奖励在经济纠纷解决中工作突出的人员，处分有不法行为的人员；

11. To liaise with foreign countries in the area of economic dispute resolution；

11. 在经济纠纷解决方面与外国进行联络；

12. To summarize，evaluate and report on economic dispute resolution activities to the government；

12. 对经济纠纷解决活动进行总结、评价，并向政府报告；

13. To exercise such other rights and perform such other duties as provided in the laws and regulations.

13. 依照法律法规行使其他权利，履行其他职责。

Article 47. Rights and Duties of Justice Offices in Provinces, Cities and Special Zones

第 47 条　省、市、特区司法机关的权利与义务

In administering economic dispute resolution，the Justice Office in provinces，cities and special zones has the following rights and duties：

在管理经济纠纷解决方面，省、市、特区司法机关有下列权利与义务：

1. To implement strategic plans，programs，laws and regulations regarding economic dispute resolution issued by the higher

authority；

1. 执行上级下达的解决经济纠纷的战略计划、方案、法律、法规；

2. To supervise the UEDR in the preparation and implementation of plans regarding economic dispute resolution in its locality；

2. 监督调解委制定实施本地区经济纠纷解决方案；

3. To administer the organisation，the budget，and inspect the performance of the UEDR；

3. 管理组织、预算，考评调解委的绩效；

4. To make proposals to the Ministry of Justice on the establishment and improvement of the office，and on the appointment，removal and transfer of the director and deputy director of the UEDR in coordination with the OEDR and relevant sectors；

4. 提请司法部设立和完善机构，并与调解司及相关部门协调，任命、免除或调动调解委的委员长和副委员长；

5. To supervise the handling of people's complaints in relation to economic dispute resolution by the UEDR；

5. 监督调解委处理与经济纠纷有关的投诉；

6. To reward UEDR staff who have outstanding performance and take disciplinary action against those who have committed a wrongful act in economic dispute resolution in coordination with relevant sectors；

6. 与相关部门协调，奖励在经济纠纷解决中工作突出的调解委人员，处分有不法行为的人员；

7. To summarize，evaluate and report on the activities of the UEDR to the Ministry of Justice；and

7. 对调解委的活动进行总结、评价，并向司法部报告；以及

8. To exercise such other rights and perform such other duties in accordance with the laws and regulations.

8. 依照法律法规行使其他权利，履行其他职责。

Article 48. Organisation Responsible for Inspection of Economic Dispute Resolution

第 48 条　负责经济纠纷解决审查的组织

The organisation responsible for the inspection of economic dispute resolution is the same as the organisation responsible for administration as provided in Article 45 of this law.

负责经济纠纷解决审查的组织与本法第 45 条规定的负责经济纠纷解决管理的组织相同。

Article 49. Rights and Duties of the Ministry of Justice in Relation to Inspection

第 49 条　司法部在审查时的权利和义务

In the inspection of the activities and performance of economic dispute resolution, the Ministry of Justice has the following rights and duties:

在审查经济纠纷解决活动和执行情况时,司法部有下列权利和义务:

1. To inspect the implementation of strategic plans, programs, laws and regulations and to inspect the state of economic dispute resolution by the OEDR;

1. 审查调解司战略计划、方案、法律、法规执行情况以及经济纠纷解决情况;

2. To inspect people's complaints regarding economic dispute resolution by the OEDR;

2. 审查人民对调解司解决经济纠纷的投诉;

3. To inspect the administration of UEDRs by the Justice Offices;

3. 审查司法机关对调解委的管理;

4. To exercise such other rights and perform such other duties as provided in the laws and regulations.

4. 依照法律法规行使其他权利,履行其他职责。

Article 50. Rights and Duties of the Justice Offices in relation to Inspection

第 50 条 司法机关在审查时的权利和义务

In the inspection of the performance of duties by the UEDR，the Justice Office in the provinces，cities and special zones has the following rights and duties：

在审查调解委履职情况时，省、市、特区司法机关有下列权利和义务：

1. To inspect the activities and work of the UEDR in implementing the strategic plans，programs，laws and regulations and the state of economic dispute resolution；

1. 审查调解委战略计划、方案、法律、法规活动和工作，以及经济纠纷解决情况；

2. To inspect people's complaints regarding economic dispute resolution by the UEDR；

2. 审查人民对调解委解决经济纠纷的投诉；

3. To exercise such other rights and perform such other duties as provided in the laws and regulations.

3. 依照法律法规行使其他权利，履行其他职责。

Part VII
Policies towards Persons with Outstanding Performance and Measures Against Offenders
第七部分　奖惩措施

Article 51. Policies towards Persons with Outstanding Performance

第 51 条 对表现突出人员的奖励措施

Mediators，arbitrators，and the staff of the OEDR or UEDR who have outstanding performance will be rewarded or policies will be granted as appropriate.

对表现突出的调解员、仲裁员，以及调解司或调解委工作人员，可酌情予以奖励或表彰。

Article 52. Measures Against Offenders
第 52 条　对不法人员的惩罚措施

A member of the staff of the OEDR or UEDR who has committed a wrongdoing in the performance of his duties such as: abuse of position, abuse of power and taking bribes, will be re-educated, will be subject to disciplinary measures or will be punished in accordance with the laws and regulations.

仲裁司或仲裁委的工作人员在履职时实施不法行为,如滥用职权、收受贿赂,应对其实施再教育和纪律处分,或依法处罚。

A mediator or arbitrator who has intentionally committed a wrongdoing in the performance of his duties such as: abuse of position, taking bribes and others will be re-educated. In the event of serious offences, the mediator or arbitrator will be removed from the list of mediators or arbitrators of the OEDR or will be punished in accordance with the laws and regulations.

调解员或仲裁员在履职时蓄意违法,如滥用职权、收受贿赂和实施其他犯罪的,应对其实施再教育。对于情节严重的,应将该调解员或仲裁员从调解司名单上除名,或依法处罚。

One or both parties who do not extend co-operation or who violate the result of any economic dispute resolution which is final shall be re-educated or punished in accordance with the law and regulations.

对不合作或者违反经济纠纷解决最终结果的一方或者双方,应对其实施再教育,或依法处罚。

Part VIII
Budget, Symbol and Seal
第八部分　预算、标识和印章

Article 53. Budget
第 53 条　预算

The budget used in the activities and work of the OEDR and UEDR is as follows:

调解司和调解委活动和工作所使用的预算如下：

The budget of the OEDR is determined by the Ministry of Justice；

调解司的预算由司法部决定；

The budget of UEDR is determined by the province，city or special zone where the UEDR is located.

调解委的预算由调解委所在的省、市、特区决定。

Article 54. Symbol
第 54 条　标识

The symbol of the OEDR and UEDR is a picture of a scale within a circle.

调解司和调解委的标识是天平，天平外有一个圆圈。

Article 55. Seal
第 55 条　印章

The OEDR and UEDR have their own seal for official use.

调解司和调解委有各自的官方印章。

Part IX
Final Provisions
第九部分　最后条款

Article 56. Implementation
第 56 条　执行

The government of the Lao People's Democratic Republic shall implement this law.

由老挝人民民主共和国政府执行本法。

Article 57. Effectiveness
第 57 条　效力

This law enters into force sixty days after the date of the

promulgating decree issued by the President of the Lao People's Democratic Republic.

本法自老挝人民民主共和国主席颁布主席令之日起 60 天后生效。

Any provisions and regulations which contradict this law shall be null and void.

违反本法的任何规定和条例无效。

Vientiane，19 May 2005

2005 年 5 月 19 日于万象

President of the National Assembly

国会主席

[Seal and Signature]

[盖章签名]

Samane VIGNAKET

沙曼·维亚吉

第七节　缅甸商事仲裁法英汉对照

ARBITRATION　LAW

《仲裁法》

The Pyidaungsu Hluttaw Law No. 5/2016

缅甸联邦议会第 5/2016 号法案

The 10th Waning Day of Nadaw 1377 ME

缅历 9 月 25 日

5th January，2016

公历 2016 年 1 月 5 日

The Pyidaungsu Hluttaw hereby enacts the following Law：

缅甸联邦议会兹立本法如下：

Chapter 1

Title, Scope of Application and Definition
第一章　名称、适用范围和定义

Title

名称

1. This Law shall be called the Arbitration Law.

    本法名为《仲裁法》。

Scope of Application

适用范围

2. （a） Subject to sub-section （b）, an Arbitration Agreement whether executed in the State or in any other country, the place where legal implementation of arbitration is in the State, the provisions of this Law shall be applicable.

    （a）除（b）款另有规定外,无论仲裁协议在本国或别国签署,只要仲裁在本国执行的,应适用本法的规定。

    （b） If the place of arbitration is at any other country, which is apart from the State, or place of arbitration is not specified or not determined, section 10,11,30,31 and Chapter 10, shall be applicable.

    （b）仲裁地不在本国的,或者未规定、确定仲裁地的,应适用第 10 条、第 11 条、第 30 条、第 31 条和第十章。

    （c） If any other existing law in force in the State is restricted on the settlement of dispute by means of arbitration, the provisions of this Law shall not be binding upon such law.

    （c）本国任何其他现行法律对仲裁解决纠纷有限制的,本法不受该法约束。

Definitions

定义

3. The expressions contained in this law shall have the same meaning given hereunder：

本法所载用语含义如下：

(a) "State" means the Republic of the Union of Myanmar；

(a) "本国"是指缅甸联邦共和国；

(b) "arbitration agreement" means an agreement in writing by the parties to submit to arbitration all or certain disputes which arise or which may arise between them in respect of legal relationship, whether contractual or not；

(b) "仲裁协议"是指各方当事人同意将法律关系中产生或可能产生的所有或某些争议提交仲裁解决的书面协议，该协议是否在合同中规定不影响仲裁协议的成立；

(c) "arbitration" means any arbitration administered by an arbitrator or arbitral tribunal；

(c) "仲裁"是指由仲裁员或仲裁庭管理的任何仲裁；

(d) "Arbitrator" means a person or a panel of arbitrators appointed with the consent of the parties to administer the disputes by arbitration；

(d) "仲裁员"是指经当事人同意指定的、通过仲裁解决纠纷的一名仲裁员或一组仲裁员；

(e) "award" means a decision of the arbitral tribunal and includes any interim award；

(e) "裁决"是指仲裁庭的裁决，包括任何临时裁决；

(f) "arbitral tribunal" means a sole arbitrator or a panel of arbitrators；

(f) "仲裁庭"是指一名独任仲裁员或一组仲裁员；

(g) "Court" means the District Court or High Court of the State or Region of original jurisdiction, having jurisdiction to decide the questions in dispute of the arbitration as if they are exercising its original civil jurisdiction；

（g）"法院"是指有初审管辖权的国家或地区的地方法院或高级法院，其具有仲裁解决纠纷的管辖权，如同行使初审民事管辖权；

（h）"domestic arbitration" is an arbitration which is not an international arbitration；

（h）"国内仲裁"是指非国际仲裁的仲裁；

（i）"international arbitration" means：

（i）"国际仲裁"定义如下：

　　（1）if, at the time of execution of the arbitration agreement，if one of the party's place of business and trading activity is situated in another country other than Myanmar；or

　　（1）执行仲裁协议时，一方的商贸活动地在缅甸以外的国家的；或

　　（2）if the place stated in the arbitration agreement or the place to conduct arbitration in accordance with the arbitration agreement is situated outside the country in which the parties have their place of business；or

　　（2）仲裁协议规定地点或根据仲裁协议执行仲裁的地点在国外，且为各方营业地的；或

　　（3）if, among the commercially related business obligations，any place where a substantial part of the obligations is to be performed or the closest place connected to the subject matter of the dispute is situated outside the country in which the parties have their place of business；or

　　（3）相关商业义务中，履行主体义务的地点或与争议标的物联系最密切的地点位于国外，且为各方营业地的；或

　　（4）if the parties of the arbitration agreement have expressly agreed that the subject matter relates to more than one country；such arbitration shall mean International

Arbitration.

（4）仲裁协议各方当事人明确约定标的物涉及多个国家的；该仲裁为国际仲裁。

Explanatory note：

注：

1. If the place of business of a party is more than one place，the place of business of the party shall be that which is the closest to the place of execution of the arbitration agreement；

1. 一方当事人营业地多于一个地方的，该方营业地为距离仲裁协议执行地最近的地方；

2. If a party does not have a place of business，reference to his place of business shall be its permanent residing place.

2. 当事人无营业地的，其营业地应当为其永久居住地。

（j）"New York Convention" means the convention relating to the Recognition and Enforcement of Foreign Arbitral Awards adopted by the United Nations Diplomatic Conference held on 1958 June 10 at New York；

（j）《纽约公约》是指 1958 年 6 月 10 日在纽约举行的联合国外交会议通过的《承认及执行外国仲裁裁决公约》。

（k）"foreign arbitral award" means an award made in the territory of the New York Convention member states other than the State in accordance with the arbitration agreement；

（k）"外国仲裁裁决"是指根据仲裁协议，在本国以外的《纽约公约》缔约国领土内作出的裁决；

（l）"place of arbitration" means a place where the arbitration is administered legally which is determined by the persons in dispute of an arbitration agreement or a person authorized by the person in dispute or arbitral tribunal or arbitration institution；

（l）"仲裁地"是指仲裁协议当事人确定的依法进行仲裁的地点，或者当事人、仲裁庭或仲裁机构授权的人确定的依法进行仲裁的地点；

（m）"party" means a party to an arbitration agreement；and

（m）"当事人"是指仲裁协议的当事人；

（n）"legal representative" means a person who in law represents the estate of a deceased person，and includes any person who intermeddles with the estate of the deceased，and，where a party acts in a representative character，the person on whom the estate devolves on the death of the party so acting.

（n）"法定代理人"是指在法律上代理死者遗产的人，包括任何有权处理死者遗产的人，以及行使代理人职责的一方死亡时继承该方遗产的人。

Chapter 2
Aim
第二章　宗旨

4. Aims of this Law are as follows：

本法宗旨如下：

（a）to settle domestic commercial disputes and international commercial disputes in a fair and effective manner；

（a）以公平、有效的方式解决国内商事纠纷和国际商事纠纷；

（b）to settle disputes by means of arbitration，and to recognize and enforce the foreign award；and

（b）以仲裁方式解决纠纷，承认并执行外国裁决；以及

（c）to encourage settlement of disputes by means of arbitration.

（c）鼓励以仲裁方式解决纠纷。

Chapter 3
General Principles
第三章　总则

Receipt of written communications

收到书面信件

5.（a）Unless otherwise agreed by the parties：

（a）除非当事人另有约定：

（1）any written communication is deemed to have been received on the date of delivered, if it is delivered to the addressee personally or if it is delivered at his place of business, habitual residence, or mailing address；

（1）书面通信亲自交给收件人的,或送至其营业地、惯常居住地或邮寄地址的,交付之日起即被视为送达；

（2）if none of those described in subsection（1）can be found after making a reasonable inquiry, a written communication is deemed to have been received on the day it is so delivered, if it is sent to the addressee's last-known place of business, habitual residence, or mailing address by registered letter or any other means which provides a record of the attempt to deliver it.

（2）经合理调查无法确认第 1 项所述情况的,如果有记录表明以挂号信或任何其他方式将书面通信送至收件人新近营业地、居住地或邮寄地址的,交付之日起即被视为送达。

（b）The provisions of this article do not apply to communications in court proceedings.

（b）本条规定不适用于法院程序中的通讯送达。

Objection and Waiver of right to object

放弃异议权

6.（a）A party who is involving in the arbitration proceeding or on processing the arbitration shall object without undue delay or if a time is provided by this Law or arbitration agreement or arbitral tribunal，within such period of time：

（a）参与仲裁程序或仲裁进行时的当事人,应毫不拖延地提出反对,或者在本法、仲裁协议或仲裁庭规定的时间内提出下列反对：

（1）Arbitral tribunal has no jurisdiction；

（1）仲裁庭没有管辖权；

（2）Procedural defect in arbitration process；

（2）仲裁程序存在缺陷；

（3）Failure to comply with the arbitration agreement or provisions of this Law；

（3）违反仲裁协议或本法规定；

（4）Detrimental impact on the arbitral tribunal or arbitration due to procedural defect.

（4）程序缺陷对仲裁庭或仲裁产生不利影响。

（b）proceed with the arbitration without stating his objection under subsection （a），shall be deemed to have waived his right to object.

（b）未根据(a)款提出异议而进行仲裁的,应被视为放弃异议权。

Extent of court intervention

法院介入程度

7. Notwithstanding anything contained in any other law for time being in force，in matters governed by this Law，no court shall intervene except where so provided in this Law.

尽管存在其他有效法律,法院不得根据本法以外的法律对本法所规定的事项进行干预。

Administrative assistance

行政协助

8. The parties, or the arbitration tribunal with the agreement of the parties, may make arrangements to acquire assistance from any suitable institution or person to facilitate administration of the arbitral process.

经各方当事人同意,当事人或仲裁庭可做出安排,从合适的机构或个人获得协助,以促进仲裁程序的进行。

Chapter 4
Arbitration Agreement
第四章　仲裁协议

9. (a) Relating with the arbitration agreement, writing agreement under section 3, subsection (b) means:

(a) 关于仲裁协议,第 3 条(b)款所述书面协议是指:

(1) an arbitration agreement shall be deemed in writing if it is signed by the parties;

(1) 仲裁协议由当事人签字的,应视为书面协议;

(2) if the information contained in electronic communication is accessible so as to be useable for subsequent reference, such arbitration agreement by means of electronic communication shall be deemed in writing.

(2) 如电子通讯所载资料可被查阅,以供日后参考,则以电子通讯方式达成的仲裁协议应视为书面协议。

(b) An arbitration agreement may be in the form of an arbitration clause in a contract or in the form of a separate agreement.

(b) 仲裁协议可以是合同中的仲裁条款,也可以是独立的仲裁协议。

Refer to Arbitration and stay of suit before court

提请仲裁和诉讼中止

10. (a) a court before which an action is brought in a matter which is the subject of an arbitration agreement shall, if a party so requests not later than when submitting his written statement on the substance of the dispute, refer the parties to arbitration unless it finds that the agreement is null and void, inoperative or incapable of being performed;

(a) 如果向法院提起的诉讼的争议是仲裁协议的标的,且一方当事人在不迟于就争议实体提出第一次申述时要求仲裁,法院应让当事各方付诸仲裁,除非法院认为仲裁协议无效、失效或不能执行。

(b) where an action referred to in subsection (a) of this article, arbitral proceedings may nevertheless be commenced or continued, and an award may be made, while the issue is pending before the court;

(b) 当一个涉及本条(a)款的案件被提起诉讼,在争议处于待决状态时,仲裁程序仍然可以被启动或继续,也可以做出仲裁裁决。

(c) If the court refuses to refer the parties to arbitration, any decision making before filing a suit relating to any matter of the arbitration contained in the arbitration agreement, shall not effect to the suit;

(c) 法院拒绝当事人提交仲裁的,与仲裁协议所载事项有关的、在诉讼前作出的任何决定,均不影响诉讼;

(d) the court shall order to stay the suit before the court, if the court refers the parties to arbitration;

(d) 如果法院将当事人提交仲裁,法院应在法庭上命令;

(e) No appeal shall be allowed against the court decision which refers to arbitration under subsection (a);

(e) 对于(a)款所述提交仲裁的法院决定,不得上诉;

（f）Appeal shall be allowed relating to the court decision refusing to refer to the arbitration.

（f）对于法院拒绝提交仲裁的决定，应予上诉。

Power of the Court to intervene in Arbitration

法院干预仲裁的权力

11.（a）Unless otherwise agreed by the parties，if a party requests the court，the court shall have power to make decision as its own jurisdiction for：

（a）除当事人另有约定外，当事人请求法院的，法院有权做出下列决定：

（1）taking evidence；

（1）取证；

（2）the preservation any evidence；

（2）保存证据；

（3）pass an order related to the property in disputes in arbitration or any property which is related to the subject-matter of the dispute；

（3）批准与仲裁纠纷或与标的财产有关的命令；

（4）inspection，taking photo for evidence，preservation and seizure of the property which is related to the dispute；

（4）对争议有关的财产进行检查、拍照、保存和扣押；

（5）samples to be taken from，or any observation to be made of or experiment conducted upon，any property which is or forms part of the subject-matter of the dispute；

（5）对属于或构成争议标的一部分的财产取样，或进行观察、实验；

（6）allow to enter in the premises owned by or under the control of the parties to disputes for the purpose of above mentions matters；

(6) 允许进入上述事项相关的争议当事人所有或者控制的处所；

(7) sale of any property which is the subject-matter of the dispute；

(7) 出售作为纠纷标的的财产；

(8) an interim injunction or appointment of a receiver.

(8) 下达临时禁令或指定接管人。

(b) If the interim measure is needed urgently in arbitration，the court may pass an order relating to preservation of evidence and related properties upon the application of a party as require.

(b) 如果仲裁中迫切需要采取临时措施，法院可根据当事人的请求，下达保全证据和相关财产的命令。

(c) If the interim measure is not needed urgently，upon the application of a party in arbitration，the court shall deal such matter after delivering a notice to the other parties and arbitral tribunal and with the approval of the arbitration tribunal or with the written consent of the other party.

(c) 如不需要采取临时措施，收到仲裁一方当事人申请时，法院应向另一方和仲裁庭发出通知，经仲裁庭批准或征得另一方的书面同意后处理该事项。

(d) The court shall only deal with the matters which the authorized person of the parties or arbitral tribunal or arbitral institution or other institution has no authority to do or not able to handle effectively.

(d) 法院只能处理当事人、仲裁庭、仲裁机构或其他机构的授权人无权或不能有效处理的事项。

(e) An order made by the court shall cease to have effect in whole or in part if the arbitral tribunal makes an order which expressly relates to the order under subsection (a).

(e) 如果仲裁庭做出与(a)款明确相关的命令,则法院下达的命令全部或部分失效。

Chapter 5
Composition of Arbitral Tribunal
第五章　仲裁庭的组成

Number of arbitrators

仲裁员数量

12. (a) The parties are free to determine the number of arbitrators. However, if the number of arbitrator is more than one, it shall not be an even number.

(a) 当事双方可自由决定仲裁员数量。但在仲裁员多于一人的情况下,仲裁员人数不能为偶数。

(b) Failing such determination as mentioned in subsection (a), the number of arbitrator shall be one.

(b) 如果没有(a)款所述决定,则仲裁员人数应为一人。

Appointment of arbitrators

仲裁员的指定

13. (a) Unless otherwise agreed by the parties, any nationality may act as an arbitrator.

(a) 除非双方另有约定,任何国籍人员均可担任仲裁员。

(b) The parties are free to agree on a procedure of appointing the arbitrator or arbitrators, subject to the provisions of subsection (e) of this article.

(b) 各方当事人有权在符合本条(e)款规定的情况下,对指定仲裁员的程序自行达成一致。

(c) Where, an appointment procedure agreed upon by the

parties, the appointment has to be made in accordance with such procedure. If a party fails to appoint or if both parties or the two arbitrators fail to agree on the third arbitrator, entrusted third party or an institution fails to perform any function and if the appointment procedure is not provided in the arbitration agreement, any party may request the Chief Justice or any person/institution selected by him to take the necessary measure.

(c) 当事人约定任命程序的,应按该程序进行。当事人不能指定的,双方当事人或仲裁员未能就任命第三方仲裁员达成协议的,被委托的第三方或机构不履行其职能的,且仲裁协议中没有规定任命程序的,任何一方可以请求首席法官或由他选定的人士/机构采取必要的措施。

(d) Failing such agreement in subsection (b),

(d) 如未能达成(b)款所述协议,

(1) in an arbitration with three arbitrators, each party shall appoint one arbitrator, and the two arbitrators thus appointed shall choose the third arbitrator who will act as the presiding arbitrator of the arbitral tribunal. If a party fails to appoint the arbitrator within thirty days of receipt of a request to do so from the other party, or if the two arbitrators fail to agree on the third arbitrator within thirty days of their appointment, the appointment shall be made, upon request of a party, by the Chief Justice or any person/institution selected by the Chief Justice.

(1) 在有三名仲裁员的仲裁中,每方都应任命一名仲裁员,并由被任命的两名仲裁员选择担任仲裁庭首席仲裁员的第三名仲裁员。如果一方当事人在收到另一方请求的 30 日内未指定仲裁员,或者两名仲裁员在接受任命后 30 日内未能就第三名仲裁员的任命达成一致,经一方请求,应由首席法官或由他选定的人士/机构任命第三名仲裁员。

(2) in an arbitration with a sole arbitrator，the Chief Justice or any person/institution selected by him shall，upon request of a party，appoint the sole arbitrator if a party fails to appoint the sole arbitrator within thirty days of receipt of a request to do so from the other party.

(2) 在由独任仲裁员进行的仲裁中,如果一方当事人在收到另一方请求的 30 日内未指定仲裁员,经一方请求,应由首席法官或由他选定的人士/机构任命独任仲裁员。

(e) The Chief Justice or any person/institution selected by him，in appointing an arbitrator，shall have due regard to the qualifications required of the arbitrator by the agreement of the parties and such considerations as being an independent and impartial arbitrator.

(e) 首席法官或其选定的人士/机构在任命仲裁员时,应适当考虑当事人协议规定的仲裁员所需的资格,以及仲裁员的独立和公正。

(f) The Chief Justice or any person/institution selected by him may perform appropriate functions entrusted to him by subsections (c) and (d) of this section.

(f) 首席法官或其选定的人士/机构可合理行使本条(c)款和(d)款所述职能。

(g) In appointing a sole or third arbitrator for international arbitration in which parties are of different nationalities，the Chief Justice or any person/institution selected by him may take into account appointing an arbitrator of a nationality other than those of the parties.

(g) 首席法官或其选定的人士/机构在任命国际仲裁中的独任仲

裁员或第三名仲裁员时,可考虑委任国籍与当事人不同的仲裁员。

(h) A decision on a matter entrusted to the Chief Justice or any person/institution selected by him by subsections (c) and (d) of this section shall be subject to no appeal.

(h) 对本条(c)款和(d)款所述的,委托首席法官或其选定的人士/机构做出的决定,不得上诉。

Explanation Notes: The Chief Justice mentioned in this section refers to the Chief Justice of the High Court of the Region or High Court of the State within their jurisdiction for domestic arbitration and refers to the Chief Justice of the Union for the international arbitration.

注:本条所述首席法官,是指国内仲裁中有管辖权的区高级法院或国家高级法院的首席法官,并指国际仲裁委员会的首席法官。

Grounds for challenge for arbitrator

申请仲裁员回避

14. (a) When a person is approached in connection with his possible appointment as an arbitrator, he shall disclose any circumstances likely to give rise to justifiable doubts as to his impartiality or independence.

(a) 可能被指定为仲裁员的人,应在与此指定有关的洽谈中披露可能对其公正性和独立性产生有正当理由怀疑的任何情况。

(b) If an arbitrator did not inform such circumstances to the parties as mentioned in subsection (a), from the time of his appointment and throughout the arbitral proceedings, he shall disclose any such circumstances to the parties without delay.

(b) 如果仲裁员没有如(a)款所述披露此等情况,则仲裁员从被指定之时起以至整个仲裁程序过程中，应不迟延地向各方当事人陈述此类情况。

(c) An arbitrator may be challenged only if：

(c) 只有在下列情况才能申请仲裁员回避：

    (1) circumstances exist that give rise to justifiable doubts as to his impartiality or independence，or

    (1) 存在对仲裁员公正性或独立性有合理怀疑的情况，或

    (2) he does not possess qualifications agreed to by the parties.

    (2) 仲裁员不被双方当事人同意。

(d) A party may challenge an arbitrator appointed by him，or in whose appointment he has participated，only for reasons of which he becomes aware after the appointment has been made.

(d) 只有是任命做出之后才意识到的原因，一方当事人才可以申请其指定的，或其参与指定的仲裁员回避。

Challenge procedure

申请回避程序

15. (a) The parties are free to agree on a procedure for challenging an arbitrator.

(a) 当事人可以自行商定仲裁员回避的程序。

(b) Failing such agreement in subsection (a)，a party who intends to challenge an arbitrator shall，within fifteen days after becoming aware of the constitution of the arbitral tribunal or after becoming aware of any circumstance referred to in the subsection 14 (c)，send a written statement of the reasons for the challenge to the arbitral tribunal.

(b) 如果未达成本款(a)条的约定，拟要求仲裁员回避的一方当事人应在他得知仲裁庭组成或得知第 14 条(c)款所列的任何情

事起 15 天内，以书面形式向仲裁庭阐明回避的理由。

（c） Unless the challenged arbitrator per subsection （b）
withdraws from his office or the other party agrees to the
challenge，the arbitral tribunal shall decide on the
challenge.

（c）除非（b）款中所述被申请回避的仲裁员辞职或对方当事人同
意回避申请，则仲裁庭应对申请做出决定。

（d） If a challenge under the procedure agreed upon by the
parties is not successful or arbitral tribunal decides subject
to the subsection （c） as there is no reason to challenge
upon the procedure of subsection （b），the party who
intends to challenge may apply to the court to decide upon
the challenge within 30 days from the date of such decision
is made.

（d）如果当事人约定中的申请失败，或仲裁庭在无（b）款所述理由
时按照（c）款做出决定，提出回避申请的一方可在该决定做出
之日起 30 日内向法院提出申请。

（e） Although the application under subsection （d） is pending in
the court，the arbitral tribunal shall continue the arbitral
proceedings and make an award.

（e）根据（d）款向法院提出的申请待决时，仲裁庭可继续进行仲裁
程序并作出裁决。

（f） If the arbitral award has been set aside subsequent to
application made under subsection （d），the Court may
decide whether the challenged arbitrator is entitled to any
fees or not.

（f）如果仲裁裁决经（d）款所述申请被撤销，则法院可以决定被申
请回避的仲裁员是否有权收取费用。

Termination of the mandate of arbitrator and appointment of

substitute arbitrator

终止仲裁员委任和任命替补仲裁员

16. (a) The mandate of an arbitrator shall terminate if:

(a) 如果出现下列情况,仲裁员的委任即告终止:

(1) he becomes unable to perform legally and actually his functions (as a matter of law or as a matter of fact) or for other reasons fails to act without undue delay;

(1) 仲裁员无法在法律上和事实上履行职能或因其他原因无法马上履行职能;

(2) he resigns from his office or if the parties agree on the termination.

(2) 仲裁员离职或双方当事人协商终止仲裁员委任。

(b) If a controversy remains concerning matters specified in subsection (a)(1), any party may, unless otherwise agreed by the parties, apply the court to decide on the termination of the mandate of the arbitrator. The decision regarding with the termination of the mandate of arbitrator, shall be subject to no appeal.

(b) 如果仍有(a)款第(1)项所述争议,除非双方另有约定,任何一方可向法院提出申请,决定终止仲裁员的委任。对终止仲裁员委任的决定,不得上诉。

(c) If, under subsection (a)(1) or subsection (c) of section 15, an arbitrator resigns from his office or a party agrees to the termination of the mandate of an arbitrator, this does not imply acceptance of the validity of any ground referred to in subsection (a)(1) or subsection (c) of section 14.

(c) 仲裁员离职或一方当事人根据第 15 条(a)款第(1)项或(c)款的规定同意终止仲裁员资格,并不意味着承认本条或第 14 条(a)款第(1)项或(c)款所述的任何理由。

17. (a) Where the mandate of an arbitrator terminates under

section 15 or 16，or because of his withdrawal from office for any other reason or because of the revocation of his mandate by agreement of the parties or in any other case of termination of his mandate，a substitute arbitrator shall be appointed according to the rules that were applicable to the appointment of the arbitrator being replaced.

（a）如果根据第 15 条或第 16 条的规定，因仲裁员由于任何其他原因而自行回避，或因各方当事人协议撤销仲裁员的委任，使仲裁员委任终止，或在任何其他情况下仲裁员的委任终止，则另一名仲裁员应按照规则程序替换被终止委任的仲裁员继续履行其职责。

（b）If an arbitrator is replaced as per subsection（a），the former hearings may be repeated at the discretion of arbitral tribunal，unless otherwise agreed by the parties.

（b）如果根据（a）款更换仲裁员，除非双方当事人另有约定，可由仲裁庭决定重新进行先前的听证。

（c）If an arbitrator is replaced as per this section，the order and decision made before the substitution of the arbitrator shall not be deemed invalid due to the re-composition of the arbitral tribunal，unless otherwise agreed by the parties.

（c）如果根据本条更换仲裁员，除非双方当事人另有约定，则更换仲裁员前所做命令和决定不因仲裁庭的重组而无效。

Chapter 6
Jurisdiction of Arbitral Tribunal
第六章　仲裁庭管辖权

Competence of arbitral tribunal to rule on its jurisdiction

仲裁庭管辖权限

18.（a）Unless otherwise agreed by the parties，the arbitral tribunal may rule on its own jurisdiction，including any objections with respect to the existence or validity of the arbitration agreement. For that purpose：

（a）除非双方另有规定，仲裁庭有权力对其自身管辖权作出裁定，包括对与仲裁协议的存在或效力有关的任何异议作出裁定。为此规定如下：

    （1）an arbitration clause which forms part of a contract shall be treated as an agreement independent of the other terms of the contract；

    （1）构成合同一部分的仲裁条款应视为独立于合同其他条款的一项协议。

    （2）a decision by the arbitral tribunal that the contract is null and void shall not be affected the validity of arbitra-tion clause under that contract.

    （2）仲裁庭作出合同无效的裁定，不应自动造成仲裁条款无效。

（b）A plea that the arbitral tribunal does not have jurisdiction shall be raised not later than the submission of the statement of defence. A party is not precluded from raising such a plea by the fact that he has appointed，or partici-pated in the appointment of，an arbitrator.

（b）针对仲裁庭管辖权的异议，不得迟于答辩书的提交。一方当事人已指定或参与指定一名仲裁员，不妨碍其提出此种异议。

（c）A plea that the arbitral tribunal is exceeding the scope of its authority shall be raised as soon as the matter alleged to be beyond the scope of its authority is raised during the arbitral proceedings.

（c）认为仲裁庭超出其职权范围的异议，应当在超出职权的事项提交仲裁后尽快提出。

（d）The arbitral tribunal may admit a later plea referred to in subsection（b）and（c）if it considers the delay justified.

（d）如果仲裁庭认为延迟是合理的，可根据（b）款和（c）款接受后来提出的异议。

（e）The arbitral tribunal may rule on a plea referred to in subsections（b）and（c）as preliminary issue or as an arbitral award. If the arbitral tribunal rules that it has jurisdiction or not，any party aggrieved by the arbitral award，may appeal to the court，subject to section 43，subsection（d）（1）（2）and section 47，subsection（b）（1），within 30 days from the date of receiving of such decision.

（e）对于（b）款和（c）款所述请求，仲裁庭可将其作为初裁问题作出裁定或仲裁裁决。如果仲裁庭对其有无管辖权作出裁决，任何不满的一方当事人可根据第 43 条（d）款第（1）（2）项和第 47 条（b）款第（1）项，在对裁决不满之日起 30 内向法院提起上诉。

（f）Although the application is pending in the court，the arbitral tribunal shall continue the arbitral proceedings and make an award.

（f）在申请处于待决状态时，仲裁庭仍然可以继续仲裁程序并作出仲裁裁决。

Power of arbitral tribunal to order interim orders

仲裁庭命令采取临时措施的权力

19.（a）Unless otherwise agreed by the parties，an arbitral tribunal shall have powers to make decision，order and instructions to any party for：

（a）除非双方当事人另有约定，仲裁庭有权对任何一方做出下列相关决定、命令和指示：

（1）security for costs；

（1）仲裁费用担保；

（2）document disclosure and interrogatories；

（2）文件开示和质询；

（3）provide evidence and take an oath；

（3）提供证据并宣誓；

（4）the preservation，interim custody or sale of any property which is part of the subject-matter of the dispute；

（4）保存、临时保管或出售属于争议标的物的任何财产；

（5）samples to be taken from，or any observation to be made of or experiment conducted upon，any property which is or forms part of the subject-matter of the dispute；

（5）从属于或构成争议标的物的财产取得样本，或对其进行观察、实验；

（6）the preservation and interim custody of any evidence for the purposes of the proceedings；

（6）为仲裁保存和临时保管证据；

（7）securing the amount in dispute；

（7）确定纠纷数额；

（8）an interim injunction or any other interim measure.

（8）临时禁令或者其他临时措施。

（b）An arbitral tribunal may have power to administer oaths to the parties and witnesses.

（b）仲裁庭有权让当事人和证人进行宣誓。

（c）An arbitral tribunal may have the power to adopt inquisitorial procedures as its consider appropriate.

（c）仲裁庭有权酌情采取审问程序。

（d）The power of the arbitral tribunal to order a claimant to provide security for costs as referred to in subsection（a）

（1）shall not be exercised solely because the claimant is：

（d）如果原告满足下列条件之一，仲裁庭不得命令原告为（a）款第

（1）项所述费用提供担保：

（1）an individual ordinarily residing outside the Republic of the Union of Myanmar；

（1）通常居住在缅甸联邦共和国境外的个人；

（2）a corporation or an association incorporated or formed under the law of the other country.

（2）根据外国法律成立或组建的公司或协会。

（e）All decisions，orders or instruction made by an arbitral tribunal in the course of an arbitration may apply to the court for the enforcement in accordance with the section 31.

（e）对于仲裁庭在仲裁过程中做出的所有决定、命令或指示，可根据第 31 条请求法院执行。

Immunity of the arbitrator

仲裁员的豁免权

20. An arbitrator shall not be liable for his act or omission which is done with due care during the course of arbitration as an arbitrator.

仲裁员对其在仲裁过程中由疏忽引起的作为或不作为免责。

Chapter 7
Conduct of Arbitral Proceedings
第七章　仲裁程序的进行

Equal treatment of parties

平等对待各方当事人

21. The parties shall be treated with equality and each party shall be given a full opportunity of presenting his case.

应平等对待各方当事人，并给予各方当事人充分陈述案情的机会。

Determination of rules of procedure

程序规则的确定

22. （a）Without contradicting the provisions of this Law, the parties are free to agree on the procedure to be followed by the arbitral tribunal in conducting the proceedings.

（a）以服从本法的规定为准，当事各方可以自由地就仲裁庭进行仲裁所应遵循的程序达成协议。

（b）Failing such agreement as specified in subsection （a）, the arbitral tribunal may, subject to the provisions of this Law, conduct the arbitration in such manner as it considers appropriate.

（b）如未能达成(a)款中所述一致，仲裁庭可根据本法选择适当的仲裁程序。

（c）In conducting arbitral proceedings as per subsection （b）, the power conferred upon the arbitral tribunal includes the power to determine the admissibility, relevance, materiality, and weight of any evidence.

（c）在(b)款中所述仲裁程序的进行中，授予仲裁庭的权力包括确定任何证据的可采性、相关性、实质性和重要性。

Place of arbitration

仲裁地

23. （a）The parties are free to agree on the place of arbitration.

（a）当事各方可以自由地就仲裁地点达成协议。

（b）Failing such agreement as specified in subsection （a）, the place of arbitration shall be determined by the arbitral tribunal having regard to the circumstances of the case, including the convenience of the parties.

（b）未达成上述约定，仲裁地应由仲裁庭根据各方便利的案件情况加以确定。

（c）Notwithstanding the provisions in subsections （a） and （b）, the arbitral tribunal may, unless otherwise agreed by the parties, meet at any place it considers appropriate for consultation among its members, for hearing witnesses, experts or the parties, or for inspection of goods, other property or documents.

（c）虽有本条（a）款和（b）款的规定,除非当事各方另有协议,仲裁庭可以在它认为适当的任何地点进行会议,以便在它的成员间进行磋商,听取证人、专家或当事各方的意见或检查货物、其他财产或文件。

Commencement of arbitral proceedings
仲裁程序的启动

24. Unless otherwise agreed by the parties, the arbitral proceedings in respect of a particular dispute commence on the date on which a request for that dispute to be referred to arbitration is received by the respondent.

24. 除非当事各方另有协议,特定争议的仲裁程序,于应诉人收到将该争议提交仲裁的请求之日启动。

Language
语言

25. （a）The parties are free to agree on the language or languages to be used in the arbitral proceedings.

（a）各方当事人有权自由确定仲裁程序中所使用的一种或数种语言。

（b）Failing such agreement as specified in subsection（a）, the arbitral tribunal shall determine the language or languages to be used in the arbitral proceedings.

（b）如无上述约定,仲裁庭应确定程序中使用的一种或数种语言。

（c）This agreement or determination, unless otherwise specified in subsection （a） or （b）, shall apply to any written statement by a party, any hearing and any award, decision or other communication by the arbitral tribunal.

(c) 除非前文另有规定,此决定应适用于各方书面陈述、开庭审理、裁决、决定或交流意见。

(d) The arbitral tribunal may order that any documentary evidence shall be accompanied by a translation into the language or languages agreed upon by the parties or determined by the arbitral tribunal.

(d) 仲裁庭可命令任何书证附具当事人约定的或仲裁庭确定的一种或数种语言译本。

Statements of claim and defence

仲裁申请书和答辩书

26. (a) The parties may agree the particulars to be stated in the claim or defence. Failing such agreement, the claimant shall state the facts supporting his claim, the points at issue and the relief or remedy sought, and the respondent shall state his defence in respect of these particulars and apply to the arbitral tribunal within the period of time agreed by the parties or determined by the arbitral tribunal.

(a) 当事人可以协商在申请书和答辩书中载明的事项。如未达成此种协议,在各方约定或仲裁庭确定的期间内,申请人应说明支持本仲裁请求的事实陈述、争议点和寻求的救济或损害赔偿,被申请人也应在其答辩书中说明上述事项。

(b) The parties may submit with their statements all documents they consider to be relevant and other evidence or may add a reference to the documents they will submit.

(b) 当事人可提交申请书和答辩书及他们认为与案件有关的全部文件和其他证据,也可以附注说明他们将来提交的文件。

(c) Unless otherwise agreed by the parties, either party may amend or supplement his claim or defence during the course of the arbitral proceedings, unless the arbitral tribunal considers it inappropriate to allow such amendment having regard to the delay in making it.

(c) 除非各方当事人另有协议,在仲裁程序进行中,任何一方当事人均可以修改或补充其申请书或答辩书,除非仲裁庭考虑到提出已迟而认为不宜允许提出这种改动。

Hearings and written proceedings
开庭审理和书面审理

27. (a) Unless otherwise agreed by the parties, the arbitral tribunal shall decide whether to hold oral hearings for the presentation of evidence or for oral argument, or whether the proceedings shall be conducted on the basis of documents and other materials. However, unless the parties have agreed that no hearings shall be held, the arbitral tribunal shall hold such hearings at an appropriate stage of the proceedings, if so requested by a party.

(a) 除非各方当事人另有约定,仲裁庭应决定是开庭审理(出示证据或进行口头辩论),还是根据书面文件和其他资料进行程序。然而,除非当事人约定不进行开庭审理。否则只要一方当事人要求,仲裁庭应在仲裁程序的适当阶段开庭审理。

(b) The parties shall be given sufficient advance notice of any hearing and of any meeting of the arbitral tribunal for the purposes of inspection of goods, other property or documents.

(b) 任何开庭及仲裁庭为检查货物、其他财产或文件而进行的任何会议,均应充分提前通知当事人。

(c) All statements, documents or other information supplied to the arbitral tribunal by one party shall be communicated to the other party. Also any expert report or evidentiary document on which the arbitral tribunal may rely in making its decision shall be communicated to the parties.

(c) 一方当事人向仲裁庭提交的一切陈述、文件或其他信息均应送交另一方当事人。仲裁庭可能据以作出裁决的任何具有证据性质的专家报告或其他文件也应送交各方当事人。

Default of a party

一方当事人不履行责任

28. Unless otherwise agreed by the parties，if，without showing sufficient cause：

除非当事人另有约定，如在不提出充分理由的情况下：

(a) the claimant fails to communicate his statement of claim in accordance with section 26，subsection（a），the arbitral tribunal shall terminate the proceedings；

(a) 申请人不按第 26 条（a）款的规定提交仲裁申请书的，仲裁庭应终止程序；

(b) the respondent fails to communicate his statement of defence in accordance with section 26，subsection（a），the arbitral tribunal shall continue the proceedings. However，such failure in itself shall not be treated as an admission of the claimant's allegations；

(b) 被申请人不按照第 26 条（a）款的规定提交答辩书，仲裁庭应继续进行程序。但不提交答辩书之事本身不应视为承认申请人的主张；

(c) any party fails to appear at a hearing or to produce documentary evidence，the arbitral tribunal may continue the proceedings and make the award on the evidence before it.

(c) 任何一方当事人不出庭或不提供书证，仲裁庭仍可继续进行仲裁程序并根据已有证据作出裁决。

Expert appointed by arbitral tribunal

仲裁庭指定的专家

29. (a) Unless otherwise agreed by the parties，the arbitral tribunal：

(a) 除非双方当事人另有约定，仲裁庭：

(1) may appoint one or more experts to report to it on specific issues to be determined by the arbitral tribunal；

(1) 可以指定一名或数名专家就仲裁庭确定的具体问题向仲裁庭提出报告；

(2) may require a party to give the expert any relevant information or to produce, or to provide access to, any relevant documents, goods or other property for his inspection.

(2) 可以要求当事人向专家提供或出示与案件有关的任何信息，或向专家提供让其查看与案件有关的文件、商品或其他财产的机会。

(b) If a party so requests or if the arbitral tribunal considers it necessary，the expert shall，after delivery of his written or oral report，participate in a hearing. In doing so，the parties shall have the opportunity to put questions to the expert and to present evidence on the points at issue.

(b) 如经一方当事人请求，或仲裁庭认为有必要的，专家可在提交其书面或口头报告后参与庭审。这时双方当事人可向专家提出问题，并就争议点提供证据。

Court assistance in taking evidence

法院协助取证

30. (a) The arbitral tribunal，or a party with the approval of the

arbitral tribunal，may apply to the Court for assistance in taking evidence.

（a）仲裁庭或经仲裁庭允许的一方当事人可以申请法院协助取证。

（b）The application shall specify the following particulars：

（b）申请书应当包含下列内容：

（1）the names and addresses of the parties and the arbitrators；

（1）当事人和仲裁员的姓名和地址；

（2）the general nature of claim and the relief sought；

（2）索赔和救济的性质；

（3）the names and addresses of any person to be heard as witness or expert witness and a statement of the subject-matter of the testimony required；

（3）被视为证人或专家证人的人的姓名和地址，以及证词所需的陈述；

（4）the document to be submitted or the description of the document to be produced or property to be inspected.

（4）拟提交的文件，拟生成的文件或待检查财产的说明。

（c）The Court may，within its competence and according to its rules on taking evidence，execute the request that the evidence be provided directly to the arbitral tribunal.

（c）法院可在其职权范围内行使其取证权力，执行请求并将证据直接提供给仲裁庭。

（d）The Court may，while making an order under subsection （c），issue the same processes to witnesses as it may issue in suits tried before it.

（d）法院在根据（c）款发出命令的同时，可以向证人发出同样的命令。

Enforcement of interim order of the arbitral tribunal by Court

法院执行仲裁庭的临时命令

31. （a） relating to arbitration，whether interim order are passed within or outside the State，Courts may enforce such interim orders passed by the arbitral tribunal as if its own order and decision.

（a） 对于与仲裁相关的临时命令，无论其在境内还是境外做出，法庭可执行仲裁庭发出的该临时命令，如同该命令是法庭自行做出的一样。

（b） in relation to arbitration exercised outside the State，when an applicant file the interim order for enforcement is unable to submit strong evidence that it is the same type of order exercised within the State，the Court shall not approve for enforcement.

（b） 对于在境外进行的仲裁，申请人提出执行临时命令时，无法提交有力证据证明其属于本国行使的同类型命令的，法院不予批准执行。

（c） When approval is granted according to subsection（a） the Court shall enforce such order.

（c） 做出（a）款所述许可时，法院应执行该命令。

（d） There shall be no right of appeal upon the Court decision on granting approval according to subsection （a） or upon refusal.

（d） 对法院根据（a）款做出的许可或拒绝决定，不得上诉。

Explanation Note：The interim order which refers to this section includes decision，order and instruction of the arbitral tribunal.

注：本条所述临时命令包括仲裁庭的决定、命令和指示。

Chapter 8

Making of Arbitral Award and Termination of Proceedings

Rules applicable to substance of dispute

第八章　仲裁裁决的制定和适用争议的终止诉讼规则

32. (a) If the place of arbitration is the Republic of the Union of Myanmar：

(a) 如果仲裁地位于缅甸联邦共和国，则：

(1) In domestic arbitration，the arbitral tribunal shall decide the dispute which to be settled by arbitration in accordance with the substantive law in force of the Republic of the Union of Myanmar.

(1) 在国内仲裁时，仲裁庭应根据缅甸联邦共和国现行的实体法，通过仲裁做出决定。

(2) In international commercial arbitration：

(2) 在国际仲裁时，则：

aa) The arbitral tribunal shall decide the dispute in accordance with such rules of law as are chosen by the parties；

aa) 仲裁庭应适用各方当事人指定的法律规则；

bb) Any designation of the law or legal system of a given State shall be construed，unless otherwise agreed by the parties，as directly referring to the substantive law of that State and not to its conflict of laws rules；

bb) 规定适用一个国家的法律或法律体系应视为直接适用该国实体法，而非该国的法律冲突规则；

cc) Failing any designation as per subsection clause (aa) by the parties，the arbitral tribunal shall apply the rules of law which it considers applicable.

cc) 各方当事人未就 aa) 所述事宜指定法律规则的，仲裁庭应适用其认为合适的规则。

(b) The arbitral tribunal shall decide the dispute with justice, equity and good conscience if the parties have expressly authorized it to do so.

(b) 各方当事人有明确授权的,仲裁庭应公正、公平、善意地解决争议。

(c) In all cases, the arbitral tribunal shall decide in accordance with the terms of the contract and shall take into account the usages of the trade applicable to the transaction.

(c) 在一切情况下,仲裁庭均应按照合同条款并在考虑该项交易所适用的贸易惯例的情况下做出决定。

Decision-making by panel of arbitrators
仲裁小组决定

33. (a) In arbitral proceedings with more than one arbitrator, any decision of the arbitral tribunal shall be made, unless otherwise agreed by the parties, by a majority of all its members.

(a) 在有一组仲裁员的仲裁中,除非当事人另有约定,仲裁庭的决定应由多数仲裁员做出。

(b) However, notwithstanding anything contained in subsection (a), questions of procedure may be decided by a presiding arbitrator, if so authorized by the parties or all members of the arbitral tribunal.

(b) 但是,如果各方当事人或仲裁庭全体成员授权,首席仲裁员可以就程序问题做出决定。

Settlement
和解

34. (a) If, during arbitral proceedings, the parties settle the dispute, the arbitral tribunal shall terminate the proceedings and, if

requested by the parties and not objected to by the arbitral tribunal，record the settlement in the form of an arbitral award on agreed terms.

(a) 如果在仲裁程序过程中当事人解决了纠纷，仲裁庭应终止程序，而且如果各方当事人请求而仲裁庭也无异议，应按和解条件以仲裁裁决的形式记录此和解。

(b) An award on agreed terms shall be made in accordance with the provisions of section 35 and shall state that it is an arbitral award.

(b) 按照和解协议条款作出的仲裁裁决应符合第 35 条规定，并应指明该和解的裁决性质。

(c) Such award on agreed terms has the same status and effect as any other award on the merits of the case.

(c) 这一协议与裁决书具有同等地位。

Form and contents of award

裁决书的形式和内容

35. (a) The award shall be made in writing and shall be signed by arbitrator or arbitrators.

(a) 仲裁裁决均应以书面形式作出并由独任仲裁员或多位仲裁员签名。

(b) In arbitral proceedings with more than one arbitrator for the purpose of subsection (a)，the signatures of the majority of all arbitrators of the arbitral tribunal shall suffice，provided that the reason for any omitted signature is stated.

(b) 在有一组仲裁员的仲裁程序中，仲裁庭多数成员签字即可，但须说明没有其余仲裁员签字的原因。

(c) Unless the parties have agreed that no reasons are to be given or unless the award is an award on agreed terms，the award shall state the reasons upon which it is based.

(c) 除非当事人同意不给予理由，或裁决是对协定事项的裁决，否则裁决应说明其理由。

(d) The award shall state its date and the place of arbitration as determined in accordance with section 23. The award shall be deemed to have been made at that place.

(d) 仲裁裁决应当注明日期和根据第 23 条确定的仲裁地。仲裁裁决视为在仲裁地作出。

(e) After the award is made，a signed copy shall be delivered to each party.

(e) 仲裁裁决作出后，经仲裁员签字的仲裁裁决副本应送达至各方当事人。

(f) Unless otherwise agreed by the parties：

(f) 除非当事人另有约定：

(1) The costs of an arbitration shall be fixed by the arbitral tribunal；

(1) 仲裁的费用应由仲裁庭确定；

(2) The arbitral tribunal shall specify the party entitled to costs，the party who shall pay the costs，the amount of costs and method of determining that amount and the manner in which the costs shall be paid.

(2) 仲裁庭应指明收取费用的一方、应支付费用的一方、费用金额、确定金额的方法，以及支付方式。

Explanatory note：

注：

For the purpose of subsection (f) (1)，"costs" means reasonable costs relating to：

(f)款第(1)项所述费用指下列合理费用：

(1) fees and expenses of arbitrators and witnesses；

(1) 仲裁员和证人的费用和开支；

（2）legal fees and expenses;

（2）法律费用和开支;

（3）any administration fees of the institution supervising the arbitration; and

（3）监督仲裁机构的行政费用;以及

（4）any other expenses incurred in connection with the arbitral proceedings and the arbitral award.

（4）与仲裁程序和仲裁裁决有关的其他费用。

Termination of proceedings

终止程序

36. （a）The arbitral proceedings shall be terminated by the final award or by an order of the arbitral tribunal in accordance with subsection（b）of this section.

（a）仲裁程序于最终裁决书作出后或于仲裁庭根据本条（b）款下达指令后终止。

（b）The arbitral tribunal shall issue an order for the termination of the arbitral proceedings when:

（b）仲裁庭应在下列情况下做出终止仲裁程序的决定:

（1）the claimant withdraws his claim, unless the respondent objects thereto and the arbitral tribunal recognizes a legitimate interest on his part in obtaining a final settlement of the dispute;

（1）申请人放弃请求,但被申请人拒绝且仲裁庭认为采取和解方式对被申请人有合法利益;

（2）the parties agree on the termination of the proceedings;

（2）各方当事人同意终止程序;

（3）the arbitral tribunal finds that the continuation of the proceedings has for any other reason become unnecessary or impossible.

（3）仲裁庭认定，由于某些原因已无必要或可能继续程序。

(c) Subject to the provisions of section 37，the mandate of the arbitral tribunal terminates with the termination of the arbitral proceedings pursuant to the section 34，subsection （a）and this section.

（c）在不违反第 37 条的情况下，仲裁庭的任务随第 34 条（a）款和本条规定的仲裁程序的结束而终止。

Correction and interpretation of award；additional award
裁决书的更正与解释；补充裁决

37. (a) Within thirty days from the date of award，unless another period of time has been agreed upon by the parties，a party，with notice to the other party，may request the arbitral tribunal to correct in the award any errors in computation，any clerical or typographical errors or any errors of similar nature.

（a）除非双方另有约定，自裁决之日起 30 日内，任何一方当事人在通知另一方当事人后，可以请求仲裁庭改正裁决中出现的任何计算、书写、打印错误或任何类似性质的错误；

(b) If the arbitral tribunal considers the request made as per subsection （a）or，its own initiative，may correct any error of the type refer to in subsection （a）and such correction shall be delivered to the parties.

（b）如果仲裁庭认为（a）款所述请求或经仲裁庭自行更正，可改正（a）款所述类型错误的，应将该项更正送达各方当事人。

(c) If so agreed by the parties，a party，with notice to the other party，may request the arbitral tribunal to give an interpretation of a specific point or part of the award.

（c）如果双方当事人有相关约定，则一方当事人可在通知其他各方当事人后,请求仲裁庭对裁决书的具体一点或部分做出解释。

(d) If the arbitral tribunal considers the request made as per subsection (c) to be justified, it shall give the interpretation within thirty days of receipt of the request. The interpretation shall form part of the award.

(d) 如果认为请求合理,仲裁庭应当在收到请求后的 30 日内做出更正。解释应构成裁决书的一部分。

(e) Unless otherwise agreed by the parties, a party, with notice to the other party, may request, within thirty days of receipt of the award, the arbitral tribunal to make an additional award as to claims presented in the arbitral proceedings but omitted from the award.

(e) 除非当事人另有约定,任何一方当事人在收到仲裁裁决后 30 日内,在通知另一方当事人后,可以请求仲裁庭对已在仲裁程序中提出,但在裁决中未得到反映的申诉事项作出补充裁决。

(f) If the arbitral tribunal considers the request made as per subsection (e) to be justified, it shall make the additional award within sixty days from the receipt of such request.

(f) 仲裁庭认为请求合理的,应当于 60 日内作出补充裁决。

(g) The arbitral tribunal may extend, if necessary, the period of time within which it shall make a correction, interpretation or an additional award under subsection (b), (d) or (e).

(g) 如有必要,仲裁庭可以根据本条(b)款、(d)款或(e)款延长其做出更正、解释或作出补充裁决的时间。

(h) The provisions of section 33 shall apply to a correction or interpretation of the award or to an additional award.

(h) 第 33 条的规定应适用于裁决书的更正与解释,以及补充裁决。

Effect of the Arbitral Award

仲裁裁决的效力

38. Unless otherwise agreed by the parties, the award made by the arbitral tribunal pursuant to the arbitration agreement, shall be final and binding on the parties and persons claiming under them respectively.

除非双方当事人另有约定,仲裁庭根据仲裁协议作出的裁决应是终局的,对双方当事人以及任何通过双方当事人进行主张的人均有约束力。

Chapter 9

Power of the Court relating to Domestic Arbitration

Determination of preliminary issue of law

第九章 法院对国内仲裁的初裁问题的确定

39. (a) Unless otherwise agreed by the parties, the Court may, on the application of a party to the arbitral proceedings who has given notice to the other parties, determine any issue of law arising in the course of the proceedings which the Court is satisfied substantially affects the rights of one or more of the parties.

(a) 除非双方当事人另有约定,经一方申请并通知其他方,法院可对其认为与当事一方或多方的权利有重大关系的、仲裁过程中出现的法律问题做出决定。

(b) The Court shall not accept and consider an application under this section unless it is made with the agreement of all parties; or it is made with the permission of the arbitral tribunal and the Court is observed that the determination of the issue is likely to incur more costs; and the application is caused delay the case.

(b) 除非本条所述申请是经各方当事人同意或由仲裁庭同意做出的,且法院认定该项问题的确定可能导致更多费用,且该申请会引起案件延迟的,否则法院不得受理和考虑该申请。

(c) The application of subsection (a) shall identify the issue of law to be determined and, except where made with the agreement of all parties, shall state the grounds on which should be decided by the Court.

(c) (a)款所述申请应指明待决的法律问题,除非在各方达成协议的情况下,应说明让法院做出决定的理由。

(d) Unless otherwise agreed by the parties, the arbitral tribunal may continue the arbitral proceedings and make an award while an application to the Court under this section is pending.

(d) 除非双方当事人另有约定,在申请处于待决状态时,仲裁庭仍然可以继续仲裁程序并作出仲裁裁决。

Enforcement of Domestic Arbitration

国内仲裁裁决的执行

40. (a) The domestic award shall be enforced under the Code of Civil Procedure in the same manner as if it were a decree of the court.

(a) 国内裁决应按照《民事诉讼法》的规定执行,与执行法院判决相同。

(b) If the respondent, who applies for the enforcement of the arbitral award, proves that the arbitral tribunal is not competent to make an arbitral award, the court shall not enforce the arbitral award.

(b) 如果申请执行仲裁裁决的被申请人证明仲裁庭无权作出裁决,则法院不得执行裁决。

(c) This section shall be applied for the enforcement of any domestic arbitral award.

(c) 本条适用于国内仲裁裁决的执行。

Particulars for the set aside the Domestic Arbitral award

撤销国内仲裁裁决的情况

41. (a) Upon the application for setting aside by one of the party, the court may set aside the domestic arbitral award only if:

(a) 只有在下列情况时，经一方当事人申请，法院才可撤销国内仲裁裁决：

(1) a party to the arbitration agreement was under some incapacity; or

(1) 仲裁协议一方缺乏行为能力；

(2) the arbitration agreement is not valid under the law to which the parties have agreed or, failing any indication thereon, under the law of the Republic of the Union of Myanmar; or

(2) 仲裁协议根据双方当事人同意的法律无效，或根据缅甸联邦共和国法律无效；或

(3) the party making the application was not given proper notice of the appointment of an arbitrator or of the arbitral proceedings or was otherwise unable to present his case; or

(3) 未将有关指定仲裁员或仲裁程序的事情适当地通知提出申请的当事一方，或该方因其他理由未能陈述其案情；或

(4) the award deals with a dispute not contemplated by or not falling within the terms of the submission to arbitration, or contains decisions on matters beyond the scope of the submission to arbitration.

(4) 裁决涉及的事项不在仲裁可解决的范围内的，或其包含的

决定不在仲裁可解决的范围内的。

Proviso：If the decisions on matters submitted to arbitration can be separated from those not so submitted，only that part of the award which contains decisions on matters not submitted to arbitration may be set aside；or

附文：如果仲裁范围内的裁决能与仲裁范围外的裁决分开，那么只有仲裁范围外的裁决才可以被撤销；或

(5) the composition of the arbitral tribunal or the arbitral procedure was not in accordance with the agreement of the parties or was not in accordance with this Law.

(5) 裁庭的组成或仲裁程序与当事人协议不一致，或与本法不符。

Proviso：Such agreement was not in conflict with a provision of this Law from which the parties cannot derogate.

附文：该协议与本法中当事人不得减损的条款相冲突的除外。

(6) the subject-matter of the dispute is not capable of settlement by arbitration under the existing law；or

(6) 根据现行法律，该争议的标的不能通过仲裁解决；或

(7) the award is in conflict with the national interest （public policy） of the Republic of the Union of Myanmar.

(7) 该裁决与缅甸联邦共和国的国家利益（公共政策）相冲突。

(b) An application for setting aside may not be made after three months have elapsed from the date on which the party making that application had received the award or，if a request had been made under section 37，from the date on which that request had been disposed of by the arbitral tribunal.

(b) 提出申请的当事一方自收到裁决书之日起，3 个月后不得申请

撤销；如根据第 37 条提出了请求，则从该请求被仲裁庭处理完毕之日起 3 个月后不得申请撤销。

（c） The court，when asked to set aside an award as per subsection （a），may，where appropriate and so requested by a party，adjourn the setting aside proceedings for a period of time determined by it in order to give the arbitral tribunal an opportunity to resume the arbitral proceedings or to take such other action as in the arbitral tribunal's opinion will eliminate the grounds for setting aside.

（c）法院被请求撤销裁决时，如果适当且当事一方也要求暂时停止进行撤销程序，则可以在法院确定的一段期间内暂时停止进行，以便给予仲裁庭一个机会重新进行仲裁程序，或采取仲裁庭认为能够消除请求撤销裁决的理由的其他行动。

Appeal against Domestic Arbitration

对国内仲裁提起上诉

42.（a）A party in dispute may，upon notice to the other parties and to the arbitral tribunal，appeal to the Court on an issue of law arising out of an award made in the proceedings.

（a）一方当事人可在通知其他当事人和仲裁庭后，就诉讼程序中作出的裁决所引起的法律问题向法院提起上诉。

（b）According to subsection （a） there is a right of appeal upon the award of the arbitration tribunal. However if there is a written agreement between the parties not to appeal，there shall be no right of appeal to the Court under this section.

（b）根据（a）款可对仲裁庭裁决提出上诉。但如果双方当事人书面协议规定不得上诉的，不得根据本条规定上诉。

（c）If there is an agreement in writing between the parties that it is not required to write down the reasons on the award， there shall be no appeal on such ground according to this section.

（c）如果双方当事人书面协议规定无需记录仲裁理由的，不得根据本条规定上诉。

（d）Filing appeal according to this section shall be effected by the facts relating to section 44.

（d）根据本条提起上诉应以与第 44 条有关的事实为依据。

（e）When filing an appeal according to this section，shall identify the issue of law to be determined and state the grounds on which it is alleged that leave to appeal should be granted.

（e）根据本条提起上诉时，应确定待决的法律问题，并说明应准予上诉的理由。

（f）Whether the Court accept or refuse the right of appeal under this section there shall be no second appeal.

（f）无论法院对根据本条提起的上诉接受与否，不得再次提起上诉。

43.（a）The Court，if satisfied and agree with the following facts shall accept the appeal：

（a）法院如果信纳并同意下列事实，则应接受上诉：

（1）the decision of the arbitral tribunal of the issue in dispute is substantially affect the rights of a party or upon the parties；

（1）仲裁庭对问题的裁决会严重影响一方或多方的权利；

（2）the decision of the arbitral tribunal on the issue in dispute is obviously wrong.

（2）仲裁庭对这个问题的裁决有明显错误；

（b）When filing appeal according to this section，the Court can pass any of the following orders：

(b) 对根据本条提出的上诉,法院可命令如下:

 (1) Approve the award;

 (1) 确认裁决;

 (2) Amend the award;

 (2) 更改裁决;

 (3) To return the decision to the arbitral tribunal to review and reconsider the whole or part of the award;

 (3) 将仲裁裁决全部或部分交给仲裁庭复议;

 (4) set aside the whole or part of the arbitral award.

 (4) 撤销全部或部分裁决。

(c) Appeal can be filed to the Court of competent jurisdiction for following court order:

(c) 可以向有管辖权的法院提起上诉,以追查法院的下列命令:

 (1) An order refusing to refer to arbitration according to section 10 subsection (f);

 (1) 第 10 条(f)款所述拒绝提交仲裁的命令;

 (2) An order granting or refusing to perform one of the interim measures according to section 11;

 (2) 第 11 条所述批准或拒绝执行其中一项临时措施的命令;

 (3) Court order passing upon the issue of law according to section (39) subsection (a);

 (3) 第 39 条(a)款所述在法律问题上通过的法院命令;

 (4) An order setting aside or refusing the set aside of domestic arbitral award according to section 41.

 (4) 第 41 条所述撤销或拒绝撤销国内仲裁裁决的命令。

(d) Following orders of an arbitral tribunal can be filed for appeal to the Court of Jurisdiction:

(d) 对仲裁庭的下列命令,可向有管辖权的法院提起上诉:

 (1) Order accepting the application according to section 18

subsection（b）and（c）；

（1）第 18 条（b）款和（c）款所述接受申请的命令；

（2）Order by the arbitral tribunal that it has jurisdiction or not according to section 18（e）；

（2）第 18 条（e）款所述仲裁庭是否有管辖权的命令；

（3）Order granting or refusing to perform the any interim measures according to section 19.

（3）第 19 条所述接受或拒绝执行临时措施的命令。

（e）There shall be no second appeal upon the order passed from filing of appeal according to this section.

（e）根据本条对命令提起上诉的，不得再次上诉。

Effect of the Appellate Court order upon Domestic Arbitration

上诉法院命令对国内裁决的效力

44. The appellate Court，when passing an order relating to the award according to section 43 subsection（b）：

上诉法院根据第 43 条（b）款做出与仲裁裁决相关的命令时：

（a）When it is decided to amend the award，such amended decision shall be effected as part of the award；

（a）决定修改裁决时，该修改决定应作为裁决的一部分生效；

（b）When the Court pass the order remitting the award in whole or partial to the arbitral tribunal for reconsideration and revision the arbitral tribunal shall revise such matters and pass the decision；

（b）法院将全部或者部分裁决转交仲裁庭复议修改的，仲裁庭应修改并通过裁决；

（c）Necessary timing for the arbitral tribunal to review and pass the decision may be recommended.

（c）可以为仲裁庭审查和通过裁决推荐必要期限。

Chapter 10

Recognition of Enforcement of Foreign Arbitral Award

第十章　承认外国仲裁裁决的执行

Particulars to apply for recognition or enforcement of foreign arbitral award

申请承认或执行外国仲裁裁决的情况

45. (a) The party applying for the enforcement of a foreign award shall，at the time of the application，produce before the court：

（a）申请执行外国裁决的当事人应当在申请时向法院出示：

（1）the original award or a copy thereof，duly authenticated in the manner required by the law of the country in which it was made；

（1）根据裁决做出国法律正式认定的原裁决书或其副本；

（2）the original agreement for arbitration or a duly certified copy thereof；and

（2）仲裁协议原本或者经正式认证的副本；以及

（3）such evidence as may be necessary to prove that the award is a foreign award.

（3）证明该裁决是外国裁决所必需的证据。

(b) Where the award or arbitration agreement requiring to be submitted under subsection (a) is in a foreign language，the party seeking to enforce the award shall produce a translation into English certified as correct by the ambassador or consular of the country to which that party belongs or certified as correct in such other manner as may be sufficient according to the law in force in the Republic of the Union of Myanmar.

（b）如果根据（a）款要求提交的仲裁裁决书或仲裁协议是外文的，申请执行裁决的一方应提交由该方国家大使或领事认证的英文译本,或者提交根据缅甸联邦共和国现行法律规定的其他方式认证的英文译本。

Recognition and Enforcement of Foreign Arbitral Award
裁决的承认与执行

46. （a） Except the application to set aside the award is refused under subsection （b） and （c）, the award shall be enforced under the Code of Civil Procedure in the same manner as if it were a decree of the court.

（a） 除（b）款和（c）款所述撤销裁决的申请被拒绝外,裁决应按照《民事诉讼法》的规定执行,方式与法庭判决相同。

（b） The court may refuse to recognize the foreign arbitral award if the party against whom it is invoked furnishes to the court proof that：

（b） 如果被申请人向法庭证明下列情况,法院可拒绝承认外国仲裁裁决：

（1） the parties to the arbitration agreement referred was under some incapacity； or

（1） 仲裁协议的当事人缺乏行为能力；或

（2） the said agreement is not valid under the law to which the parties have subjected to it or, failing any indication thereon, under the law of the country where the award was made；

（2） 上述协议根据当事各方所依据的法律无效,或根据裁决所在国的法律无效；

（3） the party against whom the award is invoked was not given proper notice of the appointment of an arbitrator or of the arbitral proceedings or was otherwise unable to present his case； or

（3） 未将有关指定仲裁员或仲裁程序的事宜适当地通知当事

一方，或该方因其他理由未能陈述其案情；或

(4) the award deals with a dispute not contemplated by or not falling within the terms of the submission to arbitration, or it contains decisions on matters beyond the scope of the submission to arbitration; or

(4) 裁决涉及仲裁范围以外的纠纷，或包含仲裁范围以外的决定；或

(5) the composition of the arbitral tribunal or the arbitral procedure was not in accordance with the agreement of the parties or, failing such agreement, was not in accordance with the law of the country where the arbitration took place; or

(5) 仲裁庭的组成或仲裁程序与当事各方的协议不一致，或无这种协议时，与仲裁所在国的法律不符；或

(6) the award has not yet become binding on the parties or has been set aside or suspended by a competent authority of the country in which, or under the law of which, that award was made.

(6) 裁决尚未对当事各方具有约束力，或作出裁决的国家的法院，或根据其法律作出裁决的国家的法院已将裁决撤销或中止。

(c) Enforcement of the foreign arbitral award may be refused if the court finds that:

(c) 法院认定存在下列情形的，可拒绝执行外国仲裁裁决：

(1) the subject-matter of the dispute is not capable of settlement by arbitration under the law of the Republic of the Union of Myanmar; or

(1) 根据缅甸联邦共和国的法律，该争议的标的不能通过仲裁解决；或

(2) the enforcement of the award would be contrary to the

national interest（public policy）of the Republic of the Union of Myanmar.

（2）执行该裁决与缅甸联邦共和国的公共政策相抵触。

（d）If an application for setting aside or suspension of an award has been made to a competent authority referred to in subsection（b）(6）of this section，the court may，if it considers it proper，adjourn its decision on the enforcement of the award and may also，on the application of the party claiming enforcement of the award，order the other party to provide appropriate security.

（d）如已向本条(b)款第(6)项所指的法院申请撤销或中止裁决，被请求承认或执行的法院如认为适当，可以暂停做出决定，而且如经要求承认或执行裁决的当事一方提出申请，还可以命令当事他方提供适当的担保。

Appeals

上诉

47. Any party to dispute：

争议的任何一方：

（a）The following orders passed by a competent court may be appealed：

（a）对主管法院通过的下列命令可以上诉：

（1）An order granting or refusing to take any measure under section 10；

（1）第 10 条所述接受或拒绝采取任何措施的命令；

（2）Any order under section 11；

（2）第 11 条所述命令；

（3）An order setting aside or refusing to set aside an award under section 46，subsection（b）and（c）.

（3）第 46 条(b)款和(c)款所述撤销或拒绝作出裁决的命令。

(b) The following orders passed by arbitral tribunal may be appealed to the competent Court：

(b) 对仲裁庭做出的下列命令可向主管法院上诉：

    (1) An order determining whether the arbitral tribunal has jurisdiction or not under section 18，subsection (e)；

    (1) 第 18 条(e)款所述确定仲裁庭有无管辖权的命令；

    (2) An order granting or refusing the interim matures under section 19.

    (2) 第 19 条所述接受或拒绝执行临时措施的命令。

48. Nothing in this Chapter shall prejudice any rights which any person would have had of enforcing foreign arbitral award in the Republic of the Union of Myanmar or of availing himself of such award to the enactment of this Law.

本章的任何规定均不得损害任何人在缅甸联邦共和国执行外国仲裁裁决的权利，或者本法生效期间利用外国裁决的权利。

No application of the Arbitration (Protocol and Convention) Act

不适用《仲裁(协议和公约)法》

49. Enforcement of foreign arbitral award under this Chapter shall not apply to the enforcement under the Arbitration (Protocol and Convention) Act，1937.

本章规定的外国仲裁裁决执行不适用于 1937 年《仲裁(协议和公约)法》中所述执行。

Chapter 11
Miscellaneous
第 11 章　其他

50. (a) In order to enforce the award made in contracting State of the New York Convention，the Chief Justice of the Union

may appoint，by notification，any officer from the Office of the Supreme Court of the Union or any person or any individual in charge of any organization to certify or authen-ticate the copy of the arbitration agreement or arbitral award.

（a）为执行《纽约公约》缔约国所作裁决，联邦首席大法官可通知任命联邦最高法院办公室的任何官员、任何机构的负责人员，以证明或认证仲裁协议或仲裁裁决书的副本。

（b）The person，who is appointed per subsection（a），shall：

（b）（a）款中被任命的人员，应：

（1）comply with the rules determined by the Chief Justice of the Union；and

（1）遵守联邦首席大法官确定的规则；

（2）not reveal，directly or indirectly，to others any fact in the arbitral award or arbitration agreement including the personal information of the parties，without the written consent of the parties.

（2）未经当事人书面同意，不得直接或间接向他人透露仲裁裁决书或仲裁协议中的任何事实，包括当事人的个人资料。

51. A sum directed to be paid by an arbitral award shall，unless the award otherwise directs，carry interest at the rate applied in the decree for payment of money，from the date of the award.

除非仲裁裁决另有指示，仲裁裁决指定支付的款项应自裁定之日起，按照法令中适用于支付款项的利率计息。

52.（a）The arbitral tribunal may fix the amount of the deposit or supplementary deposit，as the case may be，as an advance for the costs referred to in section 35，subsection（f），which it expects will be incurred in respect of the claim submitted to it. Provided that where, apart from the claim, a counter-claim has been submitted to the arbitral tribunal, it may fix separate amounts of deposit for the claim and counter-claim.

(a) 仲裁庭可根据具体情况确定存款或追加保证金的数额，作为第 35 条（f）款所述费用的预付款。但是除诉讼外已向仲裁庭提起反诉的，可以为诉讼和反诉确定单独数额的保证金。

(b) The deposit referred to in subsection (a) shall be payable in equal shares by the parties. Where one party fails to pay his share of the deposit, the other party may pay that share. Where the other party also does not pay the aforesaid share in respect of the claim or the counter-claim, the arbitral tribunal may suspend or terminate the arbitral proceedings in respect of such claim or counter-claim, as the case may be.

(b) (a)款所述保证金应由各方当事人平摊。一方未支付其需付份额的，另一方可以支付该份额。如果另一方在诉讼或反诉中未支付上述份额，则仲裁庭可以视情况中止或终止该诉讼或反诉相关的仲裁程序。

(c) Upon termination of the arbitral proceedings, the arbitral tribunal shall render an accounting to the parties of the deposits received and return any unexpended balance to the parties, as the case may be.

(c) 仲裁程序终止后，仲裁庭应向存款方出示账目并视情况返还余款。

53. (a) The arbitral tribunal shall have a lien on the arbitration for any unpaid costs.

(a) 仲裁庭对未付的费用享有仲裁留置权。

(b) If an arbitral tribunal refuses to deliver an award because of any party refuse to pay the costs to the arbitral tribunal，by application of other party，the Court may inquire as necessary and order that there shall be paid to the arbitral tribunal by the responsible party and Court may order the arbitral tribunal to deliver the arbitral award accordingly.

（b）如果仲裁庭由于一方拒绝向其支付费用而拒绝交付裁决，则经另一方申请，法院可以根据需要进行调查，并下令有关当事人向仲裁庭支付费用，相应地，法院可令仲裁庭交付仲裁裁决。

（c）An application under subsection（b）may be made by any party unless the fees demanded have been fixed by written agreement between him and the arbitral tribunal.

（c）（b）款所述申请可以由任何一方提出，除非该方与仲裁庭已有书面协议确定所要求的费用。

（d）The Court may make such orders as it thinks fit regarding the costs of the arbitration where any question arises respecting such costs and the arbitral award contains no sufficient provision concerning them.

（d）如果出现有关仲裁费用的问题，且仲裁裁决中无充分规定的，法院可就仲裁费用做出其认为合适的命令。

54.（a）An arbitration agreement shall not be discharged by the death of any party thereto，either as respects the deceased or any other party，but shall in such event be enforceable by or against the legal representative of the deceased.

（a）仲裁协议不因任何一方的死亡而解除，而应由死者的法定代表人执行。

（b）The authority of an arbitrator shall not be revoked by the death of any party by whom he was appointed.

（b）仲裁员的权力不因任命该仲裁员的一方的死亡而撤销。

55. Notwithstanding anything contained elsewhere in this Law or in any other law for the time being in force，where with respect to an arbitration agreement any application under this Law has been made in a Court，that Court alone shall have jurisdiction over the arbitral proceedings and all subsequent applications arising out of that agreement and the arbitral proceedings shall be made in that Court and in no other Court.

尽管本法其他条款或现行的其他法律中有别的规定，根据本法，针对仲裁协议向法院提出申请的，该法院即对仲裁程序享有管辖权。有关该仲裁协议和仲裁程序的后续申请只能在该法院提出。

56. The provisions under the Limitation Act which refers to the Arbitration Act（1944），shall be deemed to refer this Law.

《限制法》所指 1944 年《仲裁法》条款，应视为指称本法条款。

57. The Supreme Court of the Union may issue necessary rules，regulations，by-law，notification，orders，directives，procedures and manuals，in accordance with this Law.

联邦最高法院可根据本法颁布必要的规则、条例、细则、通知、命令、指示、程序和手册。

58. （a）Unless otherwise agreed by the parties in the arbitration agreement or other documents，the provisions of this Law shall not apply to the arbitration which commencing in accordance with the arbitration agreement before this Law had been enacted.

（a）除非当事人在仲裁协议或者其他文件中另有约定，本法的规定不适用于在本法颁布前按照仲裁协议开始的仲裁。

(b) Subject to the provision of subsection (a), if arbitration is commencing before this Law had been enacted, pending arbitration shall be proceed in accordance with the Law selected by the parties to the arbitration agreement.

(b) 在不违反(a)款的情况下，如果仲裁是在本法颁布前开始的，则应根据仲裁协议各方当事人选定的法律继续待决的仲裁。

59. The Arbitration Act, 1944 is repealed by this Law.

1944 年《仲裁法》被本法废止。

I hereby sign in accordance with the Constitution of the Republic of the Union of Myanmar.

本人依照《缅甸联邦共和国宪法》特此签署。

(S/d) Thein Sein

President

Republic of the Union of Myanmar

缅甸联邦共和国总统

登盛

第八节　越南商事仲裁法英汉对照

LAW 54

第 54 号法

ON COMMERCIAL ARBITRATION

《商事仲裁法》

(17 June 2010)

2010 年 6 月 17 日

TABLE OF CONTENTS

目录

CHAPTER 1

General Provisions

第一章 总则

Article 1 Governing scope

第 1 条 管辖范围

Article 2 Competence of arbitration to resolve disputes

第 2 条 仲裁可解决的纠纷

Article 3 Interpretation of terms

第 3 条 术语解释

Article 4 Principles for dispute resolution by arbitration

第 4 条 仲裁解决纠纷的原则

Article 5 Conditions for dispute resolution by arbitration

第 5 条 仲裁解决纠纷的条件

Article 6 Court refusal to accept jurisdiction if there is an arbitration agreement

第 6 条 有仲裁协议的情况下法院拒绝管辖

Article 7 Determining which court has competence over arbitration activities

第 7 条 确定哪个法院对仲裁有管辖权

Article 8 Determining which enforcement agency has competence to enforce arbitral awards and interim relief decisions of arbitration tribunals

第 8 条 确定哪个执行机构有权执行仲裁裁决和仲裁庭做出的临时救济决定

Article 9 Negotiation and conciliation during arbitration proceedings

第 9 条 仲裁程序中的协商与调解

Article 10 Language

第 10 条 语言

Article 11 Location for dispute resolution by arbitration

第 11 条 仲裁地

CHAPTER 4

Arbitration Centres

第四章　仲裁中心

Article 23　Functions of arbitration centre

第 23 条　仲裁中心的职能

Article 24　Conditions and procedures for establishment of arbitration centre

第 24 条　成立仲裁中心的条件与程序

Article 25　Registration of operation of arbitration centre

第 25 条　登记仲裁中心运作

Article 26　Announcement of establishment of arbitration centre

第 26 条　宣布成立仲裁中心

Article 27　Legal entity status and structure of arbitration centre

第 27 条　仲裁中心的法人地位和结构

Article 28　Rights and obligations of arbitration centre

第 28 条　仲裁中心的权利与义务

Article 29　Termination of operation of arbitration centre

第 29 条　终止仲裁中心运作

CHAPTER 5

Instituting Arbitration Proceedings

第五章　进行仲裁程序

Article 30　Statement of claim and accompanying materials

第 30 条　陈述主张和附带材料

Article 31　Time of commencement of arbitration proceedings

第 31 条　仲裁程序开始时间

Article 32　Notification of statement of claim

第 32 条　通知陈述主张

Article 33　Limitation period for initiating proceedings for dispute resolution by arbitration

第 33 条　仲裁解决纠纷的时效期

Article 34　Arbitration fees

第 34 条　仲裁费用

Article 35　Defence and submission of the defence

第 35 条　答辩和提交答辩状

Article 36　Counterclaim by respondent

第 36 条　被请求人反申请

Article 37　Withdrawal of statement of claim or counterclaim; amendment or addition to statement of claim, counterclaim or defences

第 37 条　撤销申请书或反申请书;修改或补充申请书、反申请书或答辩状

Article 38　Negotiation during arbitration proceedings

第 38 条　仲裁程序中的协商

CHAPTER 6
Arbitration Tribunal
第六章　仲裁庭

Article 39　Composition of arbitration tribunal

第 39 条　仲裁庭的组成

Article 40　Establishment of arbitration tribunal at arbitration centre

第 40 条　在仲裁中心成立仲裁庭

Article 41　Establishment of ad hoc arbitration tribunal

第 41 条　成立临时仲裁庭

Article 42　Replacement of arbitrators

第 42 条　替换仲裁员

Article 43　Consideration whether an arbitration is void or incapable of being performed and whether the arbitration tribunal has jurisdiction

第 43 条　考虑仲裁是否无效或不能执行,以及仲裁庭是否有管辖权

Article 44　Petition and resolution of petition against decision of arbitration tribunal concerning whether the arbitration agreement exists, the arbitration agreement is void, the arbitration agreement is incapable of being performed and whether the arbitration tribunal has jurisdiction

第 44 条　就仲裁庭制作出的仲裁协议是否存在、是否有效、是否能执行,以及仲裁庭是否有管辖权的决定提出申诉和处理申诉

Article 45　Jurisdiction of the arbitration tribunal to verify the facts

第 45 条　仲裁庭核实事实的权力

Article 46　Jurisdiction of the arbitration tribunal to collect evidence

第 46 条　仲裁庭收集证据的权力

Article 47　Jurisdiction of arbitration tribunal to summon witnesses

第 47 条　仲裁庭召唤证人的权力

CHAPTER 7
Interim Relief
第七章　临时救济

Article 48　Right to request application of interim relief

第 48 条　申请临时救济的权利

Article 49　Jurisdiction of arbitration tribunal to order interim relief

第 49 条　仲裁庭命令临时救济的权力

Article 50　Procedures for arbitration tribunal to order interim relief

第 50 条　仲裁庭命令临时救济的程序

Article 51　Jurisdiction of and procedures for arbitration tribunal to change, supplement or remove interim relief

第 51 条　仲裁庭更改、补充和撤销临时救济的权力与程序

Article 52　Responsibility of applicant for interim relief

第 52 条　临时救济申请人的责任

Article 53　Jurisdiction of and order and procedures for court to order，change or remove interim relief

第 53 条　法院更改、补充和撤销临时救济的权力、命令与程序

CHAPTER 8
Dispute Resolution Sessions
第八章　纠纷解决会议

Article 54　Preparation for dispute resolution sessions

第 54 条　纠纷解决会议的准备

Article 55　Composition of and procedures for dispute resolution sessions

第 55 条　纠纷解决会议的组成与程序

Article 56　Absence of parties

第 56 条　当事人缺席

Article 57　Adjournment of dispute resolution session

第 57 条　纠纷解决会议的延期

Article 58　Mediation and recognition of successful mediation

第 58 条　调解和认可成功调解

Article 59　Stay of dispute resolution

第 59 条　中止纠纷解决

CHAPTER 9
Arbitral Awards
第九章　仲裁裁决

Article 60　Principles for issuance of award

第 60 条　发布裁决的原则

Article 61　Contents，form and validity of arbitral award

第 61 条　仲裁裁决的内容、形式和效力

Article 62　Registration of ad hoc arbitral award

第 62 条　临时仲裁裁决的登记

Article 63　Rectification and explanation of arbitral award; supplementary awards

第 63 条　仲裁裁决的修正与解释；补充裁决

Article 64　Archiving files

第 64 条　文件存档

CHAPTER 10
Enforcement of Arbitral Awards
第十章　执行仲裁裁决

Article 65　Voluntary carrying out of arbitral award

第 65 条　自愿执行仲裁裁决

Article 66　Right to apply for enforcement of arbitral award

第 66 条　申请执行仲裁裁决的权利

Article 67　Enforcement of arbitral award

第 67 条　执行仲裁裁决

CHAPTER 11
Setting Aside Arbitral Awards
第十一章　撤销仲裁裁决

Article 68　Grounds for setting aside arbitral award

第 68 条　撤销仲裁裁决的原因

Article 69　Right to petition for arbitral award to be set aside

第 69 条　申请撤销仲裁裁决的权利

Article 70　Petition requesting arbitral award be set aside

第 70 条　撤销仲裁裁决的请求

Article 71　Hearing by court of petition requesting arbitral award be set aside

第 71 条　上诉法院针对撤销仲裁裁决的听证

Article 72　Court fees regarding arbitration

第 72 条　仲裁费用

CHAPTER 12

Organization and Operation of Foreign Arbitration in Vietnam

第十二章 外国仲裁在越南的组织与运作

Article 73 Conditions for foreign arbitration institutions to operate in Vietnam

第 73 条 外国仲裁机构在越南运作的条件

Article 74 Operational forms of foreign arbitration institutions in Vietnam

第 74 条 外国仲裁机构在越南的运作形式

Article 75 Branches

第 75 条 分支机构

Article 76 Rights and obligations of branch of foreign arbitration institution in Vietnam

第 76 条 外国仲裁机构的分支机构在越南的权利与义务

Article 77 Representative offices

第 77 条 代表处

Article 78 Rights and obligations of representative office of foreign arbitration institution in Vietnam

第 78 条 外国仲裁机构的代表处在越南的权利与义务

Article 79 Operation of branches and representative offices of foreign arbitration institutions in Vietnam

第 79 条 外国仲裁机构的分支机构和代表处在越南的运作

CHAPTER 13

Implementing Provisions

第十三章 执行条款

Article 80 Application of this Law to arbitration centres established prior to effective date of this Law

第 80 条 本法适用于本法生效之日前设立的仲裁中心

Article 81　Effectiveness

第 81 条　效力

Article 82　Detailed regulations and guidelines on implementation

第 82 条　执行细则和准则

NATIONAL ASSEMBLY

国会

No. 54 - 2010 - QH12

第 54 - 2010 - QH12 号

SOCIALIST REPUBLIC OF VIETNAM

越南社会主义共和国

Independence-Freedom-Happiness

独立-自由-幸福

LAW ON COMMERCIAL ARBITRATION

《商事仲裁法》

National Assembly of the Socialist Republic of Vietnam

越南社会主义共和国国会

Legislature XII，7th Session

第十二届立法会第七次会议

(17 June 2010)

(2010 年 6 月 17 日)

Pursuant to the 1992 Constitution of the Socialist Republic of Vietnam as amended by Resolution 51 - 2001 - QH10；

根据经第 51 - 2001 - QH10 号决议修订的 1992 年《越南社会主义共和国宪法》；

The National Assembly hereby promulgates the *Law on Commercial Arbitration*.

国会特此颁布《商事仲裁法》。

CHAPTER 1
General Provisions
第一章　总则

Article 1　Governing scope
第1条　管辖范围

This Law regulates commercial arbitration competence，arbitration forms，arbitration institutions and arbitrators；order and procedures for arbitration；rights，obligations and responsibilities of parties to arbitration proceedings；competence of courts over arbitration activities；organization and operation of foreign arbitration in Vietnam；and enforcement of arbitral awards.

本法规定了商事仲裁权力、仲裁形式、仲裁机构和仲裁员；仲裁的命令和程序；仲裁各方的权利、义务和责任；法院对仲裁活动的权力；外国仲裁在越南的组织和运作；以及仲裁裁决的执行。

Article 2　Competence of arbitration to resolve disputes：
第2条　仲裁可解决的纠纷

1. Disputes between parties arising from commercial activities.

1. 各方在商事活动中的纠纷。

2. Disputes arising between parties at least one of whom is engaged in commercial activities.

2. 至少有一方从事商事活动的当事方之间的纠纷。

3. Other disputes between parties which the law stipulates shall or may be resolved by arbitration.

3. 法律规定的当事人之间应当或可以通过仲裁解决的其他纠纷。

Article 3　Interpretation of terms
第3条　术语解释

In this Law，the following terms shall be construed as follows：

本法下列用语应解释如下：

1. Commercial arbitration means a dispute resolution method agreed by the parties and conducted in accordance with the provisions of this Law.

1. 商事仲裁是指当事人约定的、依照本法规定进行的纠纷解决方式。

2. Arbitration agreement means an agreement between the parties to use arbitration to resolve a dispute which may arise or which has arisen.

2. 仲裁协议是指当事人利用仲裁解决可能发生或者已经发生的纠纷的协议。

3. Parties in dispute mean Vietnamese or foreign individuals，bodies or organizations which participate in arbitration proceedings in the capacity of claimants or respondents.

3. 纠纷当事人是指以申请人或被申请人的身份参与仲裁程序的越南或外国个人、团体或组织。

4. Dispute with a foreign element means a dispute arising in commercial relations involving，or in some other legal relationships involving a foreign element as prescribed in the Civil Code.

4. 涉外纠纷是指涉及《民法》所述的涉外商业关系或者其他涉外法律关系的纠纷。

5. Arbitrator means a person selected by the parties or appointed by an arbitration centre or by a court to resolve a dispute in accordance with the provisions of this Law.

5. 仲裁员是指当事人选定的，或者由仲裁中心或者法院指定的依照本法规定解决纠纷的人。

6. Institutional arbitration means the form of dispute resolution at an arbitration centre in accordance with the provisions of this Law and the procedural rules of such arbitration centre.

6. 机构仲裁是指根据本法规定和仲裁中心程序规则，在仲裁中心解决纠纷的形式。

7. Ad hoc arbitration means the form of dispute resolution in accordance with the provisions of this Law and the order and procedures as agreed by the parties.

7. 临时仲裁是指依照本法规定和当事人约定的程序进行的纠纷解决形式。

8. Dispute resolution location means the location where the arbitration tribunal conducts the dispute resolution as agreed by the parties，or as decided by the arbitration tribunal if the parties do not have such an agreement. If the dispute resolution location is within the territory of Vietnam then the award must be deemed to have been rendered in Vietnam irrespective of the location at which the arbitration tribunal conducted sessions in order to issue such award.

8. 纠纷解决地点是指当事人约定的仲裁庭解决纠纷的地点,或者当事人没有约定的情况下由仲裁庭决定的地点。如果纠纷解决地点在越南境内,则无论仲裁庭在何地举行会议发布裁决,均应视为越南裁决。

9. Arbitral decision means a decision of the arbitration tribunal during the dispute resolution process.

9. 仲裁裁决是指仲裁庭在纠纷解决过程中做出的决定。

10. Arbitral award means the decision of the arbitration tribunal resolving the entire dispute and terminating the arbitration proceedings.

10. 仲裁裁决是仲裁庭解决全部纠纷并终止仲裁程序的裁决。

11. Foreign arbitration means arbitration established in accordance with foreign arbitration law which the parties agree to select to conduct dispute resolution，either inside or outside the territory of Vietnam.

11. 外国仲裁是指根据双方同意选择的外国仲裁法在越南境内外解决纠纷的仲裁。

12. Foreign arbitral award means an award rendered by foreign arbitration either inside or outside the territory of Vietnam in order to resolve a dispute as agreed by the parties.

12. 外国仲裁裁决是指经双方同意,在越南境内外作出的用来解决纠纷的外国仲裁裁决。

Article 4   Principles for dispute resolution by arbitration:

第 4 条   仲裁解决纠纷的原则

1. Arbitrators must respect the agreement of the parties if it does not breach prohibitions and is not contrary to social morals.

1. 如果当事人之间的协议不违反禁令和社会公德,仲裁员应尊重该协议。

2. Arbitrators must be independent, objective and impartial, and must comply with provisions of law.

2. 仲裁员应独立、客观、公正,并遵守法律规定。

3. Parties in dispute shall have equal rights and obligations. Arbitration tribunals shall be responsible to facilitate the parties to exercise their rights and to discharge their obligations.

3. 纠纷当事人应享有平等的权利和义务。仲裁庭应负责协助当事人行使权利和履行义务。

4. Dispute resolution by arbitration shall be conducted in private, unless otherwise agreed by the parties.

4. 除非当事人另有约定,仲裁应不公开进行。

5. An arbitral award shall be final.

5. 仲裁裁决是终局的。

Article 5   Conditions for dispute resolution by arbitration

第 5 条   仲裁解决纠纷的条件

1. A dispute shall be resolved by arbitration if the parties have an arbitration agreement. An arbitration agreement may be made

either prior to or after a dispute arises.

1. 当事人有仲裁协议的,应当通过仲裁解决。仲裁协议可以在纠纷发生之前或之后达成。

2. If one of the parties to an arbitration agreement is an individual who dies or who loses capacity for acts, then the arbitration agreement shall remain effective against the heir or legal representative respectively of such former individual, unless otherwise agreed by the parties.

2. 如果仲裁协议的一方当事人死亡或丧失行为能力,除非当事人另有约定,否则仲裁协议对其继承人或法定代表人继续有效。

3. If one of the parties to an arbitration agreement is an organization which must terminate its operation, becomes bankrupt, dissolves, consolidates, merges, demerges, separates or converts its organizational form, then the arbitration agreement shall remain effective against the organization which succeeds to the rights and obligations of such former organization, unless otherwise agreed by the parties.

3. 如果仲裁协议的一方是应停止运作、破产、解散、合并、融合、分解或转换形式的组织,除非当事人另有约定,否则仲裁协议对继承了该组织权利与义务的新组织仍然有效。

Article 6 Court refusal to accept jurisdiction if there is an arbitra-tion agreement

第6条 有仲裁协议的情况下法院拒绝管辖

Where the parties in dispute already have an arbitration agreement but one party institutes court proceedings, the court must refuse to accept jurisdiction unless the arbitration agreement is void or incapable of being performed.

各方当事人已有仲裁协议但一方当事人提起诉讼的,除非仲裁协议无效或不能履行,否则法院应拒绝管辖。

Article 7　Determining which court has competence over arbitration activities

第 7 条　确定哪个法院对仲裁有管辖权

1. If the parties already have an agreement to choose a specific court, then such court as chosen by the parties shall be the competent court.

1. 当事人已经约定选择特定法院的,应以当事人选择的法院为主管法院。

2. If the parties do not have an agreement to choose a court, then the competent court shall be determined as follows:

2. 当事人未协议选择法院的,则主管法院裁定如下:

(a) For appointment of an arbitrator to establish an ad hoc arbitration tribunal, the competent court shall be the court in the place where the respondent resides if the respondent is an individual, or where the respondent has its head office if the respondent is an organization. If there are a number of respondents, then the competent court shall be the court in the place where one of such respondents resides or has its head office.

(a) 任命仲裁员设立临时仲裁庭的,如果被申请人是个人,主管法院为被申请人居住地所在法院;如果被申请人是组织,主管法院为被申请人总部所在法院。如果有多个被申请人,主管法院为被申请人之一居住地所在地法院或总部所在地的法院。

If the respondent resides or has its head office overseas, then the competent court shall be the court in the place where the claimant resides or has its head office.

如果被申请人在外国居住或总部在外国,主管法院为申请人所在地的法院或总部所在地的法院。

(b) For the replacement of an arbitrator in an ad hoc arbitration tribunal, the competent court shall be the court in the place where the arbitration tribunal resolves the dispute;

（b）临时仲裁庭更换仲裁员的，主管法院为解决该纠纷的仲裁庭所在地的法院；

（c）For an appeal against the decision of an arbitration tribunal that the arbitration agreement was void or incapable of being performed or about the jurisdiction of the arbitration tribunal, the competent court shall be the court in the place where the arbitration tribunal issued such decision;

（c）针对仲裁庭制作出的仲裁协议无效或不能被履行，或仲裁庭无管辖权的决定提起上诉的，主管法院为做出该决定的仲裁庭所在地的法院；

（d）For an application to a court to collect evidence, the competent court shall be the court in the place where such evidence requiring collection exists;

（d）向法院申请收集证据的，主管法院为证据收集地的法院；

（e）For an application to a court to grant interim relief, the competent court shall be the court in the place where the relief needs to be applied;

（e）向法院申请临时救济的，主管法院为救济所在地的法院；

（f）For summoning witnesses, the competent court shall be the court in the place where the witnesses reside;

（f）传唤证人的，主管法院为证人所在地的法院；

（g）For an application to set aside an arbitral award or to register an ad hoc arbitral award, the competent court shall be the court in the place where the arbitration tribunal rendered such award.

（g）申请撤销仲裁裁决或登记临时仲裁裁决的，主管法院为作出该裁决的仲裁庭所在地的法院。

3. Courts with competence over the arbitration activities prescribed in clauses 1 and 2 of this article shall be people's courts of

provinces and cities under central authority.

3. 本条第 1 款和第 2 款规定的对仲裁活动有管辖权的法院为省和直辖市的人民法院。

Article 8　Determining which enforcement agency has competence to enforce arbitral awards and interim relief decisions of arbitration tribunals

第 8 条　确定哪个执行机构有权执行仲裁裁决和仲裁庭做出的临时救济决定

1. The civil enforcement agency with competence to enforce an arbitral award shall be the civil enforcement agency in the province or city under central authority where the arbitration tribunal rendered the award.

1. 有权执行仲裁裁决的民事执行机构为仲裁裁决作出地所在的省和直辖市的民事执行机构。

2. The civil enforcement agency with competence to enforce an interim relief decision of an arbitration tribunal shall be the civil enforcement agency in the province or city under central authority where the relief needs to be applied.

2. 有权执行仲裁庭临时救济决定的民事执行机构为救济所在地所在的省和直辖市的民事执行机构

Article 9　Negotiation and conciliation during arbitration proceedings

第 9 条　仲裁程序中的协商与调解

Parties shall have the freedom，during the process of arbitration proceedings，to negotiate and reach agreement with each other to resolve their dispute，or to request the arbitration tribunal to mediate in order for the parties to reach agreement and resolve their dispute.

当事人在仲裁程序中有权自由协商解决纠纷，或请求仲裁庭调解，以便双方达成协议并解决纠纷。

Article 10　Language
第 10 条　语言

1. For disputes without a foreign element, the language to be used in arbitration proceedings shall be Vietnamese, except in a dispute to which at least one party is an enterprise with foreign invested capital. If a party in dispute cannot use Vietnamese, then it may use an interpreter to translate into Vietnamese.

1. 对于无涉外因素的纠纷，仲裁程序中使用的语言应为越南语，但至少一方为外商投资企业的纠纷除外。如果一方不能使用越南语，则可让口译员翻译成越南语。

2. For disputes with a foreign element, disputes to which at least one party is an enterprise with foreign invested capital, the language to be used in arbitration proceedings shall be as agreed by the parties. If the parties do not have such an agreement, then the language to be used in the arbitration proceedings shall be as decided by the arbitration tribunal.

2. 对于涉外纠纷，即至少一方为外商投资企业的纠纷，仲裁程序中使用的语言应当由当事人约定。如果当事人无此类协议，仲裁程序中使用的语言应由仲裁庭决定。

Article 11　Location for dispute resolution by arbitration
第 11 条　仲裁地

1. Parties shall have the right to reach agreement on the dispute resolution location; if the parties do not have such an agreement, then the location shall be as decided by the arbitration tribunal. The dispute resolution location may be inside or outside the territory of Vietnam.

1. 各方当事人有权就纠纷解决地点达成协议；当事人没有约定的，由仲裁庭决定。纠纷解决地点可在越南境内或境外。

2. Unless otherwise agreed by the parties, the arbitration tribunal may conduct sessions at a location which it deems appropriate for mutual consultation between the arbitrators, for taking statements from witnesses, for seeking advice from experts, or for conducting evaluations of goods, assets or other materials.

2. 除非当事人另有约定,仲裁庭可以在其认为适当的地点进行仲裁员之间的协商,以听取证人陈述,征求专家意见,或者对货物、财产或其他材料进行评价。

Article 12   Service of notices and order for service of notices
第 12 条   通知送达与通知送达命令

The method and order for service of notices in arbitration proceedings shall be regulated as follows, unless otherwise agreed by the parties or otherwise stipulated by the procedural rules of the arbitration centre:

除非当事人另有约定或者仲裁中心程序规则另有规定,仲裁程序中通知送达的方式与命令应按下列规定:

1. Explanatory statements, communications and other materials as served by any one party must be sent to the arbitration centre or arbitration tribunal in sufficient copies so that each member of the arbitration tribunal has one copy, the other party has one copy, and one copy is archived at the arbitration centre.

1. 任何一方送达的解释性陈述、通讯和其他材料应以足量副本送达仲裁中心或仲裁庭,以便仲裁庭的每位成员有一份副本,另一方有一份副本,并在仲裁中心存档一份。

2. Notices and materials served by an arbitration centre and/or arbitration tribunal on the parties must be sent to the addresses of the parties or to their representatives at the correct addresses as notified by such parties.

2. 仲裁中心和/或仲裁庭就当事人送达的通知和材料应按照当事人通

知的正确地址送到当事人地址或其代表的地址。

3. An arbitration centre and/or arbitration tribunal may serve notices and materials by hand delivery, registered letter, ordinary mail, fax, telex, telegram, email or any other method which acknowledges such service.

3. 仲裁中心和/或仲裁庭可通过专人递送、挂号信、普通邮件、传真、电传、电报、电子邮件或任何其他认可的方式送达通知和材料。

4. Notices and materials sent by an arbitration centre and/or arbitration tribunal shall be deemed received on the date on which the parties or their representatives received them or they are deemed received, if such notices and materials were sent in conformity with the provisions in clause 2 of this article.

4. 如按照本条第 2 款的规定发出通知和材料,仲裁中心和/或仲裁庭发出的通知和材料应在当事人或其代表收到或被视为收到时收到。

5. The time-limit for receipt of a notice or material shall be calculated from the day following the day on which such notice or material is deemed received. If the following day is a public or other holiday as prescribed in regulations of the country or territory where such notice or material was served, then this time-limit shall be calculated from the first business day after such holiday. If the last day of this time-limit falls on a public or other holiday as prescribed in regulations of the country or territory where such notice or material is served, then the deadline shall be the close of the next business day after such holiday.

5. 收到通知或资料的期限应自收到通知或资料之日起计算。如果收到第二天是在通知或资料送达的国家或地区规定的公共假日或其他假期,则该期限从假日后的第一个工作日算起。如果该期限的最后一天属于该通知或资料所在的国家或地区规定的公共假日或其他假期,则截止时间为该假期后的下一个工作日结束时。

Article 13 Loss of right to object
第13条 放弃异议权

If a party discovers a breach of the provisions of this Law or of the arbitration agreement but continues to conduct the arbitration proceedings and does not object to such breach within the time-limit stipulated in this Law, such party shall lose the right to object at the arbitration or before the court.

当事人发现有违反本法或仲裁协议规定的情况却继续进行仲裁程序，并且在本法规定的期限内不反对的，即为当事人放弃异议权。

Article 14 Applicable law in dispute resolution
第14条 适用于解决纠纷的法律

1. For disputes without a foreign element, the arbitration tribunal shall apply the law of Vietnam in order to resolve the dispute.

1. 对于没有涉外因素的纠纷，仲裁庭应适用越南的法律解决纠纷。

2. For disputes with a foreign element, the arbitration tribunal shall apply the law chosen by the parties; if the parties do not have an agreement on applicable law, then the arbitration tribunal shall make a decision to apply the law which it considers the most appropriate.

2. 对于涉外纠纷，仲裁庭应当适用当事人选定的法律；当事人对适用法律没有约定的，由仲裁庭决定适用其认为最适当的法律。

3. If the law of Vietnam or the law chosen by the parties does not contain specific provisions relevant to the matters in dispute, then the arbitration tribunal may apply international customs in order to resolve the dispute if such application or the consequences of such application are not contrary to the fundamental principles of the law of Vietnam.

3. 如果越南法律或当事人选择的法律没有包含与纠纷有关的具体规

定,在申请或其结果不违背越南法律基本原则的情况下,仲裁庭可以申请国际海关解决争端。

Article 15　State administration of arbitration
第 15 条　国家仲裁管理机构

1. State administration of arbitration shall comprise the following items：

1. 国家仲裁管理应包括以下内容：

(a) Promulgation of legal instruments on arbitration and their implementing guidelines；

(a) 颁布关于仲裁的法律文书及其执行准则；

(b) Issuance and revocation of establishment licences and certificates of registration of operation of arbitration centres，and of branches and representative offices of foreign arbitration institutions in Vietnam；

(b) 签发和撤销设立在越南的仲裁中心、外国仲裁机构的分支机构和代表处的营业执照和注册证书；

(c) Announcement of lists of arbitrators of arbitration institutions operating in Vietnam；

(c) 宣布在越南运作的仲裁机构的仲裁员名单；

(d) Dissemination and education on the law on arbitration；international co-operation in the arbitration sector；and guidance on training and fostering arbitrators；

(d) 仲裁法的宣传和教育；仲裁部门的国际合作；指导培训和培养仲裁员；

(e) Checks and inspections，and dealing with breaches of the law on arbitration；

(e) 调查、检查和处理违反仲裁法的行为；

(f) Resolution of complaints and denunciations about the arbitration activities prescribed in sub-clauses（b），（c），（d） and（e）of this clause.

（f）解决本款(b)项、(c)项、(d)项及(e)项规定的仲裁活动的投诉和申诉。

2. The Government shall exercise uniform State administration of arbitration.

2. 政府应实行统一的国家仲裁管理。

3. The Ministry of Justice shall be responsible before the Government for exercising State administration of arbitration.

3. 司法部先于政府负责执行国家的仲裁管理。

4. Departments of Justice of provinces and cities under central authority shall assist the Ministry of Justice to carry out a number of tasks in accordance with Government regulations and the provisions of this Law.

4. 省、直辖市司法部门应依照政府规定和本法的规定,协助司法部履行职责。

CHAPTER 2
Arbitration Agreements
第二章　仲裁协议

Article 16　Form of arbitration agreements

第 16 条　仲裁协议的形式

1. An arbitration agreement may be in the form of an arbitration clause in a contract or it may be in the form of a separate agreement.

1. 仲裁协议可以是合同中的仲裁条款,也可以是单独的协议形式。

2. An arbitration agreement must be in writing. The following forms of agreement shall also be deemed to constitute a written arbitration agreement：

2. 仲裁协议应是书面的。下列形式的协议也应被视为构成书面仲裁协议：

（a）An agreement established via an exchange between the parties by telegram，fax，telex，email or other form prescribed by law；

（a）当事人通过电报、传真、电传、电子邮件或法律规定的其他形式交换订立的协议；

（b）An agreement established via the exchange of written information between the parties；

（b）当事人通过书面信息交换订立的协议；

（c）An agreement prepared in writing by a lawyer，notary or competent organization at the request of the parties；

（c）应当事人的请求，由律师、公证人或主管组织书面提出的协议；

（d）Reference by the parties during the course of a transaction to a document such as a contract，source document，company charter or other similar documents which contain an arbitration agreement.

（d）当事人在交易过程中提及的包含仲裁协议的文件，如合同、原始文件、公司章程或其他类似文件。

（e）Exchange of a statement of claim and defence which express the existence of an agreement proposed by one party and not denied by the other party.

（e）一方表示协议存在的申请书与另一方不否认协议存在的答辩状的交换。

Article 17　Right of consumers to select dispute resolution method
第 17 条　当事人选择纠纷解决方式的权利

For disputes between a goods and/or service provider ［on the one hand］ and consumers ［on the other hand］，even if such provider has drafted and inserted an arbitration clause in its standard conditions on supply of such goods and services，a consumer shall still have the right to select arbitration or a court to resolve the dispute. A goods and/or service provider shall only have the right to institute arbitration proceedings if the consumer so consents.

对于商品和/或服务提供者(一方)与消费者(另一方)之间的纠纷,即使该提供者已经在其提供商品和服务的条件中起草并插入了仲裁条款,消费者仍然有权选择仲裁或法院解决纠纷。商品和/或服务提供者只有在消费者同意的情况下才有权提起仲裁程序。

Article 18　Void arbitration agreements:
第 18 条　无效的仲裁协议

1. The dispute arises in a sector outside the competence of arbitration prescribed in article 2 of this Law.

1. 纠纷在本法第 2 条规定的仲裁范围以外。

2. The person who entered into the arbitration agreement lacked authority as stipulated by law.

2. 订立仲裁协议的人缺乏法律规定的权力。

3. The person who entered into the arbitration agreement lacked civil legal capacity pursuant to the Civil Code.

3. 订立仲裁协议的人缺乏《民法》规定的民事行为能力。

4. The form of the arbitration agreement does not comply with article 16 of this Law.

4. 仲裁协议的形式不符合本法第 16 条的规定。

5. One of the parties was deceived, threatened or coerced during the process of formulation of the arbitration agreement and requests a declaration that the arbitration agreement is void.

5. 一方在拟定仲裁协议的过程中受到欺骗、威胁或胁迫,并要求宣布仲裁协议无效。

6. The arbitration agreement breaches a prohibition prescribed by law.

6. 仲裁协议违反法律的禁止性规定。

Article 19   Independence of arbitration agreements

第 19 条   仲裁协议的独立性

An arbitration agreement shall exist totally independently of the contract. Any modification, extension or rescission of the contract, or invalidity or unenforceability of the contract shall not result in the invalidity of the arbitration agreement.

仲裁协议应完全独立于合同。对合同的任何修改、延伸或解除，以及合同无效或不能执行均不导致仲裁协议无效。

CHAPTER 3
Arbitrators
第三章   仲裁员

Article 20   Qualifications of arbitrators

第 20 条   仲裁员的资格

1. A person with all the following qualifications may act as an arbitrator：

1. 具备所有下列资格的人可担任仲裁员：

　　(a) Having full civil legal capacity as prescribed in the Civil Code；

　　(a) 具备《民法》规定的完全民事行为能力；

　　(b) Having a university qualification and at least five years' work experience in the discipline which he or she studied；

　　(b) 具有大学学历，并有 5 年以上的所学学科的工作经验；

　　(c) In special cases an expert with highly specialized qualifications and considerable practical experience may still be selected to act as an arbitrator notwithstanding he/she fails to satisfy the requirements prescribed in sub-clause (b) above.

　　(c) 在特殊情况下，尽管不符合上述(b)项的要求，仍可选择具有高度专业资格和丰富实践经验的专家担任仲裁员。

2. A person with all the qualifications prescribed in clause 1 of this article but who falls into one of the following categories shall not be permitted to act as an arbitrator:

2. 具备本条第 1 款规定的资格但有下列情形之一的人不得担任仲裁员:

　　(a) A person who is currently a judge, prosecutor, investigator, enforcement officer, or official of a people's court, of a people's procuracy, of an investigative agency or of a judgment enforcement agency;

　　(a) 现任法官、检察官、侦查人员、执行人员,或人民法院、人民检察院、调查机关、执法机构的官员;

　　(b) A person under a criminal charge or prosecution or who is serving a criminal sentence or who has fully served the sentence but whose criminal record has not yet been cleared.

　　(b) 被刑事指控或起诉的人,正在服刑的罪犯,或服刑完毕但犯罪记录尚未被清除的人。

3. An arbitration centre may stipulate higher qualifications than those prescribed in clause 1 of this article as applicable to arbitrators in its institution.

3. 仲裁中心可以将高于本条第 1 款的规定适用于其机构仲裁员的资格。

Article 21　Rights and obligations of arbitrators:

第 21 条　仲裁员的权利与义务

1. To accept or refuse to resolve a dispute.

1. 接受或拒绝解决纠纷。

2. To remain independent during dispute resolution.

2. 在纠纷解决中保持独立。

3. To refuse to provide information about a dispute.

3. 拒绝提供关于纠纷的信息。

4. To receive remuneration.

4. 领取报酬。

5. To maintain confidentiality of the contents of the dispute which he or she resolves，unless information must be provided to a competent State authority in accordance with law.

5. 除非应依法向国家主管部门提供信息，否则应对其解决的纠纷内容保密。

6. To ensure that resolution of a dispute is impartial，speedy and prompt.

6. 确保公正、快捷、迅速解决纠纷。

7. To comply with professional ethics rules.

7. 遵守职业道德。

Article 22　Arbitrators' Association
第 22 条　仲裁员协会

The Arbitrators' Association shall be a socio-professional organization of arbitrators and arbitration centres throughout the entire country. Establishment and operation of the Arbitrators' Association shall be implemented in accordance with the law on professional associations.

仲裁员协会应是全国各地的仲裁员和仲裁中心的社会行业组织。仲裁员协会的设立和运作应当依照行业协会的法律执行。

CHAPTER 4
Arbitration Centres
第四章　仲裁中心

Article 23　Functions of arbitration centre
第 23 条　仲裁中心的职能

An arbitration centre shall have the function of organizing and co-ordinating activities of dispute resolution by institutional arbitration，and of assisting arbitrators by providing administrative and office facilities and other assistance during the process of the arbitration proceedings.

仲裁中心的职能是组织和协调机构仲裁解决纠纷的活动，协助仲裁员在仲裁程序中提供行政和办公设施等。

Article 24　Conditions and procedures for establishment of arbitration centre
第 24 条　成立仲裁中心的条件与程序

1. An arbitration centre may be established if there is a request for establishment from at least five founding members who are Vietnamese citizens and fully qualified to act as arbitrators in accordance with article 20 of this Law，and if the Minister of Justice issues an establishment licence.

1. 如果有五名以上符合本法第 20 条规定的越南公民担任仲裁员并申请成立仲裁中心，司法部颁发执照的，可成立仲裁中心。

2. An application file for establishment of an arbitration centre shall comprise：

2. 成立仲裁中心的申请文件应包括：

（a）Request for establishment；

（a）成立请求；

（b）Draft charter of the arbitration centre on the standard form issued by the Ministry of Justice；

（b）符合司法部颁布的标准格式的仲裁中心章程草案；

（c）List of founding members and accompanying documents proving that such members satisfy all the conditions prescribed in article 20 of this Law.

（c）能证明创始成员符合本法第 20 条规定的所有条件的创始成员和随附文件清单。

3. The Minister of Justice shall，within thirty（30）days from the date of receipt of a complete and valid application file，issue an establishment licence for the arbitration centre and approve its charter；in a case of refusal，a written reply specifying the

reasons must be provided.

3. 司法部长应当自收到完整有效的申请文件之日起 30 日内,向仲裁中心签发成立许可证,并批准其章程;拒绝成立的,应提供书面答复并说明原因。

Article 25　Registration of operation of arbitration centre
第 25 条　登记仲裁中心运作

An arbitration centre must, within thirty (30) days from the date of receipt of its establishment licence, register its operation with the Department of Justice in the province or city under central authority where it has its head office. If upon the expiry of this time-limit the arbitration centre has failed to carry out registration, then its licence shall no longer be valid.

仲裁中心应在收到其成立许可证之日起 30 日内,将其运作情况向其总部所在地的省或直辖市的司法部门进行登记。如果仲裁中心未能按时进行登记,其许可证将不再有效。

The Department of Justice shall issue a certificate of registration of operation for the arbitration centre no later than fifteen (15) days from the date of receipt of the request for registration.

司法部门应自收到登记请求之日起 15 日内,向仲裁中心发布注册证书。

Article 26　Announcement of establishment of arbitration centre
第 26 条　宣布成立仲裁中心

1. An arbitration centre must, within thirty (30) days from the date of issuance of its certificate of registration of operation, publish an announcement in three consecutive issues of a central daily newspaper or daily newspaper in the locality where it registered its operation, with the following main particulars:

1. 仲裁中心应在其注册证书发布之日起 30 日内,在其登记注册地的中央日报或日报连续三期发布公告，主要内容如下：

(a) Name and address of head office of the arbitration centre；

(a) 仲裁中心总部的名称和地址；

(b) Operational activities of the arbitration centre；

(b) 仲裁中心的业务活动；

(c) Serial number of the certificate of registration of operation，issuing body and date of issuance of such certificate；

(c) 营业执照编号、发证机构和发证日期；

(d) Date of commencement of operation of the arbitration centre.

(d) 仲裁中心开始运作的日期。

2. An arbitration centre must display at its head office a notice of the particulars stipulated in clause 1 of this article and a list of arbitrators of the arbitration centre.

2. 仲裁中心应在其总部展示本条第 1 款规定的具体事项和该仲裁中心仲裁员名单。

Article 27   Legal entity status and structure of arbitration centre

第 27 条   仲裁中心的法人地位和结构

1. An arbitration centre shall have legal entity status，and its own seal and bank account.

1. 仲裁中心具有法人资格，自有印章和银行账户。

2. An arbitration centre shall be a non-profit institution.

2. 仲裁中心为非营利机构。

3. An arbitration centre shall be permitted to establish branches and representative offices both within Vietnam and overseas.

3. 仲裁中心可在越南境内和海外设立分支机构和代表处。

4. An arbitration centre shall have an executive committee and a secretariat. The structure and apparatus of the arbitration centre shall be as prescribed in its charter.

4. 仲裁中心设执行委员会和秘书处。仲裁中心的结构和设备按其章
   程规定。

The executive committee of an arbitration centre shall comprise
the chairman and one or more vice chairmen, and it may also
include a general secretary appointed by the chairman. The
chairman of the arbitration centre shall be an arbitrator.

仲裁中心的执行委员会由主席和一名或多名副主席组成,还可以包
括由主席任命的总书记。仲裁中心的主席应是仲裁员。

5. An arbitration centre shall have a list of arbitrators.

5. 仲裁中心应有仲裁员名单。

Article 28　Rights and obligations of arbitration centre:
第28条　仲裁中心的权利与义务

1. To formulate the charter and procedural rules of the arbitration
   centre, which shall be consistent with the provisions of this Law.

1. 制定符合本法规定的仲裁中心章程和程序规则。

2. To prescribe the qualifications required for arbitrators and the
   rules on selection and removal of the name of an arbitrator from
   the list of arbitrators of such centre.

2. 规定仲裁员所需的资格和从仲裁员名单中选择与除名仲裁员的
   规则。

3. To send the list of arbitrators of the arbitration centre and any
   changes to such list to the Ministry of Justice for announcement.

3. 将仲裁中心仲裁员名单及其变更情况报送司法部公告。

4. To appoint arbitrators to establish an arbitration tribunal in the
   cases prescribed in this Law.

4. 按照本法规定指定仲裁员设立仲裁庭。

5. To provide arbitration and mediation services and other
   commercial dispute resolution methods prescribed by law.

5. 提供法律规定的仲裁、调解和其他商事纠纷解决办法。

6. To supply administrative and office facilities and other services for dispute resolution.

6. 提供行政和办公设施及其他服务以解决纠纷。

7. To collect arbitration fees and other lawful fees relevant to arbitration activities.

7. 收取与仲裁活动有关的仲裁费和其他合法费用。

8. To pay remuneration and other expenses to arbitrators.

8. 向仲裁员支付报酬和其他费用。

9. To hold courses for arbitrators to reinforce their knowledge and skills in dispute resolution.

9. 为仲裁员开设课程,加强其在解决纠纷方面的知识和技能。

10. To report annually on the operation of the arbitration centre to the Department of Justice in the locality where the arbitration centre has registered its operation.

10. 每年向仲裁中心所在地的司法部门报告仲裁中心的运作情况。

11. To archive files and to provide copies of arbitral decisions at the request of the parties in dispute or of a competent State authority.

11. 存档文件,以及应当事人或国家主管部门的请求提供仲裁裁决副本。

Article 29　Termination of operation of arbitration centre
第 29 条　终止仲裁中心运作

1. The operation of an arbitration centre shall terminate in the following circumstances:

1. 出现下列情况时,仲裁中心应终止运作:

　　(a) In the circumstances prescribed in the charter of the arbitration centre;

　　(a) 在仲裁中心章程规定的情况下;

　　(b) Upon revocation of the establishment licence or certificate of registration of operation of the arbitration centre.

（b）仲裁中心的成立许可证或注册证书撤销。

2. The Government shall provide detailed regulations on the circumstances in which an establishment licence or certificate of registration of operation of an arbitration centre shall be revoked，and on the order and procedures for termination of operation of an arbitration centre.

2. 对于撤销仲裁中心的成立许可证或注册证书的情形，以及仲裁中心终止运作的制度和程序，政府应当提供详细的规定。

CHAPTER 5
Instituting Arbitration Proceedings
第五章　进行仲裁程序
Article 30　Statement of claim and accompanying materials
第 30 条　陈述主张和附带材料

1. In the case of dispute resolution at an arbitration centre，the claimant prepare a statement of claim and send it to the arbitration centre. In the case of dispute resolution by ad hoc arbitration，the claimant shall prepare a statement of claim and send it to the respondent.

1. 在仲裁中心解决纠纷的情况下，申请人应制作申请书并提交仲裁中心。在临时仲裁解决纠纷的情况下，申请人应制作申请书并将其交给被申请人。

2. A statement of claim shall contain the following particulars：

2. 申请书应包括下列详情：

（a）Date on which the statement of claim is made；

（a）制作出申请书的日期；

（b）Names and addresses of the parties，and names and addresses of witnesses，if any；

（b）各方当事人的姓名和地址，以及证人的姓名和地址（如有）；

（c）Summary of the matters in dispute；

（c）纠纷概况；

（d）Grounds and evidence，if any，of the claim；

（d）申请理由和证据（如有）；

（e）Specific relief sought by the claimant and value of the dispute；

（e）申请人寻求的具体救济和纠纷所涉及的金额；

（f）Name and address of the person whom the claimant selects as arbitrator or request for an arbitrator to be appointed.

（f）被申请人选为仲裁员或要求指定仲裁员的人员的姓名和地址。

3. The arbitration agreement and originals or copies of relevant materials must accompany the statement of claim.

3. 仲裁协议及相关材料的正本或副本应附在申请书上。

Article 31　Time of commencement of arbitration proceedings

第 31 条　仲裁程序开始时间

1. In the case of dispute resolution at an arbitration centre and unless otherwise agreed by the parties，the time of commencement of the arbitration proceedings shall be upon receipt by the arbitration centre of the statement of claim from the claimant.

1. 在仲裁中心解决纠纷的情况下，除非当事人另有约定，仲裁程序开始时间即仲裁中心收到申请人递交的申请书之时。

2. In the case of dispute resolution by ad hoc arbitration and unless otherwise agreed by the parties，the time of commencement of the arbitration proceedings shall be upon receipt by the respondent of the statement of claim of the claimant.

2. 在临时仲裁解决纠纷的情况下，除非当事人另有约定，仲裁程序开始时间即被申请人收到申请人递交的申请书之时。

Article 32　Notification of statement of claim
第 32 条　通知陈述主张

Unless otherwise agreed by the parties or otherwise stipulated by the procedural rules of the arbitration centre，the arbitration centre must，within ten（10）days from the date of receipt of the statement of claim with accompanying materials and a receipt of the provisional advance of arbitration fees，send the respondent a copy of the statement of claim of the claimant together with the materials prescribed in article 30.3 of this Law.

除非当事人另有约定或仲裁中心程序规则另有规定，仲裁中心应在收到附材料的申请书和临时预付的仲裁费之日起 10 日内，向被申请人送达申请书复印件，连同本法第 30 条第 3 款规定的材料。

Article 33　Limitation period for initiating proceedings for dispute resolution by arbitration
第 33 条　仲裁解决纠纷的时效期

The limitation period for initiating proceedings for dispute resolution by arbitration shall be two（2）years from the date of infringement of legal rights and interests，unless otherwise stipulated by specialized law.

除非专门法律另有规定，仲裁解决纠纷的时效期为合法权益受到侵害之日起 2 年。

Article 34 Arbitration fees
第 34 条　仲裁费用

1. Arbitration fees are the fees collected for the provision of services for dispute resolution by arbitration. Arbitration fees shall comprise：

1. 仲裁费是为仲裁解决纠纷而收取的费用。仲裁费用包括：

　（a）Remuneration and travelling and other expenses of

arbitrators；

（a）仲裁员的报酬、旅费和其他费用；

（b）Fees for expert consultancy and other assistance requested by the arbitration tribunal；

（b）仲裁庭要求提供专家咨询和其他协助的费用；

（c）Administrative fees；

（c）行政费用；

（d）Fees for the arbitration centre's appointment of an arbitrator for an ad hoc arbitrator at the request of the parties in dispute；

（d）仲裁中心根据各方请求任命仲裁员为临时仲裁员的费用；

（e）Fees for use of other necessary services provided by the arbitration centre.

（e）仲裁中心提供的其他必要服务的使用费。

2. The arbitration centre shall fix the arbitration fees. In the case of dispute resolution by ad hoc arbitration，the arbitration tribunal shall fix the arbitration fees.

2. 仲裁中心应确定仲裁费用。临时仲裁解决争议的，由仲裁庭确定仲裁费用。

3. The party which loses the case must pay the arbitration fees，unless otherwise agreed by the parties or otherwise stipulated by the procedural rules of the arbitration centre，or unless the arbitration tribunal makes some other allocation of fees.

3. 除非当事人另有约定或者仲裁中心程序规则另有规定，或者仲裁庭另行分配费用，否则失败一方应支付仲裁费。

Article 35　Defence and submission of the defence

第 35 条　答辩和提交答辩状

1. A defence shall contain the following particulars：

1. 答辩状应载明下列事项：

(a) Date on which the defence is made;

(a) 制作出答辩状的日期；

(b) Name and address of the respondent;

(b) 被申请人的姓名和地址；

(c) Grounds and evidence, if any, in support of the defence;

(c) 支持辩护的理由和证据（如有）；

(d) Name and address of the person whom the respondent selects as arbitrator or request for an arbitrator to be appointed.

(d) 被申请人选择的仲裁员或请求任命为仲裁员的人员的姓名和地址。

2. In the case of dispute resolution at an arbitration centre, unless otherwise agreed by the parties or otherwise stipulated by the procedural rules of the arbitration centre, the respondent must send the defence to the arbitration centre within thirty (30) days from the date of receipt of the statement of claim and accompanying materials. If one or all parties so request, the arbitration centre may extend this time-limit depending on the particular circumstances of the case.

2. 在仲裁中心解决纠纷的情况下，除当事人另有约定或者仲裁中心程序另有规定外，被申请人应在收到申请书及相关材料之日起后 30 日内向仲裁中心提交答辩状。经一方当事人或所有当事人要求，仲裁中心可根据案件的具体情况延长该期限。

3. In the case of dispute resolution by ad hoc arbitration, unless otherwise agreed by the parties, within thirty (30) days from the date of receipt of the statement of claim and accompanying materials of the claimant, the respondent must send the defence to the claimant and the arbitrator/s and the name and address of the person whom the respondent selects as arbitrator.

3. 在临时仲裁解决纠纷的情况下，除当事人另有约定外，被申请人应在收到申请书及相关材料之日起 30 日内向申请人、仲裁员以及被申请人选择的仲裁员送交答辩状。

4. If the respondent alleges that the dispute is outside the jurisdiction of arbitration，or alleges that there is no arbitration agreement or that the arbitration agreement is void or incapable of being performed，the respondent must specify such allegations in the defence.

4. 如果被申请人主张该纠纷不在仲裁管辖范围内，或者主张无仲裁协议、仲裁协议无效、仲裁协议无法执行的，被申请人应在答辩状中声明。

5. If the respondent fails to submit the defence as prescribed in clauses 2 and 3 of this article，the dispute resolution process shall still proceed.

5. 如果被申请人没有提交本条第 2 款和第 3 款所述答辩状，纠纷解决程序仍应继续进行。

Article 36　Counterclaim by respondent
第 36 条　被请求人反申请

1. A respondent shall have the right to file a counterclaim against the claimant on issues relevant to the dispute.

1. 被申请人有权就与纠纷有关的问题向申请人提出反申请。

2. The counterclaim of the respondent must be sent to the arbitration centre. In the case of dispute resolution by ad hoc arbitration，the counterclaim must be sent to the arbitration tribunal and the claimant. Counterclaims must be submitted at the same time as the defence.

2. 被申请人的反申请书应送交仲裁中心。在通过临时仲裁解决纠纷的情况下，反申请书应送交仲裁庭和申请人。反申请书应与答辩状同时提交。

3. The claimant must send a defence to counterclaim to the arbitration centre within thirty（30）days from the date of

receipt of the counterclaim. In the case of dispute resolution by ad hoc arbitration, the claimant must send the defence to counterclaim to the arbitration tribunal and to the respondent.

3. 申请人应在收到反申请书之日起 30 日内向仲裁中心提交针对反申请书的答辩状。在通过临时仲裁解决纠纷的情况下，申请人应向仲裁庭和被申请人提交针对反申请书的答辩状。

4. The arbitration tribunal which resolves the statement of claim of the claimant shall also resolve the counterclaim in accordance with the provisions in this Law on order and procedures for resolving a statement of claim of a claimant.

4. 仲裁庭处理申请人提交的申请书的，也应依照本法关于处理申请书的程序规定处理被申请人的反申请书。

Article 37   Withdrawal of statement of claim or counterclaim; amendment or addition to statement of claim, counterclaim or defences
第 37 条   撤销申请书或反申请书；修改或补充申请书、反申请书或答辩状

1. Parties shall have the right to withdraw their statement of claim and/or counterclaim before the arbitration tribunal issues the arbitral award.

1. 当事人有权在仲裁庭下达仲裁裁决书之前撤回其申请书和/或反申请书。

2. Parties may amend or add to their statement of claim, counterclaim or defences throughout the process of the arbitration proceedings. The arbitration tribunal shall have the right to disallow such amendments or additions if it considers they are an abuse aimed at causing difficulties or delaying the issuance of an arbitral award, or if they exceed the scope of the arbitration agreement applicable to the dispute.

2. 在整个仲裁过程中，当事人可以修改或补充申请书、反申请书或答辩状。如果仲裁庭认为这是一种旨在造成困难或拖延发布仲裁裁决的滥用权利行为,或者超出了适用于纠纷的仲裁协议的范围,则仲裁庭有权不允许此类修改或补充。

Article 38　Negotiation during arbitration proceedings
第 38 条　仲裁程序中的协商

Parties shall still have the right, as from the time of commencement of arbitration proceedings, to voluntarily negotiate and reach agreement on termination of the dispute resolution.

自仲裁程序开始之日起,各方当事人仍有权自行协商解决纠纷并达成协议。

If the parties reach their own agreement on termination of the dispute resolution, they shall have the right to request the chairman of the arbitration centre issue a decision staying the dispute resolution.

各方当事人在仲裁结束时达成一致的,有权请求仲裁中心主席中止仲裁。

CHAPTER 6
Arbitration Tribunal
第六章　仲裁庭

Article 39　Composition of arbitration tribunal
第 39 条　仲裁庭的组成

1. An arbitration tribunal may consist of one or more arbitrators, depending on the agreement of the parties.

1. 仲裁庭可以由一名或多名仲裁员组成,具体取决于当事人之间的协议。

2. If the parties do not have an agreement on the number of arbitrators, an arbitration tribunal shall consist of three（3）arbitrators.

2. 如果当事人没有就仲裁员人数达成协议，仲裁庭应由三名仲裁员组成。

Article 40　Establishment of arbitration tribunal at arbitration centre
第 40 条　在仲裁中心成立仲裁庭

Establishment of an arbitration tribunal shall be regulated as follows, unless otherwise agreed by the parties or otherwise stipulated by the procedural rules of the arbitration centre：

除当事人另有约定外，或者仲裁中心程序规则另有规定的，应按下列规定成立仲裁庭：

1. The respondent shall, within thirty (30) days from the date of receipt of the statement of claim and request to select an arbitrator as sent to the respondent by the arbitration centre, select an arbitrator for the respondent and notify the arbitration centre of same or request the chairman of the arbitration centre appoint an arbitrator. If the respondent has failed to select an arbitrator or to request that the chairman of the arbitration centre appoint an arbitrator, then within a further seven (7) days after expiry of the time-limit provided in this clause, the chairman of the arbitration centre shall appoint an arbitrator for the respondent.

1. 被申请人应自收到申请书和选择仲裁员请求之日起 30 日内选择仲裁员，并通知仲裁中心，或者请仲裁中心主席指定仲裁员。如果被申请人未选择仲裁员或请求仲裁中心的主席指定一名仲裁员，则在本条规定的期限届满后的 7 日内，仲裁中心主席应为被申请人指定仲裁员。

2. If a dispute involves multiple respondents, then the respondents shall agree on selection of an arbitrator or agree on requesting appointment of an arbitrator for such respondents within thirty (30) days from the date of receipt of the statement of claim sent

by the arbitration centre. If the respondents have failed to select an arbitrator, then within a further seven (7) days after expiry of the time-limit provided in this clause, the chairman of the arbitration centre shall appoint an arbitrator for the respondents.

2. 如果纠纷涉及多个被申请人,则被申请人应在收到仲裁中心发出的申请书之日起 30 日内同意选择仲裁员或同意请求仲裁庭为这些被申请人任命一名仲裁员。如果被申请人未选择仲裁员,则在本条规定的期限届满 7 日内,仲裁中心主席应为被申请人指定一名仲裁员。

3. The arbitrators shall, within fifteen (15) days from the date of their selection by the parties or appointment by the chairman of the arbitration centre, elect another [third] arbitrator to act as chairman of the arbitration tribunal. If such election has not taken place upon the expiry of this time-limit, then within a further seven (7) days after expiry of the time-limit provided in this clause, the chairman of the arbitration centre shall appoint the chairman of the arbitration tribunal.

3. 自当事人选定或者由仲裁中心主席任命仲裁员之日起 15 日内,仲裁员应当选举另一位(第三位)仲裁员担任仲裁庭主席。如果在此期限届满之前尚未进行选举,则在本条规定的期限届满 7 日内,仲裁中心主席应指定仲裁庭主席。

4. Where the parties agree to have the dispute resolved by a sole arbitrator but fail to select an arbitrator within thirty (30) days from the date on which the respondent receives the statement of claim, then at the request of one or all parties, the chairman of the arbitration centre shall appoint a sole arbitrator within fifteen (15) days from the date of receipt of such request.

4. 当事人约定由独任仲裁员解决纠纷,但自被申请人收到申请书之日起 30 日内未选定仲裁员的,应一方或者各方当事人的请求,仲裁中心主席应在收到该请求之日起 15 日内指定一名独任仲裁员。

Article 41　Establishment of ad hoc arbitration tribunal
第 41 条　成立临时仲裁庭

Establishment of an ad hoc arbitration tribunal shall be regulated as follows, unless otherwise agreed by the parties:

除当事人另有约定外,应按下列规定成立临时仲裁庭:

1. The respondent must select an arbitrator for the respondent and notify the claimant of such selection within thirty (30) days from the date on which the respondent receives the statement of claim of the claimant. If upon expiry of this time-limit the respondent has failed to notify the claimant of the name of the selected arbitrator and the parties do not have some other agreement on appointment of an arbitrator, then the claimant shall have the right to request the competent court to appoint an arbitrator for the respondent.

1. 被申请人应为自身选择仲裁员,并在被申请人收到申请人的申请书之日起 30 日内通知申请人。如果在此期限届满之前被申请人未将其选择的仲裁员的姓名通知申请人,且当事人之间也没有任命仲裁员的其他协议,则申请人有权要求主管法院为被申请人指定仲裁员。

2. If a dispute involves multiple respondents, then the respondents shall reach agreement on selection of an arbitrator within thirty (30) days from the date of receipt of the statement of claim and accompanying materials from the claimant. If upon expiry of this time-limit the respondents have failed to select an arbitrator and the parties do not have some other agreement on appointment of an arbitrator, then one or all parties shall have the right to request the competent court to appoint an arbitrator for the respondents.

2. 如果纠纷涉及多个被申请人,则被申请人应在收到申请人的申请书和相关材料之日起 30 日内就挑选仲裁员达成协议。如果在本期限届满时被申请人未选择仲裁员,且当事人之间没有任命仲裁员的其他协议,则一方或各方当事人有权要求主管法院为被申请人指定仲裁员。

3. The arbitrators shall, within fifteen (15) days from the date of their selection by the parties or appointment by the court, elect another [third] arbitrator to act as chairman of the arbitration tribunal. If the arbitrators are unable to elect a chairman and unless otherwise agreed by the parties, the parties shall have the right to request the competent court to appoint the chairman of the arbitration tribunal.

3. 自当事人选定或者由法院任命仲裁员之日起 15 日内,仲裁员应当选举另一位(第三位)仲裁员担任仲裁庭主席。如果在此期限届满之前尚未进行选举,除非当事人另有约定,当事人有权请求主管法院指定仲裁庭主席。

4. Where the parties agree to dispute resolution by a sole arbitrator but are unable to agree on selection of an arbitrator within thirty (30) days from the date on which the respondent received the statement of claim, and if the parties do not have an agreement to request an arbitration centre to appoint an arbitrator, then the competent court shall appoint a sole arbitrator at the request of one or all parties.

4. 当事人约定由独任仲裁员解决纠纷,但自被申请人收到申请书之日起 30 日内未选定仲裁员的,且双方未一致同意仲裁中心指定仲裁员的,则主管法院应当应一方或各方当事人的要求指定独任仲裁员。

5. The chief judge of a competent court must, within seven (7) days from the date of receipt of a request from the parties prescribed in clauses 1,2,3 or 4 of this article, assign a judge to appoint an arbitrator and notify the parties thereof.

5. 主管法院的首席法官应在收到本条第 1 款、第 2 款、第 3 款或第 4 款规定的当事人请求之日起 7 日内,指定一名法官任命仲裁员并通知各方当事人。

Article 42　Replacement of arbitrators
第 42 条　替换仲裁员

1. An arbitrator must refuse to resolve a dispute, and the parties shall have the right to request replacement of an arbitrator resolving the dispute in the following circumstances:

1. 出现下列情况时,仲裁员应拒绝解决纠纷,且当事人有权要求替换仲裁员:

（a）The arbitrator is a relative or representative of a party;

（a）仲裁员是一方的亲属或代表;

（b）The arbitrator has an interest related to the dispute;

（b）仲裁员与纠纷有利害关系;

（c）There are clear grounds demonstrating that the arbitrator is not impartial or objective;

（c）有明确的理由表明仲裁员不公正、不客观;

（d）The arbitrator was a mediator, representative or lawyer for either of the parties prior to the dispute being brought to arbitration for resolution, unless the parties provide written consent.

（d）在纠纷提交仲裁解决之前,仲裁员是一方当事人的调解人、代表或律师,除非各方当事人书面同意。

2. An arbitrator must, as from the time of his or her selection or appointment, provide written notice to the arbitration centre or arbitration tribunal and to the parties of any circumstances which may affect his or her objectiveness and impartiality.

2. 自选定任命之日起,仲裁员应向仲裁中心或仲裁庭以及当事人发出书面通知,告知可能影响其客观公正的情况。

3. In the case of dispute resolution at an arbitration centre, if an arbitration tribunal has not yet been established, then the chairman of the arbitration centre shall make the decision on replacement of the arbitrator. If an arbitration tribunal has already been established, then the remaining members of such tribunal shall make the decision on replacement of the arbitrator. If such remaining members of the arbitration tribunal are unable to make a decision or if the arbitrators or the sole arbitrator refuses to resolve the dispute, then the chairman of the arbitration centre shall make the decision on replacement of the arbitrator.

3. 在仲裁中心解决纠纷的情况下,仲裁庭尚未成立的,由仲裁庭主席做出替换仲裁员的决定。如果仲裁庭已经成立,则该仲裁庭的其余成员应做出替换仲裁员的决定。如果仲裁庭的其余成员不能做出决定,或者仲裁员或独任仲裁员拒绝解决纠纷的,则仲裁中心主席应做出替换仲裁员的决定。

4. In the case of dispute resolution by an ad hoc arbitration tribunal, the remaining members of the arbitration tribunal shall make the decision on replacement of the arbitrator. If such remaining members are unable to reach a decision or if the arbitrators or the sole arbitrator refuses to resolve the dispute, then within fifteen (15) days from the date of receipt of a request from one or more arbitrators as mentioned above, or from one or all parties to the dispute, the chief judge of the competent court shall assign a judge to make the decision on replacement of the arbitrator.

4. 在临时仲裁庭解决纠纷的情况下,仲裁庭其余成员应做出更换仲裁员的决定。如果其余成员不能做出决定,或者仲裁员或独任仲裁员拒绝解决纠纷的,则在收到上述一位或多位仲裁员或纠纷一方或全部当事人的请求之日起 15 日内,主管法院的首席法官应指定一名法官做出替换仲裁员的决定。

5. The decision of the chairman of the arbitration centre or of the court in the circumstances prescribed in clauses 3 and 4 respectively of this article shall be the final decision.

5. 仲裁中心主席或法院分别根据本条第 3 款和第 4 款规定做出的决定为终局决定。

6. If for any reason of force majeure or other objective reason an arbitrator is unable to continue his or her participation in the dispute resolution or if such arbitrator is replaced, then selection or appointment of a substitute arbitrator shall be implemented in accordance with the order and procedures stipulated in this Law.

6. 如果由于不可抗力或其他客观原因,仲裁员无法继续参与纠纷解决的,或者该仲裁员被替换的,则应根据本法的规定和程序选择或任命替代仲裁员。

7. The newly established arbitration tribunal may, after consulting the parties, review issues already dealt with in previous dispute resolution sessions held by the former arbitration tribunal.

7. 新成立的仲裁庭在与当事人协商后,可对仲裁庭以前的纠纷解决会议处理的问题进行审查。

Article 43　Consideration whether an arbitration is void or incapable of being performed and whether the arbitration tribunal has jurisdiction

第 43 条　考虑仲裁是否无效或不能执行,以及仲裁庭是否有管辖权

1. The arbitration tribunal must, prior to dealing with the merits of a dispute, consider whether the arbitration agreement is valid, whether the arbitration agreement is capable of being performed, and whether the tribunal has jurisdiction. If the case is within the jurisdiction of the arbitration tribunal to resolve, then the tribunal shall proceed to resolve the dispute in accordance with this Law. If the dispute is not within the

jurisdiction of the tribunal, or if the arbitration agreement is void, or if it is clearly established that the arbitration agreement is incapable of being performed, then the arbitration tribunal shall decide to stay the proceedings and immediately notify the parties thereof.

1. 仲裁庭在处理纠纷之前,应考虑仲裁协议是否有效,仲裁协议是否能够履行,以及仲裁庭是否有管辖权。如果该案件属于仲裁庭的管辖范围,则仲裁庭应依照本法解决纠纷。如果纠纷不在仲裁庭的管辖范围内,或者仲裁协议无效,或者仲裁协议明显无法履行,仲裁庭应决定中止仲裁程序,并立即通知各方当事人。

2. If it is discovered during the dispute resolution process that the arbitration tribunal has exceeded its jurisdiction, the parties may lodge a complaint with the arbitration tribunal. The arbitration tribunal shall then be responsible to hear such issue and make a decision on it.

2. 在纠纷解决过程中发现仲裁庭超越管辖权的,当事人可以向仲裁庭提出申诉。仲裁庭应听取该问题并做出决定。

3. If the parties have agreed for dispute resolution at one specific arbitration centre, but such centre has already terminated its operation without any other institution succeeding it, then the parties may reach an agreement to select some other arbitration centre; if the parties are unable to reach such an agreement, they shall have the right to institute court proceedings for resolution of the dispute.

3. 如果当事人约定在某一仲裁中心解决纠纷,但该仲裁中心在没有其他继任机构的情况下已经终止运作的,当事人可约定选择其他仲裁中心;当事人无法达成此种约定的,有权提起诉讼解决纠纷。

4. If the parties already have a specific agreement on selection of an arbitrator for an ad hoc arbitration, but at the time when the dispute arises the arbitrator is unable to conduct resolution of the

dispute for any reason of force majeure or for any other objective reasons, then parties may reach agreement on selection of another arbitrator in replacement; if the parties are unable to reach such an agreement, they shall have the right to institute court proceedings to resolve the dispute.

4. 如果各方当事人就选择临时仲裁的仲裁员达成了某种协议,但在纠纷发生时,仲裁员因不可抗力或其他客观原因而无法解决纠纷的,当事人可以约定选择替换的仲裁员;当事人无法达成此种约定的,有权提起诉讼解决纠纷。

5. If the parties already have an arbitration agreement but do not clearly indicate the arbitration form or a specific arbitration institution, then if a dispute arises the parties must reach agreement on the arbitration form or a specific arbitration institution to resolve the dispute. If the parties are unable to reach such an agreement, then selection of the arbitration form and the arbitration institution to resolve the dispute shall be implemented in accordance with the request of the claimant.

5. 当事人有仲裁协议但未明确说明仲裁形式或者具体仲裁机构的,在纠纷发生时,当事人应约定仲裁形式或者具体仲裁机构,以解决纠纷。当事人无法达成此种约定的,应按照申请人的要求选择仲裁形式和仲裁机构,以解决纠纷。

Article 44   Petition and resolution of petition against decision of arbitration tribunal concerning whether the arbitration agreement exists, the arbitration agreement is void, the arbitration agreement is incapable of being performed and whether the arbitration tribunal has jurisdiction

第 44 条   就仲裁庭制作的仲裁协议是否存在、是否有效、是否能执行,以及仲裁庭是否有管辖权的决定提出申诉和处理申诉

1. If the parties disagree with any decision of the arbitration tribunal prescribed in article 43 of this Law, they shall have the

right，within five（5）business days from the date of receipt of such decision，to petition the competent court to review such decision of the arbitration tribunal. The petitioner must simultaneously notify the arbitration tribunal of such petition.

1. 当事人对本法第 43 条规定的仲裁庭的决定不服的，有权在收到决定之日起 5 个工作日内请求主管法院审核仲裁庭的该决定。申诉人应同时通知仲裁庭。

2. A petition shall contain the following main particulars：

2. 申诉书应包含下列主要详情：

（a）Date on which the petition is made；

（a）申诉日期；

（b）Name and address of the petitioner；

（b）申诉人的姓名和地址；

（c）Relief sought.

（c）寻求的救济。

3. Copies of the statement of claim，arbitration agreement and decision of the arbitration tribunal must accompany the petition. Accompanying documents in a foreign language must be translated into Vietnamese and translations must be validly certified.

3. 申诉书、仲裁协议书和仲裁庭的决定副本必须随同请愿书一起提交。随附的外文文件必须翻译成越南文，翻译应经过有效的认证。

4. The chief judge of the competent court shall，within five（5）business days from receipt of the petition，assign a judge to hear and resolve the petition. Such judge must hear the matter and make a decision on it within ten（10）business days from the date of being assigned. The decision of the court shall be final.

4. 主管法院首席法官应在收到申诉书后的 5 个工作日内指定法官听取和解决申诉。该法官应在被指定之日起 10 个工作日内听取并做出决定。法院的裁定是终局的。

5. The arbitration tribunal may continue to conduct the dispute resolution while the court is dealing with the petition.

5. 法院处理申诉时，仲裁庭可继续仲裁。

6. If the court decides that the dispute does not fall within the jurisdiction of the arbitration tribunal, or that there is no arbitration agreement or that the arbitration agreement is void or incapable of being performed, then the arbitration tribunal shall issue a decision staying the dispute resolution. Unless the parties have some other agreement, the parties shall have the right to institute court proceedings to resolve their dispute. The limitation period for initiating court proceedings shall be determined in accordance with law. Calculation of the limitation period shall exclude the time from when the claimant initiated arbitration proceedings up until the date of issuance of the court decision accepting jurisdiction over the dispute resolution.

6. 法院裁定纠纷不属于仲裁庭管辖范围，或者没有仲裁协议、仲裁协议无效、仲裁协议不能履行的，仲裁庭应当做出保留仲裁的决定。除非当事人另有约定，当事人有权提起诉讼解决纠纷。启动法院诉讼的时效期限应当依法确定。时效期间的计算应排除申请人提起仲裁程序直至法院宣布接受纠纷管辖权之日止的时间。

Article 45 Jurisdiction of the arbitration tribunal to verify the facts
第 45 条 仲裁庭核实事实的权力

An arbitration tribunal shall have the right, during the dispute resolution process, to meet or hold discussions with one party in the presence of the other party, by appropriate methods, in order to clarify issues relevant to the dispute. The arbitration tribunal may on its own initiative or at the request of one or all parties, conduct fact-finding with a third person in the presence of the parties or after having notified the parties.

仲裁庭有权在纠纷解决程序中，在另一方在场的情况下，通过适当的方式与一方会面或进行讨论，以澄清与纠纷有关的问题。仲裁庭可以主动或者应一方或者全部当事人的要求，在当事人在场时或者在通知当事人后，与第三人进行事实认定。

Article 46　Jurisdiction of the arbitration tribunal to collect evidence
第 46 条　仲裁庭收集证据的权力

1. The parties shall have the right and responsibility to provide evidence to the arbitration tribunal to prove facts relevant to the issues in dispute.

1. 当事人有权利与义务向仲裁庭提供证据，证明与纠纷事项有关的事实。

2. The arbitration tribunal shall have the right，at the request of one or all parties，to request witnesses to provide information and materials relevant to the dispute resolution.

2. 仲裁庭有权应一方或者全部当事人的请求，要求证人提供与纠纷解决相关的信息和材料。

3. The arbitration tribunal shall have the right，on its own initiative or at the request of one or both parties，to seek an assessment or valuation of the assets in dispute in order to provide grounds for resolving the dispute. The party requesting an assessment or valuation shall advance the costs thereof，or the arbitration tribunal shall allocate such costs.

3. 仲裁庭有权或应一方或双方当事人的要求，对纠纷资产进行评估或估价，以便为解决纠纷提供依据。要求评估或估价的一方应预付其费用，否则仲裁庭应分配该费用。

4. The arbitration tribunal shall have the right，on its own initiative or at the request of one or both parties，to seek expert advice. Expert fees shall be provisionally paid in advance by the party requesting such advice，or shall be paid in accordance with the

allocation made by the arbitration tribunal.

4. 仲裁庭有权主动或应一方或双方要求寻求专家意见。专家费用应由提出请求的一方预先支付，或者按照仲裁庭的分配支付。

5. If the arbitration tribunal or one or both parties have already taken necessary measures to collect evidence by themselves but without success，then a petition may be made to the competent court to require other bodies，organisations or individuals to provide legible，audible or visual materials or to provide other objects relevant to the dispute. Such petition must specify the matters in dispute currently being resolved by arbitration，the evidence which needs to be collected，the reasons why the evidence has not been collected，and the name and address of the body，organisation or individual currently managing and/or holding the evidence which needs to be collected.

5. 如仲裁庭、一方或双方已采取必要措施自行收集证据但未成功，则可向主管法院提出请求，要求其他机构、组织或个人提供清楚的、可听或可视的材料或提供与纠纷有关的其他物体。此类请求必须指明目前通过仲裁解决的纠纷事项、需要收集的证据、未收集到证据的理由以及需要收集的证据的当前管理和/或主持的机构、组织或个人的名称和地址。

6. The chief judge of the competent court shall，within seven（7）business days from the date of receipt of a request for collection of evidence，assign a judge to hear and resolve such request. Such judge shall，within five（5）business days from the date of being assigned，send a written notice to the body，organisation or individual currently managing and/or holding the evidence requiring it to provide the evidence to the court，and the judge shall also send such notice to the same level procuracy in order for the latter to implement its functions and duties in accordance with law.

6. 主管法院首席法官应在收到收集证据请求之日起 7 个工作日内指派法官听取和解决此类请求。该法官应在被指定之日起 5 个工作日内，将书面通知送交当前管理和/或持有证据的，要求向法院提供证据的机构、组织或个人，该法官也应将此通知送交同级检察院，以便检察院依法履行职责。

The body, organisation or individual currently managing and/or holding the evidence shall be responsible to promptly and completely provide such evidence pursuant to the request of the court within fifteen (15) days from the date of receipt of the request.

当前管理和/或持有证据的机构、组织或个人，应在收到请求之日起 15 日内，根据法院的要求迅速、完整地提供该证据。

The court must, within five (5) business days from the date of receipt of the evidence from the body, organisation or individual supplying it, notify the arbitration tribunal and the applicant so that the evidence may be handed over.

法院应自收到机构、组织或个人提供证据之日起 5 个工作日内通知仲裁庭和申请人，以便移交证据。

If after expiry of the stipulated time-limit the body, organisation or individual concerned fails to provide the evidence pursuant to the request of the court, the court shall immediately notify the arbitration tribunal and the applicant, and also provide written notice to the competent agency or organization to deal with such failure in accordance with law.

如果在规定的期限届满后，有关机构、组织或个人未能根据法院的请求提供证据，法院应立即通知仲裁庭和申请人，并书面通知主管机关或组织依法处理。

Article 47　Jurisdiction of arbitration tribunal to summon witnesses
第 47 条　仲裁庭召唤证人的权力

1. The arbitration tribunal shall have the right at the request of one

or both parties and if the tribunal considers it necessary, to require a witness to attend a dispute resolution session. Witness fees shall be paid by the party requesting that the witness be summoned, or shall be as allocated by the arbitration tribunal.

1. 仲裁庭有权应一方或双方要求,并在必要时要求证人出席纠纷解决会议。证人费用由请求证人的一方支付,或由仲裁庭分配。

2. If a witness who has been validly summoned by the arbitration tribunal fails to attend the session without a legitimate reason, and the absence of such witness constitutes an obstacle to resolution of the dispute, then the arbitration tribunal may send a written request to the competent court to issue a decision summoning such witness to attend a session of the arbitration tribunal. Such request must specify the matters currently being resolved by arbitration; the full name and address of the witness; the reason why the witness needs to be summoned; and the time and location where the witness is required to attend.

2. 经仲裁庭正式传唤的证人无正当理由缺席会议,其缺席妨碍纠纷解决的,仲裁庭可以书面请求主管法院发布传唤该证人参加仲裁庭会议的决定。该请求应说明目前通过仲裁解决的事项;证人的全名和地址;传唤证人的原因;以及证人需出席的时间和地点。

3. The chief judge of the competent court shall, within seven (7) business days from the date of receipt of a written request from the arbitration tribunal to summon a witness, assign a judge to hear and resolve such request. The judge must, within five (5) business days from the date of being assigned, issue a decision summoning the witness.

3. 主管法院首席法官应自收到仲裁庭传唤证人的书面请求之日起 7 个工作日内,指定一名法官听取和解决这一请求。法官应自被指定之日起 5 个工作日内做出传唤证人的决定。

The decision summoning the witness must specify the name of the arbitration tribunal which requested that the witness be summoned; the contents of the dispute; the full name and address of the witness; and the time and location where the witness must attend at the request of the arbitration tribunal.

传唤证人的决定应指明要求传唤证人的仲裁庭的名称;纠纷的内容;证人的全名和地址;以及仲裁庭要求证人出席的时间和地点。

The court must immediately send the decision to the arbitration tribunal, to the witness, and also to the same level procuracy in order for the latter to implement its functions and duties in accordance with law.

法院应立即将决定送交仲裁庭和证人,并送交同级检察院,以便检察院依法履行职责。

A witness shall be obliged to strictly implement the decision of the court. Witness fees shall be paid as stipulated in clause 1 of this article.

证人有义务严格执行法院的决定。证人费应按本条第1款的规定支付。

CHAPTER 7
Interim Relief
第七章 临时救济

Article 48 Right to request application of interim relief

第 48 条 申请临时救济的权利

1. Parties in dispute shall have the right to request the arbitration tribunal or a court to order an interim relief in accordance with the provisions of this Law and other relevant laws, unless such parties have some other agreement.

1. 除非当事人另有约定,纠纷当事人有权要求仲裁庭或者法院依照本法和其他有关法律的规定下达临时救济的命令。

2. A request to a court to order an interim relief shall not be deemed

to be a denial of the arbitration agreement or a waiver of the right to dispute resolution by arbitration.

2. 向法院请求临时救济的，不应被视为拒绝仲裁协议或放弃仲裁权利。

Article 49　Jurisdiction of arbitration tribunal to order interim relief
第 49 条　仲裁庭命令临时救济的权力

1. The arbitration tribunal may, at the request of one of the parties, order one or more forms of interim relief applicable to the parties in dispute.

1. 仲裁庭可以根据一方当事人的请求，发出适用于纠纷当事人的一种或多种形式的临时救济命令。

2. Interim relief shall comprise：

2. 临时救济应包含：

(a) Prohibition of any change in the status quo of the assets in dispute；

(a) 禁止改变纠纷资产现状；

(b) Prohibition of acts by, or ordering one or more specific acts to be taken by a party in dispute, aimed at preventing conduct adverse to the process of the arbitration proceedings；

(b) 禁止一方当事人采取或下令当事人采取一项或多项具体行动，防止对仲裁程序产生不利影响的行为；

(c) Attachment of the assets in dispute；

(c) 扣押纠纷资产；

(d) Requirement of preservation, storage, sale or disposal of any of the assets of one or all parties in dispute；

(d) 要求保全、储存、出售或处置一方或全部当事人的资产；

(e) Requirement of interim payment of money as between the parties；

(e) 要求各方临时支付费用；

（f）Prohibition of transfer of asset rights of the assets in dispute.

（f）禁止转让纠纷资产。

3. If during the dispute resolution process one of the parties had already applied to a court to order one or more of the forms of interim relief prescribed in clause 2 of this article and then applies to the arbitration tribunal to order interim relief，the arbitration tribunal must refuse such application.

3. 如果在纠纷解决过程中，其中一方当事人已经向法院申请下令执行本条第 2 款规定的一种或多种临时救济形式，又向仲裁庭申请临时救济的，仲裁庭应拒绝该申请。

4. The arbitration tribunal shall have the right，prior to ordering interim relief，to require the applicant for the interim relief to provide financial security.

4. 仲裁庭在下达临时救济命令前，有权要求临时救济申请人提供经济担保。

5. If an arbitration tribunal orders a different form of interim relief or interim relief which exceeds the scope of the application by the applicant，thereby causing loss to the applicant or to the party against whom the interim relief was applied or to a third party，then the party incurring loss shall have the right to institute court proceedings for compensation in accordance with the law on civil proceedings.

5. 如果仲裁庭下令采取的临时救济的形式不同或临时救济超过申请人的申请范围，从而对申请人、被申请临时救济的一方或第三方造成损失的，受损的一方有权依据《民事诉讼法》提起诉讼，要求赔偿。

Article 50　Procedures for arbitration tribunal to order interim relief

第 50 条　仲裁庭命令临时救济的程序

1. An applicant for an interim relief must file an application with

the arbitration tribunal.

1. 临时救济申请人应向仲裁庭提出申请。

2. An application for an interim relief must contain the following main particulars：

2. 临时救济申请书应包括下列主要事项：

（a）Date on which the application is made；

（a）申请日期；

（b）Name and address of the applicant for the interim relief；

（b）临时救济申请人的姓名和地址；

（c）Name and address of the party against whom the interim relief is sought to be applied；

（c）临时救济被申请人的姓名和地址；

（d）Summary of the items in dispute；

（d）纠纷概况；

（e）Reason for requiring the interim relief；

（e）寻求临时救济的原因；

（f）Specific items of interim relief sought.

（f）寻求临时救济的具体项目。

The applicant for an interim relief must attach to such application evidence provided to the arbitration tribunal to prove the necessity for such interim relief.

临时救济申请人必须附上提供给仲裁庭的申请证据，证明该临时救济的必要性。

3. The applicant for interim relief must，pursuant to a decision of the arbitration tribunal，lodge a sum of money，precious metals，precious stones or valuable papers as fixed by the arbitration tribunal corresponding to the amount of loss that may arise due to unjustified interim relief being ordered，in order to protect the interests of the party against whom the interim relief is sought to be applied. Such sum of money，precious metals，precious stones

or valuable papers shall be deposited in an escrow account nominated by the arbitration tribunal.

3. 临时救济申请人应依照仲裁庭的决定向仲裁庭提交一笔款项、贵金属、宝石或有价证券作为担保，以免不公正的临时救济给被申请人带来损失。该款项、贵金属、宝石或有价证券应存放在仲裁庭指定的代管账户内。

4. Within three（3）business days from the date of receipt of an application，immediately after the applicant has provided the security prescribed in clause 3 of this article，the arbitration tribunal shall hear the matter and issue a decision ordering or not ordering interim relief. If the arbitration tribunal does not agree to the application，it shall provide a written notice to the applicant specifying its reasons.

4. 自收到申请之日起 3 个工作日内，申请人提供本条第 3 款规定的担保后，仲裁庭应立即听取意见并下达临时救济命令。仲裁庭不同意的，应当书面通知申请人并说明理由。

5. Enforcement of a decision by an arbitration tribunal ordering interim relief shall be implemented in accordance with the law on enforcement of civil judgments.

5. 仲裁庭裁定执行临时救济决定的，依照民事判决执行。

Article 51　Jurisdiction of and procedures for arbitration tribunal to change，supplement or remove interim relief

第 51 条　仲裁庭更改、补充和撤销临时救济的权力与程序

1. The arbitration tribunal shall have the right，at the request of one of the parties，to change，supplement or remove interim relief at any time during the dispute resolution process.

1. 仲裁庭有权应一方当事人的请求，在纠纷解决程序中随时变更、补充或撤销临时救济。

2. Procedures for changing or supplementing interim relief shall be

implemented in accordance with article 50 of this Law.

2. 变更或补充临时救济的程序，依照本法第 50 条的规定执行。

3. The arbitration tribunal shall remove interim relief already ordered in the following circumstances：

3. 在下列情况下，仲裁庭应撤销已经下达的临时救济命令：

（a）The applicant for the interim relief requests the removal；

（a）临时救济申请人要求撤销；

（b）The party subject to enforcement of the decision ordering the interim relief has already lodged assets or some other person has provided security for discharge of the obligation owing to the applicant；

（b）执行临时救济决定的一方已经提交了财产，或其他人已经为申请人提供了担保以履行债务；

（c）The obligation of the obligor has terminated pursuant to law.

（c）债务人的义务依法终止。

4. Procedures for removing interim relief shall be implemented as follows：

4. 撤销临时救济的程序如下：

（a）The applicant must file a petition for removal of the interim relief with the arbitration tribunal.

（a）申请人应向仲裁庭提出撤销临时救济的请求。

（b）The arbitration tribunal shall hear the application and issue a decision removing the interim relief and shall also issue a decision that the security prescribed in article 50. 3 of this Law be returned to the applicant unless the applicant who applied to the arbitration tribunal to order the interim relief is liable to pay compensation for an unjustified application causing loss to the party against whom the interim relief was applied or to a third party.

（b）仲裁庭应听取申请并做出撤销临时救济的决定，并应决定将本法第 50 条第 3 款规定的担保退还给申请人，除非临时救济申请人因其不正当的申请对被申请人或第三方造成损失而应支付赔偿金的。

The decision removing the interim relief must immediately be sent to the parties in dispute and also to the civil judgment enforcement agency.

撤销临时救济的决定应立即送交纠纷当事人，并送交民事判决执行机构。

Article 52　Responsibility of applicant for interim relief
第 52 条　临时救济申请人的责任

An applicant for interim relief shall be liable for such application. An applicant for unjustified interim relief which causes loss to the other party or to a third party must pay compensation for such loss.

临时救济申请人应对其申请负责。申请人因不正当的临时救济而给对方或第三方造成损失的，必须赔偿损失。

Article 53　Jurisdiction of and order and procedures for court to order, change or remove interim relief
第 53 条　法院更改、补充和撤销临时救济的权力、命令与程序

1. If after a party has lodged its statement of claim，such party's legal rights and interests have been infringed or there is a direct danger of such infringement，such party shall have the right to file an application with the competent court to order one or more forms of interim relief.

1. 当事人提交请求书后，当事人的合法权益受到侵害或者有直接的侵权危险的，有权向主管法院申请一种或多种形式的临时救济。

2. The chief judge of the competent court shall，within three（3）business days from the date of receipt of the application for

interim relief，assign a judge to hear and resolve the application. The judge assigned must，within three（3）business days from the date of being assigned，hear the application and issue a decision ordering or not ordering interim relief. The judge must issue a decision ordering the interim relief immediately after the applicant implements security measures. If the judge does not grant the application，the judge must provide written notice to the applicant，specifying the reasons.

2. 主管法院首席法官应当自收到临时救济申请之日起 3 个工作日内，指定法官听取和处理申请。被指定的法官应在被指定之日起 3 个工作日内听取申请，并决定是否发布临时救济命令。申请人提供担保后，法官应立即下达临时救济命令。如果法官不批准申请，应书面通知申请人并说明原因。

3. A party shall have the right to apply to a court to change，supplement or remove interim relief. Assignment of a judge to hear and resolve any such application to change，supplement or remove interim relief shall be implemented in accordance with the provisions in clause 2 of this article.

3. 当事人有权向法院申请变更、补充或者撤销临时救济。指派法官听取和处理申请以更改、补充或撤销临时救济的，应依照本条第 2 款的规定。

4. The order and procedures for a court to order，change or remove interim relief and for checking compliance with law during the application of interim relief shall be implemented in accordance with the provisions of the Civil Procedure Code.

4. 在执行临时救济期间，法院命令、变更或者撤销临时救济和检查法律程序的，应依照《民事诉讼法》的规定执行。

5. If during the dispute resolution process one of the parties which already applied to the arbitration tribunal for one or more forms of interim relief applies to the court for interim relief，the court

must refuse such application and return it to the applicant，unless the former application for the interim relief was beyond the jurisdiction of the arbitration tribunal.

5. 在纠纷解决过程中，如果一方当事人已经向仲裁庭申请一种或多种形式的临时救济，再向法院申请临时救济的，法院应拒绝该申请并将其返还给申请人，除非之前的临时救济申请不在仲裁庭的管辖范围之内。

CHAPTER 8
Dispute Resolution Sessions
第八章　纠纷解决会议

Article 54　Preparation for dispute resolution sessions
第 54 条　纠纷解决会议的准备

1. The arbitration tribunal shall make decisions on the time and location for holding dispute resolution sessions，unless otherwise agreed by the parties or otherwise stipulated by the procedural rules of the arbitration centre.

1. 除非仲裁协议或仲裁中心程序规定另有规定，仲裁庭应就纠纷解决会议的举行时间和地点做出决定。

2. Summonses to attend a session shall be forwarded to the parties at least thirty（30）days prior to the date of commencement of a session，unless otherwise agreed by the parties or otherwise stipulated by the procedural rules of the arbitration centre.

2. 除非当事人或仲裁中心程序规则另有规定，应至少在会议开始日期前 30 日将传票送达当事人。

Article 55　Composition of and procedures for dispute resolution sessions
第 55 条　纠纷解决会议的组成与程序

1. Dispute resolution sessions shall be conducted in private，unless otherwise agreed by the parties.

1. 除非当事人另有约定,纠纷解决会议应私下进行。

2. Parties may personally attend dispute resolution sessions or may authorize their representatives to attend; and parties shall have the right to invite witnesses and a person to protect their legal rights and interests.

2. 当事人可亲自出席纠纷解决会议,也可授权其代表出席;当事人有权邀请证人和一个人保护其合法权益。

3. The arbitration tribunal may permit other people to attend dispute resolution sessions, if the parties so consent.

3. 如果双方同意,仲裁庭可允许其他人参加纠纷解决会议。

4. The order and procedures for holding dispute resolution sessions shall be as stipulated in the arbitration procedural rules of the arbitration centre; or shall be as agreed by the parties in the case of an ad hoc arbitration.

4. 纠纷解决会议的规则和程序应符合仲裁中心的仲裁程序规则;在临时仲裁的情况下应当由各方同意。

Article 56　Absence of parties
第 56 条　当事人缺席

1. A claimant who was validly summoned to attend a dispute resolution session but fails to attend without a legitimate reason or who leaves a session without the consent of the arbitration tribunal, shall be deemed to have withdrawn its statement of claim. In such case the arbitration tribunal shall continue the dispute resolution if the respondent so requests or if there is a counterclaim.

1. 申请人被正式传召出席纠纷解决会议,但无正当理由缺席的,或未经仲裁庭同意离场的,视为撤回申请书。在该情况下,如果被申请人要求或提出反申请,仲裁庭应继续解决纠纷。

2. If a respondent was validly summoned to attend a dispute resolution session but fails to attend without a legitimate reason

or leaves a session without the consent of the arbitration tribunal，the arbitration tribunal shall continue the dispute resolution based on currently available materials and evidence.

2. 被申请人被正式传召出席纠纷解决会议，但无正当理由缺席的，或未经仲裁庭同意离场的，仲裁庭应当根据现有材料和证据继续解决纠纷。

3. The arbitration tribunal may，at the request of the parties，rely on the file to conduct a dispute resolution session without requiring the presence of the parties.

3. 应当事人的请求，仲裁庭可根据文件进行纠纷解决，而不需要当事人在场。

Article 57　Adjournment of dispute resolution session
第 57 条　纠纷解决会议的延期

One or both parties may，if there is a legitimate reason，request the arbitration tribunal to adjourn a dispute resolution session. A request for adjournment of a dispute resolution session must be in writing，specifying the reason and providing evidence，and must be sent to the arbitration tribunal at least seven（7）business days prior to the due date of commencement of the session. If the arbitration tribunal does not receive the request within this time-limit，the applicant for such adjournment must pay all costs arising，if any. The arbitration tribunal shall consider and issue a decision consenting or not consenting to the request for the adjournment，and shall promptly notify the parties.

如果有合法理由，一方或双方可要求仲裁庭延期解决纠纷会议。延期请求必须以书面形式提出，说明理由并提供证据，并且应在会议开始日期至少 7 个工作日前提交仲裁庭。如果仲裁庭在这段时间内未收到申请，申请人应支付所有费用（如有）。仲裁庭应考虑并做出同意或拒绝延期请求的决定，并及时通知各方当事人。

The period of any adjournment shall be as decided by the arbitration tribunal.

仲裁期间由仲裁庭决定。

Article 58　Mediation and recognition of successful mediation
第 58 条　调解和认可成功调解

The arbitration tribunal may, at the request of the parties, conduct a mediation in order for the parties to reach an agreement on resolution of their dispute. If the mediation is successful, the arbitration tribunal shall prepare minutes of successful mediation to be signed by the parties and certified by the arbitrator/s. The arbitration tribunal shall issue a decision recognizing the agreement of the parties. Such decision shall be final and shall have the same validity as an arbitral award.

仲裁庭可应当事人的请求进行调解,使双方就纠纷达成协议。调解成功后,仲裁庭应制作成功调解的笔录,由当事人签字并经仲裁员认证。仲裁庭应做出承认当事人协议的决定。该决定是终局的,且与仲裁裁决具有同等效力。

Article 59　Stay of dispute resolution
第 59 条　中止纠纷解决

1. Resolution of a dispute shall be stayed in the following circumstances:

1. 有下列情形的,应中止纠纷解决:

   (a) The claimant or respondent being an individual dies, without anyone inheriting his or her rights and obligations;

   (a) 作为个人的申请人或被申请人,在没有人继承其权利和义务的情况下死亡;

   (b) The claimant or respondent being an agency or organization has terminated its operation, become bankrupt, dissolved, consolidated，merged，demerged，separated or converted its organizational form without any agency or organization succeeding to the former's rights and obligations；

(b) 作为机构或组织的申请人或被申请人，在没有机构或组织继承其权利和义务的情况下，停止运作、破产、解散、合并、融合、分割、分离或改变其组织形式；

(c) The claimant withdraws its statement of claim or the claim is deemed to be withdrawn pursuant to article 56. 1 of this Law，except where the respondent requires the dispute resolution to be continued；

(c) 申请人撤回其申请书，或根据本法第 56 条第 1 款，该申请被视为撤回，除非申请人要求继续解决纠纷；

(d) The parties reach agreement on termination of the dispute resolution；

(d) 双方就终止纠纷达成一致；

(e) The court issues a decision that the dispute is not within the jurisdiction of the arbitration tribunal，or that there is no arbitration agreement or that such agreement is void or incapable of being performed in accordance with article 44. 6 of this Law.

(e) 法院裁定纠纷不在仲裁庭的管辖范围内，或者有本法第 44 条第 6 款所述的没有仲裁协议、仲裁协议无效、仲裁协议不能履行的情况。

2. The arbitration tribunal shall issue a decision staying the dispute resolution. If an arbitration tribunal has not yet been established，then the chairman of the arbitration centre shall issue such decision.

2. 仲裁庭应作出中止纠纷解决的裁决。仲裁庭尚未成立的，由仲裁中心主席决定。

3. After there is a decision staying dispute resolution，the parties shall not have the right to institute arbitration proceedings for re-

resolution of such dispute if such proceedings are not different from the former dispute in terms of the claimant, respondent and legal relationship giving rise to the dispute, except for the cases prescribed in sub-clauses (c) and (e) of clause 1 of this article.

3. 在作出中止纠纷解决的裁决后,如果新程序的申请人、被申请人和法律关系与先前解决纠纷的程序相同,则各方当事人无权就重新解决该纠纷提起仲裁程序,除非有本条第 1 款(c)项和(e)项的情况。

CHAPTER 9
Arbitral Awards
第九章　仲裁裁决

Article 60　Principles for issuance of award
第 60 条　发布裁决的原则

1. An arbitration tribunal shall issue an arbitral award on the basis of its majority vote.

1. 仲裁庭应在多数票的基础上作出仲裁裁决。

2. If voting does not result in a majority decision, then the arbitral award shall be made in accordance with the opinion of the chairman of the arbitration tribunal.

2. 如果投票没有产生多数决定,则仲裁裁决应根据仲裁庭主席的意见作出。

Article 61　Contents, form and validity of arbitral award
第 61 条　仲裁裁决的内容、形式和效力

1. An arbitral award must be in writing and contain the following main particulars:

1. 仲裁裁决应以书面形式提出,并包含下列主要内容:

　(a) Date and location of issuance of the award;

　(a) 发布裁决的日期和地点;

　(b) Names and addresses of the claimant and of the respondent;

（b）申请人和被申请人的姓名和地址；

（c）Full names and addresses of the arbitrator/s；

（c）仲裁员的全名和地址；

（d）Summary of the statement of claim and matters in dispute；

（d）申请书和纠纷概况；

（e）Reasons for issuance of the award, unless the parties agree it is unnecessary to specify reasons for the award；

（e）发布裁决的理由,除非当事人同意不必说明裁决的理由；

（f）Result of the dispute resolution；

（f）纠纷解决结果；

（g）Time-limit for enforcement of the award；

（g）执行裁决的时限；

（h）Allocation of arbitration fees and other relevant fees；

（h）仲裁和其他相关费用的分配；

（i）Signatures of the arbitrator/s.

（i）仲裁员签名。

2. If an arbitrator does not sign the arbitral award, the chairman of the arbitration tribunal must record such fact in the arbitral award and specify the reasons for it. In such a case, the arbitral award shall still be effective.

2. 仲裁员未签署仲裁裁决书的,仲裁庭主席应在仲裁裁决书中记载这一事实,并说明理由。在该情况下,仲裁裁决仍然有效。

3. The arbitral award shall immediately be issued in the session or no later than thirty（30）days from the end of the final session.

3. 仲裁裁决应立即在会议期间或最后一届会议结束后30日内发布。

4. The arbitral award must be sent to the parties immediately after the date of its issuance. The parties shall have the right to request the arbitration centre or arbitration tribunal to issue copies of the arbitral award.

4. 仲裁裁决应在发布之日后立即送达当事人。当事人有权要求仲裁中心或者仲裁庭签发仲裁裁决书副本。

5. An arbitral award shall be final and shall be of full force and effect as from the date of its issuance.

5. 仲裁裁决为终局裁决，自发布之日起生效。

Article 62   Registration of ad hoc arbitral award
第 62 条   临时仲裁裁决的登记

1. An ad hoc arbitral award may, at the request of one or all parties to the dispute, be registered at the court in the locality where the arbitration tribunal issued such award, prior to any request being made to the competent civil judgement enforcement agency to organize enforcement of the award. Registration or non-registration of an arbitral award shall not affect the contents and validity of such award.

1. 临时仲裁裁决可以在一方或所有当事人的请求下，在向主管民事判决执行机构提出请求之前，在仲裁裁决所在地的法院登记。仲裁裁决登记与否不影响仲裁裁决的内容和效力。

2. Within a time-limit of one year from the date of issuance of an arbitral award, the applicant for registration of an ad hoc arbitral award must send a petition requesting registration of the arbitral award to the competent court as prescribed in clause 1 of this article, together with originals or validly certified copies of the following materials：

2. 在仲裁裁决发布之日起一年的期限内，临时仲裁裁决的申请人应向主管法院提交一份本条第 1 款中所述的仲裁裁决登记请求书，连同以下材料的原本或经过有效认证的副本：

（a）Arbitral award issued by the ad hoc arbitration tribunal；
（a）临时仲裁庭发布的仲裁裁决书；
（b）Minutes, if any, of the session of the ad hoc arbitration

tribunal resolving the dispute；

（b）临时仲裁庭解决纠纷会议记录；

（c）Original or validly certified copy of the arbitration agreement.

（c）仲裁协议原本或经过有效认证的副本。

The applicant must be responsible for the authenticity of the materials lodged with the court.

申请人应对其提交法院的材料的真实性负责。

3. The chief judge of the court must，within five（5）business days from the date of receipt of a petition requesting registration of an arbitral award，assign a judge to deal with such petition. The judge assigned must，within ten（10）days from the date of being assigned，check the authenticity of the materials accompanying the petition and conduct registration. The judge shall refuse to conduct registration if he or she is satisfied that there is in fact no arbitral award，and in such case shall return the petition and accompanying materials and must immediately notify the petitioner and specify the reasons for the refusal to conduct registration. The applicant for registration of the arbitral award shall have the right，within three（3）business days from the date of receipt of such notice from the court，to lodge a complaint with the chief judge of the court regarding refusal to register the arbitral award. The chief judge of the court shall，within three（3）business days from the date of receipt of such complaint，hear the complaint and issue a decision resolving it. The decision of the chief judge resolving the complaint shall be final.

3. 法院首席法官应在收到仲裁裁决登记请求之日起5个工作日内指定一名法官处理该请求。被指派的法官应在被指派之日起10日内检查申请材料的真实性并进行登记。如果法官采信事实上没有仲裁裁决，法官应拒绝登记，发回请求书和所附材料，并且立即通知请求人，说明拒绝登记的理由。仲裁裁决的申请人有权在收到法院通知之日起3个工作日内向法院首席法官提出拒绝登记仲裁裁决的申诉。首席法官应在收到此类申诉之日起3个工作日内,听取投诉并做出决定。首席法官处理申诉的决定应为终局决定。

4. Registration of an arbitral award shall contain the following particulars：

4. 仲裁裁决登记应包括下列事项：

(a) Time and location of conducting registration；

(a) 登记的时间和地点；

(b) Name of the court conducting registration；

(b) 进行登记的法院名称；

(c) Name and address of the applicant for registration；

(c) 登记申请人的姓名和地址；

(d) The award which was registered；

(d) 已登记的裁决书；

(e) Signature of the authorized person and seal of the court.

(e) 授权人签名和法院印章。

Article 63　Rectification and explanation of arbitral award；supplementary awards

第 63 条　仲裁裁决的修正与解释;补充裁决

1. A party may，within thirty（30）days from the date of receipt of an arbitral award unless the parties have some other agreement about this time-limit，request the arbitration tribunal to rectify obvious errors in spelling or figures caused by a mistake or incorrect computation in the arbitral award，and must immediately notify the other party of such request. If the arbitration tribunal considers such request legitimate，it shall make the rectification within thirty（30）days from the date of receipt of the request.

1. 除非当事人另有约定,当事人可以自收到仲裁裁决之日起 30 日内,请求仲裁庭纠正仲裁裁决中由于拼写导致的或数的明显错误,或由于计算导致的错误,并且应立即通知另一方。仲裁庭认为请求合法的,应当自收到请求之日起 30 日内做出修正。

2. A party may, within thirty (30) days from the date of receipt of an arbitral award unless the parties have some other agreement about this time-limit, request the arbitration tribunal to explain specific points or items in the award, and must immediately notify the other party of such request. If the arbitration tribunal considers such request legitimate, it shall provide an explanation within thirty (30) days from the date of receipt of the request. The explanation provided shall form a part of the award.

2. 除非当事人另有约定,在收到仲裁裁决书之日起 30 日内,当事人可以请求仲裁庭解释裁决中的具体要点或项目,并应立即通知另一方。仲裁庭认为该请求合法的,应当自收到请求之日起 30 日内做出解释。该解释应构成裁决的一部分。

3. The arbitration tribunal may on its own initiative, within thirty (30) days from the date of issuance of the arbitral award, rectify any of the errors prescribed in clause 1 of this article and immediately notify the parties.

3. 自仲裁裁决书签发之日起 30 日内,仲裁庭可自行修正本条第 1 款所述的错误,并立即通知当事人。

4. If the parties do not have some other agreement, then within thirty (30) days from the date of receipt of an award, a party may request the arbitration tribunal to issue a supplementary award with matters raised during the process of the proceedings but not yet recorded in the award, and must immediately notify the other party of such request. If the arbitration tribunal considers such request legitimate, it shall issue a supplementary award within forty-five (45) days from the date of receipt of the request.

4. 如果当事人没有其他约定,则自收到裁决书之日起 30 日内,当事人可以请求仲裁庭对在仲裁过程中提出但尚未在裁决书中记载的事项提出补充裁决,并应立即将该请求通知另一方。仲裁庭认为请求合法的,应当自收到请求之日起 45 日内发布补充裁决。

5. In necessary cases, the arbitration tribunal may extend the time-limits for rectification, explanation or issuance of a supplementary award prescribed in clauses 1,2 and 4 of this article.

5. 在必要时,仲裁庭可以延长本条第 1 款、第 2 款和第 4 款所述的修正、解释或补充裁决的时限。

Article 64   Archiving files
第 64 条   文件存档

1. An arbitration centre shall be responsible to archive files on disputes over which it has accepted jurisdiction. Files on disputes resolved by ad hoc arbitration shall be archived by the parties or by the arbitrators.

1. 仲裁中心应负责归档受理管辖的纠纷案件。临时仲裁案卷应由当事人或者仲裁员存档。

2. Arbitration files shall be archived for a period of five years as from the date of issuance of the arbitral award or decision staying dispute resolution by arbitration.

2. 仲裁档案自仲裁裁决发布之日起或决定中止仲裁之日起 5 年内予以归档。

CHAPTER 10
Enforcement of Arbitral Awards
第十章   执行仲裁裁决
Article 65   Voluntary carrying out of arbitral award
第 65 条   自愿执行仲裁裁决

The State encourages the parties to voluntarily carry out arbitral awards.
国家鼓励当事人自愿执行仲裁裁决。

Article 66 Right to apply for enforcement of arbitral award
第 66 条　申请执行仲裁裁决的权利

1. If on expiry of the time-limit for carrying out an arbitral award the award debtor has not voluntarily carried out the award and has not requested that the award be set aside pursuant to article 69 of this Law，the arbitral award creditor shall have the right to request the competent civil judgement enforcement agency to enforce such award.

1. 如果裁决债务人在执行仲裁裁决的期限届满时并未自愿执行裁决，也未根据本法第 69 条的规定请求撤销裁决，则裁决债权人有权要求主管民事执法机构执行该裁决。

2. In the case of an ad hoc arbitral award，the award creditor shall have the right to apply to the competent civil judgement enforcement agency requesting enforcement of the arbitral award after such award has been registered in accordance with article 62 of this Law.

2. 对于临时仲裁裁决，裁决债权人有权根据本法第 62 条的规定，申请主管民事执法机构执行已登记的裁决。

Article 67　Enforcement of arbitral award
第 67 条　执行仲裁裁决

Arbitral awards shall be enforced in accordance with the law on enforcement of civil judgements.

仲裁裁决应依照民事判决执行法执行。

CHAPTER 11
Setting Aside Arbitral Awards
第十一章　撤销仲裁裁决

Article 68　Grounds for setting aside arbitral award
第 68 条　撤销仲裁裁决的原因

1. The court shall hear an application for setting aside an arbitral

award on receipt of a petition from one of the parties.

1. 法院在收到一方当事人的请求书后，应听取撤销仲裁裁决的申请。

2. An arbitral award which falls within any one of the following cases shall be set aside：

2. 有下列情形之一的，应撤销仲裁裁决：

（a） There was no arbitration agreement or the arbitration agreement is void；

（a）没有仲裁协议或仲裁协议无效；

（b） The composition of the arbitration tribunal was or the arbitration proceedings were inconsistent with the agreement of the parties or contrary to the provisions of this Law；

（b）仲裁庭的组成或仲裁程序不符合当事人的协议或违反本法规定；

（c） The dispute was not within the jurisdiction of the arbitration tribunal；where an award contains an item which falls outside the jurisdiction of the arbitration tribunal，such item shall be set aside；

（c）纠纷不在仲裁庭的管辖范围内；裁决含有不属仲裁庭管辖范围的项目的，应撤销该项目；

（d） The evidence supplied by the parties on which the arbitration tribunal relied to issue the award was forged；or an arbitrator received money，assets or some other material benefit from one of the parties in dispute which affected the objectivity and impartiality of the arbitral award；

（d）当事人提供伪造证据致使仲裁庭发布裁决的；仲裁员收取当事人的金钱、资产或其他物质利益，从而影响仲裁裁决的客观性和公正性的；

（e） The arbitral award is contrary to the fundamental principles of the law of Vietnam.

（e）仲裁裁决违反越南法律的基本原则。

3. When the court hears a petition to set aside an arbitral award，

burden of proof shall be regulated as follows:

3. 当法院审理撤销仲裁裁决的请求时,举证责任应规定如下:

(a) Any petitioner relying on the grounds prescribed in sub-clauses (a), (b), (c) or (d) of clause 2 of this article shall have the burden of proving that the arbitration tribunal issued the arbitral award in one of such prescribed cases;

(a) 根据本条第 2 款(a)(b)(c)(d)项规定的请求人,有责任证明仲裁裁决书是仲裁庭在本条第 2 款(a)(b)(c)(d)项所述情况下发布的;

(b) In the case of a petition to set aside an arbitral award relying on the grounds prescribed in sub-clause (e) of clause 2 of this article, the court shall have the responsibility to itself collect and verify evidence in order to decide to set aside or not set aside the arbitral award.

(b) 根据本条第 2 款(e)项规定请求撤销仲裁裁决的,法院本身有责任收集和核实证据,以决定是否撤销仲裁裁决。

Article 69　Right to petition for arbitral award to be set aside
第 69 条　申请撤销仲裁裁决的权利

1. A party with sufficient evidence proving that the arbitration tribunal issued the arbitral award in any of the cases prescribed in article 68.2 on this Law shall have the right, within thirty (30) days from the date of receipt of such award, to lodge a petition with the competent court to set aside the arbitral award. A petition requesting an arbitral award be set aside must be accompanied by materials and evidence proving that such petition has sufficient grounds and is lawful.

1. 一方有充足证据证明仲裁庭在本法第 68 条第 2 款规定的情况下作出仲裁裁决的,有权自收到裁决书之日起 30 日内,向主管法院提出撤销仲裁裁决的请求。撤销仲裁裁决的请求书应附有材料和证据,以证明该请求的合理性与合法性。

2. If a petition is lodged out of time due to an event of force
   majeure，then the duration of such event shall not be included
   when calculating the time-limit for requesting the arbitral award
   be set aside.

2. 如果因不可抗力而未能及时提出请求的，则在计算提出撤销裁决请
   求的时限时，不包括受不可抗力作用的时段。

Article 70　Petition requesting arbitral award be set aside

第 70 条　撤销仲裁裁决的请求

1. A petition requesting an arbitral award be set aside must contain
   the following main particulars：

1. 撤销仲裁裁决的请求书应包括下列主要内容：

   （a）Date on which the petition is made；

   （a）请求时间；

   （b）Name and address of the petitioner；

   （b）请求人姓名和地址；

   （c）Relief sought and grounds for setting aside the arbitral
   award.

   （c）寻求的救济和撤销仲裁裁决的理由。

2. The following documents must accompany the petition：

2. 请求书应附有下列文件：

   （a）Original or validly certified copy of the arbitral award；

   （a）仲裁裁决的原本或经过有效证明的副本；

   （b）Original or validly certified copy of the arbitration agreement.

   （b）仲裁协议的原本或经过有效证明的副本。

   Documents accompanying a petition in a foreign language
   must be translated into Vietnamese and the translations must
   be validly certified.

   随附请求书的外文文件应翻译成越南语，其译文应经过有效认证。

Article 71　Hearing by court of petition requesting arbitral award be set aside

第 71 条　上诉法院针对撤销仲裁裁决的听证

1. The competent court shall, after it accepts jurisdiction of a petition requesting an arbitral award be set aside, immediately notify the arbitration centre or the arbitrators in an ad hoc arbitration, the parties in dispute, and the same level procuracy.

1. 主管法院在接受撤销仲裁裁决的管辖后,应立即通知仲裁中心或临时仲裁的仲裁员、纠纷各方当事人和同级检察院。

2. The chief judge shall, within seven (7) business days from the date on which jurisdiction is accepted, assign a council of three judges including one judge to act as chairman of the council as assigned by the chief judge, to hear the petition.

2. 自接受管辖之日起 7 个工作日内,首席法官应指定一个由三名法官组成的委员会,包括指定一名法官担任委员会主席,以听取请求。

The council of judges must commence a session to hear the petition to set aside the arbitral award within thirty (30) days from the date of being assigned. The court must, seven (7) business days prior to the date of opening the session, transfer the file to the same level procuracy for it to review and participate in the session hearing the petition. Upon the expiry of such time-limit, the procuracy must return the file to the court in order for the court to open the session hearing the petition.

法官委员会应在被指定之日起 30 日内举行会议,听取撤销仲裁裁决的请求。法院应在开庭日期的 7 个工作日前将文件转交给同级检察院审理,以便其参加庭审。在此期限届满后,检察院应将文件归还法院,以便法院开庭审理请求。

3. The session shall be conducted in the presence of the parties in dispute and their lawyers (if any) and a prosecutor of the same

level procuracy. If either of the parties requests the council of judges to hear the petition in his or her absence, or if after being validly summoned a party is absent without a legitimate reason or leaves the session without the consent of the council of judges, then the council of judges shall continue hearing the petition to set aside the arbitral award.

3. 法官委员会应在各方及其律师(如有)和同级检察院的检察官在场的情况下进行审理。如果任何一方要求法官委员会在其缺席的情况下审理,或被有效传召的当事人在没有正当理由的情况下缺席,或未经法官委员会同意离席,则法官委员会应继续审理撤销仲裁裁决的请求。

4. When hearing the petition, the council of judges shall rely on the provisions in article 68 of this Law and the materials accompanying the petition in order to reach its decision; and shall not review the merits of the dispute which the arbitration tribunal already resolved. The council of judges shall, after considering the petition and accompanying materials, after hearing witnesses, if any, who have been summoned and after hearing the procurator provide the opinion of the procuracy, discuss and reach a majority decision.

4. 庭审时,法官委员会应依据本法第68条的规定和请求书附件材料做出决定;不得审查仲裁庭已经解决的纠纷的实质。法官委员会在审理请求书和随附材料后,听取被传召的证人证言(如有),并在听取检察官陈述检察院意见后,进行讨论并达成多数决定。

5. The council of judges hearing the petition shall have the right to issue a decision setting aside or not setting aside the arbitral award. If the petitioner withdraws the petition, or if after being validly summoned the petitioner fails to attend the session without a legitimate reason or leaves the session without the consent of the council of judges, then the council of judges shall

issue a decision staying the application.

5. 审理请求的法官委员会有权决定是否撤销仲裁裁决。如果请求人撤回请求，或者请求人被传召后没有正当理由缺席，或请求人未经法官委员会同意离席，则法官委员会应决定是否搁置该请求。

6. The court shall，within five（5）business days from the date of issuing its decision，send the decision to the parties，to the arbitration centre or to the arbitrator/s of an ad hoc arbitration，and to the same level procuracy.

6. 法院应在发布决定之日起 5 个工作日内将决定发送给当事人、仲裁中心或临时仲裁员以及同级检察院。

7. The council of judges may，at the request of a party and if the council considers it appropriate，adjourn a petition to set aside an arbitral award for a period not to exceed sixty（60）days in order to facilitate the arbitration tribunal in rectifying what in the opinion of the arbitration tribunal were errors in the arbitration proceedings，thereby removing the grounds for setting aside the arbitral award. The arbitration tribunal must notify the court when it has rectified errors in the arbitration proceedings. If the arbitration tribunal does not rectify errors in the proceedings，then the council of judges shall continue to hear the petition to set aside the award.

7. 法官委员会可应一方当事人的请求，并在其认为适当的情况下，延期审理撤销仲裁裁决的请求，期限不超过 60 天，以便仲裁庭纠正其认为仲裁程序中的错误，从而消除撤销仲裁裁决的理由。 仲裁庭在纠正仲裁程序中的错误后应通知法院。如果仲裁庭没有纠正程序中的错误，则法官委员会应继续审理撤销裁决请求。

8. In a case where the council of judges issues a decision to set aside the arbitral award，the parties may reach a fresh agreement to bring their dispute before arbitration or any one party shall have the right to institute court proceedings. If the council of judges

does not set aside the arbitral award，such award shall be enforceable.

8. 如果法官委员会做出撤销仲裁裁决的决定，双方可以达成新的协议将纠纷提交仲裁，或者任何一方有权提起诉讼。如果法官委员会不撤销仲裁裁决，则可执行该裁决。

9. In all cases，the time taken for dispute resolution by arbitration and the time taken to conduct court procedures to set aside an arbitral award shall not be included when calculating the limitation period for instituting proceedings.

9. 在所有情况下，计算诉讼时效期间时，不应包括仲裁解决纠纷的时间和法院审理撤销仲裁裁决的时间。

10. The decision of the court shall be final and shall be valid for enforcement.

10. 法院的判决是终局的，并适用于执行。

Article 72　Court fees regarding arbitration
第 72 条　仲裁费用

Fees for requests to a court to appoint an arbitrator，to order interim relief，to set aside arbitral awards，to register arbitral awards and any other fees shall be implemented in accordance with the law on legal and court fees.

请求法院指定仲裁员、发布临时救济命令、撤销仲裁裁决、登记仲裁裁决的费用和其他费用，应根据法律和法庭费用法执行。

CHAPTER 12
Organization and Operation of Foreign Arbitration in Vietnam
第十二章　外国仲裁在越南的组织与运作

Article 73　Conditions for foreign arbitration institutions to operate in Vietnam
第 73 条　外国仲裁机构在越南运作的条件

Foreign arbitration institutions which have been legally established and are currently legally operating in foreign countries, and which respect the constitution and law of the Socialist Republic of Vietnam, shall be permitted to operate in Vietnam in accordance with this Law.

根据本法,合法设立的、目前在国外合法经营的,且尊重越南社会主义共和国宪法和法律的外国仲裁机构,允许在越南境内运作。

Article 74　Operational forms of foreign arbitration institutions in Vietnam
第 74 条　外国仲裁机构在越南的运作形式

Foreign arbitration institutions shall operate in Vietnam in the following forms:

外国仲裁机构以下列形式在越南运作:

1. Branch of the foreign arbitration institution (hereinafter referred to as branch).

1. 外国仲裁机构的分支机构(以下简称"分支机构")。

2. Representative office of the foreign arbitration institution (hereinafter referred to as representative office).

2. 外国仲裁机构的代表处(以下简称"代表处")。

Article 75　Branches
第 75 条　分支机构

1. Branch is a dependent unit of a foreign arbitration institution, established and conducting arbitration activities in Vietnam pursuant to this Law.

1. 分支机构是指依据本法在越南境内设立并开展仲裁活动的外国仲裁机构的附属单位。

2. The foreign arbitration institution and its branch shall be liable before the law of Vietnam for the operation of the branch.

2. 外国仲裁机构及其分支机构应遵守越南法律,然后分支机构才可运作。

3. The foreign arbitration institution shall elect one arbitrator to act as head of the branch. The head of the branch shall be the authorized representative of the foreign arbitration institution in Vietnam.

3. 外国仲裁机构应选举一名仲裁员担任分支机构负责人。该负责人应作为外国仲裁机构的授权代表。

Article 76   Rights and obligations of branch of foreign arbitration institution in Vietnam

第76条   外国仲裁机构的分支机构在越南的权利与义务

1. To rent an office, and to hire or purchase facilities and materials necessary for the activities of the branch.

1. 租用办事处,租用或购买该分支机构活动所需的设备和材料。

2. To recruit Vietnamese and foreign employees to work at the branch in accordance with the law of Vietnam.

2. 根据越南法律,招募越南和外国雇员到分支机构工作。

3. To open Vietnamese dong and foreign currency accounts at a bank authorized to operate in Vietnam in order to service the activities of the branch.

3. 在越南授权经营的银行开立越南盾和外币帐户,以便分支机构的运作。

4. To remit income of the branch overseas in accordance with the law of Vietnam.

4. 根据越南法律将分支机构的收入汇出。

5. To have a seal bearing the name of the branch in accordance with the law of Vietnam.

5. 根据越南法律持有刻分支机构名称的印章。

6. To appoint arbitrators to establish arbitration tribunals pursuant to authority delegated by the foreign arbitration institution.

6. 根据外国仲裁机构的授权,指定仲裁员设立仲裁庭。

7. To provide arbitration，mediation services and other commercial dispute resolution methods in accordance with law.

7. 依法提供仲裁、调解服务和其他商事纠纷解决方式。

8. To supply administrative services，office and other services for dispute resolution by foreign arbitration tribunals.

8. 为外国仲裁庭解决纠纷提供行政服务、办公室和其他服务。

9. To collect arbitration fees and other lawful fees.

9. 收取仲裁费和其他合法费用。

10. To pay remuneration to arbitrators.

10. 向仲裁员支付报酬。

11. To provide training to raise the dispute resolution knowledge and skills of arbitrators.

11. 提供培训，以提高仲裁员解决纠纷的知识和技能。

12. To archive files，and to provide copies of arbitral decisions on request by the parties in dispute or by competent State authorities of Vietnam.

12. 存档文件，以及应当事人或越南国家主管部门的请求提供仲裁裁决副本。

13. To operate strictly in the sectors recorded in the establishment licence and certificate of registration of operation.

13. 严格按许可证和注册证所登记的行业运作。

14. To comply with the relevant law of Vietnam on operation of the branch.

14. 遵守有关分支机构运作的越南法律。

15. To provide annual reports on the operation of the branch to the Department of Justice in the locality where the branch is registered for operation.

15. 向分支机构注册地的司法部门提供该分支机构业务的年度报告。

Article 77   Representative offices
第 77 条   代表处

1. Representative office is a dependent unit of a foreign arbitration institution, established, and seeking and promoting opportunities for arbitration activities in Vietnam in accordance with this Law.

1. 代表处是根据本法设立的,寻求和促进越南境内仲裁的外国仲裁机构的附属单位。

2. The foreign arbitration institution shall be liable before the law of Vietnam for the operation of its representative office.

2. 外国仲裁机构根据越南法律对其代表处的运作负责。

Article 78   Rights and obligations of representative office of foreign arbitration institution in Vietnam
第 78 条   外国仲裁机构的代表处在越南的权利与义务

1. To seek and promote opportunities for arbitration activities for its institution in Vietnam.

1. 为该代表处在越南境内的机构寻求和促进仲裁。

2. To rent an office, and to hire or purchase facilities and materials necessary for the activities of the representative office.

2. 租用办事处,租用或购买该代表处活动所需的设备和材料。

3. To recruit Vietnamese and foreign employees to work at the representative office in accordance with the law of Vietnam.

3. 根据越南法律,招募越南和外国雇员到代表处工作。

4. To open foreign currency and Vietnamese dong accounts at a bank authorized to operate in Vietnam, and only to use such accounts for the operation of the representative office.

4. 在越南授权经营的银行开立外币和越南盾帐户,且只能用于代表处的运作。

5. To have a seal bearing the name of the representative office in

accordance with the law of Vietnam.

5. 根据越南法律持有刻代表处名称的印章。

6. To operate for the correct objectives and within the scope and for the duration stipulated in the licence for establishment of the representative office.

6. 在规定的范围内以及设立代表处许可证的期限内正确运作。

7. Not to conduct arbitration activities in Vietnam.

7. 不在越南进行仲裁活动。

8. To only conduct promotions and advertising for arbitration activities in accordance with the law on Vietnam.

8. 仅根据越南法律为仲裁活动进行宣传和广告。

9. To comply with the relevant law of Vietnam on operation of the representative office.

9. 遵守越南关于代表处运作的有关法律。

10. To provide annual reports on the operation of the representative office to the Department of Justice in the locality where the representative office is registered for operation.

10. 向分支机构代表处注册地的司法部门提供该代表处业务的年度报告。

Article 79　Operation of branches and representative offices of foreign arbitration institutions in Vietnam

第 79 条　外国仲裁机构的分支机构和代表处在越南的运作

The establishment，operation，and termination of operation of branches and representative offices of foreign arbitration institutions in Vietnam shall be implemented in accordance with the law of Vietnam and international treaties of which Vietnam is a member. The Government shall provide detailed regulations on the procedures for establishment，operation，and termination of operation of branches and representative offices of foreign arbitration institutions in Vietnam.

越南境内外国仲裁机构的分支机构和代表处的设立、运作和终止,应当根据越南法律和越南加入的国际条约的规定执行。越南境内外国仲裁机构的分支机构和代表处的设立、运作和终止,政府应提供详细的规定。

CHAPTER 13
Implementing Provisions
第十三章 执行条款

Article 80 Application of this Law to arbitration centres established prior to effective date of this Law

第 80 条 本法适用于本法生效之日前设立的仲裁中心

Arbitration centres which were established prior to the effective date of this Law shall not be required to conduct procedures for re-establishment. Arbitration centres must, within twelve (12) months from the effective date of this Law, amend and supplement their charters and arbitration procedural rules for compliance with this Law. If upon the expiry of such time-limit any arbitration centre has failed to amend and supplement its charter and arbitration procedural rules, the establishment licence of such arbitration centre shall be revoked and it must terminate its operation.

在本法生效之日前设立的仲裁中心不需要办理重新设立手续。自本法生效之日起 12 个月内,仲裁中心应修改和补充其章程和仲裁程序规则,以符合本法的规定。如果仲裁中心在期限届满时未能修改与补充其章程和仲裁程序规则,则撤销该仲裁中心的设立许可,并终止其运作。

Article 81 Effectiveness

第 81 条 效力

1. This Law shall be of full force and effect as from 1 January 2011.

1. 本法自 2011 年 1 月 1 日起实行并生效。

2. The Ordinance on Commercial Arbitration 03/2003/PL-UBTVQH11

shall no longer be effective as from the effective date of this Law.

2. 自本法生效之日起，第 03/2003/PL-UBTVQH11 号《商事仲裁条例》失效。

3. Arbitration agreements entered into prior to the effective date of this Law shall be implemented in accordance with the provisions of law effective as at the date when the arbitration agreement was entered into.

3. 本法生效前签订的仲裁协议，应当根据仲裁协议签订时有效的法律规定执行。

Article 82　Detailed regulations and guidelines on implementation

第 82 条　执行细则和准则

The Government，the People's Supreme Court and the People's Supreme Procuracy shall，within the scope of their respective duties and powers，provide detailed regulations and guidelines for implementation of articles and clauses assigned in this Law；and shall provide guidelines for implementation of other items in this Law necessary to meet State management requirements.

政府、最高人民法院和最高人民检察院应在各自的职权范围内，为执行本法规定的条款提供详细的规定和指导方针；并应为执行本法的其他项目提供指导，以满足国家管理的要求。

This Law was passed by Legislature XII of the National Assembly of the Socialist Republic of Viet Nam in its 7th session on 17 June 2010.

本法于 2010 年 6 月 17 日经越南社会主义共和国国会第十二届立法会第七次会议通过。

Chairman of the National Assembly

国会主席

NGUYEN PHU TRONG

阮富仲

图书在版编目(CIP)数据

商事仲裁翻译/金春岚编著. —上海:上海三联书店,2020.12
ISBN 978-7-5426-7270-4

Ⅰ.①商… Ⅱ.①金… Ⅲ.①国际商事仲裁－英语－翻译
Ⅳ.①D997.4

中国版本图书馆 CIP 数据核字(2020)第 234449 号

商事仲裁翻译

编　　著 / 金春岚

责任编辑 / 宋寅悦
装帧设计 / 一本好书
监　　制 / 姚　军
责任校对 / 张大伟

出版发行 / 上海三联书店
　　　　　(200030)中国上海市漕溪北路 331 号 A 座 6 楼
邮购电话 / 021－22895540
印　　刷 / 上海惠敦印务科技有限公司

版　　次 / 2020 年 12 月第 1 版
印　　次 / 2020 年 12 月第 1 次印刷
开　　本 / 640×960　1/16
字　　数 / 560 千字
印　　张 / 39.25
书　　号 / ISBN 978－7－5426－7270－4/D・473
定　　价 / 108.00 元

敬启读者,如发现本书有印装质量问题,请与印刷厂联系 021－63779028